Dibuja

Monstruos

con un pincel y agua

Un libro para dibujar,
concebido y realizado por
Claude Delafosse
y Sabine Krawczyk.

Traducción: Paz Barroso

Pintar con agua
es muy divertido.
En cuanto se seca,
tu dibujo desaparece.
Así puedes usar
el papel muchas veces.

sm saber / MUNDO MARAVILLOSO / **DIBUJO**

Cómo utilizar
este libro

Este libro tiene
papeles mágicos en
los que puedes pintar
todas las veces que
quieras.

Su secreto
es dibujar con agua.

Haz una prueba con este rostro: mete el dedo en el
agua, ponlo sobre el papel y observa lo que ocurre.

Para dibujar en este libro:

Moja la punta de tu pincel en agua,
mete
el papel
mágico
gris detrás
de la
página
troquelada y... ¡diviértete dibujando!

En
cuanto
tu dibujo
se seca, desaparece.
Entonces puedes
usar el mismo papel
para pintar otra vez.

Dibuja el extraterrestre
que pilota este fascinante
y veloz platillo volante.

Ahora
invéntate un personaje
para que este robot trabaje.

Pinta con cuidado
lo que este lobo ha devorado.

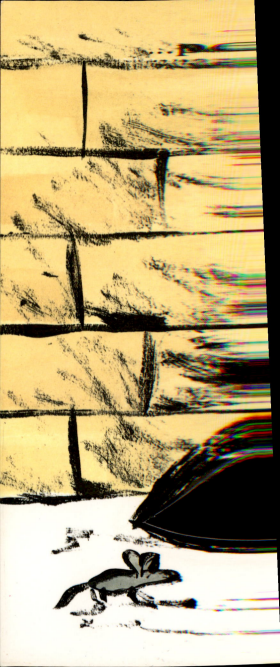

Secrets can be FATAL

Monica Heath

THORNDIKE
CHIVERS

This Large Print edition is published by Thorndike Press®, Waterville, Maine USA and by BBC Audiobooks, Ltd, Bath, England.

Published in 2003 in the U.S. by arrangement with Maureen Moran Agency.

Published in 2003 in the U.K. by arrangement with the author.

U.S. Hardcover 0-7862-6095-5 (Romance)
U.K. Hardcover 0-7540-7769-1 (Chivers Large Print)
U.K. Softcover 0-7540-7770-5 (Camden Large Print)

The text of this Large Print edition is unabridged.
Other aspects of the book may vary from the original edition.

Set in 16 pt. Plantin by Ramona Watson.

Printed in the United States on permanent paper.

British Library Cataloguing-in-Publication Data available

Library of Congress Cataloging-in-Publication Data

Heath, Monica.
    Secrets can be fatal / by Monica Heath.
    p. cm.
    ISBN 0-7862-6095-5 (lg. print : hc : alk. paper)
    1. San Francisco (Calif.) — Fiction. 2. Novelists —
Fiction. 3. Large type books. I. Title.
PS3558.E264S43 2003
813′.54—dc22
                                    2003065080

Secrets
can be
FATAL

Chapter One

I sat beside Wickerly Carver in the red Jaguar, which he called "Burro," though it was nothing like the stubborn, plodding animal for which it was named. As we sped through the mysterious and desolate Nevada desert, my thoughts turned to the events of the past two days. How much my life had changed in that short time!

It had all started in my home town of San Francisco at a fashionable garden party given by my mother's girlhood friend Adriane Montgomery. I had been feeling a little lost amid the gay crowds at the party, when I found myself being introduced to a man whose name — I was amazed to learn — was the same as my father's. Wick Carver. Wickerly Carver.

My throat tightened as I stared up at this tall, strikingly handsome man. My father had only been dead a year, and the sound of his name upset me. He had also been quite dashing, in spite of a crippled leg that caused him to walk with a slight limp. A kindly, gentle man, he had been one of the world's great dreamers and had only given up prospecting for gold after my mother died. His grand hope of finding a rich lode in the Sierra Madres was never fulfilled.

I introduced myself to this Wick as Nevada Carver, and our conversation naturally turned to the strange coincidence of the two men having such an unusual name. My father had always said he had no relatives, so I was sure we were not related. But I was intrigued by the coincidence and by the fact that this Wick Carver shared my father's interest in prospecting.

As the evening wore on, Wick Carver revealed even more surprises. He was a writer — well-known for his mysteries, which he wrote under the name Vin Savage. But now he was planning a book about the Silver Country. About a godforsaken town in Nevada named Wickerly — again the coincidence! — and an old house, called the Tower, that had once belonged to the country's most fabulous silver baron. He was determined to unearth the secrets he was convinced were buried there. His book would be a murder mystery, he said — only this time about real people!

Almost before I could recover from the shock of all this information, I found myself accepting his offer to accompany him to Wickerly to act as his secretary as he researched and wrote his grim tale.

A phone call from Adriane the next morning revealed that Wickerly Carver had not made a spur-of-the-moment decision to hire me. He was apparently obsessed by the Wickerly idea and, in fact, had been searching methodically for people who had some connection with the name. When Adriane had mentioned me, he had become terribly excited, she said, and had insisted that we be introduced.

A feeling of apprehensiveness — perhaps even fear — came over me as I prepared to leave for Nevada.

A bump in the road jolted my thoughts back to the present, and I glanced covertly at Wick. As we flew past blazing stretches of barrenness, browned by a lingering summer, I searched his face for some familiar landmark, some quirk of his handsome features that might remind me of that other Wickerly Carver, my father, who had meant so much to me.

There was no similarity and I resigned myself to his absolute strangeness, wondering why it had suddenly seemed so necessary for me to feel close to this big, intent man who was whisking me off into the Nevada wilds. I decided that it was because the stretches of parched rabbit brush and sage through which we were passing seemed so utterly remote.

In the back of my mind was the thought that I had somehow betrayed my father, for I had never roamed off like this with anyone else. I felt drawn to this Wick Carver in a rather frightening way that was alien to anything that I had ever felt before for a man. The feeling bewildered me, partly because he was forty years old, twice my age. Adriane had hinted slyly that she hoped some romantic interest would develop between us. At the party, he seemed to have noticed my black hair and blue eyes, and even the small mole near the corner of my mouth, but his glances had been just normal male admiration, I thought. Nothing seemed to indicate the sort of interest Adriane hoped might thrive.

"How far is it to Wickerly?" I asked.

"Another forty miles," he said, giving me a wry smile. "Regrets?"

"Not yet," I told him, aware that I wasn't speaking the truth.

Perhaps the small town would be different and I would like it, I thought, salving my slight twinge of conscience.

"I promise that I won't expect more of you than you can accomplish with ease," he said, in a businesslike voice.

A not uncomfortable silence fell between us, and shortly the town came into view.

Wickerly, Nevada, stood, a stark cluster of gray buildings, in the shadows of the crouching mountains. A gnarled oak held watch over a graveyard near the outskirts of the small town, showering down russet foliage, cloaking the sleeping dead with a softly rustling blanket. It was a bleak little place, almost formidable.

"It seems a proper setting for a murder mystery," I said.

"Shades of the past," Wick said. "This town, like the rest of the mining camps, has seen its share of violent death."

"And that's why you chose it?"

"Partly," he said, something in his manner suddenly secretive.

"I assume that you aren't prepared to tell me the rest of it."

"Not just yet, Nevvie," he said, calling me that for the first time. "I've an idea you'll discover my reasons soon enough for yourself," he added, more obscurely than ever.

Then he gave me a look that left me stunned, for he seemed almost hostile toward me. As quickly as it had come, that brief, cold, calculating look vanished from his handsome features, giving way to a disturbingly warm smile.

I turned my attention to the small town. Wick told me, as we drove along the main street, that the brick building, with two golden cottonwoods before it, had been the assay office. It was the sort of thing that my father would have noticed, and I felt suddenly more at ease.

There were several false-fronted buildings, with balconies extending out from them, like oversized brows, shading a high, board street. Several of the buildings were boarded up. "The Strike," a sign dangling crookedly above one of the planked doorways read. Three gruesome-looking objects, which Wick told me were sun-dried coyotes, swung above the doorway of another of the tall buildings, this one built of adobe.

The town had once boasted seven saloons, Wick said. Now there was but one, the Green Lizard. An old man sat beneath the corroded sign, watching us, idly scratching the head of a big mangy-looking dog. Otherwise, the town seemed deserted.

12

The mercilessly exposed landscape, dotted here and there with a few stunted piñon pines and junipers, slanted away from the drab mining community, down into a narrow, shadowed canyon. Much to my surprise, I glimpsed water accumulated in its depths forming a large, dark lake.

"Five Mile Canyon," Wick told me. "The Wickerly Mine is down there underneath that brackish water, enough jewelry ore to make the entire state rich. High-grade silver," he explained, when I gave him a questioning look.

"I know," I said. "But that water . . . how could they possibly have mined there beneath it?"

"That water wasn't always there," Wick said.

Then, as though he were evading my next question, he nodded toward a knoll, visible above the town through the scraggly branches of locust trees that were in the process of shedding their leaves.

I glimpsed the grim face of an old house. "Wickerly Mansion?" I asked.

"Correct, Nevvie. It was built by 'Old Silver' Wickerly — the town shortened his nickname to 'Old Sil' — the founder of the mine and the town. Old Blanche Wickerly still lives there, and in near poverty, from the appearance of things."

"But I thought the Wickerlys owned the silver," I said.

"The mine has been closed for years."

"Because the price of silver dropped?"

"Partly," he said, in that same noncommittal voice.

Wickerly Mansion was double-winged, T-shaped, its central, most substantial portion rising boldly defiant, against the backdrop of tawny hills. The cupola set astride its sloping, mansard roof pierced the almost colorless sky with a pointed weather vane that supported an immense, silver gun posed incongruously among tall, rosy chimneys.

I stared up at it in astonishment, noting that it was aimed toward the town. It seemed threatening indeed, giving a macabre touch to the already sinister atmosphere.

"Outlandish, isn't it, poised above all of that prim, Victorian grandeur," Wick said. "As incongruous as the family who has inhabited that old tomb all of these years, lording it over the town." His voice sounded suddenly bitter.

"You seem to know a good deal about this place," I commented.

"Enough to know that it will make

14

damned good reading, once I get the story down on paper," he said.

"Have you a particular murder in mind?" I asked.

"Several," he said, his face grim.

He turned the small car up the hill toward Wickerly Mansion, telling me that the reason it had become known as the Tower was because of the cupola astride its roof.

"The house was painted a dazzling shade of white during the town's heyday," he said. "Those jigsaw patterns worked into the corners of its many turrets glistened like frosting on a tiered cake."

"You sound almost as though you'd seen it," I said. "The vivid imagination of a writer, I suppose."

"Research, Nevvie," Wick commented. "A writer's forte. I've dear Fairfax to thank. She visited the museum in Carson City and came up with an old photograph of this place."

"Fairfax?" I said.

He has a girl, I thought, and was astonished by the sudden surge of disappointment that swelled through me.

"Fairfax Stanton," he said, looking straight ahead, nosing the Jaguar unmistakably toward the old house that stood defiantly above us. "A charming girl. An employee, like yourself. She's done a good deal of digging for me, groping about through the ancient annals of this town for the pertinent facts. A part of my menage as you shall be, Nevvie. One big happy family." The look he gave me seemed almost to dare me to deny it.

I sat silently, pondering his words. There were to be several of us then.

He had brought the Jaguar to a halt before the mansion.

"This is it," he said.

"You mean that we are to live here?" I asked. "But I thought Miss Wickerly . . . Old Blanche, you called her —"

"Darling child, it isn't nearly as dire as all that," he chided me. "I've arranged for us to stay here at the Tower for as long as necessary. As I told you, I've a feeling that Blanche Wickerly can use the money. Ironic, isn't it, when you think of all that silver." He glanced up at the railed veranda that skirted the front of the house. "Fairfax is here somewhere," he said, suddenly rather eager.

I had the disturbing thought that I had involved myself in something far more complicated than I had first imagined. It seemed suddenly a very foolish thing that I had done, going off with an absolute stranger, even though he was legitimately my new employer.

"I hope that I'll like it here," I said in a small voice. "A part of your happy family — living in the Tower."

He looked at me with bright eyes.

"You say that very easily," he said. "The Tower."

"It seems appropriate. Besides, it is easier to say than Wickerly Mansion, or even just the Mansion."

His eyes became shrewd. "I imagined for an instant when you called it the Tower just now that you had heard of it before."

"What a strange thing to say! I'm certain that if I had heard of this place, I'd have remembered it, if only as a precaution against coming to it. I must admit I find it quite formidable. I wonder, Mr. Carver, if I might not have a few regrets after all."

"It's too late now, Nevvie. You're here and I shan't let you go."

I tried not to think that his eyes seemed threatening above the whiteness of his smile.

"How many of us will there be?" I asked.

"Yourself. Fairfax. Blanche Wickerly, of course. Then there is Collins Stanton, Fairfax's son, a boy of about nineteen. College fellow, along for the ride, although I promised him some odd jobs around this place. It could use a handyman, from the appearance of things."

"Fairfax is an older woman, then?"

"Depending on your vantage point," he said, a hint of mischief glinting in his eyes. I wondered if she might not be his current interest, after all. "Judge for yourself," he added, gesturing toward the old house.

I glanced toward the mansion, which seemed almost alive, glaring with its many glinting windows, and saw that a woman had stepped out onto the shaded veranda. I caught the gleam of golden hair piled high above a tanned face. Fairfax Stanton was tall and slender with remarkably coltish legs, tanned below startlingly white shorts. A shower of bracelets cast a glitter from her bare arms. Even from that distance, there was something lavish about her and undeniably youthful.

Wick helped me from the small car, and when we had come near enough for me to see her face clearly, I saw that although she looked young, there was a brittleness about her. Her dark eyes glowed almost feverishly from beneath the pile of golden hair, as though, I thought, she were terribly excited about something. I wondered if it could

18

possibly be my coming. But I realized it was Wick's arrival that had aroused that tense brightness in her when she placed a long, lacquer-tipped hand on his shoulder and raised herself onto her toes to kiss his tanned cheek.

"Another assistant, I presume," she said in a throaty voice, turning her attention to me.

"Quite right," Wick told her. "Nevada Carver, my secretary."

"Incredible!" the blond woman said to me. "Another Carver! Are the two of you a clan?"

"No relation," I said. "Although I understand that Mr. Carver collects people if they happen to bear his name."

"You checked up on me, then," Wick said, giving me a quick look.

"I couldn't just go off —" I began, flushing miserably, now, with a sudden sense of guilt.

"But of course, darling," Fairfax said. "A young girl like you. Still a child, really. . . ." She gave a little shrug, apparently dismissing me as competition.

Wick seemed unaware of her gesture.

"Where is Collins?" he demanded.

"Off somewhere in this godforsaken land," she said. "Doing his best to get himself bitten by a rattlesnake." She flashed brown eyes at me. "My precious son loathes this place. A neatly executed snakebite would mean that I must whisk him away to Fallon, where, I understand, the nearest M.D. might be found. I know nothing about the place. Phoenix was our home, darling, before Wick hired me," she added. "And yours?"

I fancied that I glimpsed something more than idle curiosity in the depths of her brown eyes.

"San Francisco," I said.

"And dear Rena is from Los Angeles," she said.

"Who is Rena?" I asked.

"Rena Hill," Fairfax informed me. She glanced at Wick. "I'm curious about her, darling. She hasn't yet arrived." Her gaze returned to me. "Wick is assembling a considerable staff. Although I can't imagine why he needs so many. . . ." Her lower lip drooped in a slight pout.

"To help me write a book," Wick said calmly.

"That stock reply will have to satisfy us for the time being, darling," Fairfax said to me, as Wick disappeared through the front door of the mansion.

I guessed that he wanted to escape further questioning.

"Your husband?" I said to Fairfax, when he had gone. "Is he part of Wick's household?"

"What husband?" Fairfax retorted. Then, when I looked shocked, "Oh, I had one once, darling. I divorced him. It happened eons ago. Shortly after Collins was born, in fact. Don't be too shocked, dear, but the truth is that I have all but forgotten his name. It was that mediocre, like the man who bore it."

"And you've never married again?"

"Never," Fairfax said a bit sharply. "Though of course there have been numerous men in my life, since that first disappointment." She gave a dismissing shrug. "Wick has told you something of his methods?" she asked then, flashing me a slightly envious glance. "The way he goes about digging up facts for a book? I suppose he thought that it might be clever to list all sorts of names inside the front cover, or the back, wherever the author — or is it the publisher — decides that the little note of appreciation should go. 'Many millions of thanks to Fairfax Stanton for her invaluable aid, and to Nevada Carver for her invaluable assistance, and to Rena Hill, whoever she might be. . . .' "

I turned from her to retrieve my overnight case from the Jaguar and, as I leaned into the car, a stark shadow fell over me, briefly blotting out the sun. I glanced up and saw a buzzard wheeling on silent wings directly overhead, a dark omen against the pale sky. I turned to Fairfax, forcing a gay smile.

"I'm ready now to enter the historic portals," I said.

"I suppose Wick has told you that there are to be seven of us living in this morgue, all told, for the next . . . well, however long it may take to do what he has to do," Fairfax said, leading me inside.

"Yourself and Collins," I said. "Blanche Wickerly. Wick Carver. The Rena Hill you mentioned, and myself, of course. That's only six."

"Kev makes seven, darling. Kev Keever. Melodious name. It seems that his father once lived in this town. He was the newspaper editor here, back in the old days. Kev is a photographer-journalist, it seems. He's to take photographs of this dreary place to illustrate Wick's — history. Let's hope that he's clever with his camera, darling. He'll have to be to make this place seem appealing, even in living color. Wick wanted him, thinking that photos taken by a former local might somehow be more authentic, I suppose."

"Sounds interesting," I commented.

"Of course. Wick has no use for the dull." She gave a disconcerting little laugh. "Which speaks very well for both of us, of course. A handsome, brute type if I ever saw one. Are you interested, darling?"

I stared at her, taken aback by her abruptness.

"Not really," I said, after a slight pause.

"You will be, I promise you, and may the best woman win. Let us pray that this Rena Hill person is not a dish, darling. Let us pray that she is a witch. One less to enter into the competition." This time there was a slight edge to her laugh.

She turned and led me into the old house, which seemed to close about us like a dismal tomb.

Chapter Two

The inside of the old house *was* every bit as dismal as I had expected it to be. A heavy chandelier hung from the frescoed ceiling of a square foyer, casting down a faint and prismed glow. A wizened little woman appeared suddenly on the stairs that twined upward at one side, seeming to materialize out of the shadows. Fairfax introduced her as Blanche Wickerly.

"It's kind of you to welcome us into your home," I said.

"I've been well paid for it," the old woman snapped. "Your room is there." She pointed upward. "At the end of the corridor to your right."

There was something vital about Blanche Wickerly, something ragingly alive, in spite of her withered skin and the sunken eyes that glowed like jet beads out of their hollow sockets. An immense twist of hair stood on the crown of her small head, a miniature cupola, as black as a crow's wing. Her parched face peered from beneath it, her eyes gleaming with some incalculable fire. She had been a beauty in her day, I thought.

This was the woman, then, whose family had founded the mine that was said to be somewhere in the waterfilled canyon, below the town. I became suddenly curious about the mine, wondering if it were true that there was still silver there, enough jewelry ore to make the entire state rich. If so, I thought, why didn't Blanche Wickerly order enough of it excavated from beneath that dark water to repair her dismal mansion.

Fairfax led me up the winding stairs, into a long, dark corridor that was flanked on either side by numerous closed doors. Wick had brought up the largest of my bags, and he stood back now to allow me to enter a darkly wainscoted room. Fairfax paused beside him on the threshold, and I noticed that she allowed her tan hand to rest on his bare arm.

These gestures bothered me not a little; I told myself that I felt possessive because his name was the same as my father's, and that I must strive to overcome the bothersome feeling if the two of us were to work sensibly together.

Wick asked me if the room was satisfactory. I told him that it was, and he left us to hurry back down the corridor.

"That old woman," I began, when he had disappeared. "Will she be wandering about here, as though the house were still exclusively hers?"

"Gives you the absolute creeps, doesn't it, the way she glares at one, out of those beady little eyes; as though she somehow hoped to sort of *recognize* one of us. . . ." Fairfax broke off with a nervous laugh. "The old girl has retained free access to the parlor, darling. And of course to her own room, though God alone knows where it might be. There seem to be so many of them. All of these endless, bleak hallways. She'll take her meals with us. Wick brought his housekeeper with him, a rather jolly Mexican type. Her name is Carmen, and Wick has assured me that she will look after us all superbly."

"Wick Carver must be a rich man," I said.

"Darling, he's gambling a good deal on the success of this venture. I can tell by his attitude that he is looking forward to a great stack of money. Lucrative TV and movie sales, perhaps, though he isn't one to confide. Not yet, at any rate."

"Rena Hill," I said. "What role will she play here?"

Fairfax gave me a wide-eyed look.

"You speak as though you imagined us as characters in this bloody thriller that Wick intends to do here. Let us hope that Rena shall play the role of victim, in that case. Especially if it turns out that she is pretty!" Fairfax gave a little laugh. "I gather Rena is to file and keep track of the tidbits I uncover. A general assistant, you might call her."

"I had no idea that it ever required such a large staff to turn out a book," I said.

"Neither did I, darling. Like you, I suspect that we are gathered together here for reasons which as yet remain known only to our charming employer, and the book is merely a convenient excuse. Has it occurred to you, Nevada, that he is perhaps preparing to take a bride; that this just might be his weird way of assembling a small harem, only in a manner of speaking of course, from which to choose? Only wishful thinking, perhaps. You may as well know that I intend to lure him with all of my charms. Incidentally, darling, I have extremely long claws, like a cat."

With that bit of persiflage, which I decided not to take too seriously, Fairfax left me alone to unpack my bags.

I found my thoughts dwelling on Wick Carver, as I carried my dresses into the dark little closet and hung them on the warped pole.

I was interrupted by a light tap on my door, and when I called out, Blanche Wickerly entered, her black eyes gleaming.

Now that Fairfax had called it to my attention, I couldn't help but notice the way the old woman looked at me, as though she did indeed expect to suddenly recognize me as someone she might once have known.

"Why have you come here?" she demanded, her eyes never leaving my face. "Why are you here? First *him*. And now you. If I had guessed what he intended, I should never have let my house to him. I know now why he demanded a lease, a contract that can't be broken. He intended all along to confuse me. . . ."

"I've no idea what you're talking about," I said, alarmed by the old woman's undisguised anger.

"Carvers!" she spat. "Both of you. And one of you has to be the one. *His* daughter! Or son," she added, in a venomous voice.

"Whose son or daughter?" I asked, remembering that she must be very old, keeping my voice sensibly quiet.

"*His!* The last man to see my brother Jared alive!"

I stared at her, stunned by the bitterness in her voice.

"I know nothing at all about your brother," I said. "My father lived in San Francisco. I doubt that he ever heard of this town, or your brother."

"Are you certain?" Blanche Wickerly demanded, her eyes concentrated once more on my face, searching my features for some familiarity.

I tried to recall facts from my father's past. He had been orphaned at an early age. Or at least I had assumed that he had been, since he never spoke of having known his parents. Before he had met my mother, he had spent a good deal of time roving about, taking odd jobs — learning to live, he had called it.

"No," I said, after a slight pause. "No, I'm not absolutely certain. This — this man who was the last to see your brother alive . . . was *his* name Carver?"

The old woman nodded.

"What was he like? What did he do?" I asked.

"He was tall. Dark-haired, like the Wick Carver who has leased my house," she

29

said. "A laborer in our mine when he wasn't traipsing around the hills like a gypsy."

"What happened to your brother?" I asked.

"Murdered!" she said. "He was murdered! Do you understand now why I let him have my house, this person who calls himself Wick Carver? I thought he was the one, until you came. Now I'm not sure."

Her eyes had become openly accusing. She stared at me for a moment longer, then turned to go, rustling out into the gloomy hallway, closing the door after herself with a fierce little gesture.

I went to the window and threw wide the faded velour drapes that concealed bedraggled lace curtains. My father had been tall, dark-haired, I thought. But nothing like Wick Carver, this Wick Carver who had brought me here. My father's eyes had been blue, beneath his thick, dark hair. His face had been open. Gentle. Kind. Blanche Wickerly had been quite obvious: she suspected that the man named Carver, who had been the last to see her brother alive, had been her brother's murderer! What was more, she suspected that one of us — Wick or I — was the offspring of a killer!

I stood looking down on the town

through the holes in the ragged curtains, as Wickerlys must have done before me. He knew, I thought. Wick Carver knew that Blanche Wickerly's brother had been murdered. That particular murder was to be the basis for his book! Why else should he have arranged to rent the very house where the victim had lived? Why else would he have assembled a staff to assist him with his macabre project?

Wick Carver — the Wick Carver who had brought me to this godless place — intended to write a shocker. And what could be more shocking than an ancient crime brought to light — a killer who had imagined himself scot free for years suddenly run to ground, exposed in some dramatic manner. And if the killer himself happened to be unavailable, then some member of his family who might remain could be brought into the story in a sensational manner. It seemed the sort of thing that might fire the imagination of an omnivorous reading public.

Had my father once killed? I remembered his kindly face and thought that it couldn't possibly have been him. It had to be Wick's father, then, *if* either of the two.

Was I becoming hopelessly attracted to the son of a murderer? Or was Blanche

Wickerly mistaken about her brother's death? She was old — it was quite possible that she had lost track of the facts. I could be sure of precisely nothing.

There was little comfort in the thought.

Chapter Three

Rena Hill and Kev Keever arrived at the Tower that same evening, in time for cocktails before dinner.

Although Wick seemed very clever with the silver shaker, jolting daiquiris for Rena and Kev a careful twenty-five times, adding a dash of grenadine before he strained the drinks into cocktail glasses, Fairfax insisted on hovering about him, taking bottles from a small cabinet and making herself more than useful. I caught myself thinking rather disgustedly: if he falls for her too-obvious little tricks, he's not the sort of man I imagined him to be when I first met him.

When everyone was settled on the plush furniture with their drinks, Wick mixed a dry manhattan for himself and, glass in hand, wandered about the room, commenting knowingly on the various fixtures.

It was a large room, with a black fireplace at one end. Italian marble, Wick told us. He fondled the mantel garniture set, his lips pursed with what I took to be admiration.

"French ormolu," he announced. "What an antique dealer wouldn't give for these."

"Absolutely fantastic background for your story," Fairfax contributed.

"Agreed," Wick commented, flashing her a quick smile.

Fairfax joined Wick in his impromptu stroll, and I thought how strikingly alive the two of them looked against all that ancient finery.

A tiny twinge of jealousy threatened to intrude on my complacency, and I was relieved when Wick announced that it was time to go in to dinner.

Wick sat at the head of the long table, and Blanche Wickerly joined us to take her place at the foot. Her piercing gaze sought me, and to avoid those penetrating eyes, sunken deep into their folds of flesh, I turned to the others seated around the long table.

Rena Hill was a dark, slender girl, with green eyes and an olive complexion. I guessed her to be near my own age. She was quite lovely. Fairfax noted this fact and gave me a reconciliatory smile.

Kev Keever was a man in his late twenties, quite strikingly handsome, with sandy hair and sharp blue eyes. He caught me looking at him and gave me a slightly reserved smile. Collins Stanton was there as well, a sullen-faced youth who looked nothing at all like his mother. He had rather large features and thick, brown hair combed into a high pompadour above long peaked sideburns. I guessed that he fancied himself something of a Westerner, for he wore Western boots and slim tight jeans. A lavishly embroidered shirt completed his dinner ensemble.

When I glanced again at Blanche, I found her still watching me.

"I must warn you," she croaked suddenly. "When I discover which of you it is, I shall inform the sheriff. There are too many questions left unanswered in this town." Her words fell on the silence like a bomb. "I intend to know," she added. There was no mistaking the note in her voice; she hoped at the very least to frighten the guilty one away.

"Darling!" Fairfax exclaimed, staring at the old woman. "I do believe you've had too much sun!"

"Your father's name was Wick," Blanche accused, still looking at me. "Wick Carver."

"How strange," Rena Hill said. "The same as Wick's. But of course the two of you must be related."

"Darling!" Fairfax addressed Wick. "Perhaps you owe us all an explanation. If the two of you aren't related. . . ." She raised her tweezed brows.

"Quite simple," Wick said. "I happen to be attracted to the name."

"Ego, darling?" Fairfax said.

"But this business of calling a sheriff," Rena said. "Whatever for?"

"If you ask me, there is something strange going on here," Collins Stanton said. "Mr. Carver? Miss Carver?"

"We may as well get onto a first-name basis," Wick said, ignoring him. His eyes gleamed with annoyance, as his gaze swept the length of the table, lighting on each of us in turn. "Blanche, if you don't mind our calling you that, Miss Wickerly. And Kev, there at Blanche's right. You all know by now that Kev's last name is Keever, Nevada next. Nevvie. And Fairfax here to my right, of course. Myself. I shall gladly respond to the name Wick. And there is Collins, and Rena. A nice cozy group. No problems at all." He gave Blanche a defiant look.

"Except that one of us happens to be the offspring of a murderer," I heard myself saying.

"My God, darling!" Fairfax exclaimed.

They were all looking at me slightly aghast. The air in the dingy old dining room had become charged with some nameless suspicion.

"How did you know that?" Kev Keever asked.

I saw the same question in Wick's eyes.

"Miss Wickerly — Blanche — told me," I blurted. "The last man to see her brother alive was named Carver."

"Wick Carver," Blanche contributed, in a raspy voice.

"I grew up here in Wickerly," Kev Keever stated. "My father knew that first Wick Carver. I was just a kid when Dad used to tell about him. That first Wick Carver would be in his late sixties now. Close to seventy, I imagine." His mouth twisted in a wry smile. "That leaves our employer out."

They all turned to me.

"My father is dead," I said. "Heart attack. He — he was a tool- and diemaker in San Francisco. A kind man who loved dogs. We always had several running about. Terriers." My throat tightened with memories. "I doubt that I could bear a terrier again. Quick, darting, nimble-footed little things. You see, he walked with a little limp. The dogs' sure-footedness gave him a good deal of pleasure. He was a good man," I added. I realized that I had become nervously maudlin and gave an apologetic laugh.

"Just what in the hell are we trying to prove here?" Wick demanded. "I've got a book to write, I scarcely knew my father, and I've brought you all here to help me. Beyond that —"

"A book about Jared Wickerly's murder?" Kev interrupted. "Mr. Vin Savage," he added, his sharp blue eyes daring Wick to deny it. "Sure, I know who you really are. That's the one reason I accepted your proposition to come back here. Working with the great Vin Savage on picture layouts could make me."

"Darlings," Fairfax said. "It would be very nice if someone would tell us about this murder. Blanche, dear?" She turned her sparkling brown eyes on the old woman perched on the chair at the far end of the table. "I know that he was your brother, this Jared. But it was a long while ago. Surely you can bring yourself to tell us about it now. And I really think we should know, considering the circumstances. If it was a man named Carver who killed him —"

"I'm afraid Blanche has misled Nevvie to a certain degree." Kev interrupted. "You see, Jared's body was never found. It was only assumed that he had been murdered."

"Then there actually was no murder at all," Rena said, with obvious relief. "There has to be a body, you know, before anyone can be singled out as a killer."

"Oh, Jared disappeared, all right," Kev explained. "It's just that the water covered up any evidence there might have been, including the corpse. That is, if Jared is actually down there beneath that lake."

Fairfax's eyes lighted up with interest.

"Something tells me that my job here is going to be rather intriguing," she said. "Your father was newspaper editor here, I understand," she added, looking at Kev. "Back at the time that this . . . ah . . . murder occurred. I suppose there are still files around."

"It happens that I inherited the old *Strike* office from my dad," Kev said.

"How exciting!" Fairfax said. "Wick brought you here for more than one reason, then." She turned back to Blanche.

"Blanche, darling. Do you mind? I would like to hear your version of what happened, if you'll let me just run get my notebook." She darted from her chair, before Blanche Wickerly could reply.

The old woman's face looked as though

it had suddenly turned to stone. Only her beady black eyes were alive, focused, I noticed, on me.

"Jared was my brother," she said, in a loud accusing whisper.

For a terrifying instant I imagined that she had somehow recognized *me*. Then her glance turned to Wick.

"How can she expect me to talk about it?" she demanded. "I'm afraid I'm not well." She groped for the edge of the table with bony hands.

Wick hurried to assist her, drawing out her chair, helping her to rise. She shrugged him off.

"If you will excuse me, please," she murmured, and hurried from the room with surprising alacrity.

"Poor old thing," Rena said. "It must have been ghastly. No body to bury. Nothing but the fact that he was gone. I wonder if they were close, Blanche and her brother, Jared?"

Fairfax returned with her notebook, an expression of genuine disappointment crossing her face when she saw that Blanche had gone.

"Dear old soul," she said. "Except that there is something rather inexplicably dreary about her," she added, with a dismayed laugh.

"Kev?" Wick said. "Since everyone here seems primed for the story, would you care to tell us what you know? You must have some idea of what happened, being the son of the man who was newspaper editor here at the time."

"Silver was all this town had," Kev began reluctantly, weighing his words, deciding what to tell us. "It all started with that; with the jewelry ore buried down there in Five Mile Canyon."

"Beneath the lake," Fairfax said. "What an odd place to look for ore!"

"Silver, like gold, can be anywhere," Kev said. "Although that black water wasn't there in the canyon then. Old Silver Wickerly discovered a solid vein of silver down there more than ninety years ago, when there was only a trickle of water flowing through there. Coyote Creek, he named it. It still dribbles down off of the Humboldt. Runs into the lake. Helps to keep it full."

"I suppose Old Sil Wickerly's big bonanza ran out, like the strikes on the Comstock," Fairfax said. She gave Wick a triumphant, only partly humorous, look. "You see, I've prepared for this assignment, darling. I shall be invaluable to you."

"That damned lake," Kev continued.

"The mine is beneath it. There's an entire community submerged down there. The inevitable shacks that clustered around a prosperous mine in those days. Whim house. Ore shed. Shaft house. And the reducing mill, one of the largest in the state in its time, set down in the midst of the miner's shanties. It's all down there waiting, including the bulk of the silver."

"How did it happen?" I asked. "What caused it to be submerged?"

"Flash flood back in nineteen twenty-three, or thereabouts. The mountain slid down and formed a dam there at the end of the canyon. The lake has been there ever since. As I said, it's still fed by Coyote Creek, and it doesn't seem likely that it will ever go away, unless we get a terrific drought, the worst this country has ever seen. Nobody has ever bothered to give the lake a name. I suppose, in the beginning, the folks here figured it would go away. But forty-odd years is a hell of a long time to wait for it to happen."

"Can't they do things with powder, to help it along?" Fairfax asked. "Dynamite? Look at the way they blast down entire mountains to build roads."

"This town is still in awe of the Wickerly name," Kev said. "Strange the way a name can grip people, become almost tangible, an unalterable god overpowering them. That dam down there is Jared's grave, and Jared was a Wickerly. It would be sacrilege to disturb it, supposedly. Then, too, silver wasn't worth much, there for a while. Even the high-grade stuff. So the town has, for one reason or another, gone along with Blanche in keeping Jared's grave sacred." Kev gave a mournful smile.

"I should think that Blanche would have wanted at least to try to find the body." Rena said. "Jared's body. It doesn't make sense, just letting it stay down there beneath all that earth."

"Dynamite would have blown his bones all to hell," Kev said. "And there's no one here with enough ambition left to dig him out with a shovel. There must be a thousand tons of earth down there. Too much of it to move by hand. At any rate, the town *has* gone along with Blanche in keeping that mammoth grave sacred. Not that it's much of a town any more. Only the diehards are left here. Some setting for a murder mystery."

"Like your silver and gold, murder can happen anywhere," Wick said.

The discussion turned to other things, and later, when we went up to our rooms,

Fairfax stayed close to Wick, chatting intimately.

I turned away, so that I wouldn't have to see them starting up the stairs, and found Kev Keever beside me, his eyes shining in the gloom. Gratitude surged through me, as he took my arm, and I looked up into his face, forcing a bright, gay laugh, which came out sounding hollow and empty.

"Poor Blanche," I said, forcing myself to sound nonchalant. "Alone all of these years in this dreary place."

"Yet another reason for this town to let her hoard Jared's bones and the Wickerly silver," Kev said, with a touch of bitterness. "Harmless old lady, helpless and alone, with nothing to cling to but memories and the comfort of Jared's grave. Of course, silver really wasn't worth much there for a while. There wasn't much impetus to go against those who were all for letting Old Blanche keep that unnatural grave sacred. But that is changing, now. . . ." A secretive look crossed his face.

"The story of Jared Wickerly's death makes quite a legend," he continued. "It brings a few tourists into town to view that damned lake, locked there by that pile of clay."

"I hope Fairfax jotted it all down," I

said. "That particular legend should make an interesting addition, or part of Wick's book."

That night I dreamed of Wick Carver's book. I visualized clearly the dedication inside its front cover: "To my darling Nevvie, with love, Wick."

Chapter Four

I woke up while it was still dark, filled with an overwhelming sense of nearness and warmth, the dream seeming for an instant to be based on truth. Then I remembered what the book was to be about, and the suspicions that Blanche seemed to have about Wick and me.

There was the sound of someone passing by my door, and I realized that that was what must have wakened me. I lay still listening, wondering who was up at that time of night.

Rena Hill had the room next to my own. Wick Carver, Kev Keever, and Collins Stanton were quartered in the left wing of the huge, old house. Blanche's room was somewhere off of the dim corridor that penetrated the T portion of the rambling edifice. Fairfax was across the hall from Rena.

Whoever it was passed by again, and I called Rena's name softly, yearning suddenly for someone to talk to this first night in a strange place. The floor creaked and I called again. But no one answered.

Yet I was certain that someone was there, and the urge to speak to another human being grew stronger. I opened my door very quietly. At first it seemed as though the corridor were deserted. Then I glimpsed a woman wearing a soft, pink flowing garment hurrying away from me, around the corner of the long hallway. Was it Fairfax, hurrying to meet Wick?

Still infused with the warmth of the dream, I refused to believe that she and Wick might have arranged some stealthy rendezvous. Perhaps she couldn't sleep and was going to the kitchen for a glass of milk. Yet some dark side of my nature prompted me to follow that soft flowing of pink, with suspicion.

I came to the turning of the hallway and paused to listen for the sound of her slippers clicking softly down the worn stairs. Instead, the sound came from my right. My heart fell. Then I realized that the sounds were not coming from the corridor that led to the men's rooms, but from the central corridor that led to Blanche's quarters. My heart lurched, and I found myself gliding along that dim, dark hallway, my very footsteps almost airy with relief.

A faint scent of perfume clung to the heavy air, some sweet, cloying, old-fashioned fragrance, not at all the sort of scent that Fairfax would wear. Blanche, then? It hardly seemed likely that the strange old woman would be wandering about the halls of the Tower, clad in a seductive pink peignoir. I had imagined, when I came near her, that Blanche reeked of camphor and moth balls.

"Please," I called. "I want to talk to you."

The feminine little sounds speeded up and diminished then into the far reaches of the old house.

I came to a winding stair that spiraled upward. Thinking that the pink-clad woman had gone up there, I climbed upward and came onto the third-floor landing. There were doors opening off it at either side. The stairs continued still further upward, and I glimpsed a little patch of moonlight above me. I realized that the door opening into the cupola stood open.

"Are you there?" I called softly, mounting toward the patch of light. "Fairfax? Rena? Blanche?"

There was no answer. The cupola was empty, the windows surrounding it letting in the faint rays of silvery moonlight.

I backed down the stairs and flicked a light switch; a shaded bulb cast its feeble glow over me, illuminating what was obviously an attic room used for storage purposes.

I strained my eyes against the gloom, taking a few tentative steps into the midst of a clutter of old furniture and stacked cartons.

"Is anyone here?" I called softly.

There was a sound behind me, a creaking of the ancient boards beyond the yawning door. I turned quickly, hurrying out onto the landing. The door opposite me stood open. I caught again the cloying scent of the quaint, flowery perfume.

"Blanche?" I said; it *had* to be her.

There was no reply. Then suddenly I heard her again, the sound of her slippers growing faint below me. I realized that whoever it had been had gone back down the stairs to the second floor.

I tried to imagine what she was doing here among the rubble of the past, and I went through the door that stood open opposite me, thinking that perhaps the dingy room might contain some clue.

Like the room I had just left, it contained a clutter of castoffs — a heaped accumulation of bedroom furnishings and toilet articles. A number of dark portraits were stacked nearby, their ornate gilt frames cracked and crumbling beneath a thick layer of dust. I noticed that one of them had been removed from the stack and pushed beneath the precariously piled parts of an old bedstead. I slid it from beneath the leaning headboard.

It was a portrait of a man, painted in the stiff, darkly imposing style of a former era. The eyes of the painting seemed to draw my own, disarmingly lifelike, highlighted with white dots of oil so that they seemed almost piercing.

I stared into them, stifling a gasp, biting at the back of my hand in a sudden, stunned gesture. The eyes were shockingly familiar, a clear shade of blue, like my own, set beneath dark hair that shone with blue-black highlights.

The man in the portrait cradled a small spotted terrier, and there was a tiny dark mole near the corner of his mouth.

I shrunk away from that familiar face, with a small, involuntary sound of protest.

"No!" My voice was muffled by the accumulation of webs and dust. "No!" I repeated, this time in a harsh, aching whisper, overcome by a peculiar feeling of dread, for I had noticed suddenly that the eyes of the painting seemed to gleam with avarice and a cold, insatiable hunger.

It can't possibly be a painting of my father, I thought. Yet the portrait bore an amazing resemblance to him. And he had always been fond of terriers.

I knelt over the painting, the woman in the pink peignoir all but forgotten, as I examined the familiar features more closely. It was my father, I thought disbelievingly, except that the eyes in the painting were greedy and cruel, while his had been soft and kind. There was the same slight cleft in the subject's chin, shadowed by a stubborn growth of blue-black beard. And the tiny mole there at the corner of the mouth. There was no mistaking it — it was the same as my own.

The heavy, level brows were my father's as well. I would have recognized him, I thought, without the mole that labeled the painting, like a small, dark signature.

My eyes were drawn to a small rent in the canvas, which, I realized, with a start, had been made by a bullet that had pierced the heavy coating of oil directly between the sharp blue eyes. There were powder burns still visible around its edges, crumbling to dust when I touched the hole gingerly with the tip of my finger.

Someone had fired point-blank at the canvas, as though the man there had been real and whoever had done it had been intent on destroying him.

Had someone wanted to kill my father? Blanche Wickerly, perhaps, because he had been the Wickerly Carver who had been the last person to see her brother Jared alive? Had it been Blanche who had lured me upward to this room?

But what was a painting of a man who so closely resembled my father doing in this dire old house in the first place? The thought that it might possibly be a painting of him seemed preposterous. Yet there was no denying the likeness.

Did Wick Carver know? Was I to play some part in the shocking thriller he was writing? If Wick intended to use me, I thought, with a surge of anger at my own naïveté, why was I being so foolish as to fall in love with him?

The prying questions thronged through my mind, and I found myself running headlong down the stair, as though I could thereby escape from them. There was a movement ahead of me in the dingy corridor, and I glimpsed the woman in pink once more emerging from one of the many rooms. I called Fairfax's name.

She seemed not to hear me, hurrying on, disappearing from sight around a corner of the long, bleak corridor. Just then Wick appeared before me.

"Nevvie?" he called softly. I went toward him, feeling suddenly guilty. "May I ask you what you are doing roaming these musty halls at this ungodly hour?" he demanded, reaching to take my arm.

I let him guide me along the hallway, thoroughly conscious of the scent of his leather-and-tweed cologne, mingled still with the rich aroma of good tobacco.

"I — I couldn't sleep . . . I was looking for someone to talk to," I said feebly. "I thought I saw Fairfax. She went up there. To the third story. I thought that if she were going exploring I would like to join her. So I followed her. Except that I'm not certain that it was Fairfax at all. She didn't answer when I called."

"If it wasn't Fairfax, then it must have been Rena, or even Blanche," Wick answered, with patient amusement. "The acoustics in this rambling old house aren't the best. Whoever it was simply didn't hear you."

"I called several times," I said.

"Then it is quite simple, dear child.

Whoever it was didn't want to hear you," he said quite bluntly.

A door opened to our right, and Blanche peered through it, her black eyes gleaming with anger.

"It's *you*," she accused, looking first at me. "How can you expect a body to get their rest with people roaming about the halls all hours of the night? You thought I didn't know," she added. "You thought I didn't know that the two of you were up and snooping about."

I noticed that she wore a worn woolen wrapper, and that the smell of camphor and moth balls seemed to permeate her. How could I possibly have imagined that the mysterious woman in pink might have been Blanche? That narrowed it down then to Fairfax and Rena.

"I'm sorry, Blanche," Wick consoled the old woman. "We'll try to be more quiet —"

"It will do you no good to go nosing about," she said, cutting him off rudely. A crafty look came onto her face. "Others have tried it. I know. I know that one of you is the offspring of a murderer." She drew her head back and slammed the door.

"Wow!" Wick said. "Bitter old bitch, isn't she!"

"Apparently with reason," I said.

I thought of the portrait that I had discovered in the Tower attic. I wished that I had taken time to hide it somewhere; even destroy it. It seemed suddenly imperative that I keep this clever man from discovering it there, for it seemed to connect me, undeniably, with what had taken place in Wickerly the night Jared Wickerly had died in the slide, more than forty years before. The night Jared Wickerly had been murdered.

Wick led me along the corridor, his hand clasped firmly around my arm. If Blanche's venomous accusation had amazed him, he was clever enough to conceal it from me. The thought made me suddenly wary.

"Apparently." He picked up the thread of conversation, his voice unconcerned.

"In order to climax your book then you'll have to solve the mystery of Jared Wickerly's death," I said.

"Precisely. I plan on a startling denouement."

"It — it will involve one of us," I said, my voice trembling a little.

"Are you frightened, Nevvie?" he asked. "Don't be," he added softly, his voice becoming surprisingly tender. "You are far too lovely to be the daughter of a murderer."

His change of mood mystified me.

"I hardly view myself in that light," I said defiantly.

"You *are* frightened," he said. "Is it of me?" Without warning, he swept me into his arms. "Seeing you upset by Old Blanche's meanderings makes me feel protective, I'm afraid. I find myself extremely drawn to you all of a sudden." He bent to kiss my mouth. "Do you feel better, darling?"

"Darlings!" Fairfax had emerged silently from her room, and she stood watching us, her brown eyes flashing. For an instant I imagined that she was mocking Wick. "Just what is this about Nevvie being frightened? If something extraordinary has happened, why didn't you call me? After all, I *am* here to compile material for your book."

She wore a filmy peignoir that was, I noted, a subtle shade of green.

"Everything is fine," Wick told her. "We had trouble sleeping. I assure you that I won't hesitate to let you know any time that your services are needed."

Fairfax ducked back into her room, a little pout on her red mouth.

As I crawled into bed, Wick's kiss still burned on my mouth, and I found myself wondering what it would be like to belong to him.

Then I remembered the portrait that I had discovered in the attic room. I would get rid of it, I decided, before someone else stumbled onto it.

I dozed off at last, that pressing thought uppermost in my mind.

Chapter Five

The following day, Rena and I decided to explore the town. Wick had told us that he would be busy with Kev, and that for the time being the rest of us might feel free to do as we pleased.

As we started down the slope, Rena asked if I really believed that a man by the name of Wick Carver had been the last person to see Jared Wickerly alive. I guessed that she too wondered if Wick or I might actually be the offspring of a murderer.

I answered her absently, thinking again of the portrait in the Tower attic, with the small dark mole and the bullet hole between its cruel eyes. Because of it, I had carefully made up my face, using a complexion stick to conceal the mole near the corner of my own mouth. No one at breakfast had seemed to notice this small artifice, although I had caught Blanche Wickerly studying my face carefully, as she had the evening before over dinner.

As Rena and I made our way along the town's dusty main street, I decided I would slip up to the Tower attic at the first available opportunity and somehow destroy the dismaying likeness. I was determined that Wick Carver should not discover it.

An unbearable feeling of urgency possessed me.

"I'm sorry, Rena," I murmured. "I have a sudden headache. This glare . . . I'm not accustomed to it, coming from San Francisco where we've so much fog. Do you mind if I leave you to do your exploring alone?"

"Can I help, Nevvie?" Rena's green eyes were kind. "Do you have something to take? Aspirin? There's supposed to be a drugstore here somewhere."

"I've something in my room," I said.

I turned to start back up the hill, when Collins Stanton appeared, the heels of his boots kicking up little swirls of yellow dust.

"Nevvie. Rena." He nodded to each of us in turn. "Fine day to look over the town," he said, rocking back on his heels, surveying us from beneath the wide brim of a Stetson that looked slightly ludicrous, I must say, above his longish nose. The hat still smelled of newness in the hot sun. A clumsily hand-rolled cigarette dangled from the corner of his mouth.

"All you need is a horse," Rena commented, with a toss of her head.

"When in Rome . . ." Collins said, with a shrug. "God, what a burg!" He looked off in the direction of the lake that glimmered at the bottom of Five Mile Canyon. "Do you suppose he's really down there, like they say? Old Jared Wickerly, his bones dripping slime?"

I gave him a startled look.

"Hell, Nevvie, I'll be as irreverent as I damn please," he said, affecting a drawl. "I don't live here. If I did I'd take me some sticks of powder some dark night and go after that silver, and to hell with Old Jared's revered bones."

"I'd have to see it to believe it," Rena commented.

"Keep your eyes peeled, kid," Collins retorted. "Could be I'll figure out a way to get my hands on some of that precious silver anyway. Who do you suppose did it, murdered Old Jared? I've an idea that Old Blanche would like to know exactly who it was."

"She's just a harmless old lady," Rena said.

"She might be a little bit batty," Collins

said. "Crazy enough to try to avenge Jared, which may be why she has leased her over-sized shack to this Wickerly Carver — Vin Savage while he digs up the dirt." Collins paused, giving me a challenging glance. "Have you or Wick considered bringing out a tintype of your relative and asking this Kev Keever person, or even Old Blanche, if they can identify it as that first Wick Carver, the one who is supposed to have done her brother in? Or do either of you quite dare?"

"Collins, you are even worse than I thought," Rena accused. "Nevvie has a headache, as it is —"

"Ah, Nevvie, honey, I didn't mean nothin' by it. I swear," Collins said, in his exaggerated drawl. "It was just an idle thought. I reckon the whole thing had something to do with that heap of silver that's said to be still down there, girls. Why else should Wick's pappy, or Nevvie's, have wanted to bump off Old Jared? Toss him into that cesspool of slime?" He gestured lazily toward the lake.

"I suppose I have some snapshots of my father tucked away somewhere," I said coolly. "After he died, I couldn't bear to be reminded," I added. "But that's quite an-other story, and I still have this depressing headache. Perhaps Collins will go exploring with you, Rena, so you won't have to go wandering about alone."

I thought craftily that this would keep them both away from the Tower. And since everyone else had gone off, only Blanche Wickerly and Carmen, the housekeeper, were left in the old mansion.

Collins and Rena started off, laughing together, seeming to take to each other with remarkable casualness. I turned back toward the Tower, hurrying a little up the dusty street.

"Fine day, ain't it?" the old man whom I had seen the first day on the bench in front of the Green Lizard called out, waving. "I'm Pop. Pop Denman," he added, as I smiled.

He looked up at me with rheumy eyes that held an unmistakable spark of interest.

"And I'm Nevada Carver," I told him, unavoidably, stopping with him now.

"So I heard," he commented. "A couple of you Carvers up there at the Tower, I understand. Kin, I reckon."

"No. We're not related. At least, not knowingly."

"It ain't like Carver was any ordinary name in this town," Pop Denman said.

"I know," I said. "Wick Carver was the last man to see Blanche Wickerly's brother alive. That first Wick Carver," I added.

The old man gave me a shrewd look.

"That first Wick Carver skedaddled out of here, without telling a living soul what he'd seen," Pop Denman said. "The only way we knew for certain that Jared was dead was through a letter Wick sent five years later, or maybe six. Nobody had seen hide nor hair of him, in all of that time. We thought he'd died, too, along with Jared, down there in that big slide."

He pointed toward the arm of land that cupped the lake.

"And then one day Jay Keever — that was Kev Keever's father — got word from Wick Carver claiming he'd *seen* Jared die and asking Jay to publish a notice in the *Strike* saying so. The *Strike* was an up and coming newspaper at the time. When they read Jay's notice, folks knew that Jared was dead."

"He wasn't actually murdered, then?" I asked eagerly.

"Blanche called it that. Still does. I reckon she's got most of the town believing it by now. Seems like she had to blame someone. Wick Carver was the one she chose. There was another brother. Norman

Wickerly, his name was. Jay claimed that Wick Carver never made any mention of him in that letter, although Norman was gone too. Disappeared the same night Jared died. Both brothers gone, buried down there under that water somewhere. But it was Jared Blanche cared about. She really didn't like Norman at all in fact. He wasn't . . . much. After Jay got the letter from Wick Carver, saying for certain that Jared had died down there, Blanche had a monument erected. A monument to Jared, her favorite brother."

I followed the line of his pointing finger, and saw a marble spire rising, needle thin, on top of the earthen dam.

"Did anyone but Jay see the letter?" I asked.

"Didn't have to," Pop said. "Jay's word was sterling in this town, and everywhere else for that matter."

I gazed down at the dark lake, contemplating the old man's words, thinking at the same time of the two brothers lying dead somewhere at the bottom of the flooded canyon.

"You should have seen the two of them together in those days," Pop Denman continued, in a reminiscent voice. "Blanche as pretty as a picture, with all of that thick black hair, and her flashing dark eyes, and Jared, black-headed too, but his eyes blue. At times, there was a kind of jealousy between them, I'm thinking. The sparks would fly, then. And the next day they'd be cozy again, Jared leading Blanche off down to the mine, teaching her the ropes like she was a man, showing her how to dig and scrape and blast out the jewelry ore; that was all the two of them had left, with Old Sil dead. Jared cherished her, too, as a woman. Saw to it that none of the men there in the mine got smart with her." The old man paused to suck in a deep breath.

"Jared, Blanche, and the silver," he went on, almost to himself. "That was all this town knew. Blanche has mourned Jared all of these years. She had him a coffin built, hoping we'd find his body. We never did. She has that coffin still, there in the big house." He nodded toward the Tower. "Saving it for herself, maybe. Her grief went to her head in some ways. Made her strange."

"Grief does that sometimes," I commented, wondering where Blanche kept the coffin, if it was indeed still there somewhere inside of the old house.

"The town figured, before Jay got that letter from Wick Carver, that he'd died down there in that slide with Jared and Norman," Pop said.

"And that's why the town was willing to accept Blanche's theory that Wick Carver had killed Jared," I said. "Because Wick had disappeared without saying anything."

"I reckon that's about what it boils down to," Pop said.

"But it all happened so long ago. How can any of it possibly matter now?"

"This town died right along with Jared, in a manner of speaking," Pop stated. "Whoever killed Jared, if it was murder, like Blanche suspects, did us all in; left us here to rot, Jared down there at the bottom of the canyon, and the rest of us up here in the sun, drying up like those parched coyotes there over the door of the museum."

"You could have gotten out; gone someplace else and started over," I said. "Others have done that."

"Not so long as there's so much as an ounce of that silver still down there," Pop said. "A number of us here were interested in that ore. Still are. There was a time when every man in town worked the Wickerly mine. The silver belonged to Old Sil, and Jared after him. But it supported us all. I reckon it's the hope that it will again that holds a few of us here. We've waited more than forty years for that damn lake to go dry. Maybe it will yet, so we can get to that ore without disturbing Jared's grave." The old man suddenly looked crafty. "That, or somebody will dare to go against the name. Blow that fill up in spite of Jared's being buried there in that big hunk of clay."

"If Wick Carver saw Jared die, surely he explained how it happened in the letter," I said, my curiosity far from appeased. "Surely he cleared himself of any doubt."

"According to Jay Keever, Wick Carver didn't go into detail in that letter. He didn't say just how Jared died. Only that he had seen him die."

"Someone should have looked him up; gone to him; asked him outright how it was," I said.

"Maybe. But he must have covered his traces," the old man mused. "Then again, this town was probably afraid to know the truth. Maybe it still is. That lake is always there to remind us that there was something unnatural about the way Jared Wickerly died. Norman too, of course. All of these years, the town has gone along with Blanche, respected Jared's grave. But we all know that the town can't go on forever, like this. It takes more than legends to keep a place alive. And the government is wanting silver again now. The price is up." The old man looked down at the lake.

"A few well-placed sticks of dynamite would do it," he continued. "Blanche could set them herself. Jared taught her mining from the bottom up, when she was a girl. There's a fortune down there under that water. A regular god-damn Comstock. Maybe one of these days the town will go back to it, start digging ore again. But we'll have to find Jared first. Move his remains . . . unless *Blanche* dies pretty soon."

The old man turned back to me.

"Like I was telling that young fellow, the one in the cowboy getup. Collins Stanton, he said his name was. Like I was telling him a little while ago, if it happened that Jared wasn't caught in that slide, after all; if we should find out, say, that he'd been trapped underground, in one of the mine tunnels, then that pile of dirt wouldn't be sacred any more. That would turn the town loose. We'd blast away, drain off that damned black water."

"Why are you telling me this?" I asked.

"You ain't the only one I've told," Pop said. "Like I say, I was telling it all to that young Stanton fellow. And I'll tell it again to anybody who's got a mind to stop a minute and listen. I'm an old man. I won't be around many more years. One of these days, I'd like to tell it all to the right person. The right Carver, maybe." He paused, his eyes becoming shrewd. "The Carver with enough gravel in his craw to go against Blanche and this town. Say to hell with Jared's sacred bones. There's only one way to clear that first Wick Carver's name, and that's to get down under that dam and find what's left of Jared and his brother, Norman. There should be some evidence there to show how they died. If it was murder, we'd know. Then again, if it wasn't —"

"Wick Carver's name would be cleared," I said.

"Respect for the dead is a fine thing," Pop commented. "But the living has to look out for themselves."

I left the old man, his outspoken words ringing in my ears. It seemed incredible to think that Pop Denman might once have known my father. I wanted to turn back and question him about that first Wick Carver, but the thought of the portrait made me put this aside for the moment.

As I hurried toward the Tower, I noticed, in the midst of the bleak, crumbling miners' shacks, a brightly painted dwelling, with dormer windows set into its steeply slanted roof and a broad, sheltered veranda running protectively around it. It was painted a frivolous shade of pink that seemed to defy the prim old house above me. There was something lush and forbidden about it.

I turned back toward the Tower, my curiosity about the pink house fleeing before the sense of urgency that once more overpowered me. It seemed imperative for me now to destroy the portrait hidden in the attic as quickly as possible.

I entered the Tower, pausing inside of the front door for an instant, listening for Blanche. I detected a slight, rustling sound, which seemed to come from the large back parlor, or the dining room beyond. Carmen, I thought, going about her duties. I went toward the sound, calling her name.

She answered from the kitchen.

"I'm looking for Miss Blanche," I told her, when her face protruded around the edge of the kitchen door.

"The old woman is in her room resting," Carmen said, her black eyes questioning.

"I have a headache," I explained, remembering the excuse I had given Rena. "I thought perhaps Miss Blanche might have aspirin."

Carmen disappeared through a doorway opening off of the large kitchen, and returned with a small bottle. I thanked her, gulped two pills down with the glass of water that she brought me, and went upstairs, following the corridor that led to the third-story stair. I passed by Blanche's door, listening outside for an instant, trying to catch some telltale sound. There was nothing, and I decided that I was in luck; that the old woman must be napping.

Stealthily, I made my way up to the third floor.

Before going to the room where the portrait was hidden, I went up to the cupola, and looked down on the town to be certain that none of the others were on their way back up the hill to the silent mansion.

Through a pair of binoculars that I found on a window ledge, I was able to see Collins and Rena very clearly, standing near the dark water. Their young faces seemed surprisingly serious, and I fancied that they were arguing. Puzzled, I turned the binoculars away, focusing now on the needle-thin spire of marble.

A woman stood in the thin shadow of the spire, and for an instant I imagined that it was Fairfax. Then I noticed that her blond hair was darker, more brassy, and that she had a full-blown figure, her hips and breasts flaring out from a trim waist in hourglass fashion. As I watched her, a small, spotted animal came darting up over the ridge and leaped to lick her hand, in a startlingly familiar gesture. Stunned, I realized that it was a small terrier identical to the dog in the portrait, identical to the small dogs that my father had loved and that I had grown up with.

I lowered the binoculars, laying them carefully back on the ledge, and fled from the cupola, overcome by a sudden sense of unreality.

When I entered the attic room, I saw at once that the portrait was gone. Frantically, I rummaged about through the endless clutter, searching everywhere. Had I only imagined that I had seen it there?

Desperately, I ran back up to the cupola and snatched up the binoculars, fitting them to my eyes, focusing them quickly. The woman was still there, slumped against Jared's monument, her head resting against the rosy stone. The little dog danced sympathetically beside her. I guessed that she was crying.

Of one thing I was certain: The two of *them* were quite real. Just as the portrait had been of course. Someone had taken it.

Chapter Six

"I have made a rather incredible discovery," Fairfax announced over dinner that night. "I must warn all of you that it is a bit shocking."

"Something that will prove invaluable to my book, I assume," Wick said dryly.

"You are holding us all in suspense, Mother, dear," Collins said. "Please stop being coy and get on with it."

"This town has what was commonly known in the days of the wicked West as a fancy house," Fairfax announced triumphantly. She scanned each of our faces in turn, then tilted her head charmingly at Wick. "Just the fillip your book needs, in this day of sex obsession."

There was a small, strangling sound from the end of the table. Blanche. The old woman sat clutching her throat, her wizened face pale.

"I'll not have obscenities uttered over my table," she announced. There was a threatening note in her voice. "We Wickerlys have always stood for decency in this town that bears our name. I'll not have it, do you understand? This is still my house."

"I'm sorry, Blanche," Wick said, his voice patiently soothing. "You must understand that a writer has to deal with every aspect of life. Objectively, of course. I intend to portray happenings in this town, and the town itself, as accurately as possible. However, I will most certainly change names when necessary. So far as your own family is concerned, I'm certain that you've nothing to fear."

The old woman seemed not to have been listening.

"No!" she uttered, in a croaking voice. "I had no idea. If you will excuse me, I shall retire to my room and leave you to discuss these . . . scandalous matters, without me."

She seemed terribly eager to get away, and went scurrying out now, her long, black dress rustling about her thin legs.

"Why did the old girl agree to let you have this house if she's so concerned about the reputation of her precious town?" Collins said, after Blanche had gone. "She seemed the next thing to scared there for a minute, pardners. Methinks her honored brother must once have frequented that fancy house, and that more than this town's reputation is at stake here."

"That is a thought," Fairfax said. "Why *do* you suppose she leased to you, Wick?"

"No false pretenses," Wick said. "I suppose she needed the money. I'm paying her a fortune for the use of this place. But then I intend to glean a fortune in return."

"That book had better be good then, darling," Fairfax said. "I promise to do my share. And the natives here seem quite eager to divulge their little tidbits about the family. This Jared that everyone seems so obsessed with sounds like an absolute savage. He did his brother Norman dirt, you know. Shoved a rock onto poor Norman, it seems, when they were still tikes. Shattered poor little Norman's leg all to pieces. According to the local legend, Jared was jealous of Norman. Norman was the eldest and due to inherit the Wickerly holdings when Old Sil died."

Kev was watching me. "Nevvie should be able to sympathize with that. She told us, remember, that her father limped."

"Very slightly," I said.

Fairfax, who had paused for dramatic emphasis, continued: "And get this. Old Sil wouldn't take Norman to a doctor, after what Jared did to him."

"Sounds like a mean old bastard," Collins said.

"Old Sil, it seems, always claimed that you couldn't hurt a Wickerly. He had some notion that Wickerlys were an indestructible breed. He wrapped Norman's leg in a rag and told the poor kid that the leg would prove whether or not he was a true Wickerly. If the leg got all right, he was Wickerly stock, through and through. If it didn't . . ." Fairfax gave a shrug.

"Did it?" Rena asked, her eyes wide with disbelief.

"No," Fairfax said. "He was left a cripple. Seems that the leg healed. But it was twisted, somehow, so that Norman never walked right again. Limped, like Nevvie's father."

They were all looking at me. Wick's eyes squinted slightly, gleaming with speculation, between their creased lids.

"As I've said, my father's limp was very minor," I heard myself saying, as though the moment demanded some sort of explanation. "Besides, his name was Carver. And Norman Wickerly is dead."

"You seem absolutely touchy on the subject, darling," Fairfax said. "I suppose it was rather heart-rending to see your father hobbling about. And poor Norman

Wickerly. They say that he had to use crutches for a long while. It was that bad."

"Small wonder," Rena commented.

I sat steeped in an airy flow of relief. My father had never owned a crutch in his life! At least, not that I had known of. That small thought crept in, dashing my feeling of release. I told myself that I was being foolish about the portrait. Yet that feeling of bewilderment overcame me again, and I thought: Could my father possibly have been a Wickerly. Was the fact that he had limped much more than coincidence?

"That imperfect leg finished Norman with Old Sil," Kev Keever was saying. "Old Sil and Jared both turned their backs on Norman. They had no use for cripples."

"Charming family," Collins said. "Now about this fancy house, Mother" — a leer came onto his face — "naturally, I am interested."

Rena nudged him with her elbow, wrinkling her nose at him. "If that's the sort you are," she said, "count me out."

Collins' face became suddenly serious.

"I was only joking, kid," he said.

I was surprised by the intensity of his voice, and guessed that the two had planned something together that was important to Collins.

"You can't miss it," Fairfax said. "It's the only building in town boasting a fresh coat of paint. Pink, of all colors."

The bungalow I had noticed, near the edge of town.

Fairfax glanced accusingly at Kev.

"You knew about it all the time, darling," she said. "I can tell by that smug expression on your face."

"Rose Tibbet's Pink Cloud," Kev said.

Fairfax laughed. "What an appropriate name! I've always suspected that these drab Western towns weren't without their sense of humor. A rather delightful touch for your book, Wick." She turned back to Kev. "I assume that this Rose Tibbet you mention is madam there, then?"

Kev nodded, giving Rena and me an uncomfortable look. I felt my face flush.

"I think this discussion might wait," Wick said. He had glanced at me and caught my blush.

I looked down at my plate, trying to assume a worldly expression. Carmen came in with dessert then; and the conversation turned to lighter matters.

Later, after we had finished coffee in the parlor, Wick asked me if I might like to go for a walk. I agreed to go, surprised by the rush of eagerness that welled up in me.

Wickerly Carver. I mouthed his name silently, as we walked up the slope beyond the Tower. Had he perhaps fallen in love with me and hoped to protect me from some unimaginable unpleasantness by taking the portrait?

The yellow lights of town lay below us, reflected in the lake beyond. The Pink Cloud was gaily lighted, a bevy of Japanese lanterns suspended from the roof of the veranda.

"They're having a party down there," I said.

"I imagine so," Wick said, in a dry voice.

"Did you know about it before you came here?" I asked, for no particular reason other than to make conversation. "The Pink Cloud. Did you intend to put it in your book?"

"A reasonable facsimile thereof," he said. "All names changed to protect the innocent. After all, it is a part of Wickerly. The Pink Cloud, and the girls who live there, have had their considerable influence, on this town. In fact, they've helped keep the town alive, if you can call this living. And, as Fairfax suggested, it will give my book an added fillip. Her word, not mine."

"Do you like Fairfax?" I asked, a little shocked by my own daring.

He chuckled.

"You have just reminded me again that you are still something of a youngster," he said. "Yes, as a matter of fact, I do like Fairfax. But in a rather cynical way, I fear. I have known a good many women like her and have grown to know a little bit about how they operate, enough to be rather wary. Women like Fairfax seem to enjoy entangling unsuspecting males in their webs, but she is amusing."

He slipped an arm about my shoulders then, and I became conscious of the virile warmth of his tall, hard body.

"Do you suppose he really was murdered?" I asked, to break the silence that had fallen between us — a rather dangerous silence, for it had given me a chance to realize that my feelings toward Wick were rather eager, and even a bit daring. I caught myself hoping that he might kiss me again. "Jared Wickerly, with all his stacks of silver?" I qualified my question.

"It's rather possible," Wick said. "Just as Blanche suspects."

"Have you discovered yet which of our fathers did it?" I asked, trying to sound a bit flippant.

"No," he said, and I imagined that his voice had become evasive. "You'd never guess that this town once boasted twenty thousand inhabitants," he added rather quickly. "That was right after Old Sil Wickerly discovered silver in Five Mile Canyon. The prospectors and bonanza seekers came pouring in from all over. There were a dozen or so mines strung along these mountains, like beads on a necklace. All of them spilled jewelry ore, according to the old-timers. The San Francisco agencies located their banks and counting houses here, and carried on their business to the music of mine whistles and steam engines. These barren hills fairly echoed with the hammering of the big stamp mills."

"And look at it now," I said.

"Somehow it has managed to hang on. But barely. A few head of cattle running these brown slopes. The lake provides water for livestock, I understand. And there's the tourist trade, if you can call it that. Carloads of young men from California's military bases, with a weekend pass in their pockets, seeking Rose Tibbet's girls. It's the way of the world, Nevvie."

"It would help if someone blasted away the dam and the mine opened again. Of course, they'd be working for Blanche, I suppose. The silver would belong to her, as it has always belonged to Wickerlys. But according to town gossip, she's more interested in preserving Jared's grave than she is in the ore."

"If the silver belonged to you, what would you do, Nevvie?" Wick asked in a soft voice.

"What a strange thing to ask," I said, looking up into his face, seeing the shine of his eyes through the shadows.

"Would you be content to stay in this town? Live there in the Tower, as Blanche does, if it all belonged to you?" he persisted.

"I'd forfeit it all to town charity, and that would solve everything," I answered frivolously.

Sleep eluded me that night, partly because Wick had kissed me again, when we had returned from our walk, and it had excited me more than I had thought it would, and partly because I was still concerned about the portrait.

I comforted myself with the thought that whoever had taken the painting couldn't possibly connect it with me, not without a picture of my father with which to compare it. But I couldn't help trying to find some logical explanation for its presence. There seemed to be none. Unless my father had been involved with Blanche Wickerly, I thought. Had he once been Blanche's suitor? Had he given her a portrait of himself as some sort of love token? Had he fled because he couldn't bear to face the sister of the man he had seen die? But that wouldn't have been like him, I thought, with a foreboding, though, that bordered on despair.

In an effort to escape the jumble of thoughts that seemed intent on plaguing me, I rose from my bed and went to the window. The moon shone brightly, and I stood gazing out onto the barren landscape, lost in my thoughts, not really seeing it. I have no idea how long I had been watching, when a light appeared over the surface of the lake. I thought at first that it was perhaps a flash of lightning; the dark clouds indicated that a storm might be brewing.

Then the glow became crystallized into a single beam, and I realized that there was someone there, shining lights about, snooping. Looking for silver, I thought. At the same time, I glimpsed two vague, dark figures near the shore of the lake. There was something clandestine in their movements, and vaguely familiar.

Later that same night, I was puzzled again by the sounds of someone roaming about the old house. The faint noises seemed to come from somewhere inside the walls, as though someone were concealed there, climbing about on a secret stair. I thought at once of the mysterious woman in pink.

I climbed out of bed, and pressed my ear against the wall, feeling rather foolish even though I was alone in the room. The sounds seemed to be coming from my closet. Was it Blanche snooping about, trying to find proof that I was the daughter of the man who had murdered her brother?

I flicked on my closet light and pushed my clothes aside to peer into the corners, half expecting to see Blanche's waspish face peering back at me.

There was no one there, and I told myself that I was being hopelessly dramatic.

As I left the closet, the wall gave beneath my touch, and I sprang back, startled, knocking a dress from its hanger. I examined the wall more closely and discovered that a portion of the dark wainscoting had gone askew. The dry, acrid smell of ancient woods and mortar gushed from the crack that had appeared in the closet wall.

A feeling of excitement, coupled with a sense of apprehension, came over me. I pushed the small door slowly open, revealing rows of bricks, to which a narrow ladder was attached. I realized that I was looking at one of the tall chimneys that protruded from the mansion's intricate roof. There was room enough between the walls to allow a man access. I guessed that the opening had been placed in the closet wall, as a precautionary measure, should the chimney ever require repairs.

The sounds had stopped. Whoever had been climbing about in the dark repair shaft had apparently been frightened away by my intrusion.

I fumbled again with the small door, and this time succeeded in closing it, but not before I had detected a subtle hint of perfume — that same cloying, old-fashioned scent that had wafted from the woman in pink!

I called softly. There was no reply.

More puzzled than ever, I went back to bed.

Chapter Seven

The following morning Carmen appeared while we were at breakfast. Someone had been in her pantry during the night, she complained to Wick. She had heard them walking about. Whoever it had been had left the cellar door ajar, she said, because she had found it standing partially open, and she feared that mice might come up from the cellar, to invade her kitchen.

"Esta me está agotando la paciencia!" she said, looking wide-eyed at Wick, affronted by the invasion of the old mansion's quarters that she now considered her own personal domain. "This thing is very trying to my patience," she added, remembering that she spoke English.

A puzzled expression had come onto Blanche Wickerly's face. It changed quickly to a look that I interpreted as fear. The old woman glanced up, caught me watching her, and hurriedly lifted her cup to her lips.

"There is nothing of interest in the cellar," she said, in a voice that accused us all of prying. "Nothing!" she repeated. "I shall see that it is locked, when I finish here. There will be no further reason for you to concern yourself."

Suddenly I remembered what Pop Denman had said about Jared's death. Blanche had bought a coffin, he had told me. The cellar would be the logical place for it, I reasoned, and of course Blanche was concerned that someone might come onto her macabre relic.

My thoughts were interrupted by Wick, who was outlining the day's activities. Rena was to drive into Fallon to pick up file cards and other supplies. Collins offered to take her, his eagerness betraying the fact that the two of them had planned the trip beforehand. Wick gave them an amused smile, seeming not to mind, telling them that they might take his car.

"Any chance that Fairfax might borrow a key to that musty newspaper office of yours?" he asked Kev. "I'd like her to get started digging through the morgue."

"I'm afraid it's in a state of disarray," Kev said. "I'd intended to sort through things. At least rout out the pack rats."

"Let me help you, darling," Fairfax said.

"I suppose you could." Kev's voice was hesitant.

"Agreed," Wick said, apparently not having noticed Kev's reluctance. "The two of you get started there, then." He glanced at me. "I'll need you today, Nevvie. I want to get started dictating."

I nodded.

"Luck," Fairfax whispered, brushing against me, as we were leaving the dining room. "Loads of luck, darling." Her lips curled in a sly little smile. "You might need it. Remember what I told you? May the best woman win."

Her words shocked me a little, and I drew back.

"No need to play the innocent," she commented. "I saw you with him last night, coming down off the hill. Has it occurred to you that Kev is nearer your own age, and not unattractive?"

I started to protest, my face burning.

"Don't bother, dear, I have eyes," Fairfax commented. "Ordinarily, I wouldn't mind the competition, but Wick is different. I find that I suddenly mind. Very much. And I intend to have him, Nevada Carver," she added softly. "At least for a brief affair."

She left me standing alone in the dark foyer, the others already gone. I watched after her, wondering what her game really was.

Wick had arranged the library, a dark-paneled, high-ceilinged room, to serve as his office, and I found him there. I greeted him timidly, Fairfax's words still ringing in my ears.

He sat behind a huge desk that crouched on lion's feet clasped around large glass balls that had turned lavender with age. Reaching into a deep drawer, he brought out a portable tape recorder.

"I've something here for you to transcribe," he said. "A prologue to the book. It will require polish after it's typed out. But that will have to wait. Right now, I've several new thoughts that I want to get down before they vanish."

He began to dictate, and, although he had changed several of the names, I easily recognized the characters. Pop Denman. Jay Keever, Kev's father, and editor of the *Strike* during the small town's heyday.

It was noon before I realized it, and when Wick suggested that we ask Carmen to make sandwiches for us to take on a little picnic, I told him that it sounded like a marvelous idea. He suggested that we stroll down by the lake, and I recalled the lights that I had seen there during the night. I was on the verge of telling him about it, when something in his eyes prompted me not to. They seemed suddenly speculative, as he looked at me, his lids squinted a little over their tawny brightness.

"I'll run up and get a sweater," I said a bit nervously. "There seems to be a breeze." I turned toward the door.

"Nevvie," he said, behind me.

He had come quite close to me. I felt his breath stirring the hairs on my neck, making them tickle.

"Yes?" I turned to face him.

"I think I'm growing fond of you," he said.

Amazed by his sudden change of attitude, I forced a gay laugh.

"Fairfax won't like it," I quipped. Then, when he didn't smile in return, I added, quickly: "If you will excuse an ancient cliché, isn't this rather sudden?"

"So you suspect my motives," he said, drawing away from me.

"Should I?" I asked, feeling uneasy and even a little frightened of him.

There had been something in his voice, I thought, almost as though there actually *were* motives of a sort not ordinarily present in a relationship between a man and a woman.

"Of course," he said, becoming suddenly amiable, whirling about to face me. "After all, I am an older man. And a Carver. Wickerly Carver. That in itself, I suppose, is enough to make any intentions I might have toward you suspect."

"It occurs to me that you didn't explain much about your father that first night over dinner," I said.

"Would it shock you too much, Nevada, to know that he *was* the Wick Carver who once lived here in this town? He used to talk about this place. He even brought me here once to look at that damned, black lake down there." Wick came to stand over me, his eyes intensely bright, searching my face.

"Then *he* was the last person to see Jared Wickerly alive," I said disbelievingly. "The one who —"

"Who murdered Jared," Wick finished for me, raising his thick, dark brows. "No, darling. He wasn't. It was someone else."

"But who?" I asked, thinking suddenly of the portrait. "Who did it if it wasn't your father? And why did he run away from here and then write that letter to Jay Keever, telling what he had seen? Pop Denman must have told you about it. He seems to have told everyone else."

"My father had nothing to do with any letter to Jay. I can vouch for it. I knew him well, as a matter of fact, better than most sons ever get to know the man who sires them. Although I never knew my mother. Do you understand now why I've come to this place? Why I have to find out the truth about what happened here the night Jared died? I'll not have my father labeled a murderer, even though he is dead."

"Why have you waited so long?" I asked.

"Financial insecurity, for one thing," he said. "This is a rather costly project. Then, too, I had a certain amount of searching to do. Carver is a common name. Wickerly too, for that matter. It's the combination of the two that's rare."

"Someone took your father's name? Became an impostor?" I asked in a small voice.

"Precisely," Wick said.

"And my father was the only other Wick Carver that you found?"

He nodded, slipping a companionable arm about my shoulders, guiding me from the room.

"It couldn't have been my father," I said. "There has to be someone else. Another Wickerly Carver."

"Perhaps," Wick said quietly.

"And perhaps whoever it was thought

that Wick Carver — that first Wick Carver — died that night, as well," I said, still trying to make sense of what he had told me.

"Did your father ever say why he left this town so suddenly?" I asked Wick now. "Allowed them to think that he was . . . was guilty of murder? He must have had some overwhelming reason."

"He didn't care what they thought of him here," Wick said. "He was an easygoing sort of guy. And so long as no one came along looking for him, trying to lock him up for some crime that he hadn't committed, he was content to let things slide." Wick's voice had become bitter.

"You think someone took advantage of him, whether he knew about it or not," I said.

"I know someone did," Wick told me, his face moody.

"And now you are out to avenge him," I said. "That is your real reason for writing this book."

"Perhaps," he said, not looking at me.

We went into the kitchen, where Carmen had prepared a variety of sandwiches, tucking them into a bag with a bottle of Port.

"Didn't people recognize your father when he came back here ostensibly to show you that lake?" I asked Wick, when we were started down the hill. "Surely someone must have remembered him."

"We didn't come to the town itself. We were just passing through. We had driven over from the main highway late one evening, just as the moon was coming up. Dad told me something about this place that night. I guess I knew even then that someday I might come here. . . ." He broke off.

I glanced up to see Fairfax and Kev coming up the dusty street toward us.

"Darlings!" Fairfax called, in her usual slightly affected manner. "Kev and I have uncovered a fantastic amount of juicy material down there in his dusty old morgue. To think that his father slaved there for years, trying to put out some semblance of a newspaper. It's an absolute mare's nest. But fertile. Terribly fertile."

Kev winced at her words, his lips tightening.

"The point is, darling, I really can't jot it all down. There is far too much for that. I'd appreciate it no end if you'd come on down now and help me discriminate. All of those stacks and stacks of old newspapers, with their unbelievable stories. Killings, darling. Would you believe it? And clever little editorials on the pros and cons of Rose Tibbet's sort of business."

"Dad was wasted on this town," Kev commented.

Wick glanced at me. "How about it, Nevvie? Do you mind if I suddenly desert you? I've worked you too hard already today, or I'd ask you to bring along your notebook."

"Go ahead," Kev said, taking a key from his pocket. "I'll look after Nevvie."

"But our lunch . . ." I protested feebly.

"You take it. Share it with Kev," Wick said. "I'll grab something at the local greasy spoon."

Fairfax slipped an arm possessively through his, casting me a triumphant look over her shoulder, as the two of them started down the hill.

"So he has you captivated, too," Kev commented.

"He is a charming man," I said.

"A dangerous man," Kev said.

I gave him a startled look.

"Whatever on earth do you mean?" I asked. "I can't imagine why you'd say a thing like that about Wick."

"Male antagonism," Kev said, with a mysterious smile. "After all, I too am fond of pretty girls."

I was surprised to find myself enjoying Kev's presence, which seemed a bulwark against the overpoweringly barren landscape that expanded around us with increasing austerity as we drew near the lake.

"Apart from what I said," Kev now mused, "there is something about our employer that doesn't quite ring true. Pop Denman claims he looks familiar."

I glanced at him, quickly.

"That's not surprising," I said, unthinkingly.

Kev gave me a sharp glance.

"Quite the contrary," he said. "Unless you know something about him that he has kept from the rest of us."

"No doubt he looked this town over before he brought us here," I said quickly. "He had to come here to make arrangements for the Tower. Isn't it just possible that Pop caught a glimpse of him then. It seems that anyone bearing the name of Carver is suspect here."

"This is an unfriendly town in some ways," Kev said. "What folks really dread, I suppose, is the idea that another Wickerly might turn up. Jared wasn't exactly lovable, you know." He gestured toward the great hump of tan earth that plugged the narrow mouth of Five Mile Canyon. "And there has never been any actual proof that he died. This town has never really been able to understand how such a thing could have happened to Jared Wickerly." He gave me a quick glance.

"To Norman, yes," he continued. "For all that he was born one of them, Norman lacked the domineering qualities that Old Sil and Jared considered essential in a Wickerly. But Jared. . . . If it turned out, say, that he had somehow escaped that slide; had simply wandered off, perhaps a victim of amnesia, and he or his progeny should show up here again, especially now that Old Blanche is nearing her own end, the old pattern could very well be re-established. A male Wickerly lording it over the town again from that cupola, on top of the Tower. I've an idea it came as a relief to this town to be rid of Old Sil and Jared, even if it meant losing the silver, at least for a while."

"In other words, this town is going to go for that silver for itself, the first chance it gets," I said.

"Nothing can keep us out of that mine once Blanche is gone," Kev said. "The property will revert to the government since there will be no heirs. We'll file on it. Form a corporation. Silver is in demand again, for a good price, and with good lawyers it can be done."

"Unless Blanche leaves a will," I said.

"She hasn't made any move in that direction, so far," Kev said. "I know the lawyer in Fallon who has always handled Wickerly affairs. He mentioned, offhand, that he doubted that Old Blanche had more than the clothes on her back to leave. She hasn't been able to keep the old house up, that's for certain. And she evidently hasn't enough cash left to begin mining operations, even if that lake should suddenly go down. This town would have to raise the capital; another reason they've sat back here and let that silver stay where it is."

"Let's go up to the monument," I said on impulse, thinking suddenly of the blond woman and the small dog that I had seen there. "I'd like to read the inscription."

" 'Jared Baylor Wickerly,' " Kev quoted. " 'Eighteen ninety to nineteen twenty-three,' or thereabouts. 'Taken from us by an act of nature. May his dear soul find peace.' " He glanced at me. "Okay, if you're certain that you want to climb up there just to read Blanche's idea of a suitable epitaph to her beloved brother."

We followed a cow path around the steep

shore, Kev walking ahead of me, his shoes scuffing up the inevitable little clouds of dun-colored dust.

"Take a good look, Nevvie," Kev said now, pausing ahead of me to scan the expanse of water. "There's mystery down there. Dad knew it. It became almost an obsession with him to dig up the facts. Publish them in his newspaper." Kev looked at me. "Do you know what a story like that could have meant to him? Jared Wickerly's death made good copy in its day. They ran the story back East in the *Times*. Wickerly was a name everyone knew then. If Dad could only have come out with a good follow-up, it would have put the *Strike* right up there at the top. But all he had was that one letter from Wick Carver. Five years after it happened. It was too late then. Interest in Wickerly and its silver had waned. Dad devoted his entire life to this damned town. And not once did he receive the recognition that he deserved. Oh, he was well liked here. Revered, I suppose you might say. People came to him with their troubles, expecting him to help them out. And he was the kind of man who would do it. Good old Jay Keever. But he could have been more than just a shoulder for this town to cry on. He was a newspaperman. A damn good one. All he needed was one lousy break."

"It's not everyone who wins the admiration and respect of his fellow men," I said, puzzled by Kev's bitterness. "Don't you suppose that for him it might have been enough?"

He seemed not to have heard me. "I have a feeling that the true story of what happened here that night might have been the scoop he needed. Just one lousy break."

He turned so suddenly toward me that I stepped backward. As I did so, I caught sight of the unmistakable marks left by a small dog's footpads, molded into the soft dust. Instinctively, I knew that whoever the blond woman had been, she was a part of Wickerly's mystery.

"That's why I agreed to come back here, with this Wick Carver. Vin Savage. Whoever the hell he is."

"You're still looking for that scoop, after all these years," I said.

"I'm going to reopen the *Strike* office one of these days," Kev said, giving me a determined look.

"Does Wick know?"

"Not yet."

He took my arm, steering me up the steep slope of the dam.

"Not that it's any business of his," he added. He gazed up at the sharply pointed monument. "There was a loud clap of thunder the night Jared Wickerly died," he said, as we climbed toward it. "Dad told me about it once. And it's something that Pop Denman and a few other old-timers still talk about. Pop says that it wasn't natural, that it was an isolated sound of some sort. Maybe a manmade blast. Pop's tale has helped to give credence to the theory that Jared was murdered."

We came to the monument, and I read the strange epitaph: "An act of nature . . ."

It was eerie there on top of the dam, even in daylight; silent, with no hint of a breeze stirring. I felt suddenly eager to get away.

We started back down the slope, following one of the meandering cow paths.

"Why didn't she erect a monument to the other brother?" I said musingly, as we left the monument. "Or at least put his name on this one, along with Jared's."

"Jared was all she cared about," Kev said, repeating what Pop Denman had told me.

"Wasn't there anyone else in her life? A lover, perhaps?" I asked, thinking once more of the portrait.

"She had her beaus, I suppose," Kev said, his voice becoming suddenly guarded.

"And Jared? Didn't he ever marry?"

"The silver was his true mistress, although there were women in his life," Kev said. "Rose Tibbet, for one."

"I see." I hurried on before him, tripping over something in the path, at the base of the dam.

I regained my balance quickly, glimpsing then a brightness in the dust. I stooped to pick it up, thinking instantly of the Wickerly silver.

"What is it?" Kev asked.

"Just this," I said, disappointed, holding out a claycrusted piece of metal with bright scratches on it.

Kev scrubbed it against his shirt.

"A buckle," he said. "Replete with six guns!"

He thrust it toward me, his eyes gleaming with uncontained excitement.

"Jared Wickerly's!" he exclaimed.

I saw a proud W engraved beneath the gun emblem.

"What does it mean?" I asked.

"That Jared is dead, buried perhaps here beneath our feet somewhere," he said. "This buckle might be proof, at last. A pack rat or maybe a crow must have picked it up somewhere here along the base of the dam and dropped it on the path. Now, if we could only locate Norman's buckle! And maybe something of Wick Carver's that might disprove the theory that he murdered Jared, and even Norman."

"Both brothers had a buckle with six-shooters fashioned from their precious ore?" I asked.

"Norman's buckle had sprigs of sage on it, intertwined into something that resembled a peace symbol," Kev said. "Maybe if we are willing to wait for it the rodents will bring it out for us."

"You'll give Jared's buckle to Blanche?" I said.

Kev nodded, turning it over again in his palm. We skirted the lake and went back up the slope toward town. From time to time Kev examined the buckle, musing over it.

"Old Jared got his after all, just like they said," he told me, a note of disbelief in his voice. "He's down there somewhere. Easy to find, too, if the rats got to him."

"I know what you're thinking," I said. "Do you think Blanche would allow it?"

He was lost in his own thoughts again, not hearing me.

Chapter Eight

A boy appeared at the Tower the following morning, with a perfumed note for me. I turned the pink envelope over in my hand, trying to imagine who in Wickerly had sent it.

I dismissed the boy with a quarter and sat down to read the pink missile that exuded an unsubtle, vaguely familiar sweetness.

Blanche Wickerly appeared, curious about the boy, who was running back down the slope. She glanced at the pink envelope in my hand, and a surprising change came over her face.

"It's from *her*," she exclaimed.

"I've no idea who it's from, since I haven't had a chance to read it," I said, stunned by the look of malice in the old woman's eyes.

Blanche turned and rustled off, as though she must escape that bit of pink paper that I held in my hand.

"Dear Miss Carver," the note began.

"I've heard about Jared's buckle, and I must see you at once. Meet me at the monument this evening at dusk."

The note was signed "Rose Tibbet."

The note's urgency made me decide to keep the appointment with the owner of the fancy house. But throughout the afternoon, as I typed up my notes, the rumble of thunder came rolling across the hills, and I wondered if I'd be able to go after all.

"Going to rain," Kev Keever remarked over dinner. "Peculiar weather for this time of year. Flash-flood weather."

"Like the night Jared Wickerly died," Fairfax said, her brown eyes widening. She glanced at Wick. "This will give you the atmosphere you need, darling, for your story setting. Let us hope that it spills. What a night for murder!"

There was a small, desperate sound from Blanche's end of the table.

"I'm sorry, dear," Fairfax said gently to the old woman.

It was growing dark outside. Dusk. Almost impulsively, I excused myself.

"Leaving us so soon, Nevvie?" Wick asked, giving me a questioning glance.

I fancied that I read concern in his luminous eyes. I made a pretense of glancing at my watch.

"I've something to pick up at the pharmacy," I lied. "It closes at nine. I have to hurry."

"I'll run you down in the Burro," Wick said, starting to rise.

"It's only a five-minute walk," I protested. "I need the air."

I darted from the room before he could offer again to accompany me.

I stopped at the town's small, dusty drugstore and bought a flashlight, then ran on down the slope toward the lake, one or two splashes of rain dimpling the path before me. The sky had turned a queer slate color, tinged with a sulphurous shade of yellow along the western horizon.

"Miss Tibbet?" I called, as I started up the face of the dam.

"Up here," a voice came to me at once, and I looked up and saw her leaning against the monument.

A small dog danced about her feet. Even in that faint, sulphurous gleam, I recognized her as the woman I had glimpsed through the binoculars. She was much older than I had imagined, her hair dyed a peculiar brassy shade, her lined face seeming to sag beneath the weight of rouge, powder, and mascara.

The small dog yapped at me. She silenced him with a single word.

"You're Nevada Carver," she said.

I nodded, beneath her careful scrutiny.

"What is it you wanted of me?" I asked, a bit breathless from the climb up the steep slope.

"The buckle," she said simply. "Jared's buckle." She gave me an almost pleading look, out of eyes that were a worn shade of blue. "Where did you find it? Where is Jared lying?"

"Down there." I pointed down the slope.

"I suppose I must believe now that he really is dead," she said. "I hadn't realized before that I was clinging to some small thread of hope. All of these years, since he disappeared . . ." Her voice dwindled off on a sad note.

"You knew Jared Wickerly well," I said, remembering what Kev had told me, knowing that she had, yet wanting to hear her side of it.

"If you want to put it that way," Rose Tibbet said, the hint of a smile touching her puckered, magenta lips. "Do you have it with you? Jared's buckle?" she asked.

"Kev Keever took it," I said. "He gave it to Blanche."

"That foolish old woman!" Rose said

bitterly. "The Tower should have belonged to me, you know," she added, her voice becoming toneless with a carefully controlled fury. "It would have been mine, if it hadn't been for Blanche. Jared loved me. We might have been married." She stooped to pick up the small dog. "Prince is all I have left. Jared gave him to me a long while ago. Before —" She broke off, drawing a deep breath. "But never mind that. Actually," here she smiled, "it was Prince's great-great-grandfather Jared gave to me. Perhaps a good deal further back than that, although I've kept the strain pure. I've called them all Prince."

Her voice faltered at that, and she stood gazing off toward the old mansion, forgetting me, looking back into the past. I fancied that I glimpsed a movement behind one of the gleaming windows, someone half-hidden by the faded, stringy curtains, spying on us.

"It's going to storm tonight," Rose said, as another clap of thunder rumbled through the mountains. "Just like it did that night. The night Jared left us. A night for death." Her faded eyes sought my own. "You're his daughter? Wick Carver's daughter?" she asked.

"No," I said. "Not the Wick Carver you have in mind."

She seemed not to have heard me.

"I feel that I must warn you. There is something strange happening in this town. They — those, there in town, are growing restless. The government needs silver again. In my business, one learns to be practical," she added, when I flashed her a startled look. "I've a feeling that something is about to happen, here . . ."

"I don't understand," I said.

"Someone is after Jared's silver," Rose said.

I recalled the lights that I had seen shining over the lake.

"But who?" I asked.

She ignored my question.

"Jared's silver," she repeated. "I still think of it as belonging to him. He put in the first cyanide process plant in this state. He revolutionized the silver industry here." She gave me a look that was almost a plea again. "I've tried to do my share to keep this town alive, for his sake. Not for Blanche's sake," she added. "I want you to understand that. I've done it all for Jared. I couldn't let his town turn up its toes and die."

An undeniable glint of anger had come into her eyes. She gestured toward the spire of marble.

"Blanche put up this ugly monument to my Jared," she said. "But this town is his true monument. This town, and the mine down there beneath that water. If it hadn't been for that selfish old woman up there in the Tower, the mine would have belonged to me, as well. And Jared's body . . . I'd have ordered this town to find his body, give him decent burial beside Old Sil. Cleared Wick Carver's name, once and for all. It's foolish to imagine that Wick, or anyone else, might have even *harmed* Jared. Much less killed him and left his body in the path of the slide, to destroy the evidence."

"The town seems to think that Wick Carver had something to do with his death," I said.

"Blanche started that story," Rose said. "Wick Carver was in love with her once."

I couldn't conceal a startled look, thinking at once of the portrait that had been there in the Tower attic.

"Jay Keever, too, as a matter of fact," Rose continued. "And Buck Farrington. I mustn't forget dear Buck. He was really quite smitten. Oh yes! Blanche had her following, in her day. But still she clung to Jared."

"Who was Buck Farrington?" I asked.

"No one important," Rose said. "A drifter, at most."

"And Blanche never married," I mused.

"But she did, ducky," Rose said. "She was married to Wick Carver for a short while. Jared had it annulled very quietly, at Blanche's request. It's not common knowledge here. Jared let it slip one night when we were together. Just before our child was born," she added.

"A child?" I asked. "You and Jared had a child?"

"Yes," she said quickly. "He was born a few months before Jared died."

"But, what became of him?" I asked. Something in her voice made me suspect she was lying.

"I'd always longed for a home. Children," Rose mused. "I cared for him well, there at the Pink Cloud. Ironic, wouldn't you say? Jared built the Pink Cloud for me. A consolation, since Blanche wouldn't let us get married and live in the Tower. She had only to flash her eyes at Jared to have her way. To think of her brother's child living there in a house of sin, with the very woman that she most scorned, even feared. The ironies of this world, ducky! Ah, yes, the child lived. I've always believed that."

"You didn't raise the child, then?"

"Wick took him and left here after Jared died. I figure he must have brought up the boy — maybe even given him his name."

So that was it! But did Wick know Rose was his mother? And could he have suspected that Jared was his real father, even though he had been so close to the man he thought was his real father — the first Wick Carver?

The story seemed too incredible to be true. But why would Rose lie? I turned to her.

"It's odd that Wick Carver was so willing to adopt Jared's child," I commented. "Surely he owed nothing to the man — and, after all, it was Jared's sister who had jilted him."

"Wick *had* been in love with Blanche, that's true, and I guess he had plenty of heartache when she left him, but," her face brightened with the memory, "Wick and I had become pretty good friends, close friends, ducky, in spite of Blanche." Then, remembering my original comment, she said, almost as an afterthought, "That's why he was willing to take my child."

Was Rose telling the truth? Was Wick really a Wickerly? I couldn't be sure.

"And Norman?" I asked Rose, anxious

to find out whatever she knew about the Wickerly family.

"Norman came and went. He would have no part of the mines. He roamed these Nevada hills, searching for his own bonanza. He and Jared resembled each other in appearance only. Except that Norman was crippled, and there was a certain meekness about him. Blanche saw only Jared. *My* Jared! She was overly fond of him. Possessive," Rose added, her voice bitter again.

"Blanche was working on a portrait of Jared, just before he . . . died," Rose went on. I must have started visibly, for Rose turned toward me, in the gloom, and said: "Oh, yes, Blanche painted as a young woman. It was the stylish avocation for daughters of the genteel rich."

Rose paused among a scattering of gray boulders and continued talking. "Jared was such a handsome man, with all that crisp black hair and those flashing blue eyes. His image helps me to go on."

In spite of a reluctance to dwell on it, a picture of the portrait came into my mind. Rose's description of Jared Wickerly was a description of the man in the portrait. Except for the mole, I thought, my finger going to touch the small, covered mark be-

113

side the corner of my mouth. I wondered numbly if *I* might somehow be a Wickerly.

"Blanche still hates me," Rose said, in a musing voice. The idea seemed to please her. "I humbled myself after his disappearance. It was only a small photograph I wanted of him. Something to refresh my memory from time to time. I asked her for a photograph of him, and she flew at me in a fury. Claimed that she had burned them all. She was in such a state it actually frightened me. She said that she couldn't bear to be reminded. I believed her! To lose Jared like that. *I* know how much it hurt. And she had lost Buck Farrington shortly before Jared disappeared in that storm. Buck jilted her, of course," Rose added with a little note of relish.

"After Buck left her, Blanche became more insanely jealous than ever of my relationship with Jared. Why else would a woman destroy photographs of her own beloved brother? You see, ducky, after I asked her for a photograph, she set out methodically to destroy every photo that had ever been made of Jared. Including those Jay Keever had taken, to illustrate stories in the *Strike*; she went to Jay. Demanded that he remove them from his files. Then, there was the painting —" She broke off suddenly, as though she had said too much.

A painful silence fell between us, in the face of Rose Tibbet's memories.

We had been strolling rather aimlessly in that weird, yellow light and had come onto the ridge on the far side of the lake. It was rocky here, with ridges of loose stone sticking out from the steep slope, like the bared ribs of some mammoth, underfed animal.

An eerie silence had fallen over the ruggedly barren countryside, and suddenly it began to rain in earnest.

"Like the night Jared died," Rose Tibbet said, seeming oblivious to the downpour, still lost in her past.

She walked on, her brassy hair becoming bedraggled, her pink sweater clinging to plump shoulders, cradling the small dog to her bosom beneath it.

"There's an old mining shack just at the top of this ridge," she said. "Let's try for it, though God knows a little dampness can do me no further harm . . ." Her voice dwindled off momentarily. "Now that I know that he is actually down there, nothing can harm me," she added. "Nothing! I hope that you never have to understand this terrible empty feeling.

Hope suddenly vanished. But not quite all of it, ducky. I told that old woman up there that I would get even, get my share of everything that belonged to Jared!" A note of craftiness was in her voice.

We started up the slope, the rain stinging our faces. The small dog whimpered. It had grown nearly dark. Lightning flashed, illuminating the drab world with a blue-white light.

There was a dark movement above us, a vague form outlined briefly by the bright flash. Then suddenly a part of the ridge gave way. I screamed, as a stone bounded past us in the semidarkness, followed by another, and yet another stone.

Something grazed my ankle, filling me with unbearable pain. I fell, dazed, vaguely aware that Rose Tibbet was running on ahead.

A small flow of muddy tallus came down, the wet pebbles settling against me. I lay in the dwindling rain, clutching my throbbing ankle, waiting for the pain to subside. Rose Tibbet had disappeared, after the person who had appeared so suddenly above us. That rolling stone had been no accident, of that much I was certain. Someone had tried to kill one of us, I thought, more frightened than I had ever been before in my entire life.

Vaguely, I made out the form of the deserted prospector's cabin and lurched toward it, favoring my wounded ankle. I had nearly reached the shack, when I noticed a car parked nearby, a crouching, low vehicle. Wick Carver's Jaguar! Burro. His ridiculous name for the shining red car came irrelevantly to my mind.

I tried not to imagine what the car might be doing there. Had it been Wick who had appeared on the slope above Rose and me, to send the treacherous stones thundering down? I recalled his sudden appearance in the second-floor corridor of the old house, the night that I had followed the woman in pink. Was Wick trying to frighten me, perhaps even to kill me? But why?

I crouched, dripping wet, behind a clump of sage, watching the shack for some sign of him, certain now that he must be inside. Had Rose Tibbet caught up with him, if it *had* been Wick who had rolled the stone? Was she there inside of the cabin, perhaps in danger? That rolling stone must have revived some memory of the time that Jared had rolled a stone down on Norman in the old madam's mind. Or had she glimpsed Wick, and had he looked so much like Jared that she had mistaken him for her long dead lover? After all, I thought, Wick could very well be one of them. A Wickerly.

Suddenly, two figures emerged from the ramshackle building, unmistakably a man and a woman, although it was impossible to distinguish who they might be. I watched as they climbed into the car and drove away.

I dared to continue on to the shack, after a bit, thinking that the couple had perhaps been Wick and Fairfax, for there had been a certain youthfulness about the female. The door to the shack was carefully pad-locked. I fumbled along the splintery walls and came to a window boarded over with rickety planks. There seemed to be no way to enter. I braced myself for the long walk back down the ridge and around the lake.

I started down the slope toward the faintly gleaming water, and the Tower be-yond, darting painfully from one clump of sage to the next in an effort to conceal my-self from whatever threat the night might hold.

Chapter Nine

It had grown quite dark. I hurried up the hill toward the mansion, picking my way with the beam from my flashlight. The glow cast by the town's ancient street lamps was hopelessly diffused by the rain that continued to fall gently. There would be no flash flood, after all.

An intolerable dread came over me again. Was whoever had rolled the stone waiting there now, lurking in some dark corner, waiting to pounce?

Something prompted me to turn and look down at the lake. The light was there again now, moving over the dark surface in some mysterious exploration. Who was it, after the silver? Wick? Why else should his car have been there on the ridge, I thought, with a sinking sensation. I all but flew to the Tower.

Someone moved just inside the gloomy foyer as I entered the old house. I gasped, then realized that it was only Blanche, her small form half hidden in the shadows.

"You!" she said. Then, quickly: "Have you no better sense than to go wandering about in the rain?" She gave me a scathing look, her eyes squinted into their raddled little patches of flesh. She smelled slightly of damp wool, as though she herself had just come in from the rain.

"Darling! You're back!"

I glanced up to see Fairfax coming down the stairs.

"But where is Wick?" she demanded. "I imagined, for some odd reason, that he had followed you off."

It hadn't been Fairfax, then, with Wick there at the deserted shack. Had it been Rose Tibbet?

"I haven't seen Wick all evening," I said.

"Everyone seems to have disappeared," Fairfax complained. "Gone out into this ridiculous storm. Kev and I are the only ones with sense. And Blanche here, of course," she added, taking notice of the withered old woman.

"Fools!" Blanche spat. "All of them. If they could only guess what happens in these gullies when it rains like this." She turned abruptly and disappeared through one of the tall, ornately carved doors, her mumbling voice trailing behind her.

"Peculiar old bird," Fairfax commented. "I hadn't seen her around all evening. Then suddenly she decides to crawl out of the woodwork. And Kev . . . unsociable this evening. He hasn't so much as poked his nose out of his room. Really, darling, it was dreadfully lonesome here in this dreary old house. I can't imagine what has become of Wick. Or my precious son and Rena. He and Rena borrowed Wick's car for the evening, though I can't imagine where they find to go in this godforsaken place. Unless they've dashed off to Fallon, naughty children."

I started up the stairs with an unexpected surge of relief. So it *had* been Rena and Collins keeping some dark little rendezvous at the tumbling shack. Were they the ones who were after the silver? I recalled Collins' boast to Rena: "Keep your eyes peeled, kid. Could be I'll figure out a way to get my hands on some of that silver. . . ."

"This place is a tomb tonight," Fairfax was saying, as she followed me up the stairs. "I shouldn't be the least bit surprised to see Jared's ghost appear at any moment, replete with dripping slime."

"Don't!" I exclaimed. "I've had a rather bad experience tonight. I guess it made me jumpy."

"You saw the lights," Fairfax said.

"What?" I stared down at her.

"Down at the lake," she said. "Odd that they seem to appear only when our employer is out and wandering about. Do you suppose Wick is after the silver?"

"I wouldn't know," I said, resisting an urge to tell her that I thought it might be her son, instead, who was trying to find a way to get to all of that rich jewelry ore. It was the sort of thing that Collins would do, I thought. But would he resort to murder to keep from being discovered?

"Jared's silver," Fairfax said. "You'd think that Jared Wickerly was some sort of god the way they still talk about him here. Evidently he was some sort of tyrant. An empire builder of sorts, lording it over everyone. That kind of man is invariably exciting. Rather romantic the way they still revere his memory, here."

"I suppose so," I said, suddenly drained of strength. My ankle ached, and I wanted nothing more than to change to a dry gown and go to bed.

"Somehow, I have come to see Wick in that same light," Fairfax said. "He's utterly masculine, with that same sort of romantic aura hovering about him. Damn him! He has evidently deserted us for the evening.

What a bore this place is without him." She paused, giving me a sharp look. "Wick Carver. Do you suppose that is actually his name?"

I studied her smooth face, trying to determine her meaning.

"No need to look so shocked, Nevvie," she said, with a little shrug. "It's just that he seems rather mysterious at times. I don't really want to frighten you, darling, but Wick Carver seems —"

"Someone mention my name?"

Suddenly he was there above us on the stairs, seeming to have materialized out of the shadows.

"I thought this morgue was absolutely deserted, and you've been here all of the while," Fairfax accused.

"Up in the cupola gleaning atmosphere, for one thing," he said.

It had been Wick there, then, watching Rose Tibbet and me from behind the tall, glinting windows. Then I noticed that his hair gleamed with dampness, and I knew that he was lying — that he had been out somewhere in the storm, and for some reason wanted to keep his going and coming a secret. I felt suddenly wary of him.

When I entered my room, I noticed instantly that someone had been there.

"Who is it?" I called in a tense voice, noticing that the closet door was ajar.

I saw then that the contents of my dresser drawers were scattered. Whoever it was had been searching for something and had been thorough.

I made a quick estimate of my belongings. There seemed to be nothing missing. Puzzled, I prepared for bed and slipped between the sheets, a small sense of fear tugging at me.

Later that night I heard someone stirring about the old mansion. Was it the mysterious woman in pink? Whoever it was had made her — or his — way into the dark shaft inside of the ancient walls. I heard her crawling about on the precarious ladder and tried to imagine what she might be searching for, thinking that it had to be the same person who searched my room.

I sprang from my bed and rushed to my closet, thrusting my way past the hanging clothes to press my ear against the hidden door. The sounds grew unmistakably louder. Was it Fairfax, clad in a misty pink peignoir, while she scrambled about, searching for some secret with which to impress Wick? Impulsively, I decided to go to her room.

An ominous silence pervaded the old

house, as I crept to her door and tapped lightly. There was no response. I tapped again, this time a bit louder. The sound of my knuckles against the heavy varnished panels seemed to ring along the empty hallway.

Perhaps I had been right about Fairfax.

Back in my own room, I snuck once more into my closet. Someone was murmuring, deep in the old house, the voice so faint that it was barely audible. Silently, I forced the small door open, stifling the sharp sense of guilt that came over me.

The whisper grew louder.

"Darling," the soft, husky voice said. "Oh, my darling, what has he done to you?"

Was it Wick's voice? Was he there somewhere beyond the narrow, dark shaft, making secret love to Fairfax? I leaned against the closet wall, overcome by a perverse curiosity.

"Nevada!" the whispering voice said. "Nevada Wickerly!" the whisper clearly came from the dark shaft inside of the mansion walls. "Nevada Wickerly! That's her true name. She can't fool us with her little artifices, darling, no matter how hard she tries. I *know* that Norman didn't die there with Jared. Only *I* know."

That strange whispering voice belonged to Wick, after all, I thought, stunned. It had to be Wick. His father — at least the man he assumed was his father — had been the last to see Jared Wickerly alive. Why had he referred to me as Nevada Wickerly? Unless he believed me to be Norman's daughter, I thought, amazed. But how could he possibly believe such a thing? My father's name had been Wickerly Carver.

Or had it? I thought of the portrait again, visualizing the bullet hole between those blazing blue eyes. Suddenly, I knew for certain that my life was inexorably intertwined with the lives of the Wickerlys who had lorded it over the small town for so many years from their dire old Tower.

I quickly closed the small door inside of my closet and went back to my bed. I lay awake a long while, thinking of my father, trying desperately to ferret some clue from our years together that might link him undeniably with Wickerly and the Tower. He had been vague about the accident that had caused his limp. His leg had improved through the years, my mother had said. It seemed much more than coincidence now that Norman Wickerly had been crippled.

My father had never mentioned the

126

name Wickerly that I could recall. *Was* it because he had been the one who murdered Jared? The frightening question came unbidden to my mind. Had he killed Jared, because Jared had once rolled a stone onto him, and shattered his leg? Was my father actually a transformed Norman Wickerly?

I would ask Adriane to help me, I decided. If there were any evidence to link my father to the Wickerlys, it would no doubt be hidden somewhere in his chests and boxes at the house he had left me in San Francisco.

Chapter Ten

The storm passed during the night, and the following day dawned golden with sunlight. Miraculously, some of my fears of the night before had drained away, and I was able to work with Wick quite calmly on the book, becoming engrossed in the growing tale of Old Sil Wickerly.

We hadn't yet reached the portion of the story that would deal with Jared and his supposed murder. I tried to minimize it now.

At noon I walked down to the town's small post office and mailed my letter to Adriane. I had left a key to my house with her, and in my letter I asked her to search through my father's vast accumulation of ore specimens and mining records for some bit of information about a man named Norman Wickerly. I also asked her to send me any early photographs of my father that she might find, although I didn't really expect there to be any.

I received a wire from her the following morning, assuring me that she would carry out my request.

Wick's romantic interest in me seemed suddenly to have waned; I couldn't help but notice this. I felt both puzzled and relieved by his lack of attentiveness, telling myself that it hardly mattered one way or the other that he now seemed to be paying a good deal of attention to Fairfax. But I caught him watching me from time to time, with a strange expression that seemed a mixture of disappointment and dismay.

I thought again that it could very well have been Wick who rolled that stone down onto Rose Tibbet and me, and that perhaps he wondered how I had managed to escape that plummeting menace. I recalled that his hair *had* been damp that evening, when Fairfax and I met him on the stairs, and that he *had* deliberately denied having been out in the storm.

It seemed that he might well, in fact, have a motive to do away with me. Because if it turned out that Norman Wickerly actually had been my father's real name, a portion of the Wickerly silver that was said to be buried beneath the lake would be mine.

This night, I decided to walk down toward the lake, telling myself that perhaps Rose Tibbet would be there walking her dog. I would question her about Norman again, I decided.

I hurried down the slope in the gathering dusk, my new flashlight clutched firmly in my hand.

There was no sign of Rose or her spotted terrier near the monument. I passed by it, and continued on around the lake, staying clear of the large stones protruding above. My ankle still bore the scar of the last encounter, although the abrasion was healing nicely. I had told the others that I had stumbled on the town's uneven board sidewalk. It had seemed, at the time, that Wick flashed me a knowing look, although I couldn't be certain.

Now, I carefully avoided the deepening shadows cast by the dense clumps of sage, and found myself at the top of the ridge, not far from the deserted miner's shack. Realizing how far I had come, I turned back, searching the slopes around the lake for some sign of Rose.

There was none, and I decided to take the bull by the horns and pay a visit to the Pink Cloud.

There seemed to be no one about when I

arrived. Then I noticed, rather painfully aware of their profession, two girls lounging on the side veranda. When I asked where I might find Rose, one of them told me, in a slightly bored voice, that Rose was in her room.

"Mourning," the other offered.

"Oh? Who died?" I asked.

"Prince," the girl, who had flaming red hair, told me. "Her little dog. Someone poisoned him."

I turned to go, thinking how much the dog had meant to Rose and wondering who could possibly have done such a thing.

I walked back toward the mansion, following the town's dusty main street. Pop Denman was there, in his place before the Green Lizard Saloon. I passed beneath the swinging coyotes, answering his greeting with a wave of my hand.

"You feel it, too, hey?" the old man asked, when I had neared him.

"If you mean the absolute dreariness of this place, yes," I said, tempering my words with a smile.

"That ain't exactly what I had in mind," Pop said.

"There's something brewing. A sort of unrest. Someone's been fooling around down at the lake. They've got no business there, Kev Keever says."

"Did he say who it was?" I asked, remembering the lights.

"Nope," Pop said. "All I know is that someone is after the silver. We've had them here before. Folks who figure it might be easy to slip in and grab a few chunks of jewelry ore, and no one the wiser."

The loud hum of mens' voices issued from the swinging door of the saloon. I gave Pop Denman a questioning look.

"They're holding a meeting in there," he said.

"Is it as serious as all of that?"

"Might be, if folks in this town get worked up enough over it. There are still a few who remember the old days, and the way things were here then, with the ore pouring out of the Wickerly Mine." He pointed toward the decaying *Strike* office. "Had us a mighty interesting news sheet here, then. But there ain't any need for a paper in a dying town. Kev Keever had sense enough to realize that. He got out while he had enough change in his pocket to buy fare to the next town."

"He may not have given up the idea of coming back entirely," I said.

"Reckon not," Pop stated. "Something

about this place that gets into your blood after a while. Maybe it's the loneliness. Some part of a man craves solitude. Then again, maybe it's a kind of excitement, like something was bound to give one of these days, and when it does, all hell is going to bust loose. With the price of silver going up, maybe the time has come. . . ."

"What can they do?" I nodded toward the door of the saloon.

"Blow up the dam, maybe," Pop said. "Find out what's down there underneath all of that clay. And if they uncover Jared's bones, and Norman's, in the process, give them decent burial, as befits them that is gone. They mean no disrespect."

"And clear Wick Carver's name," I said in a wooden voice, thinking that Norman's bones might not be there for them to find.

"Mayhap," Pop said.

I left him sitting on his bench, as I made my way back to the Tower.

I wondered idly how many able-bodied men there still were in Wickerly who remembered the Wickerly Mine's bonanza days. Hardly enough, I thought, to carry out the blasting of the dam, even if what Pop Denman had hinted did happen to be true.

The old house stood as quiet as a tomb.

I went up to my room and stood gazing down at the small town. Even the Pink Cloud had succumbed to the heavy desert silence, and it seemed to my heightened imagination as though death could sweep a heavy hand over this dreary landscape with no trouble at all.

Chapter Eleven

When I walked down to the small post office the following morning to collect my own and Wick Carver's mail, there was a package from Adriane awaiting me.

A feeling of apprehension swept through me as I took it from the woman behind the barred window; I hurried up the hill toward the mansion, feeling suddenly furtive. I glanced up at the cupola, from which Old Sil and Jared Wickerly had once spied on the town below, and fancied that I saw someone behind the narrow windows. I was certain that there was someone watching me when I saw one of the faded curtains tremble, as though whoever hovered there behind it had allowed it to fall back into place.

Inside the Tower, I climbed quickly to my room and locked the door, then turned to Adriane's package, my hands trembling. There was a lengthy note enclosed, written in Adriane's slightly scrawly hand.

"Darling," the note said. "I have done my best to comply with your rather strange request. The results of my search are enclosed. I found no photographs of your father, at all, darling, a fact that I find extremely odd, since there were any number of snaps of your mother tucked away in an old cigar box. Since you mentioned the name Wickerly, I am enclosing a packet of letters that was tucked into the bottom of one of your father's ore-specimen boxes.

"What first attracted my attention to them was the postmark. Darling, you will note that they were mailed in Wickerly. Wickerly, Nevada, the very town where you now find yourself with Wick Carver or Vin Savage, if you prefer that rather titillating nom de plume.

"Do let me know what this is all about! My curiosity has been thoroughly aroused!

"And now for the silver buckle, darling," the letter continued. I read on, my heart beginning to pound.

"Your father's, no doubt. It caught my eye, and for no particular reason except that it seemed rather strange that your father should have had it engraved with his first initial rather than his last. I am enclosing it, along with the rest, prompted by some odd premonition. Dear, I am certain that there must have been some mystery in his life!"

I laid aside the note and lifted out the contents of the box. The sheaf of letters that she had mentioned was tied up with twine, the envelopes long since turned yellow. Beneath them lay a smaller box, carefully wrapped.

It contained Norman Wickerly's silver buckle, the single initial intertwined with an engraving of sage that resembled a peace symbol.

A strange feeling of detachment came over me. I untied the packet of letters, which were from Jay Keever, Kev's father, and addressed to Wickerly Carver. They were filled with questions concerning Jared Wickerly's death, along with information about the town. I knew then that it had been my father who had written the letter to Jay Keever, saying that he had been the last man to see Jared Wickerly alive. Although he had been persistent in his quest for truth, I guessed that Jay Keever's questions had for the most part gone unanswered.

I searched about for a place to conceal the evidence that I myself was actually a Wickerly. Apparently whoever had rifled my room before had guessed that I might be. Hesitantly, I tucked the box into a drawer beneath my underthings, unable to find a place that seemed more secure, and went downstairs to join Wick in the library.

The atmosphere of the town seemed to have had its effect on Wick Carver. He had allowed his beard to grow. It was dark, like his hair, a short, springy growth that made his eyes seem almost golden and slightly wicked. I sat across the huge desk from him, totally aware of his masculine perfection, feeling attracted to him against my will. The slight scent of his leather-and-tweed cologne added yet another dimension to his overwhelming presence. Even as I was drawn to him, I sensed something covert in him; something specific, in fact, that was carefully guarded. More than once I glanced up from my stenographer's pad to catch him watching me, a speculative look burning in his bright eyes.

I thought, unexpectedly: If this man *is* Jared Wickerly's son, the two of us are cousins.

The thought so startled me that I got hopelessly behind in my recording of his rambling narrative, which would be pared and polished after I had transcribed it to a working draft.

"What happened to it?" he demanded suddenly.

I glanced at him, and saw with a start that he was undeniably searching my face.

"The little mole that was there at the corner of your mouth, that first day?" he continued, his brightly flecked eyes holding my own, daring me to deny that it had been there.

"Makeup," I admitted in a cautious voice.

"You mean that it wasn't real, then?" he asked. "That it was one of those patches that women use to beguile us innocent males?"

"Something like that," I said.

"The mole was very becoming, real or otherwise," he said casually, turning his attention back to the dictation.

"Time for a coffee break, Nevvie," Wick said, after we had worked steadily for an hour. "Then I think we'll get into the next chapter. It's time I brought Wickerly Carver into the picture. That first Wickerly Carver. My father." He gave me a wry smile.

"I'm eager to learn more about him," I said politely.

"You know, Nevvie," Wick said suddenly. "I would like very much to make love to you."

I stared at him quickly, then looked as

quickly down at my notebook, my cheeks flaming at the glow that I had caught in his eyes.

"I'm hoping that after we have unraveled the secrets of this place, I shall find that I can feel free to —"

Carmen interrupted him, pushing through the door with a heavy tray, her face beaming over a pot of coffee and a plate of round little confections.

"Are you still searching for that other Wick Carver?" I asked, over a cup of steaming coffee, after Carmen had gone. "The Wick Carver who wrote the letter to Jay Keever, claiming to have been the last to see Jared Wickerly alive?" I added, not quite daring to look at him.

I tried to appear casual, in spite of the sudden, wild beating of my heart. Should I tell this keen-eyed man what I suspected? Could I trust him, after all?

"I'm working on it," he said.

I found myself changing the subject then, rather desperately rattling on about the contents of the dour library, speculating idly on the titles of the books that rambled around the walls.

When we had finished our coffee, Wick resumed his flow of narrative, starting a new chapter.

"Wickerly Carver arrived in Wickerly, Nevada, the following spring. The remorseless Nevada hills laid claim to him. He sensed their mystery at once. He had spent a lifetime roaming the Western mountains searching for ore. It was his one big passion, his dream, one that had so far eluded him." His voice was pleasant, easy to follow. My pencil flew along the green lines.

"This rugged country where the fabulous silver baron Silver Wickerly had made his big find had drawn Wickerly Carver, a siren luring. He soon found himself in the employ of the fabled Old Sil, laying up yet another grubstake toward the day when he would make his own big strike. But that day never arrived for Wickerly Carver; because of a woman. . . ." Wick's voice dwindled, and he grew silent.

"Are you going to change her name for the story?" I heard myself asking.

"Whose name?" he demanded.

"Your mother's," I said, shrinking away from him, for his face had clouded with anger.

"How can I, when I've no idea what it was?" he said harshly.

I gave him a disbelieving look, trying to determine whether or not he was serious.

"Surely, your father —" I began.

"Her name was his secret," he said. "He carried it with him to his grave."

If Rose's story was true, he carried the secret of Wick's true *father* to his grave too, I mused.

"There are records of such things," I said. "I can't imagine that you haven't bothered to look."

"Painstakingly," Wick said. "Why do you suppose I've taken up writing as a career? Partly because the majority of trades and professions require that a man at one time or another must show his birth certificate. And as incredible as it may sound to you, Nevvie, it seems that I was never born. Actually, something happened to a number of the records placed on file at the county seat the year of my birth. They simply aren't there. I know that my father was married for a short while, during the period of his life spent in this town. He mentioned it once, rather bitterly."

"There has to be proof somewhere," I insisted, scarcely able to contain the story that Rose Tibbet had related to me.

"Proof of what, darlings?" Fairfax appeared, her brown eyes curious.

"A personal matter," Wick said shortly.

He hadn't confided in the others, then, I

thought. That he hadn't seemed somehow significant.

"Don't forget that I am your chief researchist," Fairfax said. "If it is anything that I can run down for you . . ."

"I doubt that even you could ferret this one out," Wick said.

"If that's the way you feel about it . . ." Fairfax shrugged, her lips drooping in a pout. "How is it coming?" she asked, after a moment, glancing at my stenographic pad.

"As well as can be expected," Wick said.

"I've a few new tidbits to work in," Fairfax said. "Really, darling, this town is an absolute gold mine of weird facts. Did you know, for instance, that the dead seldom deteriorate in this high, dry climate which accounts for those hideous coyotes hanging over the main street of this burg? The mummified remains of Indians, or some sort of aborigines, have been found about in caves, after God knows how many billion years. Rather makes you wonder, doesn't it, about Jared — and Norman too, of course."

"You've been talking to Pop Denman again," Wick said.

"The old character is full of facts," Fairfax said. "I'm beginning to understand your fascination with the forty-niners, darling. Except that they called them 'pilgrims' here; the prospectors who came pouring onto the Comstock, a decade or two after the discovery of gold in California. Old Sil Wickerly was one of the lucky few, according to Pop, along with the men who located the Comstock. Scoundrels, one and all, I take it, but rich as Plutus to a man."

"It was a fascinating era," Wick said.

"And to think that there are still people here who lived it. Rose Tibbet, for one. Did you know that she was Jared's woman back then? Seduced by the town baron, with no choice left but to live a life of sin?"

"I doubt that it was quite that dramatic," Wick said.

"However, you must admit that my version would make good reading. Arouse sympathy for a rather naughty character," Fairfax said.

"You've talked with Rose?" I asked.

"I've an appointment with her for Thursday afternoon," Fairfax told me. "We are taking tea together, on her veranda, if the weather permits. All terribly proper and refined. Imagine the things that she must know about Jared, considering that they were once lovers!" Fairfax gave a little laugh. "I can hardly wait! According to

Pop, Blanche was jealous of Rose. She considered Jared her own exclusive property, it seems, simply because they happened to be related by blood. He was all Blanche had."

"There was Norman," I said.

"Even Pop Denman didn't have a good deal to say about poor Norman," Fairfax said. "Norman seems to have been one of those quiet, nondescript souls who never leaves much of an impression. Old Sil and Jared were the exciting men! Big! Handsome! Overpowering! Accustomed to ordering people about. Norman had the Wickerly look, I take it. Black hair. Blue eyes." Fairfax flashed me a smile. "Rather like your own coloring, darling," she commented. "It seems that he moved out of this morgue even before Old Sil died. Took up residence in some shack down by the mine. Turned his back on his father — and Jared. The Tower. This, after they had more or less rejected him.

"Imagine how he must have loathed Jared all of those years, growing up here in this house. According to Pop, it was filled with every luxury that the Wickerly silver could buy. Brazen with gilt. All of these French ormolu garniture sets, one for every marble mantle. And these hideous plush monstrosities." Her arm swept out in an all-inclusive gesture. "They were, of course, very popular then among the wealthy. Old Sil was something of a *bon vivant,* and Jared, as well, it seems. Local gossip has it that either of them could identify a vintage wine simply by sniffing the cork. There is said to be a wine cellar beneath this pile of boards, fabled in those days as one of the most lavish in the country." She gave Wick a mischievous look.

"Might be worth investigating, darling," she added. "Considering Blanche's weird attitude the morning that Carmen mentioned someone having left the cellar door ajar. Imagine how rare the vintage would be by now, if there should happen to be some bottles left down there!"

"Except that Blanche has retained all rights to that particular section of this gloomy tomb," Wick said.

Evidently Pop Denman had failed to tell Fairfax about the coffin that Blanche was said to have purchased for Jared, for she made no mention of it. It would provide a macabre touch for Wick's book, I thought, even though the coffin had gone unused. I decided to tell him about it at the first available opportunity.

Fairfax had launched into another tale about the Wickerlys, determined, it seemed,

146

to hold Wick's attention for as long as possible.

"Would you believe it, darlings," she said. "Norman Wickerly actually tooled his own silver buckle, after Old Sil had presented Jared with that fantastically intricate buckle Nevvie found down by the lake. According to Pop's version of the story, Norman high-graded some of Old Sil's precious jewelry ore; stole it out of the Wickerly Mine, with the aid of one Wickerly Carver!" She raised her eyebrows triumphantly.

An expression of intense interest had come into Wick's eyes.

"Your father?" Fairfax said then, looking at me. "Or Wick's, here?" She paused dramatically. "At any rate, that first Wick Carver helped Norman get out the rare ore, and Norman fashioned himself this strange buckle, with sprigs of sage worked into the pattern. A sort of peace symbol, I assume. You see, both Old Sil and Jared were violent by nature. They carried guns, and sometimes used them. Not so Norman. He wanted no part of bloodshed. I suppose his innocuous little buckle was a part of his rather mannerly defiance."

I listened numbly, extremely apprehensive now about the buckle hidden upstairs in my drawer. Knowing about Norman Wickerly would contribute a good deal to Wick's book. Yet I couldn't bring myself to confide in him, partly because I suspected him of knowing a good deal more about my past — and his own — than he would have me believe.

"There can be no doubt that Old Sil Wickerly was a tyrant," Wick commented. "That particular trait always makes interesting reading, perhaps because there is something tyrannical buried deep in the best of us, which few of us have the courage to exploit."

"I can imagine the little people in this town hating Old Sil, yet admiring him, in a sort of twisted, ambivalent way," Fairfax said. "He didn't trust anyone, they say, except maybe Jared. That's why Old Sil built this house here on its hill with the cupola perched on top. It gave him an eagle's-eye view of the mine. He hoped to catch some poor devil high-grading ore, their term for out and out thievery. He did catch one or two carting off his precious silver in empty powder boxes. He put a bullet through them, from the cupola, with his high-powered rifle."

"Surely there was some sort of law here!" I exclaimed, imagining the wicked old man, perched in his little nest, no doubt watching through the very binoculars that I had used to view Rose Tibbet. It occurred to me that Old Sil could very well have been my grandfather. I shivered at the thought.

"There can be no doubt that the old boy had a streak of meanness," Wick said, his voice sounding rather sympathetic, even a little envious.

"That's not the half of it," Fairfax went on. "There are still rumors about that Old Blanche was something of a belle in her day, and a rather daring one, at that. Contrary to popular belief, it was much more than Jared's death that got to her, made her the strange old woman she is today."

"What are you getting at now, Fairfax?" Wick asked, his eyes becoming a little wary, even angry.

"Well, you did want to use her in your story, didn't you?" Fairfax demanded. "Just because she happens to be our hostess, in a manner of speaking . . ."

"Go on," Wick ordered, settling back in his chair and gazing out through one of the tall windows, as he lighted a fresh cigarette.

"There was at least one other man in her life," Fairfax said. "A man named Buck Farrington. He used to slip up here to the Tower to see Blanche, while Jared was busy down at the mine. The whole town guessed what was going on. She had been seeing something of Jay Keever and Wick Carver, before that. But so far as anyone knew, there had been nothing particularly scandalous about those affairs. And even if there had been, no one would have dared to mention it, with Jared around looking after Blanche, fending off any hint of idle gossip.

"Blanche stopped seeing Jay and Wick when this Buck Farrington came along. According to Pop, Buck was a no-good. A drifter. Hardly the sort of man that Jared might have picked for his sister. Is it any wonder that the town dared to take minor notice? You can imagine Jared's reaction when he heard. The town assumed, at first, that Blanche had taken up with Buck Farrington merely to get even with Jared for his own indiscretions with Rose. Whatever her reasons, it seems that Blanche was willing to allow this Buck Farrington to hang around. And then one day he disappeared as mysteriously as he had come. Jared was caught in the slide shortly after that, and poor Blanche was left alone in this morgue to mourn. Is it any wonder the poor old soul is weird!"

"I assume that you've taken notes on all of this," Wick said, in a businesslike voice.

Chapter Twelve

The conversation over dinner that night turned to Jared Wickerly, yet again. Blanche, as usual, had left the table, to lock herself away in her room. We were free to say what we would about Jared.

"I find myself feeling slightly envious of the women who knew him," Fairfax remarked, unexpectedly. "Actually, that sort of man can be very gentle with women. Look what he did for Rose Tibbet. Lavished that marshmallow pink house on her. Paid her all sorts of attention."

"But never married her, dear Mother," Collins stated.

Fairfax ignored him.

"And Blanche. He evidently adored his sister," she continued. "Jared reeked of silver. Local legend has it that his boots were tooled with it, and even the buttons on his shirt were fashioned of pure jewelry ore. They had little six-shooters on them, to match the buckle Nevvie found. And that monstrosity on top of the Tower that passes for a weather vane. Symbol of power, darlings, here in the fabulous West."

"I'll settle for a more practical symbol, Mother," Collins said. "A car like Wick's, for instance."

"Don't tell me that you are hinting again?" Fairfax said. She gave Wick an indulgent smile. "My subtle son."

"He's welcome, of course," Wick said.

"We'll be off, then," Collins said, taking Rena's hand. "Thanks."

"You two are spending a good deal of time together these days." Fairfax commented. "Although I can't imagine what you find to do with yourselves in this dull town."

"We manage," Collins said.

I looked down at my empty plate, suddenly feeling guilty as I recalled the red Jaguar parked near the old shack the night of the storm.

"Anyone for brandy alexanders in the drawing room?" Wick asked, rising to pull out chairs for Fairfax and me. "A quick one, before I leave you. I've business to attend to tonight in town."

"Count me out," Kev said. "I've things to do."

He left us with no further explanation.

Later, I glimpsed Wick from my window, passing beneath the ancient street lamps, making his way unmistakably toward the Pink Cloud.

I put him from my mind and went to shower and prepare for bed.

When I returned to my room, the lights had appeared by the lake again.

Something prompted me to take the box containing the letters and the buckle that Adriane had sent out of my dresser. I pulled open the drawer and moved aside my clothes.

The box was gone! I stared numbly at the place where it had been, stunned by its sudden absence. Someone in the old house had taken it. Wick Carver? He could easily have returned to the Tower and slipped into my room, while I had been across the hall showering. Or had it been Fairfax? It had to be someone who had known about the box; probably the person who had been there in the cupola, as I came up the hill from the post office.

It seemed suddenly that it could have been any one of them. Even Blanche. There was something slyly furtive about the old woman.

My fear had given me a chill. I went to the closet for a jacket, noticing when I opened the door that one of my dresses had fallen from its hanger. I realized, as I picked it up, that of course someone had been there among my clothes, which had been pushed to one side of the rod, away from the small door that gave access to the space inside of the Tower walls.

Whoever had entered my room, then, had come up through the shaft beside the chimney. I pressed my ear cautiously against the small door, listening for some telltale sound.

Suddenly, the sound of a voice came to me, murmuring in barely coherent tones. It was the same whispering voice that I had heard before.

"Buck," the voice said, unmistakably. "Bucky, darling."

Buck Farrington. Blanche's lover. I was unable to believe my ears.

Was Buck Farrington hiding somewhere in the old mansion? Was he an accomplice of some sort? Wick's? I closed the small door quietly. Perhaps Buck Farrington was the person who was searching for silver down by the lake. Perhaps it wasn't Collins and Rena at all. I hurried to the window and drew open the drapes.

154

The lights had disappeared. What light there was now, falling over the shimmering water, was cast by a large silvery moon, which hung suspended in the east, above the dark shapes of mountains.

I lay awake a long while, that night, lost in the strange thoughts that poured through my mind. When I could bear them no longer, I got up and wandered out into the corridor. Even though it was quite late, I would see if either Fairfax or Rena might be up.

When I rapped at Rena's door and got no response, I gathered that she must still be out somewhere with Collins. Fairfax also failed to answer when I called softly outside her door, tapping on the carved panels.

I thought suddenly of Blanche. I hadn't taken the time to talk with the old woman, partly because I had been afraid of what she might tell me, particularly about her brother Norman, and partly because there was something so . . . awesome about her.

Still, even though it was late, I continued on toward her room, suddenly determined to talk with her. If the bits of evidence that I had uncovered proved anything at all, Blanche Wickerly could very well be my aunt. The thought startled me; I felt no hint of affection, or even liking, for the old woman.

The sound of voices came to me, from behind Blanche's closed door. I paused outside, straining to hear what was being said inside, feeling only a slight sense of guilt at so doing.

"Why have you come here?" Blanche Wickerly's voice demanded, creaky with anger.

"I've been going over a vast accumulation of notes and other invaluable material since I returned to the house this evening, and it occurred to me that you perhaps know a good deal about my father." This second voice clearly belonged to Wick.

"You've got hair like his! Like Jared's." Blanche said, her voice growing high-pitched, verging on hysteria. "But she lied! You aren't Jared's son!"

"I've just come from the Pink Cloud, where I had a most enlightening visit with Rose. I'm beginning at last to understand the force that seemed to draw me to this town, and even your reasons for allowing me and my staff to live here at the Tower. You knew, didn't you, that this is where I belong?"

"I tell you, she lied!" Blanche insisted. "She's a bitter woman. Bitter!" The old woman's voice rose on a pained note.

"I'm of the proper age to have been born here in this town, during that rather confusing period just before Jared died," Wick said.

"Jared consorting with the likes of *her!* I would never admit that you might be his son. Never! Go, before what name you have is tainted, the way that water down there in Five Mile Canyon has turned foul, with the dark secrets it hides," Blanche said ominously. "Let the name Wickerly die with me. I'll never admit that you might be his son. Never. Do you think that I would give her the satisfaction, after all of these years?"

"Norman? What about Norman?" Wick persisted, almost as though he had guessed that I was there in the corridor listening, straining, as he was, after the truth at last.

"How can I know about Norman?" Blanche said. "Except that he died, like Jared. Why are you plaguing me like this? Now go! Go before it's too late."

"Has it occurred to you that one of your brothers might have escaped death?" Wick asked.

The old woman gave an angry cry.

There was a movement on the far side of the door. I drew back in sudden fear, scurrying off down the corridor, then, running softly, on hearing the door to Blanche's room swing open.

"Nevvie!" Wick called after me.

I turned toward him, trembling with guilt.

"How long have you been out here?" he demanded.

"I just came," I lied, with surprising calm. "I was looking for Fairfax."

"Don't you imagine that she might be found in her room?" Wick asked, his eyes gleaming.

"I'll try her door again," I said, forcing my voice to sound cool.

I turned at that and hurried off, feeling him watching after me until I was past the corner.

Chapter Thirteen

In the black hours just before dawn, something woke me up. I had managed to put the conversation I had overheard between Blanche and Wick from my mind enough to doze, though fitfully.

Now I sat up in my bed, suddenly wide awake, but not at all certain what kind of sound I had heard. I tiptoed to the door, opened it, and looked down the corridor.

If someone had been there, they had gone. Or had it been only a restless dream that had startled me awake? I opened the door. There was no one outside in the shadows of the long corridor.

I started to close the door, when I caught a movement farther down the corridor. I thought at once of the woman in pink.

A sweeping sense of determination, coupled with anger, now possessed me; I slipped into my robe and went boldly out into the hallway. I had brought my flashlight, and I turned it on now, although the dim ceiling light was burning.

Whoever had been there had disappeared. I continued on, turning into the corridor that led past Blanche's door, and pausing outside of her room for an instant to listen.

I was too thoroughly awake by now to go back to sleep. I decided, on impulse, to go up to the attic room where I had discovered the portrait. Perhaps it had been returned. Had the person who had taken it been the same person who had entered my room and taken the small box containing the possible evidence of my father's past?

The door to the third-floor attic room loomed before me; I pushed it open and stepped tentatively inside. Flashing my light about, I saw that the portrait was still missing.

It occurred to me that someone might have hidden it elsewhere in the dusty room, and I began a methodical search among the endless clutter that was banked against the walls, moving aside boxes, exploring every nook and cranny that might possibly conceal it.

I stooped to sort through a stack of ancient, gilt-framed pictures pushed against the wall, and noticed that a section of the wall was hinged. Then I discovered another of the small doors that opened on to the shaft that gave access to the towering chimney.

It seemed suddenly credible that who-ever had taken the portrait had simply hidden it somewhere inside the dark repair shaft, and I pulled open the little door, more determined than ever to find it. If the woman in pink could clamber about on the steep ladder, clad in her flowing peignoir, so could I, I told myself stubbornly. I tried to convince myself that it could not have been Fairfax, using this treacherous and rather romantic route to rendezvous with Wick.

Taking a deep breath, I stepped bravely through the small opening, my foot groping for the ladder rungs. This is sheer folly, I thought. Yet something urged me on. One step downward . . . and then an-other. It became easier after a time, and I found myself moving rather freely down through the Tower walls, past more of the little doors, opening no doubt into dark, dingy little closets identical to my own.

There was a much larger door opening off the bottom of the shaft, this one a fire door made of iron. I tried it, slowly. It swung easily, almost as though someone were there beyond it, expecting me.

Trembling with fear, I stepped through into a small, dark chamber. I directed the beam of my flashlight about. I could see at once that it was Old Sil's wine room. The walls were lined with racks, several of them containing dusty champagne bottles tipped carefully to keep their corks properly moist.

I noticed a long narrow box standing against the far wall, its lid flung back, lined with maroon-colored velvet. Jared's coffin. It stood dustless, silver-tooled, gleaming, and I moved toward it, drawn by a macabre sense of awe.

Something lay in it, covered with a soft velvet throw. Unsuspecting, I lifted back a corner of the velvet. A shriveled brown object lay there. I thought at first that it was one of the dried coyotes that had hung above the door of the town museum. Then I realized that this face had once been human, and that I was gazing at a mummy. Perhaps because I had grown accustomed to the dried coyotes, or perhaps because the object lying there had long since lost any resemblance to humanity, I felt surprisingly little horror.

I covered the dried object and moved slowly about the small room. Suddenly there was sound behind me. I turned quickly, in time to see the fire door slam closed, shutting me into the small, airless room; and I caught briefly the unmistakably masculine scent of Wick's cologne. I tried the door, calling his name.

There was no reply.

Numbly, mesmerized by that closed door, I listened for some sound, and I imagined that I heard him climbing upward on the far side of the dark shaft.

Quite frightened by now, I groped along the walls, discovering another of the iron doors; this one, I guessed, led outward into the main cellar. It, too, was bolted on the far side.

It occurred to me that I must conserve the batteries in my flashlight, and I snapped it off. Surprisingly, I felt more secure in the pitch blackness, with the sight of the coffin obliterated. I tried not to think about the object it contained; it had seemed so impersonally piteous, like the sad, shriveled remains of an animal lying by the roadside.

I have no idea how long I huddled inside the small room, before a sound reached me, this one coming from outside the larger of the two fire doors. I caught the rasp of metal grating against metal, and realized, with surges of panic and relief,

163

that someone was opening the door.

Blanche Wickerly stood there in the faint rectangle of light.

"Darling Bucky," she said. She moved toward the coffin.

"Miss Wickerly?" I said.

"Call me Blanche, dear," she said, clanking the iron door closed behind her.

I had the presence of mind to snap on my light. Boldly, I flashed it over her.

"Blanche!" I said.

"It's *you*," she hissed, aware at last of my presence. "Nevada Wickerly!"

"Nevada Carver," I said defiantly.

"Never mind," she said, moving past me toward the coffin. "Bucky, darling, I won't let her tell." She drew back the velvet covering, exposing the mummified being. "They'll never know about us!"

"Buck Farrington?" I asked, moving toward her.

Her hand darted into the folds of her long black dress. Something flashed from beneath the draped material. It was a gun, clutched determinedly in Blanche's birdlike hand. She pointed it at me.

"Jared taught me to shoot," she said, in a voice that sounded quite lucid. "And I shall, if you attempt to leave this room."

The silver-plated pistol glowed evilly.

"This is what happened to your lover," I said. "Buck Farrington."

She reached to touch the mummy.

"Don't worry, Bucky, darling," she said. "I won't let her get away. I won't let her tell them about us. We've fooled the town all of these years, Bucky. All of these years, and not a one of them has suspected our little secret." She gave a mad-sounding cackle. "I won't let her spoil it now. Nor him, darling. The one who *calls* himself Wick Carver." Her eyes gleamed like coals, in the beam from my light. I knew, without a doubt, that she was quite hopelessly mad.

"I leased him this house," she continued. "I knew who he was and that sooner or later I would have to kill him."

"But he's the one who closed me in here," I said, the sound of my own voice startling me a little.

"However you came, I have you now," Blanche said. "I shall have to kill her," she whispered over her shoulder to the thing in the coffin. "And the rest of them, if they should start to realize. . . . All of them!"

She turned, compelled to gaze at her dead lover, the gun still wavering in her hand, pointing dangerously at me.

"I tell you again, there was never any-

165

thing, really, between Wick Carver and me, Bucky," she said. "I want you to believe that, sweetheart. I didn't mind, when he turned to Rose. I was glad, do you understand? Glad to be rid of him. Glad that he kept her from Jared, at least for a while!" Her eyes blazed as she spoke to the coffin.

"I forgot Wick Carver when you came to this town, Bucky," she continued. "He meant nothing to me, after I met you. I fooled Rose, and Jared, too; he put her up to luring Wick away from me. I had you to turn to, Bucky. I had you!" Her voice ended on a piteous sob. "I had you, until Jared found out about us," she added, her voice becoming suddenly harsh. "Rose must have told him, out of spite. Jared had no call to do what he did to you, even though he was my brother." She was whispering again, in a voice that suddenly sounded shockingly familiar; the voice that I had heard coming through the little door in my closet. It *had* been Blanche.

"What are you going to do?" I demanded, when she grew silent. "You can't keep me here forever. Someone will come looking for me. Even if you kill me. . . ." I made myself say it, inching a little toward the iron door.

Blanche noticed, and wagged the gun dangerously.

"Let them," she cried. "Let them come! Bucky and I will hold them off. We won't let them discover our secret." A new realization seemed to cross her small face. "You don't know my Bucky, Nevada. You've never met my handsome Bucky."

She motioned me near, with the heavy gun. I crept toward her; perhaps I could snatch it away, if I obeyed this sudden whim.

"Look at him," she demanded, seeming uncannily to read my mind, and shrinking away from me into the shadows. "Meet my handsome Bucky!"

She reached to lift a shriveled hand from the velvet depths, pressing it into mine. It might have been the dried paw of a desert animal. I looked closely now at the thing in the coffin. Buck Farrington's body had warped into a grisly shape. The brown skin had dried to parchment, following the empty contours of long, hollow bones. I saw that the grimacing little face had a small, jagged hole in its forehead, the edges of the unnatural orifice shriveled.

"This is the one I've caught spying," Blanche said to him. "Her name is Nevada. And now we must decide what is to

167

be done with her. She can't go free to tell the town about us. They would think us evil, darling, lovers all these years, and keeping it from them." Her face turned suddenly bitter, and she looked at me, her black eyes accusing. "Bucky wanted to marry me. We'd have been married long ago if it hadn't been for Jared. He didn't want Bucky to have me. Or any other man. Why do you think he annulled my marriage to Wick Carver?"

"But I thought you —"

"You thought I wanted it? It was Jared! Jared, do you understand? He made me do it. Rose helped him, by playing up to Wick, when Jared told him to stay away from me. She was there waiting to comfort him." The old woman paused, a triumphant gleam coming into her eyes. "But I had my Bucky then. I had my Bucky to comfort me. She can't take Bucky away from me, although God knows she has tried, slipping up here at night in that scandalous pink wrapper! Wandering through this house, as though it belonged to her." Blanche leaned toward me. "I've let her slip around all of these years, just to prove to her that she can't steal my Bucky away from me. She had Jared and Wick Carver, but she can't have my Bucky."

The woman in pink, I thought. Rose Tibbet.

Blanche reached behind the coffin and brought out a large, bulky object. It was the portrait that I had discovered in the third-floor room.

"This is what she's after," Blanche said. "But she knew better than to steal it from me. She's had to slip up here at night all of these years, just for a glimpse of Jared! And Bucky . . . I know that she's after my Bucky. Except that she can't steal him away from me, the way she did Wick. . . ." Blanche's bright eyes grew vague. "I shall never forget the look in Jared's eyes when I admitted that Wick Carver and I were married! That cruel look came onto his face. I had no choice but to let him arrange the annulment."

"Is that Jared, then?" I asked, knowing that the portrait had to be he.

"He was against us," Blanche said, her voice filled with her ancient hatred. "He tried to take Bucky away from me, just as he denied me Wick Carver."

"But you had turned to Buck Farrington, even before Jared — and Rose — took Wick away from you," I said.

"I was desperate for happiness," Blanche said. "I knew that none of it could ever last. Not so long as Jared lived."

"Did Jared kill Buck Farrington?" I asked.

"He was against all of them," Blanche said, her black eyes blazing.

"You hated your brother," I accused. "You hated Jared, while all the time this town thought you cared too much for him."

"Yes, I hated Jared," Blanche said. "And Rose Tibbet. I hated both of them."

She flung down the portrait and ground her heel into the painted face.

"I wanted Rose to see this. Jared, with a hole in his head. Dead, do you understand? Dead. I let her slip up here at night, knowing that she would never dare tell anyone. You see, she saw how Jared hurt my Bucky. She came here and saw. She knew Jared was responsible, and I knew that she would never tell."

"Jared killed Buck Farrington, then." I said. "Did Norman know?" I asked, thinking of the man I knew was my father.

Blanche's small eyes grew crafty.

"You ask too many questions, Nevada," she said. "As if you didn't know. As if Norman Wickerly hadn't told you the whole sad story. Ah, yes, I saw that mole there on your cheek that first day, and I recognized you for a Wickerly! It's a

Wickerly mark. Those Wickerlys who bear it are cursed. Do you hear me? Cursed! It will do you no good to try to hide it. You can't escape, though you've changed your name."

"If I am to die anyway, why don't you tell me the whole story?" I asked; I might distract her a little. "Your accusations against me give me a right to know the truth about my father, the truth about what happened here the night Jared died."

"Norman didn't tell you about Jared and my Bucky? Norman didn't tell you that Jared warned Bucky to stay away from me. Bucky stood up to Jared. Bucky loves me." She gave a pleased nod, her voice becoming childish.

A picture of what must have happened so long ago began to take shape in my mind. Jared Wickerly forbidding Blanche to see any man. And Blanche slipping out and making her choice, in spite of him. She had chosen Wick Carver first, and had turned to Buck Farrington when Jared intervened.

"Jared called it self-defense," Blanche mused. "But I knew. I knew he wanted to keep Bucky and me apart any way he could. He said Bucky was a wanderer. Fiddle-footed. Not good enough for me.

He wanted to keep Bucky and me apart. But no one could do that, could they, darling?" She actually patted the mummy. "No one could keep us apart."

"Where did it happen?" I asked. "Where did Jared . . . hurt Bucky?"

"Up on the hill, in one of the worked-out mines," she said. "Bucky and I used to meet there. Jared followed me one night. He had his gun. This gun." She waved the ominous weapon dangerously. "He drew on Bucky. But Bucky stood up to him. He had his own gun, and he aimed it at Jared. Then something went wrong. Bucky fell bleeding at my feet. Jared said he was dead. But I wouldn't let Bucky die!"

"Did Jared help you bring him here?" I asked.

"Jared went to get the coroner." Blanche said. "He thought Bucky was dead. While he was gone, I ran down to Rose's for Wick Carver. I asked Wick to help me. I told him that I would swear that he was the one who had shot Bucky if he didn't help me get Bucky out of there before Jared returned. We took Bucky to another old tunnel, on the other side of the ridge, and when Jared came with the coroner, Bucky was gone."

"How long has he . . . lived with you,

here in the Tower?" I asked.

"I cared for him there in the tunnel. Bathed him. Kept him warm," she said. "And when Jared died, I brought him here."

"Jared never found out, then, that Bucky . . . hadn't died?"

"He knew!" Blanche said, with sudden vehemence. "He spied on me from the cupola and followed me one day when I went to care for Bucky. He found Bucky lying on the pallet I had made for him. Jared said he was going to take Bucky away. He said I couldn't go there again to see Bucky!" She flashed me an outraged look. "And then that same night, the storm came, and the water threatened to flood the mine. Jared had to leave. But I knew he would remember and that as soon as the storm was over, and he knew that his precious silver was safe, he would come back to the tunnel and take my Bucky away."

"But the storm killed Jared," I said. "And Wick Carver never told anyone what he knew about Buck Farrington. So you were safe."

Blanche nodded. "Jared died in the storm. Jared died, and I was glad, do you hear? Glad! No one had a right to try to keep me and Bucky apart. Least of all

Jared. Spawning children by a whore. She said the child was Jared's!"

"Rose Tibbet?"

"She lured Wick away from me and bore his son, and then tried to pass the child off as Jared's!" the old woman ranted, in horrified tones.

Suddenly I believed her, realizing at the same time that Rose had lied after all.

"And after Jared died, you brought Buck Farrington here," I said numbly, wondering if Wick had any inkling of this part.

"I've lived with him all these years," Blanche said.

What did one do, in the face of stark madness? I drew slightly away from the old woman.

"Norman," I persisted. "I want to know about Norman."

"Dead," Blanche said. "Both of them dead. Even the dog, Prince. This one was descended from the one Jared gave her. I killed it. Gave it rat poison. And now I must kill you. I tried once. You and that awful Rose Tibbet, out walking . . . She wouldn't stay away from Jared. It wasn't enough that she had him. She had to have Wick. . . . And now she wants Bucky, slipping around half-naked. . . ."

"The stone," I said. "You rolled it down

174

the hill the night it rained."

"I saw the lights on the lake," she said. "You were after the silver. You and Rose. I won't have it, do you hear? I won't have his grave disturbed."

"But if you hated him . . ."

"This town doesn't know that," she said. "They've respected my feelings. Revered the dead. That can't change. It must never change."

"Why?" I asked.

Her small face grew crafty. "Bucky and I know," she said.

"It wasn't Rose and I after the silver," I said.

She stared at me, her black eyes glittering.

"Who was it? Who was it?"

"I've no idea," I said.

That wasn't quite true. I was almost certain now that it had been Collins and Rena.

"But I must know," Blanche insisted. "I must stop them. They mustn't disturb the grave. Jared's grave. Norman *isn't* down there. I know that now."

Then she took my flashlight and moved, with a flourish of the heavy pistol, to the iron door. Before I could spring forward, the door swung into place, sealing me in.

Chapter Fourteen

My thoughts turned to Wick Carver. Had he discovered that I was Norman Wickerly's daughter and, as such, entitled to a share of the Wickerly ore? Believing that he was Jared's son and heir, had he turned on me?

I huddled in the blackness. I probably had been drawn to a man who had all the while been plotting against me. I had thought myself capable of a far keener judgment than that.

A frantic feeling of fury came over me. I groped my way through the darkness to the iron door and pounded on it, not stopping until my fists were bruised and aching.

The door refused to open. I thought of Wick's Mexican housekeeper, Carmen, and called her name. There was no sound of life outside that impregnable door.

I sank down against the web-covered wall, overcome by my desolation.

Then, like an echo of my futile efforts to

escape, a sound, faint at first, began to grow louder.

"In here!" I cried.

Thinking that it might be Blanche returning, I grew silent, crouching, some part of my mind plotting to spring at her, to overpower her and somehow secure her weapon.

The door swung open. It was Blanche, still clutching her gun.

"They're down at the lake! They'll find Jared!" she cried to the mummy in the coffin. "What shall we do, Bucky? What shall we do?" She seemed beside herself with her fear; she had forgotten me.

I lunged suddenly, knocking her off balance. The gun went clattering across the dusty floor. I snatched my flashlight from Blanche and darted out through the fire door.

Blanche had left the cellar light burning. The dust-caked bulb cast a gloomy light over the cluttered room. Quickly, I threaded my way through it and ran up the stairs, wishing belatedly that I had dared to take the time to lock Blanche into the tiny room.

I plunged down the hill, away from the mansion, fancying that I heard Blanche beside me. I didn't stop running until I had reached the bottom of the slope, where the main street of the town began. Only then did I dare to glance behind me, next turning the beam of my light onto the dusty street. There was no one about.

I made for the lake then. The lights glowing across the water had grown very bright. I glimpsed dark figures moving furtively; clearly the shapes of men involved in some stealthy task indeed.

I recalled the angry voices that I had heard coming out of the Green Lizard Saloon; what Pop Denman had hinted, about the townspeople blowing up the dam, must be coming true. I started down the slope toward them.

My knees shook a little, and I realized that I was still afraid. When a crackling noise sounded close by, I turned sharply, flashing my light quickly over the clumps of sage that seemed to glow, in that concentrated beam, with a silvery sheen.

"Who is it?" I called.

"Nevvie?" A voice answered out of the shadows, sounding muffled and only slightly familiar.

Suddenly a man emerged, frightening me and causing me to cry out.

"Be quiet!" he warned.

He wore a battered topcoat, and a mask

concealed his face and hair. I shrunk away with a small, strangled cry.

"Wick?"

He snatched my light, flicking it off.

"You'd better get back up to the Tower," he said, his voice distorted by the mask.

He gripped my arm with a gloved hand and turned me about, pulling me along through the night.

"I know who you are," I announced bravely. He *couldn't* be truly malicious.

I fancied that he stiffened with displeasure, although he refused to reply, urging me rather roughly up the incline toward the mansion.

"I know that you believe yourself to be Jared's son," I said, trying to sound matter-of-fact. "I know that you've come here hoping to claim the Wickerly silver for yourself, as his heir."

This time, he responded.

"Who told you that?" he demanded, the harshness of his voice penetrating the rubber folds of the all-enveloping mask.

"I overheard you talking with her, when you came out of her room and caught me there in the corridor," I said. "Surely you guessed that I had —"

"Of course," he said, in that same muffled voice.

"What are you going to do with me?" I asked.

I was in real danger again, and I was amazed by the sense of calm that seemed to envelop me.

"We might be cousins," I persisted, when he failed to reply. "We might both be Wickerlys."

The man dipped into the pocket of his topcoat and held forth something bright and shiny.

"Is this what you're getting at, Nevvie?" he asked.

The object in his hand was Norman Wickerly's buckle. My father's buckle.

"You're the one who took the box from my room," I said. "I thought it was Blanche. But how did you know . . . ?"

"I saw you from the cupola," he said. "Trudging up the hill from the post office, looking rather furtive, as though that little package you had contained some sort of damning evidence. I guessed. And you'd mentioned that your father had walked with a limp. I put two and two together. It was as simple as that."

"First Blanche threatening to kill me, and now you," I said, marveling at how totally a mask could conceal a man; he had become a genuinely frightening stranger.

"Did you expect her to finish the job for you, when you locked me in that dungeon of a cellar?"

The man turned toward me now, apparently startled, although it was impossible to be certain. All that I could see of him was the faint shine of his eyes through the small holes.

"How did you get away from Blanche?" he asked.

"I knocked her aside and ran," I said.

"Where is she now?"

"I have no idea," I said.

We were circling the old house, staying in the shadows, and coming around to the rear. I looked up at its faintly gleaming windows, wondering if the others were there inside, sleeping, unaware that the town and the Tower had come suddenly alive, simmering with threats.

Suddenly I cried out, upward, toward the narrow windows.

The masked man grabbed me then, clamping a gloved hand over my mouth. He half dragged me down the cellar stairs, toward the fire door at the far end of the cluttered basement room, and shoved me inside with an almost feverish haste, as though he had become suddenly repelled by what he was doing and couldn't finish the task quickly enough.

Again, the iron door clanked shut; I fell to my knees inside the airless room.

At the last moment, my captor rolled the flashlight lightly inside, out of some vague sense of pity, perhaps. It rattled gently across the floor for a second. I followed the sound, groping for it, flicking it on and breathing a sigh of relief to discover that it still worked.

There was no sign of Blanche. The lid of the coffin still stood open, although I saw now the casket was empty. She has *taken* Bucky, I thought crazily.

I went to the smaller of the two doors, the one that led into the repair shaft beside the towering chimney. It was still bolted on the far side.

There seemed to be nothing for me to do but to sit down and wait for a cruel fate that must overtake me this time.

After a while, I sensed that the house above me had awakened. I wondered if it was morning and if the deed at the dam had been completed. Or had the town's reverence for the dead, and the name Wickerly, overcome them at the last moment, so that they had scurried away in shame without having accomplished it? I had heard no sound of dynamite exploding.

Perhaps Wick had somehow stopped them, I thought. The worst of the Wickerly blood seemed to have found its way to the surface in him; might he be, in spite of Blanche's vehement denials, Jared's son?

As though my very thoughts had conjured it, the smaller of the two doors swung open, and Wick stood there, gazing at me, looming larger than life.

"You've come back," I said, numb.

"Nevvie! For God's sake! I had no idea that it was you," he said, coming quickly toward me.

"What are you going to do with me?" I asked, still in that same stunned voice.

"Get you out of this musty hole, for one thing," he said, his voice sounding amazingly kind.

"After all of your trouble of bringing me here," I said. "Pushing me so rudely inside," I added, in spite of myself.

"What in the hell are you rambling on about, girl?" he demanded. "Have you suddenly lost your senses?"

"Hardly," I said. "I smelled your cologne, when you closed me in here that first time."

"My God, do you think I shut you in

here purposely?" he asked. "I didn't know it was you! I swear it."

"You've changed your mind," I said. "You've decided to let me have a share of Old Sil's silver. Am I now to have the pleasure of refusing it?"

"You're raving!" he said. "Unless . . . Is it possible that Jared, or even Norman, somehow lived?"

"As if you haven't the proof right there in your pocket," I said, refusing to trust him, perhaps because he looked so fierce, standing there in the half-light, his eyes gleaming much as I had imagined that they might.

"This is no time for clever little games, Nevada," Wick said, jerking me roughly toward him, drawing me into the narrow, dark shaft between the mansion walls. "In a few minutes, that damned lake is going to be gone! I want to be there when it happens. What a chapter it will make! The town of Wickerly springing to life again, after forty-odd years!"

"Then you didn't try to stop them?" I asked.

"Put a stop to the most interesting bit of action in the whole book?" Wick exclaimed. "You underestimate me, Nevvie. Now, come on, give me your hand. Up the ladder like a good girl. Careful, now. I'll be right here above you, something substantial for you to cling to."

He intends to push me when we reach the top, I thought. He has it all planned. Get rid of me. Wait until the dam is gone, and then claim the silver.

We reached the top of the ladder, and a sudden, atavistic instinct gripped me. I clung to the rungs of the narrow ladder, until my hands ached, daring the darkly glowering man above me to pry them loose.

"Hurry up," he ordered. "I don't want to miss anything." Then, when I still clung there, "Come *on,* Nevvie." He leaned down, reaching for me.

"No!" I cried. "No!" A shrill scream tore at my throat. I recognized it as hysteria.

Wick Carver loomed over me. I opened my mouth to scream again. Suddenly he slapped me across the face, and at the same time, I felt his big hands prying at me, loosening my numbed fingers.

They came free and I dangled in his hands over that narrow, black pit for a paralyzing instant.

Then he was tugging at me, drawing me upward, pulling me close, as we stepped out into the cluttered attic room.

I looked up at him, puzzled.

"Was the climb out of that dark hole as bad as all that?" he demanded. "Come on, now. There's no time to lose."

Stunned, wholly confused, and still afraid, I let him draw me from the room.

Chapter Fifteen

A crowd had gathered around the lake. Amazed, I glimpsed Collins Stanton wearing a shining black diving suit. Rena clung, white-faced, to his arm. And Fairfax stood beside them.

"Now we know why Collins and Rena have been slipping out so often together," Wick commented. "Collins has been watching too many diving-for-treasure episodes on TV. He had some idea that he could get a share of the silver, with Rena to help him. He's been diving every night into that black water, probing around for chunks of ore."

"And you've let him?" I asked numbly. Could I run away, if he got interested in all this?

"Another fillip for my book, to borrow Fairfax's word," Wick said. "I came onto Collins' diving gear stored in an old shack there above the lake. I guessed then what was going on. And, of course, I saw the lights down at the lake. They only confirmed my theory about Collins and Rena."

There were men working along the face of the dam. I noticed that they wore masks that hopelessly disguised them.

"All very anonymous," Wick commented, pausing in the shadows, still holding my arm. "No one wants to show his face while in the process of desecrating Jared's grave."

The scene around the lake seemed suddenly and totally unreal, a strange panorama indeed in the stark, shadowed colors of night.

"It won't be long, now," Wick continued.

"Why are you letting them do this?" I asked.

"I've told you," he said.

"But I thought you were one of them. The mask . . . And my father's buckle, Wasn't it you?"

"I've no idea what you are running on about," he said. "I'm afraid it will have to wait. . . ."

Suddenly, a dark shadow came toward us out of the sage. Whoever it was lunged at Wick, knocking him off balance. He let go of my arm as he fell, and I bolted off at last, leaving him there, struggling in the dust.

"Nevvie! What in heaven's name?" Fairfax cried, when she saw me.

"Wick tried to kill me," I blurted. "Someone . . . someone saved me. . . ." My voice caught on a sob of relief.

"Wick? My God, darling, you are absolutely hysterical!" She stared at me aghast, then reached and began frantically to rub my arms. "You can't expect me to believe a thing like that."

I pointed up the slope toward the two struggling figures rolling on the ground. One of them rose now and then reached down for the other, who knelt, nursing a mask-encased jaw. So the victor was Wick.

He pulled the masked man up by his collar and drew him, on staggering feet, toward us. Just as he reached us, Wick snatched the mask from the man's head.

It was Kev Keever, looking very sheepish.

"What in the hell is going on, Kev?" Wick demanded.

"*You're* the one who took the box from my room!" I accused Wick now, in a disbelieving voice. "*You're* the one who pushed me back into that awful dungeon!"

"I locked you in there the first time, Nevvie," Wick said. "As I tried to tell you.

Do you think you can forgive me?"

"But why?" I asked. "I don't understand any of this."

"I knew someone was slipping around the Tower at night. Some woman. I intended to trap whoever it was. I followed you and slammed that damn door. Then, when I came down here to the lake, where all of the excitement was, and realized that you were the one who was missing. . . . Darling, I'm sorry. I got back to you as soon as I could."

"I may as well confess," Kev said. "It was me, Nevvie, herding you up there, locking you in the second time. I meant no harm by it, if you can possibly believe that. And I took the box. I may as well confess to that crime, too. I went up to the cupola a couple of times and happened to see you with it. I knew you were actually a Wickerly, and I wanted to keep you away from the lake until we'd done what we had to do, just in case you knew who you really were and should take it into your pretty head to try to stop us. In the name of Wickerly," he added. "Although you couldn't possibly have been as tyrannical as Jared."

Wick gripped me suddenly by the shoulders, turning me to face him.

190

"Nevada! Is it true that you're a Wickerly? That we're cousins?" he asked.

"No," I said. "No, we're not."

My voice was lost in the shrill sound of Fairfax's cry, which was unmistakably joyous.

"Cousins?" she shrieked. "But how absolutely marvelous! Blood relatives. That means that there can't possibly be anything like romance between you, darlings." She laughed then, pretending to have been joking.

Wick ignored her.

"You've got a lot of explaining to do," he said to Kev. "You'd better get started."

"Well," he sighed, "Dad suspected that one of the Wickerly brothers had escaped the slide that was supposed to have killed Jared," Kev said. "Then that letter came, supposedly from Wick Carver. Actually, it was a confession, of sorts, from Norman Wickerly. Someone in the post office had seen the name Carver on the envelope, though, and the rumors got started that Wick Carver had killed Jared. There wasn't anything Dad could do to stop them, short of giving away some secrets that Norman had entrusted him with." Kev shrugged.

"I know it sounds confusing," he said. "But that's how it was. Dad let me in on just enough of this town's secrets to make me suspicious of both of you Carvers. Then the day that Fairfax and I went down to the *Strike* office, I happened on to some old photographs of Norman. He had the Wickerly mark, the same as Jared — and you, Nevvie. Dad had done a little human interest story on it, long before this town fell apart, and I came onto that, too. The fact that you suddenly started hiding your own mole, Nevvie, sort of gave you away. You had also mentioned that your father limped. I figured that you had to be a Wickerly, whether you knew it or not. Then that little box, with Dad's letters and Norman's buckle inside, arrived to clinch it. I just didn't want you bothering around down here at the lake, maybe trying to stop what we've decided, after all of these years, has to be done. In spite of Jared's grave," he added ruefully.

"You were determined to have the Wickerly silver for yourself," I said.

"Hardly." Kev emitted a short, bitter laugh. "Don't you see? I wanted the town to have it. God knows the people here have 'respected' Jared's bones, and the name Wickerly, long enough. Yes, come to think of it, in a way I did want it for myself. I wanted this place to thrive again, so I could open the *Strike* office. Revive the paper. Print Dad's scoop. You see, I also found Norman's confession there in the *Strike* office, the same day that I found the photos."

"But, darling, why didn't you show it to me?" Fairfax demanded. "Why were you so secretive?"

"As I said, I wanted the scoop for myself. For Dad's sake," he added. "Beyond that, my plan to blow up the lake, revive this town, was entirely philanthropic."

"It was you calling a meeting there at the Green Lizard," I said. "Working the townspeople up."

Kev nodded. "I visualized a library. A decent school. A hospital. Such mundane necessities as that. Then, too, I guessed that someone had started fooling around down at the lake, trying to high-grade some of the ore." He glanced at Collins and Rena. "I found Collins' diving gear in that old shack there on the other side of the lake. Brought in from Fallon, no doubt, on one of his mysterious trips with Rena in Wick's car. I followed them one night, as a matter of fact. And then I started laying my plans to blow up the dam, inciting the town, if that's a crime," he added, with another careless shrug.

"We were just messing around," Collins said. "We never meant any harm."

Kev had mentioned a confession sent to Jay Keever by Norman Wickerly. I wanted to ask about it, but a strange qualm prevented me from it, and I said instead: "Blanche? What about Blanche? She tried to kill me."

"Darling!" Fairfax said. "That shriveled old woman? I imagined something vicious about her. But to kill you . . ." Her voice dwindled off in amazement.

Suddenly, someone shouted down near the dam.

"We'll attend to Blanche later," Wick said, laying a comforting arm along my shoulders.

"She's my aunt," I said, in a dismayed voice.

"I know, darling," Wick said, his own voice grim.

It came to me that he still believed himself to be Jared's son.

"They've found what's left of Jared!" someone shouted below us.

The crowd moved in a body toward the group of masked men, bent now over something lying at the base of the dam.

"They were digging to plant the powder, and there he was," a man near us said.

A small pile of ivory-colored bones lay near the men's feet. Rose Tibbet appeared, supported by the two girls that I had seen on the veranda of the Pink Cloud, the evening that I had gone there. I saw, with a start, that Rose was wearing a filmy pink peignoir. I remembered what Blanche had told me, and visualized Rose slipping about the Tower in the dead of night, seeking some keepsake of Jared.

I became aware of Wick standing beside me, staring numbly at the remains of what he believed to be his father.

Rose Tibbet glanced up suddenly at the two of us. "I lied," she said. "He was my son. My son and Wick Carver's." Tears spilled from her faded eyes. "I wanted so much to be Jared's wife, to live in the Tower," she continued. "I thought I could force him to marry me by making him jealous. That's why I gladly lured Wick away from Blanche when Jared asked me. Let him continue to see me, long after Jared told me that Blanche had lost interest. I comforted him, and bore his son. And it was all a plot to get even with Blanche and to have Jared and the silver. That's why I tried to make them both believe that the child was Jared's. Neither of them believed me. At least, they pretended not to. Then, when Jared disappeared, I sent the baby away with Wick, because of Blanche. She came to me that same night. She threatened to kill the child if I tried to keep him here. She — she threatened his life that night, before Wick came up from the mine. I fended her off. . . ." Her voice faltered.

I shall never forget the expression that came onto Wick's face. He started to speak, just as one of the men crouched near the bones shouted: "He's been shot! Jared's been shot. See, there!" He jabbed his finger at the fleshless skull. "Somebody put a hole square between his eyebrows. Murdered, just like we've thought all these years!"

"Wick Carver! Just like we suspected." Another of the men cried. "By God, that bastard was a murderer, after all."

"Darling!" I gripped Wick's hand, fear surging through me, as I attempted to draw him away.

"What do you want to bet he did them both in," someone else said. "Norman and Jared, both. I'll bet Norman's bones are rotting somewhere underneath this damned fill, with a bullet hole through the skull, same as Jared, here."

"Get back, all of you!" someone screamed above us.

I looked up and saw Blanche, a small, white-faced figure standing defiantly above the crowd, near the monument. The silver pistol glinted in her hand.

"So now you know the truth," she cried. "I'll kill all of you, do you hear me? I'll fire that powder you've got planted, and blow you all to hell."

"It's Blanche! Blanche Wickerly." The crowd murmured her name nervously.

"Get back, for God's sake, like she says," a man near us said. "The old fool's gone crazy. Brooding all these years for Jared . . . It's affected her mind."

"We'll see that he's laid away in a proper grave, Blanche," the same man called up to the old woman, in an effort to pacify her. "We'll help you lay him away next to Old Sil, where he belongs."

"I hated Jared!" Blanche cried, in her crackling, old woman's voice. "Do you hear me? I hated my brother!"

There was a stunned silence.

"He tried to take my Bucky away," she cried. Then, in a twisted effort to redeem herself, she said, mostly to the unknown speaker, "That's why I had to kill him. This is the gun I used." She waved the shining weapon. "I took dynamite to one of the old tunnels that night. The rocks were always loose along this slope, hanging out over the mouth of the canyon. Jared had taught me well, and I used the knowledge he had given me to seal his doom. I knew how much power it would take to bring that canyon wall rolling down. Norman tried to stop me. But he was nothing but a cripple. Wickerly Carver came, too. But he was too late. I'd already shot Jared, and the fuses were lit. The sounds of the storm covered the blast. . . . That slide buried Jared. . . . I thought it had killed Norman, too, and maybe, if I was lucky, Wick Carver. But Wick must have helped Norman, and the two of them got out." The old woman paused, seeming to single me out of the crowd now. "I knew when that letter came to Jay Keever that Wick had escaped. And I knew, when I laid eyes on her" — she *was* looking directly at me, I cringed against Wick — "that Norman had somehow got out, too."

"Who does she mean?" someone asked.

"God knows," another person said. "Crazy as a coot."

"She knew too much," Blanche went on. "I had to kill her."

Did she actually believe that she had killed me in the wine room? I wondered.

"I hate to think what's going to happen if

198

that gun goes off," Kev said, beside us. "All that powder we've got planted, right there under her feet, and that crazy old woman, with a loaded gun!"

"Move the crowd back," Wick said quietly. "We've got to get people away from here. There'll be a massacre if that powder goes off."

Wick and Kev moved along the edge of the crowd, urging them back. Stunned to a man, they obeyed.

Blanche stood now with something clutched desperately to her side. I knew what it was, even before someone flashed a bright light on her to illuminate the shriveled remains of Buck Farrington.

"My God!" a woman screamed, "It's a mummy, like those they've got in the museum. The crazy old fool!"

"You think you can take my Bucky away!" Blanche's shrill voice sounded again. "Jared Wickerly. You think you can take my Bucky away. But I won't let you. Do you hear me, Jared? I won't let you!"

She raised her arm, pointing the gun at the pitiful pile of bleached bones, all that remained of Jared Wickerly. Suddenly, Rose Tibbet tore herself away from the two girls who were trying to comfort her, and ran, her pink peignoir billowing, to throw herself across the small heap.

Then the world seemed to explode, in a thunderous roar. The earth trembled, and a shower of clay fell. Wick's arms closed about me, protecting me from the pelting clods.

When the sound and the dust had died away, there was nothing left where the dam had been.

"You've got your scoop," I said to Kev.

We were in the Tower dining room, the six of us, having coffee.

"Too bad I can't print it," Kev said, looking at me over the rim of his cup.

"No one's trying to stop you," Wick commented.

Kev flashed him a grateful look.

"Dad worked for over forty years trying to make this town a decent place to live," he said. "I thought I could take up where he had left off, but I went about it all wrong. Barging in. Inciting violence. I'm responsible for Blanche's and Rose's deaths."

"Blanche died a long time ago," Wick said. "And maybe Rose did, too. That's something we'll never know."

"It was Rose slipping about the Tower at night," I said. "She thought it should have belonged to her. I suppose that was the nearest she could come to living here."

We were all silent for a moment; then Kev said:

"I'll not undo all Dad did, by coming out with a batch of sensational, yellow journalism about the dark secrets of this town. I'll wait until you open the mine. Then I'll have my story. Right now, I think it's time that I gave Nevvie something that belongs to her."

He took an envelope from his pocket and handed it to me. Norman's buckle was there inside, along with a yellowed letter.

I unfolded the worn sheet.

It read: "I was the last man to see Jared alive. You can be sure that he's dead, for I saw him die with my own eyes. I tried to stop what happened that night, but maybe I didn't try hard enough. That big mud slide came rolling down the walls of the canyon onto us, and it would have gotten me if a friend of mine hadn't been on hand to help me out. You remember Wick Carver, Jay? That's who it was. Suffice it to say that both of us had seen too much that night."

I had motioned to Wick to come read over my shoulder. I glanced at him, now.

"They both saw," I said. "Wick Carver,

and Norman. . . . My father. Both of them knew it was Blanche who killed Jared."

"You know, Jay, how I hated Old Sil and Jared," the letter continued. "I guess everybody knew why. Well, I've begun to get over that, now. The leg's getting better all of the time. I found a good doctor who went to work on it, breaking and re-setting the bones. But enough of that. At the time, I had no desire to remain in Wickerly. That's why I left town the night Jared died, and took Wick Carver's name. I'd had enough and more of being a Wickerly."

I glanced at Kev. "Your father had his scoop all the time," I said.

"And was decent enough not to print it," Kev said. "I hope I can be half the newspaperman he was for this town."

I turned back to the yellowed sheet.

"We made a bargain between us," it went on. "Wick's name for the mine. Old Sil fixed it a long time ago so that only his male heirs could inherit the silver. You might be inter-ested to know that Blanche can never claim any of it. Only the house belongs to her. The mine belonged to me, with Jared gone. I went to the lawyers in Fallon and had the papers made over in Wick Carver's name. The papers are laid away safely in a box at the United States Bank in San Francisco, until such a time as Wick's son turns up to claim them."

Wick — this Wick — caught his breath.

"Didn't your father ever tell you?" I asked, as stunned as he was.

He shook his head, his eyes still on the letter.

"I'll find my own silver," Norman Wickerly — my father — had written, hopefully. "I don't want the Wickerly ore that belonged to Old Sil and Jared. The real Wick Carver has no use for it either, after what happened between him and Blanche. But maybe his son will someday. Maybe young Wick will show up to open the mine, and run it like a man instead of a tyrant. And that's my main reason for writing this letter. So you'll know, when and if young Wick shows up, that he is legally entitled to all of it. He'll have the papers to prove it."

"It's time someone besides a Wickerly had a chance at the silver, buried there in Five Mile Canyon," I read on, speaking the words aloud, when Fairfax flashed me an impatient look. "I think the town will someday appreciate having someone besides a Wickerly running the mine, and that's why I'm giving it to Wick Carver, in exchange for the use of his name, and for saving my life the night Blanche killed Jared."

"The mine no longer belongs to Wickerlys, then," Kev said, in an awed voice. He looked at Wick Carver with new respect. "It will take some getting used to, after all these years under the Wickerly influence."

"My father, Norman Wickerly, then, deeded the Wickerly Mine to the real Wick Carver, in exchange for his name, and because that first Wick Carver saved him from the slide that buried Jared. After Blanche had already shot Jared," I added, with a sense of amazement, trying to get it all straight in my mind.

"If you had known Old Sil, or Jared, you'd understand why your father figured the town might appreciate having someone else running the mine," Kev said. "My father told me plenty about Old Sil and Jared. They both had a mean streak. And look what they did to Norman. Your father, Nevada. Jared breaking his leg like that, and Old Sil going along with Jared in his meanness. Is it any wonder Norman felt inclined to bargain for a new name. And, of course, he would have been grateful to Wick Carver for getting him out of the way of that slide. Being a cripple, Norman could easily have been buried right along with Jared — or what remained of Jared, after Blanche finished with him."

I glanced up at Wick.

"Your father must have been a fine man," I said, thinking at the same time that fate had strange ways. If it had not been for that first Wickerly Carver, I might not have been here now, falling in love with his son.

"He was," Wick was saying.

"What does it all mean?" Fairfax demanded.

"That Nevvie and I aren't cousins, after all," Wick said. "I think I like it better this way," he added, giving me a look that made my face glow.

He looked at Kev.

"I'm incorporating the mine," he said. "Just as soon as I can get to San Francisco to collect those papers Norman signed over to Dad, in exchange for services rendered. Shares for everyone who is interested in helping to revive the Big Bonanza. I'll reserve a number for myself, of course. A writer's income is rather sketchy, at times, and I understand that a wife has a habit of longing for security."

He was looking at me again, his eyes

bright. I remembered something that he had said to me, about wanting to make love, and my face flamed.

"Darlings!" Fairfax said, in an impatient voice, looking from one to the other of us. "I do wish someone would explain."

"We are going to paint the Tower white," I said.

"And tear down that damned cupola," Wick added, taking my arm.

The employees of Thorndike Press hope you have enjoyed this Large Print book. All our Thorndike and Wheeler Large Print titles are designed for easy reading, and all our books are made to last. Other Thorndike Press Large Print books are available at your library, through selected bookstores, or directly from us.

For information about titles, please call:

(800) 223-1244

or visit our Web site at:

www.gale.com/thorndike
www.gale.com/wheeler

To share your comments, please write:

Publisher
Thorndike Press
295 Kennedy Memorial Drive
Waterville, ME   04901

MARION—THE PROPHECY

MARION— THE PROPHECY

M J Finn

Book Guild Publishing
Sussex, England

First published in Great Britain in 2006 by
The Book Guild Ltd,
25 High Street,
Lewes, East Sussex
BN7 2LU

Typesetting in Baskerville by
IML Typographers, Birkenhead, Merseyside

Printed in Great Britain by
Antony Rowe Ltd, Chippenham, Wiltshire

A catalogue record for this book is available from
The British Library.

ISBN 1 84624 048 4

Prologue

Lamplight flickered on the rippling water of the Thames and on the far embankment the occasional passing car disturbed the stillness of the night, but the woman slowly walking to the centre of Putney Bridge heard and saw nothing, her deep inner despair inuring her to everything around her. It was three o'clock in the morning and the city slept, but this woman didn't sleep, for sleep was a luxury that had long been denied her, so she came to the bridge in search of a more permanent sleep, a sleep that was eternal. The strident wail of a distant police siren dimly pierced the night and the woman looked up briefly before continuing on, her eyes cast to the ground as if she were counting her footsteps or making doubly sure that each foot preceded the next in her grim resolve to see this through to its bitter conclusion. At the bridge's centre she stopped and turned her eyes to the darkly sparkling water, her hands lightly resting on the cold parapet, and as she raised her head the lamplight caught the twin tracks of tears that seared her cheeks, glittering like diamonds before they fell unnoticed, just as she would fall unnoticed, and at last find peace.

A tug hooted on the water behind her and she mentally discarded the sound, the tug too far away to affect the outcome of her intentions, yet it acted like a spur, instilling within her a need for haste, and she clambered up onto the parapet and stood for a moment looking down at the river surging beneath her. It had a hypnotic quality, inviting the leap into its welcoming embrace, and the woman stepped off the parapet without a second thought, boldly accepting its deadly promise, and as she fell she screamed … a scream as old and primordial as time itself.

Chapter 1

'There's a Miss Douglas from social services to see you Doctor,' Sister Barrett said, poking her head round the door, and Doctor Charles Levington looked up irritably.

'What, now? I need to go through these case notes with you before morning rounds. Can't it wait 'til we've finished?'

'Apparently not.' Sister Barrett shook her head, making the starched cap tremble precariously on her dark hair. 'She says it's important that she sees you before you do your rounds.'

Doctor Levington sighed. 'All right. Show her in ... but tell her I can only spare her five minutes. I'm running late as it is.'

Miss Douglas was a very intense middle-aged woman, her eyes constantly shifting and blinking behind huge spectacles, but it was her sheer bulk that surprised Charles Levington the most, giving him the instant impression this was how people on safari felt when they were being charged by a bull elephant or a hippopotamus, and he sat up in alarm as she strode purposefully towards him, a thick beefy hand outstretched in greeting.

'Doctor Levington?' she boomed. 'Carmel Douglas. Fulham Social Services. Sorry to burst in on you like this.'

He half rose from his seat and shook her hand, casting a meaningful glance at his watch as he waved her to a chair, and she plumped herself down heavily, talking to him absently as she rummaged in her briefcase.

3

'I won't keep you long, I hope ... Now where's that damn file? I know you're a busy man, Doctor, but aren't we all these days? Ah, here it is.' She rested the file on her voluminous lap and blinked at him through her spectacles, nodding at the paperwork piled on his desk. 'Are those your patients' files?'

'I was going through them prior to my morning rounds,' he said pointedly, and she ignored him just as pointedly.

'Got to the Marion Harting file yet?'

'Sorry?'

'Marion Harting? She is your patient, isn't she, Doctor?'

'I don't ... I've been on holiday. This is my first day back.'

'I know.' She grinned at him. 'I came in last week, but they said you were in Barnsley.'

'Actually it was Bali,' he said stiffly, and she blinked at him.

'Really? I could have sworn they said Barnsley. Never mind ... Marion Harting came in while you were away and I'm on the case.'

'Case?' He stared at her. 'What case?'

'The Marion Harting case.' She said it as if she were talking to a three-year-old. 'Perhaps if you were to find the notes?'

'What? Oh ...'

The file was the next one in the heap of folders and he extracted the notes and glanced at them perfunctorily, raising his eyes questioningly at the woman sitting across from him, and she shook her head in exasperation, tapping the file on her lap with a meaty finger.

'Well, Doctor? What do you make of it?'

'Make of it?' It was his turn to blink back at her. 'Make of what?'

'The Marion Harting case,' she repeated earnestly. 'Intriguing, eh?'

'I'm sorry, Miss Douglas,' he said quickly, 'I'm afraid I'm not at liberty to discuss my patients with you ... Perhaps you've some information for me that might aid her recovery?'

4

He waited expectantly and Carmel sighed wearily.

'She was a jumper,' she said, as if that explained everything, and Charles gaped at her.

'She was a what?'

'A jumper … Marion Harting … Threw herself off Putney Bridge at three o'clock in the morning.'

Charles's face remained blank and Carmel raised her eyes to the ceiling as if he were a stupid dullard and she was wondering when the penny would finally drop.

'It was a suicide attempt, Doctor.' She spelled it out for him slowly and succinctly so he wouldn't miss a thing. 'And not the first time, either.'

'She's tried it before?'

'Three times before to be precise,' Carmel nodded. 'That's how social services came to be involved. Like I said, Doctor, I'm on the case.'

Charles Levington looked at the medical notes more thoroughly, noting that Marion was admitted at 3:57 last Wednesday morning … wet and bedraggled, but alive.

'A tugboat crew saw her jump and pulled her out,' Carmel said as if reading his mind. 'Just some broken bones, so I was told last week.'

'Mmm.' Charles looked up from the notes. 'One or two fractures. Cuts and contusions. Nothing serious or life-threatening.'

'I spoke to Doctor Penny last Thursday. He was on duty when they brought her in, but as she'd be your patient when you returned from holiday, he suggested I speak to you.'

'What else did he suggest?' Charles asked dryly, and Carmel shrugged.

'He suggested that as a suicide attempt it could have done with a bit more planning. The water level was too high, you see, and she didn't have that far to drop. Another few feet and she'd have killed herself for sure.'

'Perhaps it wasn't a suicide attempt,' Charles offered carefully. 'Perhaps it was a cry for help.'

'Nevertheless, it could have ended in her death … just like the other times. Were they cries for help too, Doctor?'

'Possibly.'

'And the cries were heard, Doctor. Social services have been trying to help Marion Harting for the last three months.'

'Three months?' Charles stared at her. 'Marion's attempted suicide four times in three months?'

'Yup.' She nodded at the open folder on his desk. 'It should all be in there. On all three occasions she was treated in the accident and emergency department right here in this hospital.'

Charles skipped back through the file and read through the notes quickly. Slashed wrists on the first occasion, treatment for a bruised and swollen windpipe and larynx where she'd tried to hang herself on the second, and the utilisation of a stomach pump after an overdose of pills on the third. Marion Harting was determined to end it all, that was for sure. Or was she? A plaintive cry for help that had gone unheeded? Maybe social services wasn't the help Marion craved.

'… resources.' Carmel looked at him with an inquisitive smile, and he realised he hadn't been listening.

'Sorry?'

'I said, "Perhaps we should pool our resources." Work together to get to the bottom of it.'

'Tell me what you know about her,' Charles said, and Carmel shrugged her huge shoulders.

'She's twenty-five … Pretty little thing. Lives with her boyfriend, Terry Newell, in a two-bedroomed flat in Fulham.'

'Parents?'

'Emigrated. Went to live with Marion's sister in Canada.'

'Any other family in England?'

6

'There's an older brother, Ronald, who lives in Tooting. Drives a van or something ... and there's an aunt or someone still alive and kicking down in Devon or somewhere. I'm sorry to be a bit vague, but Marion is rather reticent where her family are concerned.'

Maybe she just didn't like talking to social services, Charles thought, *or maybe she didn't want anyone's help at all and the suicide bids were genuine.*

'So, how did you get involved this time?' he asked, and Carmel squinted at him through her spectacles.

'The boyfriend, Terry, phoned me. He thought I'd have more clout convincing the people here to put Marion under strict supervision in case she tries something untoward while she's in here.'

'I see,' Charles nodded, his mind working overtime. 'So I take it she's being supervised?'

'Twenty-four-hour watch,' Carmel nodded. 'They had a policeman here for the first day or so; then they got the League of Friends involved. Marion's under constant surveillance.'

'Right.' He'd have to discuss the arrangements with Sister Barrett. 'Tell me,' he said after a moment, deciding on a different approach. 'Did you find out why Marion is persistently attempting suicide?'

'Nope.' Carmel shook her head, the movement making her jowls quiver. 'We could never get to the bottom of it. We asked her often enough, but she'd just give us a blank look and totally ignore the question.'

'I see.' He didn't know what else to say. What else *could* he say?

'I've got to go,' Carmel said, lumbering to her feet. 'I've a woman to see in the Broadway. She's got seven kids, a parrot, two hamsters and a gerbil ... and she's got a drink problem. Listen, Doctor, I'll leave my notes here for you and if I can be of help just give me a call.'

Suddenly their roles were reversed and it was Carmel Douglas in a hurry to get on and Doctor Levington who wanted to prolong the meeting, but once again she thrust out her hand, gripped his palm in a three-second vicelike grip, then turned away, talking over the bulwark of her shoulder as she bustled towards the door.

'Sorry to call unannounced, Doctor, and thank you for your time ... Let me know how Marion gets on, won't you?' At the door she stopped and turned to face him, her eyes finally stilled as she gazed levelly at him, and her voice took on a note of gravitas as she delivered her parting shot. 'There's more to Marion than meets the eye,' she said solemnly. 'There's a reason behind these suicide attempts, you know. A deep-seated reason that we can only guess at. I've only scratched the surface in getting to the bottom of it, but you're a doctor, a professional, so I'm hoping you can do better. Look after her, Doctor ... she needs your help and it's not just her bones and flesh that need mending ... it's some break in her make-up that needs putting back together and looking after. Must dash. 'Bye.'

The ensuing silence was a palpable thing and Charles stared dumbly at the door as it closed on her retreating back, her folder cast nonchalantly onto the pile on his desk, and he thumbed through it idly—the whole concept of a patient's mental problems was too far removed from his sphere of knowledge to have any meaningful impact. He was accustomed to dealing with the tangible: broken bones and torn flesh that he could administer and treat until all was healed and renewed, but Marion Harting, the patient in Room Five, required help of a different kind, the kind of help that only a psychiatrist could offer.

There were three psychiatric reports from Marion's previous suicide attempts, but they were inconclusive and merely suggested depression as the root cause and recommended antidepressants as a remedy. It was a classic

8

case of a woefully inadequate health system failing the patient and the consequences were predictable to say the least.

Sister Barrett came in then and they reviewed all the patients' notes prior to his rounds, but he deliberately kept Marion's file until last, wanting more time to delve and probe into the mind of a woman who was determined to kill herself.

'Marion Harting,' he finally said, his voice neutral, betraying nothing. 'She's been put on a suicide watch, I believe.'

'That's right,' Sister Barrett nodded. 'Came in on Wednesday morning. Attempted suicide. We've had the boyfriend, the police and social services giving us grief ever since. Her left leg was broken in three places and she's got a plaster from her ankle to her crotch; her left shoulder was severely dislocated and her arm's in plaster from a shattered elbow, but they still think she's going to jump out of the window or something. We've got the League of Friends feeding her with a plastic spoon and the duty nurse has to check her mouth after every medication to make sure she's swallowed it and isn't saving it until she's got enough to do herself any mischief. We really don't need the aggravation.'

'What's she like?' Charles was curious after all he'd heard about her, and Sister Barrett shrugged noncommittally.

'She's nice enough, I suppose. She rarely speaks, but she's no bother. Let's face it, she can hardly do much harm to herself in the state she's in at the moment. Even so, Hospital Admin insisted that the window was secured and we keep her under continuous surveillance. I expect they're afraid of someone suing the arse off them if she manages to top herself while she's in here, but it's all a bit dramatic, if you ask me.'

'You're probably right,' Charles said diplomatically. 'Anything else I should know?'

'She's pregnant.'

It was said so matter-of-factly that Charles almost missed

the significance of it, and he was about to speak when he paused, wondering if that was the reason for the suicide bid, before remembering that the attempts on her life had started three months ago. Unless, of course, she was more than three months pregnant.

'How far advanced is the pregnancy?' he asked after a moment, and Sister Barrett gave a light shrug, a mere rise and fall of her shoulders.

'We're not sure … A month? Maybe five or six weeks, but without discussing it with her it's difficult to pinpoint exactly. She'd lost some blood and was in shock when she came in last week and Doctor Penny gave her a transfusion just to stabilise her. We did a routine check on her blood sample and it came back positive for pregnancy. Doctor Penny didn't think it was the right time to broach the subject with her and he was more concerned with getting her settled and comfortable. Having said that …'

Charles waited for her to continue and when she said nothing he cocked his head at her, raising his eyebrows expectantly.

'Go on.'

'Well … I worked in maternity for six years and whether the mothers wanted the baby or not, they still talked about them—it was the main topic of their conversation … but Marion hasn't mentioned it. Not one word, which is strange to say the least.'

'Well … you said she doesn't speak much.'

'Even so, you'd think she'd ask if the jump off Putney Bridge had harmed the baby, wouldn't you?'

Charles considered that for a moment until another thought wormed its way into his head.

'Do you think she doesn't know that she's pregnant?'

'It's possible, I suppose. I mean … committing suicide is one thing, but killing your unborn child as well is quite another.'

10

'Has anyone mentioned it to her since she's been here?'

'No.' Sister Barrett shook her head emphatically. 'Only Doctor Penny and I were aware of it, anyway, and at the time his prime concern was fixing the breaks and making sure she was stable. He didn't want her unduly stressed, especially in her state of mind, so he decided we should say nothing.'

Probably the wisest course of action in the circumstances, Charles thought, and until they had more information it was probably best to let it remain so.

'Okay.' He came to his feet, the recent holiday in Bali forgotten as he immersed himself in his work. 'Let's take a look at the patients.'

Chapter 2

Room Five, on the third floor of the Mountbatten wing, was like a hundred others in St Christopher's hospital, with one glaring exception: it was basically empty. There was a bed with a small cupboard alongside it for personal effects, against the far wall was a chair that was occupied by an elderly woman from the League of Friends, and that was it. No pictures, no vase of bright flowers, no cleaning utensils, no curtains round the bed for privacy, no medical equipment stored in a corner, not even a bedpan, and Charles realised just how seriously Admin were taking the threat of Marion's compulsion to harm herself, and had left absolutely nothing to chance. The room was stark, bare and spartan, which he thought was hardly conducive to the well-being of one of his patients, but he said nothing as he nodded to the elderly woman and stepped over to the bed, focusing all his attention on the girl who lay silent and still, her eyes closed as if she were asleep.

Charles was aware of the elderly woman leaving the room, but he kept his eyes on the girl, studying her closely and putting a face to all the information he'd gathered about her in so short a time. Carmel Douglas said Marion was a pretty little thing and Charles had to agree with her. She had long dark hair that was a tangled riot over the pillows, giving her a wild, unkempt look that had an appeal all of its own, and she had a good shape to her body that not even the rumpled blankets could conceal. Her face was soft in repose, her pale cheeks slightly hollowed, the cheekbones prominent, and she had a delicate nose set above a well-defined mouth and a small chin that bore the faintest shadow of an indentation as if it had been added as an afterthought. On her left temple, between her eye and her hairline, was the trace of an old scar or a birthmark, a pink smear that was barely discernible, a small puckering of the flesh, like a burn, and Charles absently wondered if she was conscious of it, and if she was, whether she made an effort to cover it with her hair. Her eyes flicked open and he noticed they were a deep hazel, but they appeared unfocused, seeing nothing except a faraway space somewhere on the ceiling.

'Good morning, Marion,' Charles said conversationally. 'I'm Doctor Levington and I'll be looking after you from today. I was on holiday when you came in, but you saw Doctor Penny last week, didn't you?'

Her eyes seemed to clear, turned towards him, studied him dispassionately for a few seconds then returned to examine the ceiling, her whole demeanour one of utmost boredom, and Charles sighed softly.

'How are you feeling today?' he went on, and regretted the words instantly. They sounded trite and meaningless. She'd been dragged from the river where her suicide attempt had been foiled and she now suffered the pain and discomfort of broken bones, cuts and bruises. How did he think she'd feel? On top of the world?

'I'm sorry,' he said sincerely. 'That was a stupid question to ask, wasn't it?'

She gave a barely audible derisive snort and Charles smiled. At least he'd managed to exact a response. He looked at her chart and nodded with a degree of satisfaction. She was eating, albeit sparingly, but her fluid intake was good and she was responding to treatment, which all pointed in the right direction for a full recovery.

'I'll see if we can find a plastic vase,' he continued, passing the chart to Sister Barrett. 'Get some flowers in here—brighten the place up a bit, eh?'

Marion ignored him totally and Charles shrugged.

'Right then.' He turned to go. 'I'll pop in again and see you later.'

Marion said nothing, not even stirring on the bed, and Charles walked briskly from the room.

Charles Levington turned the last page of the file and sighed, his lips pursed thoughtfully as he gazed at the open folder in contemplative silence, his long-boned fingers drumming absently on his desk. After twenty-eight years as a doctor and surgeon he had finally met a patient that he didn't know how to cure. He could mend her broken bones and heal the lacerations, but he couldn't heal the disquiet that was eating away at her mind. He flipped back through the file and scanned the first page, absorbing the personal details in search of some clue to explain why Marion Harting was hell-bent on committing suicide, but all he found were clinical facts, a name, an age, an address that gave no hint of the personality or character of the person they described, for they lacked the warmth of knowledge, coldly written by a hospital administrator simply doing a job.

Yet in the last three months Marion had tried to kill herself four times.

Why?

Even the previous psychiatrists hadn't come up with a suitable answer.

Marion was an attractive young woman, Charles thought, with everything to live for, so why was she so determined to end it all? What compulsion drove her to slash her wrists, take an overdose of sleeping tablets, try to hang herself, or, as in this latest example of dogged persistence for self-destruction, throw herself off Putney Bridge in the hope of either breaking her neck or drowning?

That she'd suffered only broken bones and minor cuts and bruises was a miracle in itself, but Charles knew it was only a matter of time before she succeeded in her bid, that the time would come when there would be no one on hand to stem the flow of blood, pump out her stomach, cut the rope before it was too late, or just happen to be passing in a boat to save her from drowning. She'd been very fortunate so far, to say the least, but when would fortune fail? When would the luck run out? How much time did they have to save her from herself?

He sighed wearily as he deposited the file in the desk drawer and came to his feet, glancing at his watch as he stepped into the corridor and made his way to Room Five, mulling over the one thought that just might make Marion Harting sit up and take notice, the one piece of information that just might make her want to live again. Assuming she wanted to be pregnant, of course. It just might give her another reason to kill herself, a decisive factor that could make her more determined than ever to succeed when all the previous attempts had failed. Should he tell her? Would she welcome the news or would it send her spiralling down into a well of despair from which she would never recover? He needed answers into the workings of her mind, and he knew just where to get them. But that would come later. First he had to get to know her and he had to make her trust him. That was the basis for every doctor/patient relationship: trust. And without it he would get nowhere.

The woman from the League of Friends smiled hello when Charles entered the room then made herself scarce, and he pulled the chair closer to the bed, settling himself comfortably as he waited for Marion to become aware of him. She cleared her throat and blinked and Charles thought that was as good a sign as any that she was receptive, so he smiled, making his voice light.

'Good afternoon, Marion,' he said airily. 'I was here this morning. Doctor Levington ... Remember?'

She gave a slight shake of her head as if she considered him an idiot for thinking she'd forget so soon, and Charles's smile broadened.

'You do remember. Good. I've been studying your case today and although I'm pleased at the way you're responding to treatment, there's another problem that needs treating, wouldn't you agree?'

She blinked twice, her attitude one of bored indifference, and Charles shrugged.

'Maybe you'd like to talk to me about it?'

She said nothing, her face betraying no emotion whatsoever.

'Why did you do it, Marion?' he went on softly, persistently. 'Throw yourself off the bridge last week? And the other times, too? Why, Marion?'

She could have been a statue, cast from stone, and the only indications she was alive were the slow rise and fall of her chest and the occasional flicker of her eyelids.

'What's so bad in your life that makes you so determined to end it, Marion?'

She gave the slightest shake of her head and Charles leaned closer, almost willing her to respond to him as he sought to penetrate the barrier she'd erected around herself, a barricade of sullen silence.

'Why, Marion?' he repeated earnestly. 'Just tell me, please. Why are you doing it? Why don't you want to live anymore? Why? Answer me, please, Marion ... Why?'

She closed her eyes as if to shut him out of her private world, and he sighed softly as he came to his feet and returned the chair to its position against the wall, turning to look at her one last time. The scar on her temple seemed more visible now, a dark smudge on the expanse of pale flesh, a mark whose vividness he'd been unaware

16

of earlier, and he wondered if it changed with her mood just like a person's cheeks coloured when they were embarrassed. He made a mental note to look into it.

Charles paused by the door and turned, all his instincts telling him that Marion wasn't a lost cause and she was worth a parting shot, something for her to think about in her world of self-imposed silence.

'I want to help you, Marion,' he said sincerely. 'I want to see you walk out of here a happy young woman with everything to live for. I want you to live your life as it was meant to be lived and I want you to enjoy every last second of it, not throw it away and destroy it like you seem determined to do. I want to see you married with kids and a loving family around you … Perhaps a good job and holidays in the sun … Maybe you don't want those things. Maybe that's the stuff of ultimate boredom as far as you're concerned, I don't know. I don't know because you won't talk to me. But what I do know, Marion, is that you're a very attractive young woman and you deserve better than floating down the Thames as a bloated corpse, another suicide statistic just because life got a bit tough and you couldn't handle it. You know what a tough life is, Marion? Take a look at the people dying of motor neurone disease or suffering with MS … Peek into the children's ward and see the kids with leukaemia. Take a peep at the ones who've got a life of cerebral palsy to look forward to yet still manage to laugh, who still manage to get on with it and would never consider for one second that life wasn't worth carrying on with. I believe you're worth it, Marion … I believe you deserve a life and I believe you're worth living it. It's just a pity you don't.'

He turned and yanked the door open, his eyes scanning the corridor for the League of Friends woman, his breathing heavy and his heart pounding as if he'd run a marathon, and he hesitated on the threshold, failing to see the woman and knowing he'd have to wait until she returned.

17

'I don't know.'

It was the sudden sound of Marion's voice rather than its content that brought Charles up short and made him spin on his heels, his heart lurching in his chest as he realised that something in his tirade had reached out and touched her and brought the response he'd been hoping for.

'Sorry?'

She shook her head disconsolately, all the pain and agony of her dilemma mirrored in the brown depths of her tortured eyes.

'I don't know why,' she repeated in a hoarse whisper. 'I just know I have to do it.'

'To kill yourself?'

'I have to end it … finish my life.'

'And you don't know why?'

He stepped back into the room, the door swinging shut behind him, and he waited at the foot of the bed, not daring to come too close and shatter the fragile and tenuous link that had somehow been forged between them.

'It's as if …' She swallowed hard as though the words were choking her. 'As if a light has gone out in the world and there's no point anymore … no reason to carry on. It just seems … It just seems the right thing to do … the *only* thing to do.'

'Marion … let me help you.'

She shook her head dismissively and closed her eyes, her voice betraying a resigned conviction that she was past help and he was wasting his time.

'You want to help me, Doctor?'

'You know I do.'

She nodded wearily. 'Then get me well enough to walk out of here so I can do what I've got to do.'

'*Got* to, Marion?' His voice was harsh, stung to anger by her casual acceptance of her fate. 'Why have you got to?'

But the barricade had come back up and she ignored him,

18

severing the flimsy link that had bound them for so short a time. Charles felt the presence of the woman from the League of Friends behind him and he strode from the room with a lighter heart than when he'd entered. He'd breached Marion's barriers once, and he'd do so again.

He passed a young man in the corridor, heading in the opposite direction, and impulse made Charles stop, studying the bulletins pinned to the wall, yet he watched from the corner of his eye as the man entered Room Five, and a few seconds later the elderly woman emerged, allowing Marion her privacy as she was trained to do.

'The man who's just gone in to see Marion ...' Charles smiled at the woman as she approached him. 'Do you know him?'

'Oh, yes, Doctor,' the woman grinned. 'That's Marion's boyfriend, Terry Newell. He always comes in about this time.' Her face took on an uncertain look and she peered at Charles fretfully. 'It was okay to leave them together, wasn't it? I was told I had to vacate the room when anyone else was in there. He won't give her a knife or something, will he?'

'I'm sure everything will be fine,' Charles said reassuringly. Terry Newell had had plenty of opportunity before now to provide Marion with the means to dispose of her life and Charles had no reason to suspect that today would be any different. 'How long does he stay?'

'An hour usually. Gives me time to get a cup of tea and a sandwich.'

'Then please, don't let me stop you.' Charles stepped aside, and with a grateful smile the woman shuffled away.

Professor Leon Macleod was semi-retired from teaching psychiatry at Guy's Hospital, London, but he was still considered to be a leading authority in deep trauma syndrome, and in between lecturing on the subject he was in

19

the process of writing a book that he hoped would cover all aspects of the many-faceted area of mental distress. Students of old dubbed him 'The Absent-minded Professor' and everything he did suggested the description was very apt. He was prone to wearing rumpled suits and wildly patterned ties that never quite managed to hang straight, and well-worn shoes that hadn't seen polish since the day he first put them on his feet. He was in his late sixties and his grey wispy hair was in constant disarray, at odds with a neatly trimmed goatee beard that he believed gave his features a certain distinguished look. He wore thick-lensed spectacles which he peered through with myopic eyes, and his thin cheeks had a strange pallor as if they hadn't felt the sun's rays in a very long time, confined as he was indoors with books of learning and students in waiting, the slog of research filling his mind and the dust of academia filling the cracks in his shoes. His voice came as a complete surprise and he spoke with a soft Scottish lilt that carried a tranquillity and serenity all of its own, a deeply soothing quality that he had used to good effect over many years, subduing rowdy students just as efficiently as calming distressed patients. He was also a close personal friend of Doctor Charles Levington and had been for more than twenty years.

'Charles, my boy!' His delight was evident as soon as he recognised Levington's voice on the telephone. 'It's lovely to hear from you.'

'How are you, Leon?'

'I'm well … very well. And you?'

'I just got back from three weeks in Bali so I'm fit as a fiddle.'

'It's good to hear it. Are you keeping busy then?'

'You know orthopaedics, Leon,' Charles laughed. 'There's always another bone to set somewhere.'

'Aye. That's true enough … So, what can I do for you, Charles?'

'You know me too well, Leon. It might have been a social call, you know.'

'You didn't phone me to discuss your wee holiday, did you now?'

'You're right, I didn't … It's about a patient of mine. She's in a bit of a state mentally, and I thought I'd pick your brains, if that's okay?'

'You're not after stealing my patients, are you now?'

'Not at all,' Charles said quickly 'It's just a problem that I need guiding through, really.'

'Well … fire away then.'

Charles wondered where to begin and how much to reveal over the telephone without breaking patient confidentiality, and he decided to keep it simple, sticking to the bare bones of the case.

'Like I said, she's in a bit of a state and has a compulsion to commit suicide. They ran some tests when she was admitted here and she was found to be pregnant, but I don't think she knows, Leon. My dilemma is, do I tell her? Do I risk giving her a reason to live against the chance that the knowledge might tip her over the edge and I lose her completely?'

'You know, Charles,' Leon said conversationally, 'this is a bit like me phoning you and saying I've got a patient with a slipped disc and asking whether I should operate or give manipulation treatment. You'd want an X-ray at least, would you not?'

'Probably. Yes, you're right, Leon. It was silly of me to expect an appropriate answer when you've got so little to go on.'

'Let's not be too hasty, here. If I told you more about my patient with the slipped disc you might be able to advise me what to do. Now, does she want children? Does she even like the wee beggars?'

'I've no idea.'

'Well, it might be a good idea to find out. If she hasn't a

21

problem with bairns then I can't see there's any harm in disclosing the information. What have you got to lose?'

'My patient,' Charles said simply, and Leon snorted derisively.

'You'll lose her anyway if she's that compulsive, Charles. If she's determined to go, then, by God, she'll find a way.'

Charles thought it through and it made a kind of sense. It was worth the risk if it halted her headlong flight towards self-destruction.

'She might need other help, Leon,' he went on soberly. 'The sort of help that only someone like you can give.'

'Aye, well … It'll not be the first time I've brought a would-be suicide back from the brink.'

'That's what I thought … Thanks, Leon. Listen—do you think this might be something you'd want to get involved in?'

'Sounds an interesting case. Might be worth a chapter or two in my wee book.'

'I thought it might,' Charles laughed. 'Thanks again, Leon. I'll get back to you if I need your help, okay?'

'Aye. You do that—you know where I am if you need me.'

Chapter 3

Charles looked at his watch for the eighth time in two minutes, then came to his feet and stepped from his office, striding briskly down the corridor in his eagerness to be in the right place at the right time. He was a little early, but so too was Terry Newell, and Charles spotted him at the coffee vending machine at the head of the stairs and waited for him to turn towards him before he stepped forward with a smile and an outstretched hand. Charles's outwardly calm demeanour belied an inner wariness, for he was all too aware of the delicate nature of discussing a would-be-suicide's mental state with the one person she was closest to. But his choices were limited, seeing as Marion herself wasn't very communicative, and he needed some answers if he was to be of any help to her at all.

'Mr Newell,' he said pleasantly. 'I'm Doctor Levington, Marion's doctor. Could you spare me a few minutes?'

'Sure,' Terry nodded, juggling the coffee as he shook the proffered hand, and Charles led him back along the corridor to his office.

Terry Newell was a well-dressed man in his late twenties, tall and personable with serious blue eyes that were at odds with his easy smile and open features; he had a bland expression that never seemed to change whatever the circumstances. He was softly spoken, polite and considerate, and Charles couldn't help thinking that Marion would be hard-pressed to find a more suitable companion and partner, which made her

23

attempts at suicide all the more baffling. He waved Terry to a seat and sat behind his desk, taking a moment to collect his thoughts before launching into the unknown, maintaining the balance between concerned professional duty and intrusive questioning with the utmost care.

'I didn't get much chance to speak to you when you came to visit Marion yesterday,' he said guardedly, and Terry eyed him over the rim of the plastic cup.

'What did you want to speak about?'

'Well, Marion, obviously … Have you known her long?'

'About three years.'

'How did you meet?'

'I run a boutique on Fulham Broadway. She came in and we got talking about the different colours and styles that go with dark hair.'

'Mr Newell … I don't mean to be rude or inquisitive, but Marion has a serious problem and it's only by trying to get to the bottom of it that gives us any chance of helping her.'

'I understand.' He sipped the coffee slowly then shrugged. 'If I can be of any help at all …'

'These suicide attempts … is it a new thing?'

'You mean did she try it before, when we first met?'

'Yes.'

Terry shook his head and sighed heavily. 'No. She seemed perfectly balanced, you know, well adjusted just like any other girl of that age. We got on well together.'

'And when did she move in with you?'

'Last summer.'

'When exactly?'

'August Bank Holiday. Her brother, Ron, helped us shift the furniture and bring her stuff over. He works for a parcel delivery firm and he borrowed one of their vans.'

'Perhaps I should speak to him,' Charles mused thoughtfully. 'He might be able to shed some light on Marion's recent behaviour.'

24

'I doubt it,' Terry shook his head. 'He was just as bewildered as I was after the first time she tried it. You know … When she cut her wrists.'

'Three months ago?'

'That's right. It came as a shock to both of us.'

'What about Marion's parents?'

'They emigrated to Canada about five years ago.'

'I see … And you've no idea what triggered this off? I mean, something pretty drastic must have happened to make her so determined to take her own life all of a sudden.'

'No idea at all. Everything was going fine. The boutique was doing well and Marion had just started a new job.'

'A new job?' Charles's ears pricked up. 'When was this?'

'April.'

'And she cut her wrists in …?'

'May.'

'What was the job?'

'You think there's a connection between the new job and her suddenly wanting to end it all? I don't buy that, Doctor. Marion loves that job.'

'What does she do exactly?'

'She works behind the scenes at Wembley Arena.'

'And you say she likes the job?'

Terry nodded. 'She couldn't get enough of it. Just before … just before she cut her wrists, I remember she came home full of excitement because Robbie Williams was to do a concert there. She got to meet a lot of famous people and Robbie Williams is one of her favourites.'

'So why try and kill herself? What brought it on like that?'

'I wish I knew,' Terry murmured. 'I asked her … you know … after the first time … I asked her why and she couldn't tell me.'

'Couldn't or wouldn't?'

'To be perfectly honest, Doctor, I don't think she knows herself. I was the one who cut her down when she tried to hang herself. We both cried, you know? I cried because I wanted to help her, and she cried because she didn't know why she was doing it … It was like something inside her was controlling her and making her do it. As the weeks went by she became more and more depressed until in the end I couldn't reach her. It was as though she'd withdrawn into some deep part of herself and no one else was allowed in.'

'But you never sought medical advice?'

'Not voluntarily, no. She'd seen psychiatrists before and they were pretty useless. Besides, it's like … like an insanity thing, isn't it? I didn't want them to take her away from me.'

'You think she's mentally ill?'

'Well, something in her mind is making her do these things, isn't it?' he shrugged helplessly. 'What else am I to believe?'

'Well … I don't doubt that you care for Marion very much …'

'Care for her?' Terry interrupted. 'I love her, Doctor. We planned to get married … start a family … She's my life.'

'Start a family?' Charles disguised his sudden interest with a professionally detached voice. 'Marion wanted children then?'

'Oh, yes,' Terry nodded emphatically. 'She said she wanted three kids. Two girls and a boy.'

Charles smiled across the desk at him, the way ahead suddenly clearing like a dawn mist evaporating in the warmth of the rising sun.

'Is Marion taking the contraceptive pill?'

'Mmm.' Terry nodded round a mouthful of coffee. 'She hates condoms. So do I, as it happens.'

'Not one of the best things ever invented,' Charles agreed with a grin, then he sobered. 'I think we have to be practical in this situation, Mr Newell, and whatever your depth of feelings are for Marion, I'm afraid we can't allow her compulsion to go unchecked.'

'You mean you want to lock her away in a mental home?'

'I didn't say that.'

'It's what you meant.'

Charles sighed wearily and ran his fingers through his hair in a tired gesture, groping for the words to ease the man's torment. It was always difficult to tell someone that the person they loved was mentally ill.

'Marion needs expert help, Mr. Newell,' he said softly. 'Psychiatric help.'

'And if she doesn't get it?'

'If she doesn't get it ...' He shrugged expressively. 'You can't guarantee to be there to cut the rope next time, Mr Newell.'

They were silent for a long moment, reviewing the options and considering the consequences of each one, then Charles cleared his throat pointedly.

'I think Marion would benefit from seeing a psychiatrist, Mr Newell. Not like the ones she saw before, but a specialist ... someone who can delve into her mind and find out why she's behaving the way she is. I believe it's the only realistic chance we've got of saving her life.'

Terry drained his cup and swallowed hard, emotion fighting common sense in the bubbling cauldron of his mind, but in the end common sense prevailed and he gave a quick nod of his head, praying with all his heart that he wasn't consigning Marion to a life in an institution.

'All right,' he whispered. 'If ... if you can get Marion to agree ... then it's all right with me.'

And this was the easy part, Charles thought bleakly. Getting Marion to co-operate would be a much more difficult task, but he had an ace up his sleeve now, the last card to play if everything else failed.

Marion gave no indication that she was aware Doctor Levington had entered the room, her eyes staring fixedly at the ceiling, and she remained motionless as he pulled the chair close to the bed, her breathing shallow and even. Charles studied her carefully, noting that the birthmark on her temple was barely discernible, the angry hue of before now faded to a mere hint of colour like a trace of darker shadow at the edge of her eye.

'I've been thinking about what you said yesterday, Marion,' he began hesitantly, feeling his way. 'Even you have to admit it's rather worrying to know that you want to end your life, but have no idea why. Wouldn't you like to find out?'

She said nothing and Charles cleared his throat, forming the words painstakingly in his mind before they slipped from his tongue.

'I can help you find out, Marion ... but only if you want to. And that's the whole crux of the matter, you see, because if you don't want to be helped then there's not a lot I can do about it. I'm a doctor, Marion, and it's my job to make you well again, but I can only go so far. I can't cure the real reason why you're here, but I know someone who can ... Do you understand?'

She remained silent, simply staring at the ceiling, and Charles sighed wearily.

'Marion ... I'd be failing in my job as a doctor if I didn't offer you the best chance of a full recovery, but I can't do it on my own. I need some help to get to the root cause of why you're lying in that bed right now. I want to help you, Marion, and in return you've got to help me.'

She blinked several times in quick succession as if she was digesting his words and running them through her mind, picking them apart and disseminating their content, and Charles leaned forward in his chair, closer to her inert form, the better to reach her and make her take notice.

'We need to find out why you keep harming yourself, Marion.'

She closed her eyes as if trying to shut him out, but he

28

persisted doggedly, his voice taking on a harsher tone as he strove to elicit a reaction from the seemingly lifeless woman who so blithely ignored him.

'Talk to me, Marion. You spoke to me yesterday so speak to me today. For Christ's sake let me help you.'

'What do you want from me?' she whispered fiercely. 'Why don't you just go away and leave me alone?'

He'd breached the barricades for a second time and he hid a sigh of relief 'Because I want to help you,' he said earnestly. 'I want to find out why you're so determined to end it all, and I think deep down inside, you want to find out, too.'

She blinked and frowned at him, her dark eyebrows coming together on the bridge of her nose. 'Do I?'

'Yes. We need to probe the reason behind this morbid death-wish you seem to have developed. Now, I can't do it, Marion. I'm not qualified … but I know someone who is. A very eminent psychiatrist called Leon Mac—'

'A psychiatrist?' She turned her head to stare at him, her deep brown eyes boring into his with grave intensity. 'I've been that route before, remember? Fat lot of good they did me.'

'This one's different, a specialist. I believe he stands a good chance of getting to the root cause of your problem.'

'You think I'm mad.' She made it sound like a statement of fact, not a question, and Charles shook his head adamantly.

'No, I don't think you're mad, Marion, but I think you're very disturbed. Don't you? Don't you find it at all disturbing that you keep trying to take your own life and you haven't a clue why? Doesn't that disturb you, Marion?'

'Go away,' she said tiredly, her eyes returning to the ceiling in an act of finality. 'Just … just go away and leave me in peace.'

'Please, Marion.' He almost begged her, desperately seeking her co-operation. 'Think about it, that's all I'm asking of you. Think about the possibility that Leon Macleod just might unlock the secret to why you crave your own death. Will you do that for me? Will you at least think about it?'

But Marion had rebuilt the breached barricades and he was talking to himself.

'Did we get the latest update on Marion Harting's blood analysis?' Charles asked, and Sister Barrett nodded.

'It's on your desk, Doctor.'

'Thanks. I'll be in my office if you need me.'

He read the report with interest then spent another twenty minutes going over Marion's file, cross-referencing dates and known facts with the notes from social services, searching for a motive, a catalyst that had acted as a trigger for her recent behaviour, but he was chasing shadows, seeking answers where there were none. He sat in contemplative silence for a while then came to his feet decisively, striding along the corridor with a confident step, all the uncertainty of the past few days cast aside, renewed purpose surging within him. It was a battle of wills, a contest of strength, and he refused to go down without a fight. Marion might be determined to kill herself, but he was just as determined to save her.

'Good afternoon, Marion,' he said briskly as he entered Room Five and smiled at the woman in the bed. 'How are you today?'

She ignored him and he studied her chart, pausing to examine the plaster cast on her leg and feeling her toes for signs of circulatory problems, but she gave no indication she was aware of him. She was totally oblivious to him as she stared at the ceiling with bored eyes, and he moved round the bed to study her closely.

Her long dark hair was its usual tangled mess on the pillow, framing her features in a dark swathe that seemed to add to her attractiveness rather than detract from it, giving her a wild, untamed look that he found oddly appealing. He had noticed the curious way she had when she frowned, the drawing together of her eyebrows over the bridge of her nose, and it reminded him of something, something familiar, yet something that he couldn't quite put his finger on. He shrugged aside the feeling that he should know what it was, turning instead to bring the chair to the side of the bed.

'Now, Marion,' he said conversationally. 'I know you want to get out of here, but we'd like to carry out a few more tests first. Will that be all right?'

Her eyes flicked up at him suspiciously then she looked away, finding a sudden fascination in the flowers on the locker beside the bed.

'They're nice,' Charles murmured, seeing for the first time the plastic vase and its colourful array. 'Did Terry bring them in for you?'

She frowned at the mention of Terry's name, her eyebrows meeting in a thin line, but she said nothing, her eyes flitting from petal to leaf, from stem to vase as if the answers to all life's mysteries were contained in that one bunch of flowers, and Charles sighed as he tried again, waiting for a reaction as he laid out the alternatives.

'I want you to see the man I talked about yesterday. Doctor Leon Macleod. Actually, he's a professor, and he's damn good at his job.'

'The psychiatrist.' She snorted with derision and Charles cocked his head at her with interest. The barriers had crumbled easily today.

'Yes, a psychiatrist. Did you think about what I said yesterday, Marion?' he went on. 'Don't you want to know why you keep trying to do away with yourself?'

'Pointless,' she whispered, and Charles started at the hidden despair in her voice, perfectly sane, perfectly rational, yet without inflection, dull and lifeless in the quiet of the room.

'What's pointless, Marion?' he urged softly, and she shook her head as if it didn't matter.

'Psychiatrist.'

'Why, Marion? Why is it pointless to see a psychiatrist?'

'He won't stop me.'

'Stop you from doing what?'

'You know,' she murmured, and nodded at her fractured leg. 'I'll make sure next time.'

'You're going to try again?'

'Go away,' she said wearily as if the whole thing bored her to tears. 'We've been through all this before … Just go away and leave me alone.'

'I want to know why you keep doing this to yourself, Marion,' he persisted gently. 'Don't you want to know, too?'

'I don't care,' she shrugged, the slightest movement of her shoulders. 'I'm still going to do it.'

'But why, Marion? You're young … beautiful … You've got a good job and a man who loves you immensely. Doesn't any of that mean anything to you?'

She shook her head, dark hair shimmering over the pillow, then she closed her eyes as if to say she was terminating the conversation and going to sleep.

'Marion? Marion, I know you can hear me. You haven't got to answer, just listen, okay? You might not think too highly of yourself and you might not give two hoots about your job. You might not even like where you're living and for all I know you could hate the man you've been sharing your life with … Lots of reasons to end it all, Marion, lots of perfectly good valid reasons to chuck it all in and do away with yourself. But listen to me, Marion … listen very, very carefully because I'm going to give you one perfectly good valid reason not to … one reason why you should cling to life and not throw it all away. Are you listening to me, Marion?'

She remained motionless, her eyelids tightly closed, shutting him out, but she couldn't shut her ears and

Charles leaned even closer, making sure she heard every last syllable.

'You're pregnant, Marion. You've a seven-week-old baby inside you. I reckon you've been a bit too preoccupied these last few weeks to even have noticed, probably too distraught to have even thought about taking the pill … but it's true. Now, you might not want to live for all the reasons I mentioned, and a thousand others that I don't even know about, but can you not want to live for the life of the baby that's growing inside you? Isn't that worth living for? Marion?'

Her eyes clicked open and she slowly turned her head to stare at him, their faces inches apart, and Charles resisted the sudden overpowering temptation to kiss her, watching her closely as the full gamut of emotions flickered across her dark eyes.

'You're lying,' she whispered, and he shook his head quickly, holding on to the initiative with both hands while he still had it.

'I'm not lying, Marion,' he said sincerely. 'I wouldn't lie to you about something as important as this.'

'Preg…nant?' She struggled with the word, and he nodded, his eyes holding hers as he fought to impart this truth, making her believe him.

'Seven weeks,' he said with authority. 'Isn't that worth living for, Marion?'

She seemed to consider his words with deliberate concentration, examining her emotions and feelings as she absorbed the news that she was carrying a child, maternal instincts filling the gaps left by despair and heartache.

'Isn't it, Marion?' he insisted softly. 'Isn't a baby worth living for? Or do you want to kill that, too?'

'Baby.' She said the word as if she was tasting it, savouring it, trying it on for size to see how it fit, then a flare of panic crossed her eyes momentarily before the dullness returned and she looked away.

'It doesn't matter,' she whispered lifelessly. 'No one can do anything about it. I'll end up killing myself and the baby will die, too … It's all a complete waste of time.'

'It doesn't have to be, Marion,' Charles urged vehemently. 'What have you got to lose? If there's a chance the psychiatrist can save you *and* your baby, why not give it a try? What have you got to lose, Marion?'

'Nothing.'

He barely heard it and he strained to listen, his ear close to her mouth as he sensed the first glimmer of hope in a hopeless cause. He was convincing her. Slowly, that was true, but bit by bit she was coming round to the idea of seeking help for the problem that dogged her, and the first tentative step was always the hardest one of all.

'Marion? Will you do it? Will you speak to a psychiatrist? See if he can help you?' The silence seemed to go on for an eternity and Charles hardly dared breathe as he watched Marion with mounting excitement, willing her to agree, fervently praying that her maternal instincts were a stronger, more compelling force than the one that currently drove her to destruction. Marion's eyes, he noticed, were mere pinpoints of light that held a deep mystery, mirrors of a soul in torment, focused somewhere far away and distant; then a shudder seemed to pass through her and she nodded, the barest movement of her head as the life of an unborn baby brought victory over the magnetic pull of death.

'All right.'

It was a whispered sigh, her breath warm on his face, and he felt a surge of triumph that he'd been able to reach her, touching some deep chord within her and nurturing the will to live. It was a small beginning but he was content, two lives now standing on the edge of salvation when but a moment ago he had nothing.

One day he would hear Marion's laughter, he thought with unaccountable joy, and he realised he'd wanted to hear her laugh since the moment he'd first seen her. He would see her smile and hear her speak coherent words of everyday conversation. He would see her live a normal life and she wouldn't die until she was a grandmother in her dotage. Charles Levington promised it to himself, and he wasn't prone to breaking promises.

Chapter 4

It was a week later when Marion met Professor Leon Macleod, a week in which Charles had witnessed a dramatic change in the patient in Room Five. She was eating more, the colour had returned to her cheeks, and she was sitting up and taking notice of the life around her, even attempting a conversation of sorts with the elderly woman from the League of Friends, and the ward nurses no longer avoided her, taking a renewed interest in bathing her and seeing to her needs. The biggest change, perhaps, was in her eyes, that now glowed with an inner fire, a spark of hope where once was only despair, and the torment of a tortured soul had been subtly replaced with the glimmer of nurturing life, the hope that perhaps she wasn't doomed after all and could be miraculously saved from herself.

She knew Leon Macleod was coming that day: Charles had sat with her and told her what to expect, but she still found the professor strangely disconcerting, until he spoke and his soothing voice worked its well-practised magic.

'You must be Marion Harting,' he said with a little smile. 'I'm Professor Macleod, but you must call me Leon.'

She nodded to acknowledge him but said nothing as he produced a notebook and pencil, poised expectantly as he probed the way ahead.

'Do you mind if I record our session, Miss Harting?' he said, producing a little tape recorder and setting it on the bed between them. 'I'm not as young as I used to be and it

36

saves trying to remember everything.'

She gazed meaningfully at the pad and pencil on his lap and he gave an effacing laugh.

'I make notes as well,' he explained, and she sighed softly.

'Do what you want.'

'Doctor Levington has told me a little about you,' he went on carefully, 'but perhaps you'd like to tell me again in your own words.'

'There's nothing really to tell,' she shrugged offhandedly and his smile deepened.

'I'm sure there is, and if I'm to help you, I'll need all the information I can get.'

'It's pointless.' She shook her head. 'I told him that.'

'Doctor Levington?'

'Yes.'

'You told him it was pointless?'

'Yes.'

'And why would you tell him that?'

'Because it's the truth ... You can't help me ... No one can.'

'Maybe not ... but I thought the object of the exercise was to at least try. Is that not the case, Miss Harting?'

'I suppose so,' she murmured grudgingly, and he nodded.

'Good. Well, perhaps if I start by asking you a few questions about yourself ... Would that be better?'

'Suit yourself.'

'I will then. We'll just have a friendly chat. Imagine we'd just met and were having a quiet drink somewhere ... Getting to know about each other. All right?'

'Does that mean I can ask you questions as well?'

'Do you want to?'

She shrugged as if she didn't care one way or the other. 'Maybe.'

'Fine,' Leon nodded. 'Ask me what you like.'

She didn't answer him and he made a note on the pad, his writing quick and precise, then he looked up and smiled.

'Right then … Where were you born?'

'Farnborough.'

'That's in Surrey, isn't it?'

'It isn't, actually, but does it matter?'

'No. I don't suppose it does. Did you spend all your child-hood there?'

'We moved to Middlesex when I was four.'

'Did that bother you?'

She gave an exasperated shake of her head, her hair shimmering on the pillow. 'Why should it? I was four, for Christ's sake. It didn't bother me one way or another.'

'When you get used to somewhere, it can be a bit traumatic if you have to move somewhere else. Did you know that moving house is one of the most stressful occurrences in someone's life?'

'Not to a four-year-old, it isn't.'

'Perhaps not. Were you an only child?'

'Nope. One brother and one sister. Both older than me.'

'Were you close?'

'As close as any other family, I suppose.'

'Do you still see them?'

'I see my brother sometimes.'

'But not your sister?'

Marion sighed and shook her head.

'Shirley got married and they emigrated to Canada.'

'What about your parents?'

She frowned at him and shrugged. 'What about them?'

'Are you still in contact with them?'

'When my dad retired they emigrated to be with Shirley.'

Leon peered at her thoughtfully, lightly tapping the pencil against the side of the pad, then he made a quick note and cleared his throat expressively.

'Did you resent your parents moving away like that?'

'No, I was happy for them. They could have a better quality of life out there.'

'You didn't think it was unfair that they should desert you and your brother and go to live with Shirley in Canada?'

'Unfair?' She frowned at him, her dark eyebrows coming together over the straight sweep of her nose. 'What was unfair about it? They wanted a better life and I was happy for them. They could have chosen anywhere … Australia. South Africa. New Zealand. It didn't matter to me where they went just as long as they were happy.'

'But they chose Canada … where Shirley was. Sibling rivalry can be a powerful force, Miss Harting.'

'You think I was jealous of Shirley?' She snorted derisively. 'You think that's the cause of my problem?'

'Aye, it might be,' he shrugged, and she stared at him, her eyes taking in the dishevelled suit and dusty shoes.

'Then why didn't I try to kill myself when they first emigrated five years ago?' she said with irrefutable logic. 'Why would I wait until now before making my protest?'

'Sometimes, Miss Harting,' he said deliberately, 'these things simmer just beneath the surface for years and years before they make themselves apparent. Cause and effect aren't necessarily locked in the same timescale.'

She turned her eyes to the ceiling, knowing he was wrong but not knowing *how* she knew, just a certain awareness that he was barking up the wrong tree, and Leon watched her carefully, noting the boredom and lack of interest in her posture, body language saying more than words ever could.

'Tell me something,' he said after a long moment. 'Has Shirley got any children?'

'Two girls.'

'I see. Did she have them before your parents emigrated, or after?'

'Before.'

'So … do you think having grandchildren on the other side of the world influenced your parents' decision on emigrating to Canada?'

'Who knows?' Marion shrugged. 'I expect it had something to do with it.'

'Quite.'

He tapped his teeth with the pencil, putting two and two together and making five, and he took a mental step backward, all too aware of the folly of a hasty diagnosis and seeking another way to prove his theory.

'You didn't really want treatment for your condition, did you, Miss Harting?'

'What?'

'At first,' he nodded, 'all you wanted was for your leg and your arm to heal so you could get back out there and attempt suicide again, isn't that right?'

She didn't answer and he pressed on, looking for some reaction as he probed the unknown recesses of her mind.

'You were all set to ignore everyone and throw yourself under a train or something. Right?'

Again she said nothing and Leon nodded thoughtfully. 'So what made you change your mind?'

She blinked at him.

'What?'

'Why did you agree to let me see you? Why the sudden change of heart?'

'You know why,' she murmured, and he smiled softly.

'You're pregnant. You're having a bairn.'

'Right.'

'Another grandchild for your parents,' he went on relentlessly. 'Give them a good enough reason to come home … get one over on your sister and have your parents back where they belong. If you can achieve that, then there's no further need to commit suicide, is there?'

'You're still on the sibling-rivalry thing, are you?' she snorted. 'Well, you're wrong.'

'Am I?'

'Yes.'

'How do you know I'm wrong?'

'I just do,' she shrugged. 'I feel it … I know it.'

'Interesting,' he murmured, then he folded the notebook and stuffed it in his briefcase, making ready to leave. 'I think we've done enough for one day, don't you, Miss Harting? I'll come and see you again tomorrow.'

'Please yourself.' She gave a half smile. 'It'll be a waste of time though, won't it?'

'Will it?'

'You've already got me labelled and pigeonholed, haven't you? You've solved my problem and all you've got to do now is convince me that you're right, then "hey presto" I'm cured. … Wonderful.'

'There's a way to prove it, you know.'

'Is there?'

'Regression.'

'Ah … hypnotise me and take me back to when my parents emigrated … Analyse my emotions and feelings at the time until you find something that fits your theory. Another successful case for the brilliant Professor Macleod.'

'Don't knock it,' he said lightly, switching off the recorder and tucking it in his jacket pocket before coming to his feet. 'It's a proven method, Miss Harting.'

'Yeah, sure. Whatever you say.'

'I'll see you tomorrow.' He stepped to the door and smiled over his shoulder at her. 'Bye, Miss Harting.'

Chapter 5

Charles Levington waited until he was at home in the quiet of his study before reading the transcript of Leon Macleod's recorded session with Marion that afternoon, and the more he read the more sceptical he became. No matter how successful the psychiatrist's past triumphs were, no matter how impeccable his reputation was or how high the esteem in which he was held in the medical profession, Charles couldn't help but agree with Marion that in this instance the professor was wrong. It was a gut feeling, an intuition that there was more to Marion Harting's problem than a compulsive desire to be reunited with her parents, more than sisterly jealousy that made her want to kill herself— there was some compelling drive deep within herself that told her her life was not worth living.

He thought again of the conversation he'd had with her boyfriend, Terry, and wondered if Leon had purposely ignored the fact that Marion's troubles began soon after taking the job at Wembley Arena. Leon was in possession of all the facts, all the data, yet he seemed hell-bent on solving Marion's problem in one quick session, arriving at a solution with impossible haste and convincing himself of its truth without further ado or examination. Perhaps that was where his brilliance lay, not in a rapid analysis with half-guessed-at motives, but in making the patient believe he'd arrived at an answer, and beneath that wrongful guise making them open up and allow the truth to emerge.

And where was the truth? Where was he to find the catalyst that had set in motion a train of events that had culminated in Marion's four attempts at suicide? Wembley Arena was the key, he was sure of it. Was there a connection perhaps? A link between the two? A Phantom of the Opera character perhaps, a Svengali hidden behind the scenes who bewitched and beguiled with mesmerising effect until Marion's only escape was suicide?

'This is stupid,' he muttered to himself harshly. 'You've been watching too many horror films. Get a grip.'

He still considered the link, though, a connection, a definite dividing line between sanity and stability before Marion had started working there compared with depression, four suicide attempts and a changed character since.

'Something must have triggered it,' he murmured aloud. 'Something must have set the wheels in motion ... and Wembley Arena's all I've got.'

Charles waited until after lunch the following day, then he signed himself out of the hospital and drove to Wembley, finding a space in the Arena car park before heading to the main entrance, where he was stopped by a security guard, all polite insistence as he barred the doctor's way.

'Can I help you, Sir?'

'I don't really know,' Charles said honestly, looking about him uncertainly. 'I'm Doctor Levington and I'm researching some background for one of my patients. She works here.'

'Oh?'

'Miss Harting ... Marion Harting.'

'Never heard of her, but that's not unusual. There's hundreds work here. I could get someone from personnel to have a word with you. They'd know her.'

'Fine.' Charles nodded eagerly. 'Would you mind?'

The guard spoke into his radio and Charles wondered how

he understood the reply amid the crackling and white noise that accompanied a garbled message, but the man seemed to hear perfectly and he turned back with a smile.

'Someone's coming down now. Shouldn't be long.'

'Thanks ... I'll wait here.'

The guard sauntered away, keeping a discreet distance but not for one second letting Charles out of his sight as he circled the entrance hall, checking doors and ticket booths with single-minded purpose. A woman appeared at the far end and the guard moved to intercept her, their voices low as he pointed to Charles, then the woman crossed the wide expanse of floor to him, smiling warmly as she held out her hand.

'Doctor...?'

'Levington,' he supplied, shaking the proffered hand, and she nodded.

'Sharon Thomas. How can I help you?'

'I'm researching some background on a patient of mine ... I can't go into details of course.'

'Of course. And she works here?'

'Mmm. Harting. Marion Harting.'

'Ah, yes ... Poor Marion. She's had a pretty rough time of it just lately.'

'You know about ...'

'The suicide attempts?' She sighed and nodded. 'Oh, yes. She could hardly keep them secret really. She's lucky we kept her on. If we hadn't been so short-staffed ...'

She let the sentence hang unfinished and Charles nodded sympathetically.

'I understand. Can you tell me anything about her?'

'Not really. She hasn't been here long. A good worker, conscientious, got on well with everyone as far as I know.'

'What did she do here?'

'Props department. She settled in well and I believe she was happy in her work.'

44

'That's the impression I got,' Charles agreed solemnly. 'Listen ... I can guess how busy you are here, but would it be possible to talk to someone Marion worked with? Someone she was close to, perhaps?'

'It's a bit difficult at the moment with a matinee in progress ... but come with me and I'll see if I can find someone to talk to you.'

He smiled gratefully and followed the woman through a side door that led them around the auditorium to the area backstage, an ants' nest of people scurrying about their business to attend to matters concerning lighting, sound, curtains and props in the labyrinth of corridors and passages that criss-crossed in a confusing maze. They came to a halt before a doorless workshop filled with a million artefacts stowed in mindless profusion on overstuffed racks that lined the walls.

'Props,' Sharon smiled, and Charles followed her inside.

It was a veritable Aladdin's cave with everything imaginable spilling from boxes and trunks or hanging from the racking in colourful array, and Charles wondered how they ever found anything in the confusion where nothing was marked or labelled, a seemingly impossible abundance of everyday items mixed with the exotic with no thought to ever finding them again.

Sharon had stopped to talk with a young girl whom she introduced to Charles as Linda Beavis, and he shook her hand warmly.

'Linda was particularly friendly with Marion,' Sharon told him, and his eyes lit up with interest.

'Can you spare me a few minutes to tell me something about her?' he asked, and the girl glanced at her watch and nodded.

'I'm not needed until half-past. Will ten minutes be enough?'

'It's a start,' he smiled, then nodded his thanks to Sharon

45

as she left them to it, disappearing into the mayhem of the corridor.

'Right then,' Linda said, turning to face him. 'What do you need to know?'

'I'm not sure really … I'm trying to get to the bottom of why Marion wants to commit suicide. Is there anything you can think of that she might have been upset about or was worrying her?'

'Not that I know of,' Linda shrugged. 'When I asked her she couldn't think of a reason either.'

'That's what her boyfriend said. What was she like?' Charles changed tack, searching all the angles. 'Tell me about when she first came here.'

'She loved it,' Linda smiled. 'It's sort of exciting meeting famous people every day. She couldn't wait to get here in the mornings and she stayed on after her shift to watch the show and meet the stars.'

'And she was a happy person? Not depressed or gloomy or anything?'

'She was no different from anyone else. We all have our off days, don't we? But she seemed happy enough and she thoroughly enjoyed her work.'

'So what changed? What happened to turn a bright, vivacious young girl into a depressed suicidal compulsive? When did it all start to go wrong, Linda?'

'Don't ask me,' she shrugged. 'One day she was fine and the next she was quiet and moody. She got steadily worse after that.'

'After what? What day, Linda? What happened in one day to alter her so much?'

'I don't know really. It was a Monday and we only had a matinee to do. It was an ice-show extravaganza, I think …'

'Go on.'

'Well … when we wrapped it up I said about going for a drink somewhere and she was all for it … Her boyfriend,

Terry, was working late, or something. Marion wanted to go for a drink straight away, but I'd got make-up all down my front so I had to go home and change first. I only live five minutes away so it wasn't a problem, and I said for Marion to come with me.'

'And she agreed?'

'Mmm. She asked if she could borrow a blouse and we had a sort of fashion show, trying things on in my bedroom.'

'What happened then?'

'We were about to go out when my mum came in, so I stopped to make her a cup of tea. Marion was in the sitting room waiting for me and I was in the kitchen.'

'So when you went out … where did you go?'

'We didn't.'

Charles blinked at her.

'Didn't what?'

'We didn't go out.'

'Why not?'

'Marion changed her mind. I came back into the sitting room and it was like she was in a trance. She was just sitting there staring into space and I had to speak to her three times before she heard me. I made her a cup of tea and when she was finally talking sense she asked about the ornaments on the mantelpiece and mentioned the photos on the wall. Then she said, 'Who are they?' I said, 'Who?' and she said, 'The sailors.' I said it was a group shot of my older brother, Tim, and some of his mates who were on the same ship together. He was in the Royal Navy … He died in the Falklands when his ship was bombed. The only one in the photo who survived was his friend Sam. I don't know if it sort of saddened her, but she suddenly said she didn't want to go for a drink after all, and she almost ran out of the house. She was very quiet the next day … subdued, and I thought she was still thinking about the Falklands and how sad it was that so many sailors and soldiers were killed … but she never

47

seemed to get over it. She got worse day by day until she slashed her wrists.'

'But you asked her,' Charles frowned. 'Both you and Terry asked her and she said she didn't know why she did it. If she was depressed by the Falklands War, why didn't she simply say so?'

'I asked if it was the Falklands, and she said no. She said she didn't have a clue why she did it. She just felt that her life was over and she wanted to end it all.'

'Very strange,' Charles mused. 'And there was nothing else you can think of that might have caused the sudden change in her?'

'Nothing at all.' She glanced at her watch and shrugged. 'Look, I've got to go. Has that helped you at all?'

'Yes, thanks, Linda ... How do I get out of here?'

Linda told him how to get back to the car park, and he thanked her again.

'No problem,' she smiled. 'Bye.'

'And you believe an ornament or a photograph triggered it all off, do you?' Leon Macleod asked sceptically, and Charles spread his hands in a helpless gesture.

'I don't know. It's a possibility. Either that or something else in that room. I only know that Marion wasn't quite the same after going round to Linda Beavis's house.'

'If it was the photograph, what was the trigger? A naval uniform perhaps?'

'I don't know,' Charles repeated testily.

'Hmm ... Not a lot to go on, is it?'

'No, but ...'

'But what? Speak up, man.'

'Well ... it's a bit more than the sibling-rivalry theory, isn't it?'

'Is it? Aye, well ... you'd be surprised just how many people can thank family squabbles and jealousies for being responsible for their disturbed state of mind.'

'I don't doubt it,' Charles agreed with a shake of his head. 'I just don't think it's responsible in this particular case.'

'And you're basing this theory on what?'

'Instinct … A sixth sense … I don't know … The same thing as Marion herself, perhaps. She's not convinced about sisterly jealousy either.'

'Well, she wouldn't be, would she. She's not very likely to come right out and admit it, is she?'

'She would if you think about it,' Charles pointed out logically. 'If you ask me, she's got two choices—she either co-operates or she doesn't, she either wants to be cured or she doesn't. Let's assume she doesn't. Let's assume she wants nothing more than to be let out so she can kill herself. If that's the case then she'd agree with you, accept treatment and get released from hospital as soon as possible so she can make attempt number five. Why throw a spanner in the works and make it difficult for you? No, she obviously wants to get better and she genuinely doesn't buy your sibling-rivalry theory.'

'Unfortunately, Charles,' Leon said dryly, 'disturbed minds don't think with such clarity of purpose as yours. The processes of logic are, um, somewhat out of touch with reality.'

'What's the answer, then? You could spend months wasting your time by going down the wrong road.'

'I'm a great believer in hypnotherapy.'

'Hypnotism? Do you think it would work in this case?'

'Well, I've found over the years that a relaxed patient is more responsive than a highly strung one,' Leon said. 'And you have to admit, Charles, that Marion Harting is one very highly strung lassie.'

'She does seem to be living on her nerves a bit … So, how do you intend to use hypnotherapy to get to the root cause of her problem?'

'Regression,' Leon said promptly. 'It's our best chance of getting to the bottom of it.'

'Will she respond?' Charles wondered aloud. 'I mean, hasn't the subject got to be receptive to suggestion for it to work?'

'Precisely,' Leon smiled. 'We'll find out just how much she wants to be cured, won't we?'

'She's not the easiest of patients.'

'It doesn't matter.' Leon shook his head. 'If she genuinely wants to get better, as you seem to believe, then she'll allow herself to be regressed. She's got nothing to lose, has she?'

Chapter 6

'Good afternoon, Marion,' Leon smiled, carefully placing the tape recorder on the bed. 'You don't mind if I call you Marion?'

'Call me what you like,' she said offhandedly, and Leon shrugged as he settled on a chair beside her, pad and pencil at the ready as he studied her calmly.

'I seem to remember,' he murmured in his soft Scottish lilt, 'that yesterday we were talking about your past. Tell me about your partner, Terry.'

'What about him?'

'Doctor Levington thinks he's a nice laddie … Is that how you see him?'

'Terry's all right.'

'He thinks the world of you.'

She looked away, unable to meet Leon's eyes, and he sighed softly. 'Describe your feelings for him.'

'Like I said,' she mumbled quietly, 'Terry's all right.'

'You don't love him?'

Marion squirmed awkwardly and bit her lower lip as though she were ashamed of feelings she couldn't control, and Leon made a quick note on the pad.

'That's a strange phenomenon,' he observed softly, and she swung her eyes to him, her eyebrows meeting in a frown.

'What is?'

'Well, normally,' he said conversationally, 'lassies like to talk about their boyfriends. You obviously think something of

51

him or you wouldn't live with him … and I hear you plan to get married, is that right?'

'Yes,' she whispered, and Leon nodded.

'That's what I thought … Hence the question … do you love him?'

She turned her head away, facing the wall, and Leon wondered at the reaction. What was she feeling guilty about?

'Marion? Tell me, have you ever been unfaithful to him?'

She paused for a long moment then shook her head, but the pause wasn't wasted on Leon and he latched onto it straight away.

'When you say you haven't been unfaithful, Marion, you mean you haven't been to bed with anyone else, is that right?'

She nodded, her eyes to the wall, and Leon smiled gently.

'What about … what about in your thoughts, Marion?' he probed. 'Have you ever been unfaithful in your thoughts?'

'I … I don't … No, I …'

'What about the photograph of Tim Beavis and his shipmates, Marion? Did you want to go to bed with any of them?'

'Who?'

'Tim Beavis … Linda's brother … You saw a picture of him and his friends when you went to her house after work, remember?'

'No, I …'

'You don't remember?'

'Linda and me … we were going out.'

'Aye, that's right, but you saw the picture or something else in that room and you changed your mind … Why was that?'

'I don't … I can't …'

'It's all right, Marion,' he soothed gently, and he waited for her to calm down, fully aware that he now had two avenues of approach into her mental unrest: sibling rivalry and guilt, each powerful enough to have sent her over the edge and

52

tumbling into a maelstrom of uncertainty, unbalancing her mind into the chaos of traumatic distress.

'Marion … I think I can help you. You *do* want me to help you, don't you? If not for your sake, then for the sake of your baby, isn't that right?'

She nodded fretfully and he let out a long sigh.

'I want to try you with regression … but it only works if you're in total agreement. Do you understand, Marion? We'll be wasting our time if you don't co-operate with me on this.'

She gave a little shrug, the barest movement of her shoulders beneath the counterpane, and Leon shook his head.

'Was that a yes, Marion?' he asked softly. 'Are you prepared to help me with this?'

The question seemed to hang suspended in the air for an eternity, then she took a long, ragged breath and nodded.

'Yes.

'Good.' Leon switched off the tape recorder. 'We'll make a start on Monday.'

'I've just read the transcript of your last meeting with Marion,' Charles said carefully, and Leon smiled thinly.

'Interesting, don't you think?'

'It's … disconcerting to say the least.'

'In what way?'

'Well, it seems to me that the deeper you delve, the more possibilities you're faced with. On Friday morning you were convinced that sibling rivalry was the cause of Marion's mental state, but by the afternoon you'd added guilt to the list. What's next? The fact that she wasn't breastfed as a baby? Rejection by her first boyfriend? Where does it all end?'

'It ends when we reach the truth, Charles,' Leon said pragmatically. 'Mental diagnosis isn't an exact science, you know. It's not like setting a broken arm or repairing a torn ligament, and we can't take X-rays of a person's mind to see where the problem lies. You put your finger on it with your first sentence—they're just "possibilities", avenues to explore in our search for the real cause, pointers to direct us, but until we know for certain, that's all they are ... possibilities.'

'So ... this regression you've planned for this afternoon—how far are you taking her back?'

'To her childhood. I'm interested in the time the family moved to Middlesex.'

'How does it work?' Charles frowned. 'You just said psychiatry isn't an exact science, so how do you get her back to when she was four?'

'I don't get her there, *she* does. I merely suggest it to her and she does the rest.'

'Can you control it?'

'How do you mean?'

'Well ... can you control her mind to where it takes her?'

'Of course not,' Leon scoffed. 'It's *her* mind, Charles. All I can do is direct it through the power of suggestion.'

'But you can wake her up if she becomes distressed?'

'Usually.'

'What do you mean, "usually"? Either you can or you can't.'

'It's not as simple as that, Charles, not as cut and dried. You underestimate the awesome power of the mind. It's how Fakirs walk on burning coals or push six-inch nails through their bodies and feel no pain. It's why Lourdes has become a Mecca for healing the sick, not because of any religious intervention, but because people believe it and their minds tell them so. They heal themselves by sheer willpower alone. If mankind had the full use of every part of the brain then we could move objects simply by willing it. We would have immense strength. We would read thoughts as easily as we listen to the spoken word. Our learning capabilities would increase a hundredfold, Charles, and even the simplest child

54

would make Einstein look like an imbecile. In other words, if the mind wishes it, then so shall it be.'

'So … if Marion's mind decides not to respond to your "wake-up" commands, then she stays wherever it is you've sent her?'

'Wherever it is her *mind* has sent her,' Leon corrected forcibly. 'I can only *suggest* where she goes.'

'It's all rather … hit and miss really, isn't it?' Charles sighed, and Leon spread his hands expressively.

'Like I say, it's far from an exact science, but we have a remarkably high success rate. The subject is in no danger and it's not often we encounter any difficulties.'

'How long will it take?' he asked softly, and Leon shrugged.

'A couple of hours, maybe three.'

'That's not long to review a childhood,' Charles murmured. 'It'd take me longer than that to remember half of what happened to me when I was a kid.'

'The mind doesn't work on the same timescales,' Leon remarked, absently stroking his goatee beard with long, tapering fingers. 'It's the same when you dream while asleep. A great deal happens and you think the dream lasted hours when in actual fact it lasts seconds. That's how drowning people see their whole life flash before their eyes in a matter of moments. To the patient—to Marion—she'll be seeing it as it happened, minute by minute, day by day, and when she wakes up she might even assume that months or even years have gone by when the reality is that it's all taken place in a few hours.'

'But if her mind's experiencing weeks …'

'Yes?'

'Well … it would take her weeks to describe it all to you, wouldn't it? Telling it as it happens in her mind. Her brain might work at lightning speed, Leon, but her mouth can't.'

'No, that's right. We just pick up key words and build the picture from there. If we think we've hit on something important, we can slow the process down and get her to be more specific.'

'I see … What time are you starting?'

'Three o'clock. I'll meet you here at six if you like and we can go through the tape together.'

'Thanks, Leon,' Charles nodded with a smile. 'I'd like that very much.'

Leon thought Marion was asleep when he first entered the room, for she neither moved nor spoke nor gave any indication that she was aware of him, her recumbent form still and unmoving beneath the rumpled counterpane. Her eyes were closed and her breathing was deep and even, but she stirred lethargically as he pulled up a chair and sorted through his things, watching him through sorrowful eyes as he switched the recorder on and fiddled with his notebook.

'Good afternoon, Marion,' he said politely. 'Did I wake you?'

'I wasn't asleep,' she mumbled, and he smiled.

'Ready to begin?' he asked quietly, and after a moment she nodded.

'As ready as I'll ever be.'

'Good. Now, I believe we have a significant point in your life when you were four, the time you and your family moved to Middlesex, and that's where I'd like to take you back to. You understand, Marion? When you were four years old. Now then …'

'Before you start,' she interrupted him, and he blinked at her.

'Yes?'

'These tapes.' She nodded at the cassette recorder. 'Do I get to hear them?'

'That depends.'

'On what?'

'On their content.'

He gazed at her steadily then gave her a little sympathetic shrug of his shoulders, his mouth twisted in a rueful line.

'What you have to realise, Marion,' he said carefully, 'is that these tapes may contain something harmful to you ... something that you'd rather forget. It would be pointless if I cured you one minute only for you to have a relapse once you heard the tapes ... Do you understand?'

'Yes.'

'Good.'

'But I still want to hear them.'

'I thought we just agreed ...'

'Once I've heard them, I'll decide what you erase from my mind. You can do that, can't you? Get rid of the bad bits by hypnosis?'

'Aye ... but it's not that simple, Marion.'

'But that's the deal ... Take it or leave it.'

'You're hardly in a position to bargain, now, are you?' Leon sighed with exasperation. 'I'm the doctor and you're the patient. If you want to be cured you have to accept my diagnosis and treatment.'

'No I don't.' She shook her head, a shimmer of dark curls on the pillow. 'If I'm the patient then I have all the rights afforded to any patient in the country, and that includes the right to refuse treatment.'

'But I thought you wanted this, Marion, for the sake of your baby. What's changed?'

'The thought of you delving into my mind,' she said softly. 'The thought of you learning more about me than I know myself ... Some things, Professor,' she added with slow deliberation, 'are worth more than the life of an unborn child.'

'But even so ...'

'We'll listen to the tapes together,' she conceded. 'When

we come to a part that you think is damaging to my mind then we'll discuss it and if I agree with you I'll let you hypnotise it out of me ... That way I get to hear the tapes and you get to cure me ... Deal?'

'I don't know ...'

'Deal?'

He stared at her long and hard and he could see the resolve in her eyes, grim determination that brooked no argument, and he nodded with a resigned shrug, the newly installed Patient's Charter allowing her free access to all her files without compromise or consideration.

'Promise?' she insisted, and he forced a wry smile.

'I promise, Marion. Now ... can we get on?'

'All right,' she whispered, the tremor in her voice carrying all her fears and misgivings. 'Let's do it.'

Chapter 7

EGYPT, 1223 BC

The high priest, Ki-Un-Rah, straightened from the entrails of the recently slaughtered sheep and nodded thoughtfully, his thin fingers absently caressing the ebony shaft of his ivory-tipped staff of office as he gazed up at the rising sun, long black shadows stretching out behind him and casting eerie patterns on the temple wall.

'Tukka,' the priest, Husash, muttered, and Ki-Un-Rah nodded.

'Yes ... Two ... Found to the west before the Nile turns south. I can read the signs, Husash.'

'You will tell the Pharaoh?'

Ki-Un-Rah gave him a withering look and turned away, his sandals kicking up the dust as he strode purposefully down the slope to the temple courtyard, his staff clicking on the flagstones to the beat of his long strides, flowing robes trailing in his wake like billowing sails in a sea breeze. He paused at the antechamber and signalled an attendant with a jerk of his head before stepping inside, standing aloof and disinterested as he emptied his bladder in the pot she held, then he nodded and turned away, settling himself at the wooden desk as another attendant brought his breakfast of figs, freshly baked bread and water from the coolest well.

He examined the scrolls as he ate, checking and cross-referencing the signs and omens with deliberate care until he was sure the portents were correct—no room for error in his calculating mind—and he scratched markers on the scroll at the relevant points so he could find them easily when he conveyed his findings to Ramesses himself.

The Pharaoh God Ramesses was a remarkable man, but it wasn't his imposing height that stood him twelve inches above the average Egyptian that made him remarkable, nor was it the fact that he had fathered in excess of one hundred children. It wasn't the dubious honour of having eight wives, even if two of them were his own daughters, that made Ramesses remarkable either. What made Ramesses II remarkable was his age. In the year of the Habat, or 1223 BC if calculated by modern standards, Ramesses was seventy-three years old and had been God and Lord of all Egypt, of the Upper and Lower Nile, for fifty-six years. When most of his subjects could look forward to three or four decades of life, Ramesses had outlived them all and was the only pharaoh that any of them could remember.

Since defeating the Hittites at Qadesh in his youth, Ramesses had brought many years of peace and prosperity to Egypt, and he had set about a vast building programme that had culminated in the temple in Abu Simbel that he had built in honour of his favourite wife, Nefertari, and his own mortuary temple in Thebes was nearing completion.

But it was Ramesses' advancing years that concerned Ki-Un-Ra, for even the great Pharaoh God himself couldn't live forever. He was still sprightly, that was true enough, but he was becoming forgetful of late and his towering form had begun to stoop, his once-confident footsteps now hesitant and faltering. How much longer did they have? Time enough, the high priest thought, to secure the afterlife of their great leader and ensure he lacked for nothing when he passed from this life to the next.

He heard the summons just as he ate the last of the fruit, the low note of the trumpet echoing down the valley, and he quickly gathered the scrolls together and snatched up his staff, blinking in the sudden glare of the sun as he hurried from the antechamber. It was a short walk from the temple to the palace and he was admitted with reverent respect and directed to the pharaoh's bedchamber, where he found the old man at his ablutions, dutifully attended by three serving girls who were oiling the wrinkled body with infinite care.

'Ki-Un-Rah,' Ramesses muttered as the priest bowed into the room. 'Did you slaughter your sheep?'

'Indeed, Lord,' he nodded eagerly. 'The portents are most favourable.'

'Portents,' he sniffed. 'What would you priests do without your portents?'

'Or a pharaoh without his priests?' Ki-Un-Rah said softly. 'We labour only for your good, Lord.'

'So I am led to believe,' Ramesses said dryly. 'Well? Get on with it, man.'

Ki-Un-Rah consulted the scrolls, taking his time as he gathered his thoughts and put them in order to appease a slow old mind, referring back to a history that had occurred before the priest was even born.

'I have studied the account of the accursed Hebrew, Moses, Lord,' he began, and Ramesses snorted with derision, not so forgetful that he couldn't remember the event with alarming clarity.

'Moses and that interfering brother of his. What was his name? Aaron? I was not so wise in those days, Ki-Un-Rah. Had I been better advised, they would never have reached the Sea of Reeds.'

'All the same, Lord,' the high priest went on deferentially, 'the power of the Hebrew God is not to be denied.'

'I fear no god, priest. Am I not the mightiest god of all?'

'Indeed you are, Lord,' Ki-Un-Rah said hastily, 'and your prowess is admired from Persia to Nubia ... while you live.'

'Meaning?'

61

'Meaning, Lord, that I seek only your protection when your life is no more … when the Hebrew God might prevail and gain the upper hand.'

'You think his power is that great?'

'I think his power is as nothing compared to your great power, Lord, but I merely seek a precaution. You were witness to the dreaded vengeance of the Hebrew God through the accursed Moses. Who can guess at the vengeance the God might bestow upon you in the afterlife?'

'Go on.'

'The portents insist on two companions, Lord, to accompany you on your journey through the afterlife … Two companions imbued with all the power of gods so that together you might defeat the Hebrew God. Two children whose innocence and purity are not in doubt. They alone can protect you against the most vengeful of gods.'

'Children?' Ramesses scoffed. 'You expect me to entrust my afterlife into the care of children?'

'Children now, Lord, to ensure their innocence, but grown enough by the time they are needed. Grown and instilled with all the power of the gods Bastet and Anubis.'

'I see… And where are you to find such children?'

'In Abydos, Lord, where the Nile turns south.'

'Why Abydos?'

'I have read the omens, Lord, and know the signs to seek … They will be found in Abydos.'

'Be about it, then.' Ramesses waved him away with an arthritic hand. 'Inform me when you have found them.'

Abydos was a thriving city to the east of Dendera and the Valley of the Kings, hugging a tributary of the Nile with dogged persistence, the high walls and ornate temples surrounded by rich farmlands that teemed with labourers tilling the soil and tending cattle in a never-ending cycle that ensured its continued existence and financial security in an uncertain world. Ki-Un-Rah was well aware of its importance in the grand scheme of things, but even the people of Abydos had no inkling of the elevated status their city was about to enjoy when two of its lowliest citizens were to be bestowed with the honour of serving their Pharaoh for eternity.

The high priest's arrival caused a great stir in the city and he was afforded the most luxurious apartments in the Temple of Osiris, the minor priests and minions scurrying to see to his comfort, the rumours flying thick and fast as he was bathed and fed, whispered questions and muted gossip echoing from chamber to chamber as each guessed the reason for the high priest's visit. He made them wait, of course, as was his way, and it was four days before he made it known that he wished to inspect every child in the city. On the fifth day the population lined the streets, a thousand rumours turning the mass into a babbling cauldron of curious voices as they stood in the heat of the day, mothers clutching their children in excited expectancy.

So they brought their offspring to the throne of Ki-Un-Rah, leading them forward one by one to be examined closely by the priest before being dismissed with a jerk of his head, a twisting column shuffling along the dusty street to submit their sons and daughters to deliberate scrutiny by the emissary of their God.

As the ninety-eighth child stepped forward, Ki-Un-Rah stiffened in his seat, his hand reaching out slowly, and with consummate care he turned the boy's face to the light, his eyes staring unblinking at the mole on the side of the child's neck. There, unmistakably, was the sign he was seeking, the dark mole forming the definite shape of a dog, Anubis, the god of mummification, plainly visible like a beacon in the night. The priest's eyes flicked up to the boy's mother and he studied her closely, wondering if she were Isis herself come to pay tribute to their Pharaoh; then he nodded, beckoning her forward with a long finger.

'Your name?'

'Dumea, Great One,' she murmured, and Ki–Un-Rah smiled.

'And the boy?'

'Nedemin, Great One.'

'How old is he?'

'He has seen seven summers, Great One.'

'The boy's father … what does he do?'

'He has an ox and a plough, Great One. He tends the soil.'

'Not any more,' Ki-Un-Rah murmured. 'Your family will be taken to Thebes, where servants and slaves will tend you. Our Pharaoh, Ramesses, has need of your son.'

Dumea's mouth dropped open and she gaped at him in amazement, her whole world turned upside down by this great honour, and she could only nod fitfully as temple guards escorted her away, clutching the hand of the son who had changed their lives for ever.

Ki-Un-Rah nodded and the procession shuffled forward once more, children being proffered and presented with varying degrees of pride and hope, every mother seeking the same reward as the fortunate Dumea. The high priest counted a further seventy-two infants before the little girl was ushered to his throne, her dark hair and flashing eyes making him wonder, indecision creasing his brow as he tilted her face to the sun. She wrinkled her face against the sudden glare, eyebrows meeting on the bridge of her nose, looking for all the world like a contented kitten, and the high priest gasped as the cat goddess, Bastet, was revealed to him in all her glory, the omens fulfilled just as he'd read them.

'Are you the girl's mother?' he said, and the woman nodded, taking a hesitant step forward.

'I am, Great One.'

'And you are …?'

'I am Teqa, Great One … My daughter is called Moona.'

'How old is Moona?'

'Four summers, Great One.'

'Assemble your family, Teqa,' Ki-Un-Rah murmured. 'You travel to Thebes, where you will live until our Pharaoh has need of the girl.'

The high priest came to his feet, his task completed, and he waved away the hordes that still lined the street, ignoring the disappointment in their eyes as he swept majestically into the temple and disappeared from sight.

THEBES, 1221 BC

It was two years before Ki-Un-Rah played any direct part in the development of Moona and Nedemin, content until then to allow the minor priests to watch over them and govern their progress in the Grand Temple at Thebes. The two families were given sumptuous apartments above the rear courtyard and wanted for nothing, servants and slaves seeing to their every comfort, but more than a close eye was kept on the two chosen children, ensuring they came to no harm and remained free of taint or blemish to their innocence, their purity guaranteed by the very lives of the people who watched over them.

Five days before the full moon was due in mid-September, the high priest crossed the Nile in his ornate barge and immediately ordered a period of fasting for six-year-old Moona and her nine-year-old companion, Nedemin, their bodies to be washed and scented every three hours whether night or day, and their heads to be shaved ready for their initiation of eternal servitude. On the evening of the fifth day he had them brought naked to the inner sanctum of the temple, where he stood in his finest robes before the statue of the god Osiris flanked by the ornate statues of Bastet and Anubis, candlelight flickering on gold and ebony, bringing life to dead eyes, the crouching dog and erect cat seemingly alive, stilled forms that appeared to breathe in the uncertainty of the shifting shadows.

Past hunger, too weary for coherent thought, the two children stood on quivering legs, swaying with exhaustion as they turned tired eyes to the high priest, who raised his arms slowly, all his power and might and majesty transfixing them in the aura of his will.

'One heart,' he intoned loudly. 'One mind. Together in life. Together in death. Anubis and Bastet, keepers of our God Ramesses. Together for all time. Together in all things. Ever shall it be and only a light brighter than the sun god, Ra, shall part them. One heart. One mind. Together in life. Together in death … Hear me, High Priest Ki-Un-Rah, for I have spoken and so shall it be. One heart. One mind. Together in life. Together in death. Together in all things for all time.'

He nodded to the priests who waited in the shadows and they came forward to hold the naked children as the ceremony peaked to a climax, the high priest's eyes searching the domed ceiling as the moment drew near, the first glimmer of the moon seen through the aperture, a lance of silver that pierced the gloom with its incandescent light.

'One heart. One mind,' he repeated, beseeching the heavens. 'Together in life. Together in death. Together in all things until the sun god, Ra, is surpassed. By the power invested in me by the great god Osiris I call on the gods to imbue within the chosen ones the spirit and power of Bastet and Anubis. I call on Sekhmet and Hathor, Amon and Mut. I call on Atum and Horus, Isis and Seth. I call on Taweret and Thoth, Osiris and Ra, to instil within the chosen two all the powers of the goddess of the sky, Bastet, and the god of mummification, Anubis. One heart. One mind. Together in life. Together in death. To protect our God, Ramesses for all time in the afterlife until the sun god, Ra, is surpassed.'

He turned to the smoking brazier at his side and withdrew

a glowing firebrand, the metal tip a bright fiery orange, and as the moon filled the aperture and the beam of light intensified, he nodded and stepped forward quickly, arms aloft as he brought all his mighty power to bear.

'One heart,' he hissed, and touched the firebrand to Nedemin's chest, ignoring the boy's screams as he turned to the terrified girl.

'One mind,' he chanted, intoxicated by the stench of burning flesh as he placed the firebrand to Moona's temple, just missing her left eye as she struggled in abject terror.

'Together in life. Together in death. Together in all things for all time. Only when the sun god is overshadowed shall you be parted, driven asunder by a light brighter than Ra. Protect our god Ramesses against all who seek to defeat him. This is your charge for all eternity and all the gods bear witness to this night. So shall it be, for I, Ki-Un-Rah, High Priest of Upper and Lower Egypt and all the lands therein, so decree it.'

The moon passed overhead then and the silver lance faded and died, the flickering candles once more holding sway and casting the room in an eerie glow, and Ki-Un-Rah turned and walked slowly from the chamber, his duty completed and the safety of his lord assured for all time.

THEBES, 1213 BC

'But other children play in the courtyard, Mother,' Moona said with all the logic of a fourteen-year-old. 'All I am ever allowed to do outside is thresh corn.'

She had matured into a rather striking young girl with long dark hair and piercing almond eyes, the scar on her temple taking nothing away from her natural beauty, but seeming to add character and strength to features already blessed with personality and charm. She was tall and lithe and her femininity was in no doubt beneath the flowing shift she wore, curves to tempt and beguile, much to the growing discomfort of the priests who safeguarded her innocence, for her purity was sacrosanct and not to be sullied by word or deed if their God, Ramesses, was to enjoy a long and trouble-free afterlife.

Her mother, Teqa, sighed softly and smiled, all too aware of the attractions to be found outside the temple walls, but she too was held responsible for Moona's conduct and she was not about to dismiss the trappings of luxury for a few moments of wayward impetuosity on her daughter's part.

'But you are like no other child, Moona,' she murmured, 'except the boy Nedemin … You are both chosen. … special, and therefore cannot act like the other children. You know all this. It has been explained to you time and time again.'

'Until I tire of it,' Moona sighed. 'All day I sit with Nedemin and the priests and they teach us to be worthy, yet no one tells us what we are to be worthy of.'

'Worthy to serve the Pharaoh,' Teqa explained patiently. 'I thought you knew all this?'

'But we have never even seen the great Pharaoh, Mother. How are we to serve if we are kept a day's ride from where he rules? He has seen eighty-three summers and I have to wonder if he will live long enough for Nedemin and I to serve him at all.'

'Then you must serve him in the only way possible to you … By your obedience. You have been ordered to seek no company other than your family, Nedemin and the priests, and you serve our great God by doing just that.'

'But what harm can come with playing as the other children do? I was watching them in the courtyard below and they have tethered a wild donkey to the latch-post and are taking turns to see who can mount it … It looks such fun.'

'And if your fun results in a shattered spine, how will you serve your Pharaoh then?'

'I know, I know … I just wish …'

'I know you do, Moona, and wishing was ever a young girl's pastime. But children put aside a wishful youth when they are groomed for higher things. Now, sit with me and teach me more of the writing the priests have shown you so I can read the inscriptions in honour of our Pharaoh.'

A commotion in the antechamber brought their lesson to an abrupt halt, and it was Nedemin himself who brought the news, breathless with anticipation yet bearing all his confused uncertainty as he blundered into the room.

'Moona, have you heard?' he cried, and she frowned, dark eyebrows coming together on the bridge of her nose as she peered at him quizzically.

'Heard what, Nedemin? What brings you here in such haste?'

'Our work is over. … Our duty to our God is done before it has even begun.'

'How so? What nonsense is this?'

'Ramesses the Great is dead, Moona,' he said in a shocked whisper. 'We serve a corpse and I hear the high priest comes this way tonight to relieve us of our task.'

'Who told you this?' Teqa demanded, coming to her feet. 'If this is market gossip you tell us, Nedemin …'

'No gossip, Teqa,' he insisted. 'I heard it from the priest, Husash, himself.'

'What does it all mean, Mother?' Moona asked in a small voice. 'Are we to return to Abydos? Are we to simply be sent away to the city of our birth with no recognition for our sacrifices over the last ten summers?'

'I know as much as you, child,' Teqa murmured, unable to keep the note of concern from her voice. 'We must wait and see what Ki-Un-Rah has to tell us, if indeed he comes this way … There is more to keep him from Thebes if Nedemin's news is true.'

'Husash said the high priest will be here by nightfall,'

Nedemin said knowledgeably. 'You forget that Ramesses is to be buried here in Thebes and Ki-Un-Rah will come to prepare the way.'

'I must tell your father, Moona,' Teqa said, hurrying to the door. 'We must prepare to leave.'

Moona crossed to the aperture and peered down to the courtyard below, the urgent bustle of the priests filling her with unaccountable fear, the uncertainty of their future making her heart race and the blood pound in her veins. Nedemin came and stood beside her, his hand reaching for hers in a comforting gesture, and he squeezed her fingers gently, sharing his nearness and his warmth.

'It will be all right, Moona,' he murmured softly. 'Ki-Un-Rah will tell us we are no longer required to serve the Pharaoh and we will be sent home.'

'Will we?' she whispered, her hand unconsciously touching the scar on her temple. 'I think we are destined for higher things, Nedemin.'

'What further use can they have of us?' Nedemin wondered with a frown. 'Even the high priest cannot serve a dead pharaoh.'

'Well, we shall soon see ... Look.' She pointed across the city to a stretch of the Nile glistening in the far distance. 'The high priest's barge. He comes, Nedemin ... Our fate is about to be revealed to us.'

Ki-Un-Rah went straight to the inner sanctum of the temple where he spent the next three hours preparing for the ritual to come, dispatching priests with his instructions before falling to his knees at the statue of Osiris, arms spread in supplication as he battled for the afterlife of his God, Ramesses. Satisfied he had pacified the gods, he came to his feet and moved the effigies of Bastet and Anubis until they were arranged before Osiris, standing like sentinels guarding the gateway to the afterlife, keeping the terrors at bay until the ritual was concluded and more fitting measures could be taken to ensure the Pharaoh's safety. When all was done, he signalled to Husash and the priest opened the great door, allowing the solemn procession to file into the chamber, and the priests came with their burning torches and incense, filling the room with a pungent odour that stung the eyes and dulled the senses.

Moona and Nedemin were brought forth, the simple white shifts they wore in stark contrast to the robes of mourning worn by the priests who flanked them, and they were led to stand before Osiris, their backs to the statues of Bastet and Anubis as they faced their destiny, their very existence culminating in this one moment of time.

Priests held Moona and Nedemin's arms tightly as Ki-Un-Rah swayed before them, his ivory-tipped staff of office glinting in the torch light as he waved it hypnotically before their eyes, his booming voice echoing round the chamber in urgent appeal.

'One heart. One mind. Together in life. Together in death. Safeguard the afterlife of our God Ramesses. Bastet and Anubis personified and dispatched to guard our greatest Pharaoh against the power of all the gods. Until the sun god, Ra, is surpassed, you shall watch over our Lord.'

He stepped to one side, the long blade hidden in the folds of his robe as he touched his staff to the scar on Nedemin's chest, avoiding the boy's gaze as he lifted his eyes skyward to beseech the heavens.

'One heart ... Go, Anubis, and protect your God.'

The blade flashed and Nedemin's throat was a gaping hole, blood gushing in a crimson tide that stained the priests who held him, supporting his weight as he sagged on legs that would no longer hold him, glazed eyes losing sight of this world as they stared into the next.

Priests stood between Moona and Nedemin and she saw nothing of his death, but she heard Ki-Un-Rah approach her, his voice appearing at her side as if coming from the mouth of Bastet herself, and she felt his staff touch her temple and his breath on her cheek as his final words dispatched her to the afterlife.

'One mind … Go, Bastet, and protect your God.'

Everything seemed to happen in slow motion then, and she caught the merest glimpse of light reflected on a slashing blade before her head seemed unable to support its own weight and flopped onto her shoulder, her bulging eyes staring incredulously at the spurting blood that turned her shift into a shimmering mass of crimson that paled, dimmed, grew an incandescent white before the blackness descended and blotted everything out for ever.

Chapter 8

'Four years old, you said,' Charles Levington muttered as the tape ground to a halting silence, and Leon Macleod shrugged, his fingers pensively stroking the goatee beard.

'Well, she *was* four years old, wasn't she?' he pointed out logically. 'It was just the timescale that was wrong.'

'So what was all that about? The ancient Egyptian thing? Was that real? Did it actually happen or was Marion simply repeating something she'd heard?'

'It was rather too … exact, too precise … too personal to be anything other than a real experience.'

'You think … you think Marion actually experienced all that?'

'Who knows?' Leon spread his hands. 'Like I said before, the mind is a very complex organ and it will go where it will.'

Charles was thoughtful for a moment, then he sighed.

'I suppose it depends on whether you believe in reincarnation, doesn't it? I mean, we've got to decide whether we think Marion was Moona in a previous life, or whether she was making it all up.'

'Well, that rather simplifies things, but basically, yes, our beliefs don't really come into it. You delve into the mind and you work with what you get no matter what you believe. A real experience or an imagined one makes little difference if they affect her in the same way.'

'What do you think? Personally, I mean? Was her story real or imagined?'

Leon removed his spectacles and cleaned them thoughtfully, leaning back in his seat as he probed the mysteries of the mind with deliberate care.

'Well … it would explain the birthmark on her temple, wouldn't it?'

'That's hardly a basis for psychoanalysis, is it? A birthmark?'

'You have to admit, Marion does rather resemble a cat when she screws her face up.'

'I knew it!' Charles clicked his fingers as though he'd suddenly realised something. 'When she frowns like that … I knew it looked familiar, but I couldn't place it. It's a cat. When she does that, she looks just like a cat.'

'Aye, well … No doubt we all get our mannerisms from somewhere.'

'This gets worse,' Charles laughed humourlessly. 'And there was me thinking you were a psychiatrist. I thought you delved into the mind, not formed opinions from birthmarks and the way people look.'

'What you fail to realise, Charles—what we can't know at this stage—is that Marion's mind may have invented the story to explain the birthmark. She may also have decided on Bastet to explain the way her eyebrows meet in the middle when she frowns. It's the chicken-and-egg syndrome. What came first, the scar or the story that explains it?'

'You're playing devil's advocate here,' Charles murmured, shaking his head. 'One minute you're suggesting Marion repeated a real experience, and the next you're saying she invented the story to explain her features. Talk about hedging your bets. You're onto a winner whatever way it turns out, aren't you?'

'One has to keep an open mind,' Leon smiled. 'When you're dealing with an inexact science, as we are, it pays to hear all the evidence before jumping to any conclusions.'

'So what's the next step?'

'Marion wants to hear the tape.'

'Is that wise?' Charles wondered, and Leon grimaced.

'Probably not, but patients have rights these days. If she wants to hear the tape, there's not much I can do to stop her.'

'But if you considered it damaging for her to hear it, surely you could refuse?'

'Hardly!' Leon closely examined his spectacles then put them back on. 'Under the present laws could you prevent one of your patients reading their medical records?'

'It's not the same though, is it?' Charles shook his head. 'Reading their records isn't likely to send them over the edge.'

'It could do, especially if they had a terminal illness that they weren't aware of.'

'I suppose so,' Charles sighed. 'Is Marion aware of what she said under hypnosis?'

'Most patients remember a certain amount after regression. When I brought her out of it, she couldn't stop crying. It was as though she was remembering something that happened a long time ago.'

'Well, if it really did happen, it *was* a long time ago, wasn't it?'

'More than three thousand years,' Leon said, a note of awe in his voice. 'I've heard of people regressing to the English Civil War, but never as far back as this.'

'It's a bit mind-boggling really,' Charles agreed. 'So, what happens after she's heard the tape?'

'I want to discuss it with her, see if there's anything deep-rooted in there.'

'Then what?'

'Regress her again. Bring her forward in time.'

'To when she was four in this life?'

'I don't think it'll be as simple as that, Charles. I think Marion's mind has decided where it wants to go and all I can do is follow as best I can. It'll get to the present in its own good time, and I'll have to be content with that.'

They fell silent, each lost in their own thoughts, but the

ghosts of Bastet and Anubis seemed to haunt them, the luckless Moona and Nedemin pawns in a master game of which they were unaware, playthings of the gods and victims of whim, chance and religious endeavour.

'When…' Charles cleared his throat and tried again. 'When are you seeing her?'

'After lunch.'

'Isn't that rather soon after…'

'She's had all night and all morning to think about it,' Leon murmured. 'Besides, I want to get to her while things are still fresh in her mind … while the emotions are still mixed up with the clinical facts.'

'You'll keep me informed?'

'Of course.' He came to his feet, stuffing papers into his briefcase. 'We'll meet up for dinner tonight, if you wish? I take it you'll be paying?'

'Typical Scotsman!' Charles laughed. 'Okay … Eight o'clock?'

'I'll see you back here,' Leon nodded. ''Bye, Charles.'

'Good afternoon, Marion,' Leon smiled, sitting beside the bed and casting her an appraising glance. 'How are you today?'

'All right,' she murmured woodenly. 'I'll be glad to get rid of this plaster cast, though.'

'Aye. No doubt you will, but it's early days yet.'

'It wouldn't be so bad if they'd let me get out of bed … give me some sticks so I can walk about a bit.'

'I know.' He nodded sympathetically. 'But you're not only undergoing medical treatment, you know—you're not only here because of a few wee broken bones.'

'They think I might try and jump out the window or something, don't they?'

'Aye, well … Your past record does tend to suggest you might try something like that.'

She sighed wearily and turned to look at him, the frown bringing her eyebrows together, then she nodded at the tape recorder on the bed between them, her dark eyes searching his face as she studied him carefully.

'Have you heard it?' she asked softly, and he nodded.

'Aye. I've heard it, lassie.'

'I see.'

'Do you?'

'I think so … It's a bit … disconcerting really.'

'In what way?'

'To think that might have been me … Moona … Sacrificed to protect a pharaoh.'

'How much of it do you remember?'

'The things I said?' She shrugged lightly. 'Most of it. It's like the way you remember a dream when you wake up—bits and pieces. I'd like to hear the tape to fill in the blanks.'

Leon peered at her intently, absently wondering if he were gazing at the same face that Ki-Un-Rah had seen three millennia ago, then he cocked his head to one side, studying her over the rim of his glasses.

'Are you sure you want to?' he asked softly. 'Considering how upset you were after the last session? Are you sure you really want to bring it all back?'

'It's back already, isn't it?' she said simply. 'Most of it, anyway.'

'And how do you feel about that?'

'My life in ancient Egypt? It's a bit hard to believe really.'

'Do you think she was you? Moona?'

'Mmm.' Marion nodded slowly. 'I … I *feel* it was me. When I was reliving it … it felt real somehow. That it actually happened.'

'Dreams can sometimes feel like that,' Leon nodded. 'You must have had dreams in the past that appeared so real you'd swear they really happened to you.'

'Not like this ... The colour ... the sights and smells ... the innocence and ... and at the end, the fear.'

'You were fearful of the high priest?'

'He was a very imposing man. I didn't know why I feared him ... just that he was a very powerful man who should be feared.'

'I dreamt I was being attacked by a tiger once,' Leon said conversationally, his Scottish lilt softening the words. 'The fear was real enough then, but it was only a dream ... not real.'

'Did you feel the tiger's breath on your face? Did you feel his claws rip into your body? See the blood spurt from your veins?'

'No, but...'

'I did, Doctor,' she whispered. 'I felt the priests holding me. I felt Ki-Un-Rah's breath on my cheek. I could smell the incense and I felt it when he cut my throat ... not at the time. It was like a delayed reaction ... like when you hit your thumb with a hammer—you don't feel the pain at first, but you wait, knowing it's going to hurt. It was a bit like that. When my head drooped and I saw the blood ... then I felt the slit in my throat ... too late to acknowledge it ... like an echo ... too late to even be aware of it, because by the time I felt it, it was all over and I was dead.'

'And then?'

She blinked at him.

'What do you mean, and then? Then there was nothing. Nothing that I can remember, anyway. Just a black void.'

He held her eyes for a long moment then he nodded, satisfied she was stable enough to hear the tape, and he switched the recorder on without another word, settling back in his seat to watch her as she listened intently.

It took three hours to play it all back, rewinding some parts so she could hear them again, her eyebrows knitted together in a frown as if she sought a message behind the words, some

78

distant thought that eluded her like a vaporous dream, ethereal and unreal, a will-o'-the-wisp as elusive as shadows. Sometimes she wiped tears from her eyes as though the emotions were now and not a part of yesterday, felt in modern times and not simply a part of a forgotten history, and other times she smiled as though recalling a love for an ancient mother or the joy of an innocent childhood in some far-off land where the sun shone on the sparkling waters of the Nile and children played in the shadows of high temples.

Leon gave her a minute to compose herself when the tape had finished, leaving her to her past while he fetched two cups of tea from the cafeteria, setting Marion's on the locker beside her before quietly resuming his seat.

'So,' he murmured after taking a tentative sip of tea. 'What do you make of it all, Marion?'

'The same as before,' she whispered. 'Hard to believe.'

'It could be just a dream, you know. It doesn't matter how real it feels, the mind is more than capable of making us believe the impossible.'

'The mind can create an image,' she agreed with a little nod, 'but can it create a smell? Can it create sounds I've never heard before?'

'Oh, yes,' Leon nodded emphatically. 'All that and more. Believe me, lassie, the mind is its own master and isn't dictated to by conscious thought. We all like to believe we control our minds, but the truth is, it's the other way round— our minds control us.'

She touched the birthmark on her left temple as if recalling the firebrand's caress, a terrified six-year-old with a shaven head and no robes to clothe her, Nedemin naked beside her, the stench of burnt flesh in her nostrils and the awful words going on and on. 'One mind. One heart. Together in life. Together in death.' On and on like a mantra, and she knew with sudden awareness that if Leon was right and we were controlled by our minds, then it was also true that strong minds could control weaker ones and impressionable young children could be governed by the iron will of a high priest at the zenith of his power.

'Tell me,' Leon said, interrupting her thoughts. 'What did you think of the young lad, Nedemin? As a person, I mean?'

'He was ... nice. Sweet and innocent, like me.'

'You didn't feel ... closer than that?'

'You mean, did I love him?' She shook her head. 'No. We were brought together to complete a task and that's all there was to it.'

'To protect a pharaoh in death?'

'Seems like it.'

'But no one told you that, did they? No one actually said, "Right, Moona, we've turned you into the cat goddess, Bastet, and together with Anubis it'll be your job to protect Ramesses in the afterlife", did they?'

'Not in so many words, no, but we heard it often enough in the various rituals we underwent.'

'And you weren't there when Ki-Un-Rah spoke to Ramesses about it, were you.'

'No, but ...'

'So how did you know?'

'What?'

'You've just listened to the tape, Marion, and you've also admitted that no one took the time to spell out what your role was in all this ... So how did you know?'

'I ...'

'There's no possible way you could have known, is there?'

'I ... I felt it. It's ... it's like when you wake up and your head's under the duvet and you can't see anything, but you just know it's morning, or still dark outside—you feel it. You just know. Besides, we were always in the company of priests. They were always instructing us and telling us things.'

'I agree that's a possibility,' he nodded wisely, 'but the most logical explanation is that it was all a dream, because things don't require explanations in dreams, do they? That's why you could be dreaming of walking down a street and it would seem perfectly natural to see a fish riding a bicycle or something equally ridiculous, because if you need explanations, the mind conjures one up for you.'

'It's not that simple.'

'Oh, but it is, Marion. You needed an explanation for the sacrifice in your dream, so your mind invented the protection-of-Ramesses theory.'

'But ... but why would I do that? Why would I bother with such an unlikely story as that? Why would I make it so elaborate and complex? What would be the purpose of it?'

'That's what I intend to find out,' he said briskly, gathering his things. 'I'll see you again in a couple of days and we'll see if we can't get to the bottom of it.'

'More hypnosis? More regression?'

'Would you mind?'

'I suppose not,' she shrugged. 'I'm not going anywhere, am I?'

'Is that what you believe, then?' Charles asked as they finished dinner and settled back with coffee and brandy. 'It was all a dream?'

'What other explanation is there? There's no way she could have known all that stuff, things she wasn't a party to, yet she tells it like she was there. In Ramesses' bedchamber, in the inner sanctum preparing for the rituals. It's too pat, it's too perfect—she knows too much, Charles. Stuff she wouldn't know at all if her story was true.'

'Unless ...'

'Unless what?'

'Well ... it's just a guess. Something I read in the *Lancet*.'

'Go on.'

'Doctor Bukerov in the Ukraine produced a paper about death. His theory was that when a person dies, all knowledge

81

is available to them—the dead know everything. He did some work with the Italian psychiatrist, Giovanni Angletti ...'

'Aye, I read the article,' Leon smiled. 'They thought that if they found a person who'd lived before and had been reincarnated, they could tap the knowledge that was imparted in his mind during the period of his death. It didn't work, of course.'

'That doesn't mean the information wasn't there,' Charles pointed out. 'All it proves is they couldn't extract it.'

'So you think that's how Marion knew the reasons behind Moona and Nedemin's sacrifice? Knowledge imparted after death?'

'It's a possibility, isn't it?'

'Anything's possible, I suppose,' Leon shrugged, 'but highly unlikely. It's more probable that she either dreamed it or she read something about it and it stuck in her mind.'

'Two possibilities, then,' Charles mused. 'Three, if you count the 'knowledge-in-death' theory. Will you be able to prove one or the other by regressing her again?'

'The more information I can get from her, the more likely it'll be that I can tie it down to something specific. At the moment I'm no nearer to finding out why she wants to kill herself than on the day I started, but it all takes time. I'll get there eventually.'

'You're confident of discovering the cause, then?'

'She's very susceptible to hypnosis,' Leon nodded, reaching for his coffee. 'I had no trouble regressing her at all.'

'When's the next hypnotherapy session?'

'Thursday. I'm tied up until then.'

'Perhaps ...'

'Of course,' Leon grinned, knowing what Charles was going to say. 'I'll bring the tape to your office as soon as we're done.'

'All set, then, Marion?' Leon asked brightly as he switched on the tape recorder, and she shrugged, the slightest movement of her shoulders.

'I suppose so.'

'Good girl. Just relax and let yourself drift. You know what to do. I'm going to take you back into the past again, but not as far back as last time. Understand?'

'Yes.'

'Splendid. Just concentrate on my voice and let yourself go with the words … Back in time, Marion … Not Egypt … Not the time of the pharaohs … Another time when you were young … Another time, Marion … A time before all this … Let your mind go back … back in time …'

Chapter 9

BABYLON, 540 BC

Darius glanced at the fading light and came to his feet, sheathing his sword and reaching for the helmet with the feathered commander's plume as he strode to the door, the rasp of his boots on the stone floor alerting the outer guards of his approach, and they fell into step behind him, the nightly ritual carried out with military precision. The fire carriers were already busy lighting the torches and the colonnade was well illuminated as darkness descended, the first pinpricks of distant stars visible in the eastern sky, but Darius paid them no heed as he made his rounds, inspecting the Royal Guard with a commendable devotion to duty that had earned him the respect of his men and the gratitude of his king, Nabonidus.

At the age of twenty-four, Darius was considered by many to be too young to have attained the commander's plume, but his prowess in battle together with his quick mind and ready wit had brought him to the attention of his superiors, not least the king, who immediately had him transferred to the Royal Guard. Darius spent the next two years at Tema in the Arabian desert, protecting Nabonidus as the king fought to control a rebellion, but even royal guards had no need of two commanders and when Darius reached that lofty rank he was dispatched to guard the king's son, Belshazzar, who had been left to rule Babylon in the king's absence.

The posting suited Darius well, for he had a wife and two children in quarters behind the high walls of that magical city, and he was even pleased to be the custodian and wagon-master of a great number of plants that Nabonidus had gathered to restore the hanging gardens established by Nebuchadnezzar many years before, so overjoyed was he to be going home after so long.

He had been in Babylon for more than a year now, his duties, as always, not taken lightly, and he showed as much loyalty and integrity towards his prince, Belshazzar, as he ever did to the king, and his dedication and unstinting vigilance were often commented on at court, much to the wry amusement of Darius's wife, Lindinia.

'They will promote you to chancellor next, Darius,' she laughed. 'With all these compliments abounding, it is a wonder your head has not swollen to twice its size. Are you sure your helmet still fits you?'

'I shall raid the coffers of gold to buy a new one if that is the case,' he countered with a grin, 'and my lovely wife will have to forego the pleasures of a new gown this year.'

'Ah … well, perhaps I am mistaken after all,' she giggled. 'I am sure the old helmet will serve you a while longer yet.'

'Just as I thought it might,' he nodded knowingly. 'So tell me, Lindinia, which cloth has caught your eye in the marketplace today?'

'It is the bluest blue you have ever seen, Darius, and it shimmers and shines with every twist of light. The thread is as fine as spiders' webs and sits on the body so lightly, I might as well be naked.'

'An interesting thought,' he laughed. 'And a sight to make Belshazzar and all his courtiers sit up and take notice.'

'I can have it, then?' she asked eagerly. 'Will I send the body slave, Arak, to the market tomorrow and secure a length?'

'As if you have not already instructed her to do so,' Darius chided good-naturedly. 'I have no doubt the tailor, Gendenimus, has already been told to expect its arrival.'

'Ah, you know me too well, my love. I can keep no secrets from you.'

And it was true, Darius thought as he checked the sentry outside the royal apartments—neither could keep a secret from the other, and it seemed as if they shared every thought, every emotion, every deed, and it had been so for as long as he could remember.

They had been born within days of each other in the town of Rarran, and Darius's mother, Taramet, had despaired of the child's fretful behaviour in those first traumatic weeks—his incessant wailing and his failure to respond to all her tricks and guile, enough to try the most patient of women. Thinking fresh air might quieten his constant screeching, Taramet had taken him with her to fetch water from the well, and there, as soon as baby Darius came into contact with Perdeus and her new baby daughter, Lindinia, he ceased his crying abruptly.

Believing him to be cured of his ills, Taramet returned home, only to find Darius resuming his ceaseless shrieking before they had travelled a dozen paces, and she was forced to invite Perdeus and Lindinia to her home until her baby slept in peaceful silence.

When the same thing happened the following day and again the day after, it quickly became apparent that Lindinia had a calming effect on the wearisome Darius and the two mothers contrived to spend as much time as possible together, for in return little Lindinia seemed to flourish and shine whenever Darius was present. So it was that the two children grew up together, seemingly inseparable, two parts of the whole, and it was only natural when they came of age that they were married and built a home together, sharing everything just as they had from birth.

Lindinia grew into a very attractive woman with long dark

hair and flashing almond brown eyes overshadowed by thick eyebrows that met in the middle when she frowned. Small and slight, she was the perfect complement to Darius's large frame, her delicate hands and lithe figure in total harmony with his muscled strength, femininity and masculinity walking side by side and facing the world together.

The only blight on their marital bliss was the amount of time Darius had to spend away with the army and at first Lindinia had joined the throng of camp followers, making a home wherever Darius served, but after the arrival of their second child they decided that a more secure and permanent home was required and they had taken quarters in Babylon itself. Darius's recent posting to the city had been a dream come true for all concerned and they wasted no time in adding a third child to their brood, their daughter Veronius sharing a room with her two older brothers, Halezzar and Victomus.

'Soldiers for a future king,' Darius mused as he made the last of his inspections and turned for home, the anticipation of seeing Lindinia again never failing to send a thrill of pleasure rippling down his spine.

Darius was a tall man, broad-shouldered and heavily muscled with finely chiselled features partially concealed by a thick beard, curled lovingly into the latest fashion by Lindinia herself, who made a point of teasing the edges of the moustache into the cheeks of the beard until one was indistinct from the other. He had long auburn hair that glistened like gold in the sunlight, and Lindinia loved nothing better that to wash and comb it for hours on end until it shone like burnished copper, burying her face in the silken tresses as she revelled in the very smell, the very essence, of the man she loved above all other.

Taking the steps two at a time, Darius lightly descended the palace wall and turned into the congested street, squeezing his way through the market before stepping into a side alley and pushing open the door to his house, the aroma of cooked meats and mulled wine assailing his senses as he removed his helmet and unbuckled his sword belt.

'There you are, my love,' Lindinia smiled, arms out-stretched to hug him in welcome as she kissed his cheek. 'Is our lord, Belshazzar, safe for another night?'

'Safe enough, I think,' Darius smiled. 'I saw Calamar, our noble prince's servant of the bedchamber, enter the palace with four concubines for our lord's pleasure. He'll be safely locked between a pair of willing thighs by now.'

'Do I detect a note of envy, Darius?' Lindinia teased with a frown, her eyebrows coming together on the bridge of her nose and transforming her features into that of an inquisitive kitten. 'And all the while I believed I was more than a match for your passions.'

'Indeed you are, Lindinia,' he laughed, tapping her bottom lightly. 'And when I have bathed and eaten I will allow you to prove it.'

'Such consideration,' she grinned. 'Am I worthy of such love?'

'Probably not ... but you have it all the same.'

'Then I am indeed fortunate to have a husband such as you,' she said, taking his hand and leading him into the house. 'Now, spend a moment with your children while I prepare the table.'

They ate together as they always did, Darius telling them of his day as they fed titbits to the boys, making a game of it and laughing when the baby, Veronius, regurgitated her mother's breast milk with an ear-splitting belch that Darius said was loud enough to wake the gods. Later, when the children were abed, Lindinia took great delight in stripping Darius of his leather armour and wool tunic and bathing him tenderly, scrubbing away the sweat and the grime with a coarse cloth soaked in scented water, her fingers delicately tracing the scar on his chest that was a replica of the birthmark on her left temple. One heart, one mind, together for always.

'So, Lindinia,' Darius said as he absently caressed her breast with a wet hand, 'what gossip have you gleaned from the market today?'

'You think I tell you gossip, husband?' she said impishly. 'I tell you only truths and matters of fact—I leave gossip to the washerwomen and commanders of royal guards.'

'Impudent camel,' he chided with a smile. 'I am sure you could hear the merest whisper from five hundred paces.'

'Oh, a thousand at least,' she laughed. 'Do not sell me short of my station.'

She washed his face with the cloth, thinking for the hundredth time how the mole on his neck resembled a dog, then her hands moved down to his shoulders and upper arms, gentle touches and tender caresses that said more of her love for him than words ever could.

'Well, then?' Darius went on. 'What news have you got for me?'

'So, I was right, then? Commanders of royal guards *are* party to idle gossip and tittle-tattle?'

'It always pays to hear the word from the market, Lindinia,' he said seriously. 'Who knows who plots the life of the lord I am sworn to protect?'

'Who indeed, my love? Well, you may find your allegiance split in two, for the word in the market is that our good king, Nabonidus, is to return to Babylon before the year is out and he intends to restore the moon god, Sin, to the temple at Harran.'

'I forever wonder how these rumours are spread,' Darius frowned. 'How is it that news of such importance can reach the ears of market-goers, but fails to reach the courtiers in the palace? You would think that Belshazzar would be the first to know of his father's arrival.'

'Perhaps he keeps it secret,' Lindinia suggested. 'Or

perhaps the merchants in the market travel faster than the king's messengers. Whatever the reason, my love, I am assured the rumour is true.'

'And he comes with more plants for the gardens, I expect,' Darius said dryly, and Lindinia laughed.

'Would you rather he came with a thousand slaves, Darius, and coffers filled with the plunder of his wars? He seeks only peaceful settlement and even you have to admit to liking the colour and the beauty of the hanging gardens.'

'Ha!' Darius scoffed lightly. 'The place smells like a concubine's chamber. Give me the smell of the stables anytime. It is far more wholesome than the sweet petals of the gardens.'

'Then I shall remind you of that when you come to me in our bed after I have smothered myself in horse dung in preference to the scents and perfumes I am accustomed to— we shall see then which smell you think the more wholesome.'

'Now you, my love,' he laughed, capturing her in his great arms in an affectionate bear hug, 'could spend two moons with a herd of goats and camels and still smell as fresh as the morning dew. I sometimes wonder if your body acts like other women's. I have to hold my nose when I pass through the market, the stench is that bad at times.'

'I refuse to reveal the secrets of my bath chamber,' Lindinia chuckled, nibbling the flesh of his shoulder. 'It is not wise for a husband to know everything.'

'You and I have no secrets, Lindinia,' Darius murmured softly, kissing her cheek. 'I know everything about you.'

'And I you, my love,' she whispered, then laughed aloud, her hand snaking down to grope between his legs in a gesture as familiar and as old as the sands of time. 'Including when you desire me, so dry yourself and let us to bed before such a mighty phallus is reduced to nothing in the waiting.'

BABYLON, 539 BC

True to the word of the gossipmongers on the streets, King Nabonidus returned to Babylon before the year was out, and after five days of ceremony and feasting he restored the moon god, Sin, to the temple at Harran before celebrating the New Year festival in Babylon, taking the hand of the statue of Bel et Marduk to show his divine kingship to the citizens beneath his reign.

It was to be a good year, Lindinia decided emphatically. The king was returned and the gods were in their rightful place. The times of drought were over and the watercourses were full after abundant rainfall. Soon the fields would be rich with corn and barley and the granaries would overflow with their yield, the labourers working well into the night to bring in the harvest. The children would prosper and Darius would gain further promotion in the service of Belshazzar. It would be a good year, she nodded to herself, perhaps the best ever.

But it would turn out to be the worst.

Three days later, the rumours had it that King Cyruss II of Persia was preparing to launch an attack on the city of Babylon.

'Will they come, Darius?' Lindinia asked worriedly, concerned for the children, and he shrugged wearily, his duties pressing upon him with insistent urgency.

'Our patrols report a large Persian force to the south, but their intentions are unclear. The Governor of Gubaru leads them, but he is merely an emissary of King Cyruss. His name is Guti, but the gods alone know what his orders are.'

'Can they breach the city walls?'

'They have few siege engines, Lindinia, and Belshazzar thinks we can hold them at bay.'

'What does King Nabonidus think? Is he in agreement with his son?'

'Who knows what Nabonidus thinks? He does not seek my

91

counsel, Lindinia, and I am not party to the gossip at court.'

'But you must have heard something, Darius,' she persisted. 'You command the Royal Guard. What instructions have you been given?'

'Instructions?' he scoffed, shaking his head. 'My instructions are to protect the lives of my king and my prince.'

'Is that it? Is there no plan afoot to thwart the invasion?'

'What would you have us do, Lindinia? Sally forth and meet the Persians in open combat?'

'I do not know how to wage war, Darius,' she said softly, touching his cheek with her fingertips. 'I only know that I love you and our children and I fear for the safety of you all.'

'There is a team of wagons leaving later today,' Darius said carefully. 'Nabonidus seeks the welfare of his wives and concubines … I can find places for you and the children. You must go to your mother's house at Harran.'

'Will I be safer there than in Babylon?'

'Who is to say which city is safer than the next?' Darius murmured. 'But the Persians can enter Harran with no opposition. There will be no fighting and the bloodlust will be contained. They will treat you fairly.'

'Are you to escort the wagons?'

'I told you, Lindinia,' he said deliberately. 'I am to guard Nabonidus and Belshazzar.'

She held his eyes for a long moment, her fingers absently touching the scar at her temple, then she shook her head slowly, all her convictions and her love displayed in the quiet authority of her voice.

'Arak will take the children. My place is beside you.'

'If I have to fight, Lindinia …'

'Then I fight at your side.'

'Lindinia …'

'Hush now. It is decided. If the Gods decree it then we shall fall together. I will share my death with you just as I have shared my life.'

'I cannot ask this of you, my love,' he said solemnly, and she smiled sadly.

'It is not necessary for you to ask, Darius,' she murmured, rising on tiptoe to kiss his cheek. 'The decision is mine and I have made it. Now, when do the wagons leave?'

'Just before sunset.'

'Then Arak must make ready. Will you see the children before they go?'

Darius sighed heavily and nodded, holding back the tears with difficulty as he fought to maintain his composure.

'I will eat with you at midday, then … then I am expected at the palace.'

'So be it, then.' She nodded with finality. 'I will have a meal prepared for you.'

Babylon was a city in chaos, the citizens fleeing in droves and clogging the narrow tracks with oxen and mules or trundling handcarts laden with possessions, while others barricaded their homes, eyes fearful as they scanned the horizon for the Persian hordes, ever mindful of the rape and pillage, plunder and death that awaited them if the walls were breached.

Darius was kept busy seeing to the defences of the palace, organising patrols and positioning the guards, but everything rested with the army who manned the thick walls, and he put his trust and his faith in the governor, Amitzar, who led them, his capabilities, or lack of them, put to the ultimate test.

That evening Darius watched from the west tower as the column of wagons carrying his children and his future creaked through the lower gate, snaked its way through the fields of ripening corn and headed toward the setting sun, the last hope of Babylon escaping a doomed city, for after the final wagon was clear, the gate would be closed and sealed against the enemy without. But it was not the departure of his children, distressing though it was, that saddened Darius so much, it was the disheartening sight of the wagon bearing

93

King Nabonidus himself that filled Darius with a desperate melancholy, their king looking to his own while the fate of Babylon hung in the balance.

As evening turned to dusk, the first Persian campfires could be seen in the hills to the south and as the night wore on, more became visible to the east and north, a circle of flickering light that gradually encompassed the whole of the countryside until it appeared as if a ring of fire surrounded them, a flaming omen of the furnace heat of battle to come.

It was late the following morning before Darius managed to return home, the market strangely deserted and still, his footsteps resounding eerily on the empty streets and echoing back to him from abandoned homes and bare stone walls. He found Lindinia sitting on the front step as though whiling away the time in peaceful contemplation, and he smiled tiredly as he approached, all his love for her welling up inside him until he thought it would overwhelm him, her unstinting devotion to him touching his heart.

'What ails you, wife?' he said, his voice affectionately gruff, and she came to her feet slowly, shrugging her shoulders and spreading her hands in a gesture of bafflement, a puzzled frown knitting her eyebrows together and creasing her forehead.

'I went to draw water,' she murmured apologetically, 'but the watercourses were empty. How can this be, Darius, when yesterday they flowed full to the top?'

'Empty?' He blinked at her. 'Are you sure?'

'You think I have not the wherewithal to know if I can draw water or not?' she said more sharply than she intended. 'The courses are empty, Darius. I tell you it is so.'

'Did you try more than one, Lindinia, or just the course by the market?'

'I have walked the length and breadth of Babylon in my search, Darius. The city is without water.'

94

'The Persians,' Darius breathed. 'It must be their intention to drive us out by cutting our water supply. Is there none in the barrels?'

'A little,' she nodded with a sigh. 'Arak had the good sense to fill them before she departed, but it will last us little more than a day. Two at the most.'

'Belshazzar has a good supply at the palace,' Darius said wearily. 'If I can obtain some, I will.'

'How goes it out there?' she asked, leading him into the house, and he grimaced as he threw off his helmet, sprawling on the cushions and closing his eyes.

'The Persians are without and we are within … No change from last night. They still make no move to attack.'

'Well, if thirst drives us from the city, they have no need to attack. Why take by force a city that we would give to them willingly and undamaged by war? They have the measure of us, I fear.'

'There is truth enough in that, Lindinia. We sit helpless behind our high walls while they plunder our crops and slaughter our cattle.'

'Has the king no answer for them, Darius?' she asked plaintively, stooping to pull his boots free, and Darius snorted with derision.

'Have you not heard? And I thought the fair Lindinia was the first to hear all the rumours.'

'Heard what?' she frowned. 'I have been too busy searching for water to pay heed to gossip today.'

'Our good and noble king, Nabonidus, has fled the city … He was with the wagons last night.'

'Deserted us?' She blinked at him incredulously. 'Our king has gone?'

'Gone and left Belshazzar to face the Persians alone.'

'How is it you were not sent to escort him? Is that not the purpose of a royal guard, Darius?'

'I was not even told, Lindinia,' he scoffed. 'See the high

esteem in which they hold their commander? The first I knew of it was when I saw half my force flanking the king's wagons yesterday—reduced me to three thousand men when I was depleted enough to begin with.' He sighed heavily. 'I fear mine is a lost cause, Lindinia. I was stretched to the limit before, but now...'

'They have yet to breach the walls, my love,' she said hopefully. 'You have no duty to protect a prince if he is not threatened.'

'You forget the water, Lindinia,' Darius reminded her gently. 'Or rather our lack of it. If Belshazzar decides our plight is hopeless, he may have no option but to sally forth and engage the Persians in the field ... My duty is by his side.'

'As mine is by yours,' she murmured, and smiled grimly. 'And shall be for ever.'

It was in the early hours of the following morning that the alarm was raised, the sentries bellowing from the towers as the truth dawned, guile and cunning succeeding where a fruitless siege might fail. Rather than blunt their forces against the mighty walls of Babylon, the Persians had redirected the water, and once the courses were dry they simply used them to enter the city, climbing from the deep gullies like demons from hell as they ransacked the city.

Darius heard the commotion from his bed and he dressed hurriedly, fingers fumbling with buckle and harness as he strapped on his armour, firing instructions to Lindinia as he snatched up his helmet and sword and ran to the door.

'I must go to Belshazzar ... Barricade the door after me and take to the cellar. I will return if I can.'

'DARIUS!' Lindinia screamed, but he was gone, out into the fray to protect his lord, and she scrambled for her tunic, foregoing sandals and belt as she dashed after him, her feet slipping on the splashes of blood that littered the streets in crimson pools.

The fighting was fiercest around the palace and she ran toward the noise, following in Darius's wake and pausing only to retrieve a sword still gripped in a dead guard's hand before charging on, her heart pounding madly and her breath coming in painful gasps. She reached the top of the steps and her eyes widened in fear as she caught sight of Darius at the palace gate, his back to the wall as he held a snarling mob of the attackers at bay, his sword slashing and hacking with deadly efficiency, and Persian after Persian fell victim to the flashing blade, the screams of the dying filling the air with their terrifying cry.

A giant Persian swung with his sword and Darius parried the thrust with difficulty, slewing his body to one side as he absorbed the force of the blow, and a second Persian, seeing his chance, lunged with his spear, piercing leather, wool, flesh and bone in one agonising moment of time. Darius's sword fell from lifeless fingers, the blood spurting and his eyes glazing in death before his body touched the ground.

'AAAAAIIIIIEEEEE,' Lindinia wailed like a banshee, the scar on her temple throbbing with a fierce intensity, and she threw herself into the battle, the borrowed sword whirling about her head as she hacked her way to her fallen beloved, mindless of the slashing blades about her.

Wounded in a dozen places, she finally reached the body of Darius and she fell to her knees, hugging him tightly as the Persians closed in, and she buried her face to his neck, closing her mind and her eyes to the horrors around her as the swords rose and fell and the spears jabbed until there was no longer any pain and she lost herself to the eternal darkness that slowly descended and engulfed her for ever.

Together in life. Together in death. For always.

Chapter 10

'This gets more complicated the more it goes on,' Charles Levington muttered, shaking his head as if to clear it. 'What the hell was that all about?'

'It's very strange, I must admit,' Leon said thoughtfully. 'Most interesting. I've never heard anything quite like it in my life.'

'I know you wanted to bring her forward in time, but ... well, it was hardly a giant leap, was it?'

'No, but ... I think it's the correct way to proceed. Whatever's giving Marion these suicidal tendencies is obviously related to the past somehow.'

'So what will you do? Keep edging her forward until you get to the bottom of it?'

'That's about all I can do, really,' Leon sighed. 'It could be a long process.'

Charles stared at the tape recorder as if willing it to reveal all its secrets, a hundred questions passing through his mind with no ready answers to any one of them, riddles and mysteries that they could only guess at, pure conjecture in the twilight world of the unknown.

'So ...' he ventured carefully, 'do you think the two stories are linked? Are they the same people as Moona and Nedemin?'

'Well, the people are different, that's for sure ... but whether they share the same memories is another matter entirely. Perhaps it's something in the genes, in the physical make-up of a person, that we carry from life to life … a part of our subconscious that we're totally unaware of.'

'You believe all that reincarnation stuff, then?'

'It's not a question of what I believe,' Leon said with a hint of exasperation. 'It's what the facts tell us that count. You don't have to be reincarnated to carry the genes of an ancient ancestor. I once read somewhere that the majority of the population of Europe could trace their family tree back to the Roman Emperor, Nero. If the genes we inherit carry a memory, then it's possible to tap that memory. In Marion's case, it might just be that the gene memories are breaking through into her mind. It isn't *her* life she's recounting, but the life of an ancestor.'

'That works in the case of Lindinia because she had children, people to pass on her genes, but Moona had no offspring, did she? And even if you're correct, Lindinia's children wouldn't be able to be so graphic about her death, would they, because they weren't there to witness it.'

'Aye, well … We seem to be going round in circles here,' Leon murmured. 'It's like walking along a narrow, twisting path, and if we put a foot wrong we end up in quicksand. There's no firm ground to build any basis of hypothesis on. We're just groping in the dark.'

'There is …' Charles paused, deliberating over his choice of words, then he shrugged lightly, tossing caution to the wind. 'There is a perfectly logical explanation for Marion's stories, of course.'

'There is?'

'Mmm … They happened … and they happened to her.'

'That's very convenient, is it not?' Leon said dryly. 'If you can't find a valid reason, accept the most obvious. That's a bit like the ancients accepting the theory that the sun revolved around the earth simply because it appeared that way, or assuming the world has to be flat because you'd fall off if it wasn't round. All very logical, but equally misled. When it comes to analysing the mind, Charles, logical explanations get thrown out the window.'

'But it is possible, isn't it?'

'Of course it's possible—possible, but highly improbable. We're trying to resolve a very complex issue here and it's never wise to leap on the first logical explanation just because it's convenient and saves us a bit of bother. And even if you happen to be right, that still doesn't explain why Marion's hell-bent on self-destruction, does it?'

'I suppose not,' Charles sighed. 'When are you seeing her again?'

'Monday.'

'Okay. Listen, I might have another word with Marion's boyfriend, see if he can throw some more light on all this.'

'Please yourself,' Leon shrugged. 'Just be careful what you say. I don't want Marion thinking we're discussing her problems to all and sundry behind her back, and I don't want Mr Newell saying something to her that'll put her treatment even further behind than it is.'

'I understand,' Charles nodded. 'I'll talk to you again on Monday morning and let you know if I learn anything.'

'Right. Enough for one day, I think. Have a good weekend, Charles.'

The two-bedroom flat in Fulham was tastefully furnished and well maintained, the pastel shades and discreet lighting giving the place a homely, warm atmosphere that was both calming and pleasing on the eye. Photographs and knickknacks added personal touches of lives shared, and Charles was surprised to see vases of dried flowers in the hearth and a soft old clown sitting in an armchair, Marion's influence that belied the troubled state of her confused mind.

Terry let him in with a welcoming smile and ushered him to a seat, his head cocked to one side quizzically as he eyed the doctor cautiously, a hint of understandable concern in his voice.

'I didn't think you doctors worked on Sundays,' he ventured with a tentative smile. 'There's nothing wrong, is there?'

'No, no.' Charles shook his head. 'I just thought you might be able to fill me in with a bit of background … Help us to find the cause of Marion's behaviour. I thought I was more likely to catch you at home on a Sunday.'

'You were the last person I expected when you phoned this morning. I got a bit worried in case Marion … you know.'

'Nothing to worry about, I can assure you, Mr. Newell.'

'I'm glad to hear it … and call me Terry. Can I get you a coffee or something?'

'Coffee would be fine. Black with one sugar, please.'

Terry busied himself in the little kitchen, talking through the open hatch as he switched on the percolator and prepared the cups.

'I thought it had to be something important if it couldn't wait until I visited Marion tonight,' he said warily, and Charles smiled.

'Well, it could have waited, I suppose, but I wanted a quiet chat with you and I'm not back in the hospital until the morning.'

'I see. How's her leg and her arm coming along?'

'Fine. They itch a bit, but that's always the case. You always get an itch where you can't reach it. A lot of people stick a knitting needle down the plaster and have a good scratch.'

'Makes sense. Who's the other doctor Marion's been seeing? He's a shrink, isn't he?'

'Professor Macleod? He's very good. Had a lot of success in the past.'

'Let's hope he can help her. Is he making any progress?'

'Getting there slowly. You know how these things are,

101

Terry. Nothing seems to happen for a while, then you make a breakthrough and it all comes together pretty quickly.'

Terry stepped into the sitting room and offered the tray to Charles.

'There you go. Black coffee, one sugar … Sorry, you were saying?'

'Thanks. I was only saying that we shouldn't expect too much too soon. These things take time.'

'I guess so.' He sat on the couch, coffee cupped in his hands, and he gazed at Charles over the rim, peering at him through the rising steam.

'You wanted some background information, I believe,' he pressed, and Charles shrugged lightly, keeping it low-key and informal.

'Just bits and pieces, really—anything that can throw some light onto Marion's compulsive disorder. Tell me … has she ever mentioned the scar on her temple?'

'Not really. Only to say it was a birthmark. I never took any notice of it.'

'I notice she touches it quite a lot. Is that a habit?'

'Not that I know of.' Terry shook his head. 'It's just something people do, isn't it? You know, scratch their head or rub their nose or something.'

'Well, she seems to do it more when she's distressed.'

'You mean like a comfort thing?'

'Mmm.' Charles nodded, sipping the coffee slowly. 'Is she prone to having nightmares?'

'Lord no!' Terry laughed shortly. 'I always said Marion could sleep for England.'

'What about … Perhaps I shouldn't ask this.'

'Ask what?'

'Your sex life … Would you describe it as good?'

'Up until the first attempt at suicide it was.'

'Then what happened?'

Terry sighed softly and peered down into his cup, taking

his time as he thought it through and sorted the real from the imagined, then he looked up and held Charles's eyes in a steady gaze, a hint of a frown creasing his brow.

'We still ... you know ... did it, but ... but there was something missing ... It's as if her heart wasn't in it anymore and she just went through the motions to keep me happy. We were doing it less and less and this last month we stopped altogether. It was obvious she wasn't in the mood and I wasn't going to force her.'

'Did that bother you?'

'Of course it bothered me. I'm a bloke and I like sex as much as the next man, but I didn't make an issue of it. I was more concerned about Marion ... worried about her. I just wanted the old Marion back again.'

'She'd changed that much then?' Charles asked, taking a sip of coffee, and Terry shook his head in a gesture of despair.

'It became like I hardly knew her. The face was the same and the same body wore the same clothes. She ate and drank the same things and slept in the same bed ... but it was like something had died inside her. The spark, the life, everything that was there before, just seemed to have been extinguished. Apart from her behaviour she was the same person on the outside, but something had changed inside, something that made her moody and irritable ... something that made her uncommunicative and sullen ... something that made her want to kill herself.'

'Must've been difficult to live with,' Charles murmured softly, and Terry shrugged.

'After the first suicide attempt I was constantly on edge, watching her like a hawk all the time. And she knew that, of course, she was aware I was always checking up on her, making sure she was all right, and that wouldn't have helped, would it? You soon get fed up with someone watching your every move, don't you? And that made it even worse, made her more irritable ... even more difficult to live with.'

103

'It's a vicious circle,' Charles agreed with a nod. 'What about the second suicide attempt?'

'When she tried to hang herself? Jesus!' He shook his head as if he couldn't quite believe it. 'You think you've done everything possible to prevent it happening again … After the first time I hid everything sharp, every knife, every pair of scissors, every razor blade, but I came home one day and found her hanging from the bedroom ceiling. We had beams put in there to give it a cottagey feel and there was a hook where we hung one of those wicker chairs that you suspend so that you can relax while you're swinging about.'

'And she'd hanged herself?'

'She must have thought about it first because she'd untied the rope from the wicker chair and made a sort of noose in the end. She used the laundry basket to stand on and she just jumped off. Christ! It's a wonder she didn't break her neck.'

'Was Marion expecting you home at that time?' Charles asked, fully aware that when a suicide attempt was merely a cry for help it was usually carried out when there was a good chance of discovery before death occurred. Genuine cases made sure they wouldn't be interrupted.

'No.' Terry shook his head, shattering the 'cry-for-help' theory. 'I never get home before seven o'clock most evenings, but I was meeting a supplier at five and I'd left their sample books in the flat, so I dashed home to get them just after four-thirty that afternoon. I didn't even know Marion was at home. She was supposed to be at work, but she took the afternoon off.'

'And that's when you found her?'

'Yeah. When I think … If I'd have been ten minutes later … Jesus! I don't even want to think about it.' He gave Charles a bewildered look. 'When it's just sharp objects, you know, knives and stuff it's relatively easy to put everything out of harm's way, but when someone tries to hang themselves … every item of clothing is a potential weapon. Every belt, every tie, every pair of tights. You even have to consider sheets and table cloths. It was a nightmare.'

'And the third time?'

'The tablets? It got to the point where I was afraid to let her out of my sight, but she seemed to be a bit better and like a fool I let her go shopping on her own. It's like I was saying about constantly checking up on her. She was getting fed up with it and we'd had a few rows over it and she accused me of not trusting her, and in a fit of pique I said "Okay. Fine. Go shopping, but I'm trusting you to be home by six." So off she went. I think that's all she intended to do when she left home. Do some shopping, maybe have some lunch in town … just get out of the flat for a while where she was under close scrutiny. She went into Boots the chemist and she must've seen all the pills and stuff and I think it was a spur-of-the-moment thing. She bought a couple of packets of this and a couple of packets of that, then locked herself in the ladies loo and took the lot. Luckily, a member of staff had seen her go in and got a bit concerned when she didn't come out.'

'And raised the alarm,' Charles murmured, and Terry nodded.

'Got her to hospital and they pumped her stomach out.'

'But she still didn't know why she was doing it?'

'She didn't have a clue … At least, that's what she said. I believe her, but …' He shrugged despairingly. 'Who knows?'

They sipped their coffee in thoughtful silence and Charles wondered what the answer was.

'What about Marion as a person?' he ventured, trying a different approach. 'What are her likes and dislikes?'

'She likes the normal stuff, I suppose,' Terry shrugged. 'White wine, chocolate … nice clothes. Robbie Williams and Antonio Banderas.' He smiled fondly, remembering Marion as she used to be. 'She loves dogs. I think she had a dog when she was younger. She kept pestering me to get an Alsatian, but

105

there's not much room here in the flat, and with both of us out at work all day, it just wasn't practical … not fair on the dog.'

'Anything else?'

'Nothing that readily springs to mind. Marion was just a normal girl with normal tastes. Maybe if I thought about it, you know, sat and analysed every facet of her character, something else might come to light, but you don't take too much notice at the time, do you? You just accept a person for who they are and simply get on with enjoying each other.'

'I suppose so,' Charles murmured, then fell silent, mulling things over in his mind. It seemed to him that the deeper they delved, the more complicated it became, the more bizarre that Marion would contemplate suicide, and he wondered if they'd ever reach the truth, the final piece of the jigsaw puzzle that explained everything with abundant clarity and allowed them to lay to rest the ghosts of the past that appeared to feature so strongly in Marion's subconscious mind.

'What about … what about her interests?' he asked, believing that the more he knew about her, the more chance he had of gaining an insight into the forces that drove her. 'Did she have any hobbies or pastimes?'

'She liked to play draughts and she was bloody good at chess, but apart from that … but that was strange, too.'

'What was?'

'She used to get sudden fads for things … I don't mean like a craving for chocolate or something, but … out of the blue she'd have this sudden urge to do something. It was almost like an obsession with her.'

'Can you be more specific?'

'I remember once we were watching TV and they advertised a Tutankhamun exhibition at the British Museum. She nagged me to death over it until I promised her we'd go and see it, but it had never bothered her before. I didn't even know she was interested in that sort of thing, and I don't think she was, really … it was just an impulsive thing, a one-off, but once it grabbed hold of her she wouldn't let it go.'

'Was that it?'

'I don't know.' Terry shook his head, confused between what might be taken as normal avid interest and obsessive behaviour when he was in no position to judge, and he loathed the idea that he might be making more of it than it really was, but he ploughed on gamely, hoping that any information, however innocent in appearance, might lead to Marion's recovery.

'She hated Western films, especially if it was a typical cowboys-and-Indians thing … I didn't think there was anything odd in that because she was no different to most girls in that respect … but she hated those films with a passion that went beyond the norm.'

'You never discussed it with her?'

'Not really. Not the cowboy thing, anyway.'

'But something else?'

'King Arthur.'

'What about him?'

Terry shrugged and shook his head.

'I don't even know how we got on the subject, but I remember saying something like, "He was a great king and it was a pity they couldn't find the site of Camelot." She sort of stared at me and said that history had a way of making heroes out of villains and I shouldn't be swayed by romantic nonsense. I asked her if she knew something that the rest of us didn't, and she just looked at me. I wondered where she got her notions from, you know, out of step with everyone else, but she couldn't say. She just said she'd never been one for believing all the hype that we tend to lavish on "heroes" like Robin Hood and Dick Turpin, and King Arthur was no exception.'

Charles wondered if Marion was simply expressing an opinion or whether she spoke with the voice of bitter experience, for who was to say what governed our likes and dislikes? Why does one man love tea and another hate it? Why does one man climb mountains when another might fear their height? One man might swim like a fish while another has an inherent fear of water, yet no one questions where these fears and phobias stem from. They just are. A part of our make-up. A fraction of the whole that makes each individual the person they are. And who is to say our likes and dislikes, our loves and our hates, are not predetermined by past lives? Who can say with such certainty that we haven't all experienced it before and merely carry our predilections, our likes and our hatreds, with us? Personality and character as diverse as snowflakes, one person moody and sullen, and the next person carefree and bright. One man a mass murderer, and the next a missionary of God. Opinions and notions formed for no rhyme or reason and with no valid cause for their existence. It was an interesting concept and one that Charles would have to discuss with Leon on Monday.

'Another coffee?' Terry asked, and Charles shook his head.

'No, thank you. I'd better be going.' He came to his feet and passed Terry his empty cup.

'Thanks for sparing me your time today.'

'Has it helped?'

'Who can say?' Charles shrugged, moving to the door. 'But every little helps, I suppose. Thanks again, Terry.'

Leon Macleod listened with interest as Charles recounted his meeting with Terry Newell the previous day, but a look of scepticism crossed his face as Charles expounded his theory of past lives causing present behaviour, shaking his head as he patiently waited for him to finish.

'As a theory,' he murmured, 'it has its merits, but as a workable concept it's got more holes than a sieve.'

'How come?' Charles frowned. 'No one can rationally explain what makes one person differ from another.'

'Of course they can,' Leon scoffed. 'Upbringing. Schooling. Parental control, or lack of it. There are a thousand reasons, Charles, and you know it.'

'In its simplified form, yes, but you could have two people brought up together in the same house, at the same time, and they'll be as different as chalk and cheese. Personality. Likes and dislikes. Opinions and beliefs. Foibles and idiosyncrasies. No two people are identical, Leon, and there has to be a reason for it.'

'The reason is because our thought processes are different from those of anyone else. No two people *think* the same, so no two people can *be* the same.'

'But thought processes can't make someone have an inherent fear of spiders, can they? It isn't thought processes that produce fears and phobias, is it? People don't consciously think they hate heights, it just is ... and there has to be a reason for it.'

'And you believe the reason lies in a past life, do you, Charles? A past experience that we carry with us in a reincarnated life?'

'Well, it's possible, isn't it?' Charles pressed, and Leon smiled

'Let's take the facts one at a time.' He ticked them off on his fingers. 'One, you believe that every person has lived before.'

'Yes, it's possible.'

'No, it isn't, actually.'

'Why not?'

'Because, my dear Charles, there are more people alive in the world today than have ever died. Ergo, we couldn't all have lived before.'

'Are you sure about that?'

'Positive. Unless there are some lost civilisations that no one even knows about, but 1 think that's pretty unlikely, don't you?'

'What about the Buddhist thing?'

'What Buddhist thing?'

'Well, the belief that animals and creatures are all part of the same system.'

'Oh, you mean you might have been an ant or a horse in a past life?'

'Yes,' Charles nodded. 'Then it would work, wouldn't it?'

'Well, it might explain why some people like rolling about in the hay,' he said dryly, 'but it's a bit of a long shot, don't you think?'

'I don't know,' Charles shrugged. 'At least it means we could have all lived before.'

'Very convenient, but you're suggesting that Marion's lived twice before. Once in Egypt, and once in Babylon, not to mention her present life. So why give her three lives as a person when others have to be content with being a goat or something first?'

'I'm not saying I know all the answers, but ...'

'So that's fact number two. Three, who decides if you come back again?'

'I don't ...'

'Four, who decides whether you come back as a pig or a person?'

'It's not ...'

'Do you get a choice?'

'A choice?'

'Mmm. What you come back as ... or even if you come back at all? Can you say, "No thanks, I've had enough of that"? Can you choose if you're to be a man or a woman? Can you choose where you're to live, or who your parents are going to be? You see, Charles, what you're suggesting is fraught with pitfalls, because if there's any choice at all, no one would come back to live in a squalid slum in India or a mud hut in Africa, would they?'

110

'Perhaps it's part of the process,' Charles ventured. 'You know ... first a bug or a beetle, then a cat, then a horse, then you're born into poverty somewhere, and so on, working your way up the chain.'

'Very neat. The only problem is, if your theory is right, Marion should be Queen of England by now, not some menial worker earning a living at Wembley Arena.'

'Like I say,' Charles sighed, 'I don't know all the answers. It's just ... thinking aloud ... possible reasoning.'

'Mmm,' Leon nodded. 'Possible, but not very plausible. There are too many unknowns, Charles. Too many areas where you're groping in the dark. Let's just stick to the facts, shall we?'

'All right. Fact one. Marion was Moona in ancient Egypt. Fact two ...'

'Just a minute,' Leon interrupted. 'You're jumping to conclusions again. We've heard two stories that might or might not be linked in some way, but you can't prove it one way or another. Stick to the facts, and the facts are that Marion is very disturbed and wants to terminate her life. Under hypnosis she's recounted two tales that are just as likely to be wild imagination as anything else, which only goes to prove how inventive she can be. You've heard some titbits from Marion's boyfriend which are no more strange or outlandish than any of us have experienced and if you're putting all your faith in her opinions or her likes and dislikes then you're going to be sadly disappointed. It's how people are, Charles. It's what makes them individuals. It's what sets each of us apart from the next person.'

'I suppose so,' Charles sighed wearily. 'I just thought it might explain a few things.'

'Aye, and if we could prove it, it would, but unfortunately we can't ... Not yet, anyway. So in the meantime we'll just carry on and see where it leads us.'

'When are you seeing her again?'

111

'I'm on my way to her now. It'll be interesting to hear what she dreams up this time.'

'Well … keep me informed.'

'Will do. See you later, Charles.'

Chapter 11

POMPEII, AD 79

Emperor Vespasian's ten-year reign was coming to an end, but no one could have guessed that in those first few months of 79. He had patronised the arts, reformed the army and began building the great Coliseum in Rome, but he was getting old now and his days were numbered, the ambitious who coveted his power busy plotting and scheming their own advancement at his demise.

The citizens of Rome had never had it so good and there was wine and food in plenty, a time of peace when they could enjoy the fruits of their labours, safe behind their strong walls and conquering armies, rulers of the world and the recipients of homage from all corners of the far-flung empire. The suburbs and countryside also basked in the glory of Rome, and vast villas and estates dotted the hills or vied for space within view of the Bay of Naples. The slopes of Vesuvius were a rich mixture of farmland, vaulted mansions and grazing cattle that overlooked the twin towns of Pompeii and Herculaneum in the valley below.

Gaius Vorteus had not been slow to recognise the merits of Pompeii and he had moved his family from the congestion of Rome many years before when property was cheap and the choices were many, taking his pick from a hundred prime sites and securing for himself a palatial villa on the edge of the town where he was close enough to conduct his business, yet far enough away to escape the stench of the privy ducts from the mass of humanity below. He was a cloth merchant by trade, slowly expanding his influence until he owned his own fleet of ships, and nothing gave him greater pleasure than to stand on the slopes of his estate and watch his vessels enter the bay, carrying the cargo that would find its way into the finest houses of Rome and beyond and making him infinitely richer in the process.

Thirty years before, he had met and married the beautiful Veronia, a noble Senator's daughter, and the following year she bore him a son, the sickly Parlian, whom Gaius hoped might die of his ills before he reached puberty. That the child not only lived but seemed to prosper and thrive was a constant source of amazement to Gaius, and to his dying day he wondered at the sudden transformation in the boy when he was but five years old.

Had Gaius taken the trouble to ask his son he might have learned the answer, but he died in ignorance when Parlian was seventeen and he went to his grave none the wiser about his son's change of fortune.

It has to be admitted that Parlian's early years were beset with illnesses and a wearisome lethargy that left him sullen and morose, and to alleviate his precocious nature he developed a spiteful and vindictive streak that had the slaves and servants cowering in fear before he'd even reached his fourth birthday.

By the time he was five, little Parlian was almost out of control, striding about the villa like Gaius himself and issuing orders to all and sundry with no thought to their practicality or consequences, and even the most slow-witted of slaves found it prudent to avoid the screaming brat of a child and seek a place to hide for safety until the horror had passed.

Finding no one to castigate one bright afternoon, Parlian made his way to the kitchens, where he surprised the terrified staff with his sudden appearance, pounding the

114

flagstones with his wooden sword and making them leap back in alarm.

'Idlers,' he ranted 'Menfolk hiding with the washerwomen and cooks to escape your duties! You, Guriat. Should you not be attending my father's horse? And you, woman …' he jabbed his sword at a sallow-skinned field slave. 'Why do you stand and stare? Have you no work in the gardens today?'

She cowered back, fear in her eyes, and as she did so a young girl, no older than Parlian himself, stepped from behind her mother's skirts and stood square-on to the young firebrand, eye to eye as she viewed him with a quiet calmness that left him deflated and ill at ease. She reached out a tiny hand and her finger touched the dark mole on the side of his neck, the one shaped like a dog, and then she frowned.

Parlian blinked at her, totally mesmerised by the way her brows came together on the bridge of her nose, his eyes flicking trance-like to the birthmark on her left temple, then without a word he opened his tunic to reveal a similar scar on his chest, drinking her in as she gazed at him silently. They seemed to hold the moment for an eternity, each totally absorbed in the other, then the girl held out her hand and Parlian dropped the mock sword in a clatter of wood on stone before taking her hand in his and leading her up to the sunlit courtyard above.

Her name was Shera and she was daughter to the slave woman from Gaul known as Nadia. She had been born on the estate five years before, after her mother was raped by a Roman centurion following her capture. Nadia was four months pregnant when Gaius bought her from the market in Herculaneum, reasoning that he would have two slaves for the price of one, and she was sent to work in the fields, where she barely paused to give birth before tending the vines once more, her thighs awash with mucus and gore and the bloodied infant strapped to her back.

Like Parlian, Shera was a sickly child, which was

115

understandable considering the nature of her birth, and her stick-thin frame seemed to wander like a wraith amid the elders, eating little and saying even less as she clung to a tenuous life in the harsh world of servitude and serfdom. But as with Parlian, that chance meeting in the bowels of the villa was to change her life for ever, and from that day she began to fill out and grow, her character altering from quiet subservience to gay abandon just as Parlian changed from a surly brute to a considerate and sensitive young man, each complementing the other like two halves of the same coin, forever together as they prospered and grew.

Parlian immediately had Shera transferred to the upper quarters where they could play uninterrupted, and she quickly became his confidante and his friend, sharing all the things they enjoyed to the exclusion of all others in the blossoming bonds that bound them irrevocably together. He taught her Latin and later Greek, imparting his knowledge as fast as he absorbed it himself, and when he was taught to play the harp he showed her also, watching intently as her delicate fingers plucked lightly at the strings. They roamed the fields and the streets together, exploring the world around them with growing wonder, each discovery made all the more delightful by the presence of the other, and it was a fatalistic inevitability that they should fall in love, the merchant's heir and the slave girl, one heart and one mind in perpetual union.

'Yet for all we express it, Parlian,' Shera murmured one afternoon as they lounged on the slopes of Vesuvius when they were barely in their teenage years, 'ours is a hopeless love. For all that we might wish it to be different, I am a slave and a betrothal cannot exist between us.'

'I will set you free, Shera,' he promised solemnly. 'When I am old enough to govern my own household, I shall take you in and free you.'

'I am your father's slave, Parlian, and he will not give me to you lightly.'

'Then I shall pay for you. However much the price, Shera, you will be mine.'

'And you would set me free?'

He hesitated and she grinned impishly, tickling his nose with a barley stalk as she crouched at his side.

'I guessed it,' she laughed. 'You would forever hold me as a slave just so I might do your bidding.'

'No, Shera,' he said earnestly. 'I would never use you in that way. But ...'

'But?'

'But ... if I were to free you, you might take your leave and I would never set eyes on you again. Would I chance that? Would I gamble losing you in return for your freedom?'

'Parlian ...' She gazed at him seriously, all her love and intent mirrored in her dark eyes. 'Were you to free me or shackle me to the wall of your villa, the outcome would be the same—I would be here for you. Free me or not, I go nowhere without you.'

'In that case I will free you,' he decided with a nod. 'Then we shall be betrothed.'

'And I shall bear you lots of children.'

'Of course,' he laughed. 'You will be known in Pompeii as the pregnant woman who lives on the hill, the wife of the merchant Parlian, who is envied by everyone for possessing such a beautiful wife.'

'Ah, you turn my head,' she blushed. 'It is I who shall be envied for having such a considerate and thoughtful man at my side ... even if he does simply use me to breed his children.'

'Never that, Shera,' he shook his head. 'Loved and honoured, but never used as a brood mare. I swear it.'

'And I believe you. Come, it is hot and I can hear a stream

117

nearby. Let us drink and cool our toes in the water before I melt in the heat.'

'Race you there,' he said eagerly, clambering to his feet and straightening his tunic, and they streaked across the field, whooping and laughing with the sheer joy of youth, stride for stride beneath the relentless Mediterranean sun.

Gaius died when Parlian was seventeen, a damp sea chill reaching his lungs until he could scarcely breathe, propped in his bed and coughing up blood in a never-ending torrent that left him debilitated and weak, his heart giving out mercifully after fifteen days and dispatching his soul to eternal rest and peace. They buried him in the family mausoleum in the town, Parlian holding the arm of his mother, Veronia, and supporting her through the dark days, the weight of his father's business resting squarely on his young shoulders. But he neither faltered nor complained, assuming the mantle as head of the house with hardly a pause, bearing the responsibility with a maturity and a quiet confidence that belied his tender years.

'We need to discuss the slaves, Mother,' he said when the period of mourning was over. 'We have far more than we know what to do with.'

'One can never have too many slaves, Parlian,' she murmured softly. 'Would you sell them all and have us tend the fields ourselves?'

'We possess more than enough to attend all our needs and the others are barely gainfully employed. Whether they are profitable or not, they still have to be fed.'

'What do you intend to do, then, Parlian? Sell them at market?'

'I thought … I thought as a gesture in memory of Father we might …'

'Yes?'

'Free some of them.'

She blinked at him.

'Free them?'

'Not all of them, Mother. Just a select few.'

'A few?'

'Yes … in honour of Father.'

'I see.' She nodded slowly. 'And how many are you planning to free?'

'Oh, I thought five or six.'

'And have you anyone particular in mind?'

'Well, Guriat is past his best, and Lengor, the cattleman, has served us well since before I was born.'

'Anyone else?'

'The field woman, Nadia, and her daughter perhaps.'

'Ah.'

'What does "Ah" mean?'

'It means, Parlian, that we have come to the bones of the matter. It is Shera you wish to free and you disguise the fact with noble intentions of your father's memory.'

'The result is the same,' he argued patiently. 'A number of slaves set free as a gesture of goodwill.'

'As long as Shera is one of them.'

It was a statement, flatly spoken, and Parlian shrugged, feeling the colour rise to his cheeks.

'She is no more a slave to me than you are, Mother,' he said quietly. 'It has always been so.'

'I fail to think why. She is but a Gallic whore's offspring with who knows who for a father and she is a slave into the bargain. Yet I know how much she means to you. What will you do when she is gone from you, Parlian?'

'She will not go,' he said with certainty. 'She will stay here with me.'

'I see. Tell me, do you simply seek comfort in your bed or do you aspire to greater things?'

'If I wanted a slave for my bed, Mother …' He left the

119

sentence unfinished, shaking his head in annoyance, and Veronia laughed incredulously.

'You want more than that? You would elevate her to your side, Parlian? My, how your father would find amusement in your stupidity. Shera is a slave girl, Parlian, and always will be. Look to the women of the town or noble daughters if you seek more than a bed companion.'

'I need to look no further than these very walls to find all that I seek, Mother. All that I ever wanted is to be found in Shera.'

'You think so?' Veronia scoffed. 'Does she know how to entertain senators and noblemen? Can she converse with highborn womenfolk and discuss anything but the tending of goats or how to harvest a crop of corn? Does she know how to dress or how to conduct herself in noble company? Will she assist you in your work, Parlian, or will she make you the laughing stock of the whole town? You are thinking with your heart and not your head. Consider again, Parlian, I beseech you. Keep her for your bed by all means, but take another as your wife.'

'I want no other than Shera,' he insisted adamantly. 'She is all and more than I could ever wish for.'

'Now, perhaps, Parlian, while you are young and head-strong, but pause to think of the future. Who would you rather have to promote your cause with senators and nobles? A highborn woman of quality, or the bastard daughter of a Gallic slave?'

'I can promote my own cause and need no woman to speak on my behalf,' he said hotly. 'Like it or not, Mother, I will free Shera and take her for my wife.'

'Then all your father's efforts have been in vain, for you will destroy his business and be the ruin of us all.'

Despite Veronia's prophetic words of doom, Parlian's marriage to Shera led to neither catastrophe nor ruination

120

and the cloth trade he had inherited flourished over the next twelve years, with profits soaring to greater heights and new markets opening up as the Empire expanded. Shera bore him two sons and three daughters during that time, the villa on the hill ringing with children's laughter, and for all Veronia's initial objections she doted on her grandchildren to the exclusion of all others, forever in their company and delighting in their sweet innocence and affable nature.

Vespasian had been emperor since 69, but since his recent death Titus now ruled the Empire, and Rome's finances had never been better, every citizen benefiting after years of sound government, and Parlian took full advantage of the booming economy by opening a store in the capital's most affluent sector and employing tailors to deal directly with the city's most wealthy and discerning patrons.

The Vorteus family prospered on the hill overlooking Pompeii and Herculaneum and, contrary to Veronia's misgivings, Shera proved to be an accomplished hostess at the lavish parties they gave at every opportunity, entertaining the Empire's rich and powerful with a natural ease that both surprised and delighted the devoted Parlian.

'You are my Queen of Sheba,' he said one August morning, making her laugh.

'And you are my King Solomon. Patient, kind and ever considerate to me.'

'To think … if I had not gone to the kitchens that day, I might never have met you.'

'Oh, I think our paths would have crossed at some point, Parlian. You might have seen me in the fields and had me whipped for slacking in my work.'

'Never,' he laughed. 'You would never slack and I would never have you whipped. Your flesh is far too precious to me to have it torn under the lash.'

'Well, I have to admit you are as patient with the slaves as you are with me. I have never known you yet to raise your fist or your staff at our people. We are all fortunate that it is you who govern this house.'

'I am the fortunate one, Shera,' he said seriously. 'You are my light and my life.'

'Aah, I love you so, my lord and master, Parlian. The gods and the Fates smiled down on me the day you came into my world.'

'And took you from the kitchens to a splendid apartment,' he grinned, and she poked him playfully in the ribs.

'And stopped you from terrorising the whole household, you mean,' she quipped. 'Someone had to stand up to you.'

'Yet who would think it would be you? Skinny waif that you were, as I recall.'

'Skinny waif or not, I had the measure of you. You just wanted a little friend to occupy you.'

'And you have done so ever since! Come, Shera. We will pack treats for the children and eat in the fields. What say you?'

'I say you have forgotten we are to dine in Pompeii today, Parlian. Quiglus Antimus is hosting a party to mark the birth of another son.'

'Oh, yes. I had put it from my mind.'

'I know you hate the town, my love, but the children are looking forward to it and it will do you no harm to drink a wine or two in honour of the newborn. Besides, have you seen how Vesuvius smokes today? We would be choked to death if we sat in the fields. It is like a witches' cauldron out there.'

'No doubt you are right, as always.'

'You know it ... Now, Luciana has laid a fresh toga for you on the bed, so once you are ready we will be gone.'

'Are you not changing?'

'Mmm.' she nodded. 'I had Sagramin fashion me the most wonderful garment from the batch of Persian silk you imported last week. I will change once I have seen to the children.'

'If you came to our chamber now ...'

'Yes?'

'Well ... we could change together.'

'Ah. You wish to see my surprise as soon as I put it on?'

'Not exactly, Shera ... I was hoping to see you *before* you put it on.'

'We have little time, Parlian. We are expected at the house of Quiglus very soon.'

'I had not planned on needing much time,' Parlian smirked, and Shera smiled knowingly.

'Is it fast and furious you want, my love? Very well, then. Give me a moment to check on the children and I will join you in our chamber. Get aroused and ready for me.'

'Always that, Shera,' he murmured lovingly. 'Always that for you.'

The house of Quiglus Antimus hugged the wall of Minerva's temple, a sprawling villa with secluded courtyards alive with the tinkle of fountains and bedecked with trailing plants and vines, urns and statues taking up every available space in the marbled halls, the high columns festooned with bunting and flowers to mark the festive occasion. A large number of guests had already made themselves at home by the time Parlian and his family arrived at the porticoed entrance and they could hear children's excited laughter and the buzz of murmuring adult voices as they greeted their host and his elegant wife, Turana, now fully recovered from the birth of her latest son.

They joined the throng in the outer courtyard, sipping wine as they eyed the smouldering summit of Vesuvius, the flying sparks and hiss of white steam adding to the party atmosphere as though the very gods had added their weight to the celebrations.

'A pretty show, Quiglus,' Parlian grinned. 'I always believed you had the ear of the gods.'

'And I always believed Turana was blessed by them,' the wine merchant grinned. 'Now I know for sure.'

'Some said it was not to be trusted,' Shera remarked, waving her goblet at the billowing clouds. 'I have seen several leave the town in a panic today. Are we quite safe, do you think, Quiglus?'

'Quite, quite safe, my dear,' he smiled. 'It is but the rumblings of a dissatisfied mountain and no more than we mere mortals experience after a night of feasting.'

'Yet were Parlian to belch such noxious fumes after a night of feast, I would be wise to show concern for his health.'

'She worries about me,' Parlian chuckled. 'Do not fret so, Shera. If the Governor of Pompeii sees fit to remain in the town I am sure we are in no danger.'

'And should the need arise,' Quiglus added with a nod, 'we can retreat to one of Parlian's ships and make our escape by sea.'

'Of course,' Parlian said magnanimously. 'We shall continue our party on board.'

'The smoke thickens,' a voice said behind them, and they turned to watch as the steam changed to curling black smoke that hung suspended against the blue of the sky, an ominous cloud that brooded over the valley like a disapproving father.

Ash had begun to fall, layering the streets in a thick mantle, and they retreated from the courtyard into the house, closing the doors against the noxious fumes and swirling ash that made the outer air unbearable and impossible to breath.

'Perhaps we should return home,' Shera said anxiously, but Quiglus would not hear of it.

'Nonsense,' he boomed. 'The smoke is thicker on the hill than it is in the city. It will pass soon enough and you are as well to remain here than to fight your way through it. Come, my friends. Drink up. I refuse to let the mountain ruin this day.'

Yet the day was already ruined, turned dark as evening by the gathering mass of ash and pumice that filled the sky and lay twenty inches thick on the paved streets. They could hear small stones and debris clattering onto the roof, spewed forth from the billowing volcano, adding to the weight of ash that rained down in a never-ending torrent, and the revellers became increasingly concerned as the roof beams creaked beneath the weight as larger and heavier rocks joined the storm. Within the hour ten feet of ash, pumice, stones, rocks and debris made escape impossible, piled high against the doors and barring the exits, the streets an inferno of scorching heat that tortured the lungs with every breath.

'Where are the children?' Shera said, looking about her in sudden fear. 'We must get out, Parlian.'

'We are safer in here than outside, Shera.' Parlian reached for her hand, squeezing the fingers tightly. 'I am sure you worry over nothing.'

'IS THAT NOTHING?' Shera screeched, and all eyes turned to the raging flames that flared like lightning flashes, illuminating the spouting smoke clouds as if the very air was on fire.

The buildings shook, great tremors rocking the foundations beneath their feet, and someone screamed as a marble statue shook free of its anchor and tumbled in a crash of broken masonry.

'By the gods, look.' Parlian stared in awe as an avalanche of lava spewed from the mountain and hurtled down on Herculaneum below, engulfing the town in the blinking of an eye. Then panic set in and the shrieks and screams rose to fever pitch as the building trembled once more, shaking and juddering as though the bowels of the earth were stirring. Then a mighty explosion turned day into night as millions of tons of molten ash rained down upon them, suffocating and crushing and sealing twenty thousand people in its searing embrace for ever.

And in the house of Quiglus Antimus the roof finally collapsed under the awesome weight, and five thousand tons of ash and pumice and stones and tiles and rafters engulfed and obliterated the partygoers below.

Chapter 12

The silence was a palpable thing, a tangible force that was felt by both Charles and Leon as the tape ground to a halt, a mind-numbing silence that seemed to mushroom and grow with each passing second until it became almost unbearable, and Charles cleared his throat with difficulty, forcing his limbs to move as he stirred in his seat.

'One mind. One heart,' he whispered fearfully, quoting a long-dead high priest. 'Together in life, together in death.'

'It's ...' Leon swallowed hard and tried again. 'It's a nonsense, of course.'

'Is it?' Charles said wearily. 'Somehow, Leon, I don't think it is.'

'It has to be.'

'The two birthmarks? The mole? Eyebrows that meet in the middle when she frowns?'

'Appearance fixation. She has those traits set in her mind and she can't let go of them. Hence their reoccurrence in every dream.'

'Dream?' Charles stared at him. 'You call them dreams?'

'What else would you call them?'

'Past experiences.'

'It's too pat ... too simple.'

'So why has it got to be complicated? Why look for deeper meanings when the simple truth is staring us in the face?'

'Because we don't know if it *is* the truth, Charles,' Leon

pointed out softly. 'They could be the product of an overactive imagination.'

'But these … these stories are so vivid. The names … the cultures … the very essence of Roman life spelled out for us. Surely that goes beyond an overactive imagination?'

'Perhaps.'

'And it was the same for the Babylon thing, wasn't it? And the Egyptian beginning? Christ, I could almost feel Ki-Un-Rah breathing down my neck.'

'You're too impressionable,' Leon remarked, reaching to remove the tape from the machine. 'In this line of business, Charles, you have to remain detached … remote. You're taking everything at face value without question or doubt and becoming worked up in the process. Not everything is as it first appears, you know, laddie.'

'But a lot of things are. This reeks of reincarnation, and you know it.'

'I know no such thing,' Leon said stiffly. 'I might guess at it or presume it, but that's a world away from *knowing* it. Knowledge only comes with detailed study and scientific analysis, and so far I've done neither. It's too soon to jump to conclusions, Charles, and we must both be patient until we know where it's all leading.'

Charles sighed and sat back in his seat, a thousand questions resounding in his head.

'Has Marion heard that yet?' he asked quietly, nodding at the tape, and Leon shook his head.

'Not yet—but like the other times, she's got a pretty good idea what it contains.'

'When are you seeing her?'

'Tomorrow. I thought she should rest until then.'

'Then what? Try again? Bring her forward a bit more in time?'

'I'm trying to reach the present, Charles, but it's taking longer than I anticipated.'

'Yeah, well.' Charles rubbed his eyes tiredly. 'I think it's taking longer than anyone anticipated. This one could run and run, couldn't it? I mean … if it is a reincarnation thing, how many appearances have we missed in between times? You know—between Egypt and Babylon, or between five thirty-nine BC and seventy-nine AD? There could have been dozens.'

'That's true … if it's a reincarnation thing.'

'Which you don't believe.'

'I'm keeping an open mind, Charles. The human brain is too intricate to simply jump at the first obvious choice. We have to remain objective and detached. It's the only way forward.'

'So when's the next session?'

'Not for a fortnight.' Leon smiled apologetically. 'I'm off on holiday to Malta at the weekend.'

'Perhaps I'll see if I can dig up any more information while you're away … see if we can throw some more light on Marion's depressed state.'

'Aye, well,' Leon came to his feet, 'Best of luck. I'll see you when I get back.'

'Right.' Charles shook his hand. 'Have a good holiday.'

'Marion, are you all right? Marion? Breathe … Breathe, dammit … Take a breath … That's good.' Leon relaxed in his chair, the sudden worry lines disappearing from his forehead as Marion took a whooping gulp of air. 'That's better. I was quite concerned there for a moment. That's the end of the tape so you can relax now.'

'I …' She stared at him blankly. 'I couldn't breath. The choking ash … I could feel it. Hot … burning … it was everywhere … no escape … as though it filled the room. Smothering … burying … so much of it.'

'You're all right now,' he soothed. 'It was just auto-suggestion brought on by the tape.'

'Was it? It felt so real—suffocating me … crushing me.'

'You could actually feel it?'

'Oh, yes,' she said with certainty. 'It was so black. I couldn't find Parlian ... or the children. All gone, Professor ... all gone in a matter of seconds when the roof caved in.'

Together in life, together in death. Leon thought of Charles' irrational reasoning, believing that the characters of Moona and Nedemin returned again and again, like lost spirits wandering aimlessly through time, sharing everything together, even the moment of death, and he shuddered as if a chill wind had reached out and touched his soul.

'You can remember it?' he ventured carefully, and Marion gave a little shrug, her narrow shoulders barely moving the coverlet.

'It's like ... like you remember a dream when you wake up in the morning ... never quite sure where the real bit ends and the unreal takes over.'

'So what *can* you remember?'

'Standing there ... a goblet in my hand ... Parlian's shocked face. Then a tremendous weight seemed to land on top of me and it all went black. There were seconds, fractions of time when sensations were still felt ... as though the body was dead but the mind took a bit longer ... clinging to life. And I felt very hot—not like you do on a summer's day, but ... extremely hot ... like I was in an oven being baked alive ... and my mouth was full of ash. I could taste the sulphur ... and I couldn't breathe. There was no air left around me ... every last particle of space taken up by the ash. So much of it ... tons of it. Then there was nothing.'

Leon didn't know what to say. Even overactive imaginations had their limits.

'What were your children's names?' he asked suddenly, and Marion didn't even pause for thought.

'Marcus, Theonus, Gurian, Portea and little Tibby. Her name was Tiberana, but we called her Tibby. Such lovely children. Such a shame they had to die like that—no mother to comfort them or take their hand to still their fears. It's just as well it was quick.'

'Do you remember it as fact, like you remember your childhood or how you met Terry, or do you remember it like you remember a dream, sort of hazy and vague?'

'A bit of both, really,' she murmured softly. 'It's hazy and vague, but I know it's a fact … I *feel* it.'

'Dreams can be very powerful, you know. They can appear so real, you'd swear they were true.'

'I know that … It's a bit like …' She frowned thoughtfully. 'It's a bit like when you remember some things about when you were very young—you sort of half-remember. You know they happened to you, but you can't quite put your finger on it.'

'An elusive memory.'

'Yes. But I thought that's why we were doing the hypnosis thing—to bring the memories to light so they're not elusive anymore.'

'Aye, well, that's the theory.'

'You don't believe me, do you?' she said flatly. 'You think I'm making it all up.'

'And are you?'

'No. What's the point of doing all this if you're not going to believe me?'

'It's not a question of belief, Marion,' Leon said forcibly. 'Like I said before, the mind is a very complex structure. It can make us believe in all sorts of strange things, but just because you believe it doesn't make it true. It's what leads people to think they hear voices telling them what to do, or makes a person think they're Napoleon Bonaparte. They believe it utterly, but it's all nonsense.'

'Was it put to the test?'

'Was what put to the test?'

'The person who thought he was Napoleon? Was he regressed like me?'

131

'I don't know.'

'And if he was, would he have been able to describe every battle, every campaign, just as it happened? Would he be able to tell you what his generals looked like? Would he be able to describe to you exactly how he felt when he was being shipped to Elba or what he had to eat when he got there?'

'Of course not,' Leon smiled indulgently. 'It's an illusion, a misconception ... a state of mind that makes him believe something that isn't true.'

'Not like me, then?'

'I don't know ...'

'Because when you take me back in time I can remember everything exactly as it was and I can describe it in fine detail. So there's a difference, isn't there?'

'Marion,' he said earnestly, 'I don't know your history. I don't know your likes and dislikes. I don't know what your interests are or what books you've read or the television programmes you've watched. So let me paint a picture for you ... present you with a hypothetical scenario. At the age of five, you go to Sunday school and the teacher mentions Babylon. Three years later, in a totally different context, someone mentions the name Darius. Two years later there's a programme on television about the ancient city itself. You're not particularly interested, but you can't make yourself not listen, and unknown to you, your mind absorbs the information. Six years later you read an article in the newspaper about some Persian artefacts being found on the site of old Babylon. Once again, you're not really interested, but the information still goes in and gets stored away. So now we come to the present day and I put you in a trance and take your mind back to the past, and hey presto it all comes together, all those pieces of useless information coupled with an active imagination that weaves a feasible story around the facts, a story that can neither be proved or disproved—and it seems real. Just like a vivid dream, you can convince yourself

132

it actually happened. It's what the mind is capable of Marion, and we must never lose sight of that.'

'I knew about the water ducts,' she said obstinately. 'It's how the Persians got in.'

'Information received along the way,' he shrugged lightly. 'The same can be said for all of it.'

'Darius was killed. How did I know that?'

'Who says Darius was killed, Marion? Who says Darius even existed?'

'I was there. He was a commander of the Royal Guard and he was killed.'

'Well, since you told me that story I went to the library and looked it up. It's true that King Nabonidus fled the city, but the Persians were pretty lenient on the townspeople and they were left pretty much alone. Now if you'd heard the same thing, you'd also know that the king's son, Belshazzar, was killed during the Persian attack. It's a pretty safe bet to guess that some of the Royal Guard whose job it was to protect him were also killed, so your mind puts Darius in the forefront of the fighting, protecting their prince, and you have the perfect solution to the problem. Like I say, a feasible story can be invented to fit the facts.'

'I don't ...'

'What?'

'I don't want it to be a dream ... I want it to be real.'

'Of course you do. Just the same as we'd like the dreams of being a millionaire to be real, or the ones where we're irresistible to the opposite sex, or we're rich and powerful ... but unfortunately, life's not like that and that's all they are ... dreams.'

'But ... but I gain nothing by any of it, do I?'

'What do you mean?'

'Well ... what do I gain by inventing the story? How am I better off if it was real? There's no purpose to it, is there?'

'Something has deeply upset you—so deeply that it led to a

133

depressed state of mind that views suicide as the only option. For some reason, Marion, you've lost the will to live and we're trying to discover what that reason is.'

'And you think it's all linked to these ... dreams? These stories I'm supposedly inventing?'

'It's possible.' He smiled brightly. 'And when we get to the end, we'll know.'

'And cure me?'

'That's the plan. Half the battle is recognising the problem and coming to terms with it.'

She sighed wearily and closed her eyes, the images of Egypt, Babylon and Pompeii so clearly etched in her mind that they could have happened yesterday, all the emotion and fear, all the sights and sounds just as real as the hospital room around her, and for all Professor Macleod's cautionary words, she believed in them implicitly—they were as much a part of her life as her parents and her childhood and the solid warmth of Terry Newell.

'When ... when are you regressing me again?'

'Not for a couple of weeks, I'm afraid.' He shrugged apologetically. 'I'm away on holiday for a fortnight.'

'Oh ... holiday ... I sort of forgot that ...'

'That the world's still turning and people are getting on with their lives?' He smiled gently. 'That's understandable considering the circumstances. I expect Doctor Levingron will be in to see you during my absence, so if anything's bothering you ...'

'Yes ... I'll speak to him.'

'Right then, I'll be off. Don't worry about anything and just try and relax. We'll carry on when I get back.'

Then he was gone and Marion was left with confused thoughts of ancient rites, Persian guile and the acrid stench of sulphurous ash falling like torrential rain and blotting out everything she held dear.

Chapter 13

'Terry?'

'Yes.'

'It's Charles Levington,' he said into the phone. 'How's everything going?'

'Oh, you know. Okay, I guess. Is this about Marion? Nothing's happened, has it?'

'No, no. Everything's fine. There have been no developments.'

'I see. Well …'

'Professor Macleod's away for a few weeks so I thought I'd see if I can fill in more of the background before he returns.'

'Well, I think I told you everything when you came to see me. I haven't thought of anything new.'

'That's okay. Listen, Marion's brother. What was his name? Ron?'

'That's right. What about him?'

'I thought he might be able to tell me something.'

'It's possible, I suppose, but I doubt it. We must've gone over it a dozen times together since this all started and he's just as confused by it as I am.'

'Pity,' Charles sighed. 'I was hoping to learn something about Marion's childhood.'

'Well, Ron's only a year older than Marion so it's not as if he was in a position to have noticed anything unusual. He'd have mentioned it to me if he had. There's an aunt, though. Ron said she's always been close to the family.'

'Oh?' Charles flipped through Carmel Douglas's notes. 'Ah, yes, lives in Devon.'

'Cornwall, actually I think she was a bit of a black sheep in her day. Skeletons in closets and all that. They don't talk about her much.'

'I see. Will she speak to me, do you think?'

'I'm sure she'd do anything to help Marion, Doctor Levington. She phones me now and again to find out what's going on. She's got multiple sclerosis and is confined to a wheelchair. That's why she hasn't been in to see Marion. I've been keeping her updated on things.'

Was that how he'd managed to breach Marion's defences that first time? Charles wondered to himself, that time when he mentioned the sick and the lame who still found a reason to live? He'd struck closer to home than he'd realised.

'How's the aunt taken it?'

'She's very concerned and wishes she could be here.'

'Perhaps I'll drive down and have a word with her.'

'It's best if you phone her first, Doctor. If she's having a bad day you'll have wasted your time.'

Fowey was a cluster of buildings hugging the river and the sweep of the hill, the old and the new sitting comfortably side by side above the little harbour, the jetty alive with fishing vessels and pleasure boats and the air filled with the plaintive cry of wheeling gulls that gave the place an ageless quality as though time had stood still and bypassed this tiny corner of the world completely.

Charles left his car in Bodinnick and caught the ferry across, then walked up the hill to Number 38, enjoying the afternoon sunshine and the weather-beaten look of the grizzled fishermen in their high boots and turtleneck sweaters, true Englishmen at one with their surroundings. He rang the bell and waited, hearing the whirr of an electric wheelchair in the hall, then the front door opened and he peered down at the woman before him, an older, shrunken version of Marion who appraised him frankly as he stepped inside.

The house was tastefully decorated in a style more associated with the older generation with pale shades on the walls and chintz curtains at the windows, vases of freshly cut flowers on the side and a lack of furniture to allow wheelchair access in the tight confines, modern needs pressing shoulder to shoulder with a yen for the past.

'Doctor Levington,' she smiled. 'Good of you to come. Please go through and sit down.'

'Call me Charles,' he nodded, stepping into the sparse sitting room and finding a vacant armchair. 'It was good of you to see me at such short notice, Miss Harting.'

'Rosalind,' she acknowledged with a wave of her hand. 'Roz … Cup of tea?'

'Lovely. Thank you very much.'

She disappeared into the kitchen and Charles studied the photographs above the fireplace, a picture of Marion and Terry, another of Marion as a child and several depicting groups of people with an older man who Charles assumed was Marion's father, smiling faces and sparkling eyes that knew nothing of the nightmares to come, bliss discovered in ignorance of a future only half guessed at.

'Milk and sugar, Charles?' Roz called, and he shook himself as though coming awake, returning to the present with a bump.

'Yes, please, Roz—one sugar.'

He heard the rattle of cups and the whistle of the kettle and in no time at all Rosalind joined him, passing him a full cup and positioning her wheelchair where she could face him, eyeing him through the steam as she sipped her tea slowly.

'So how is Marion, Charles?' she asked softly. 'I speak to Terry on the phone, but I'm not so sure I'm getting the full picture.'

137

'Well, I can't say it's an easy case, Roz, You must understand I'm only dealing directly with her broken limbs, but I'm working in close consultation with Professor Macleod, who's treating her other problems.'

'The suicide attempts?' she sighed heavily. 'Do they know what's making her behave like that?'

'Not yet. That's partly why I'm here. I was hoping you could throw some light on her present behaviour.'

'Well, I have to admit I've given it a lot of thought these past few months. The truth is …' she shrugged helplessly, 'I can't think of anything that'd make her behave like that. I know she could be a bit strange at times, but not *that* strange. Not strange enough to suddenly start becoming suicidal.'

'What was her childhood like?'

'Pretty much like anyone else's. She did well at school …'

'But she was never any trouble?'

'Not at all. I remember Archie, Janice and me talking about it—that's Marion's parents. Archie's my brother. They were quite worried about her at first, you know, when she was very young. She appeared to be preoccupied somehow … as if she was waiting for something to happen, sort of looking about her as if she expected someone else to be there, but she seemed to grow out of that after a while.'

'When you say she seemed preoccupied, what exactly do you mean?'

'It's hard to say exactly … Marion wasn't their only child so they had a reasonable idea what to expect, but those first few months she cried incessantly and they didn't know what to do for the best. In the end she seemed to grow out of it, but she was never interested in toys, she just didn't want to know. She was perfectly content to just lie in her pram and watch the world go by. She used to study every new face that came along, and they used to laugh at the way she inspected them, frowning that funny frown of hers. Later, when she got a bit older, she used to spend hours at the window, just looking out as though it fascinated her, and I remember Archie and Janice talking to the doctor about it, you know, saying how concerned they were that she wasn't like other kids and spent so much time on her own.'

'What did the doctor say?'

'Not a lot.' Roz shrugged. 'The opinion was that as long as she was healthy and was eating all right, there was nothing to worry about. It was just a phase that she'd grow out of in time.'

'*Was* she eating all right?'

'She had her fads,' Roz smiled fondly. 'Tell me what kid doesn't? But some weeks she'd eat like a horse and the next she'd hardly touch a thing. It didn't seem to do her any harm, though. She was strong and healthy enough.'

'But she eventually grew out of all that?'

'Mmm,' Roz nodded. 'She was always quiet and sort of withdrawn, but she was a happy kid generally. There was just ...'

'What?'

'I don't know. It's hard to pin down precisely ... It was as if she was patiently waiting for something. As if she'd thought something through and had settled down to wait. It was uncanny really. Sort of eerie.'

'In what way?'

'I can't say exactly.' Roz shook her head, peering at him over the rim of her cup. 'Archie changed his job when she was four and they moved to Middlesex. They thought that might upset her seeing as she was always sat at the window like that, but she took it all in her stride and she couldn't get enough of the new place once they moved, looking into every nook and cranny until she'd inspected everything, then she settled down to wait again, sort of poised as if she was constantly listening out for something. It gave me the creeps sometimes. Before I developed MS, I used to stay with the family quite a lot and sometimes I used to go up and tuck her in of a night, but no matter what time it was, she was always awake, her eyes opening the second I walked into the room. She'd sort of eye me up and down as if she was inspecting me, then she'd go back to sleep again.'

'What about when she was older? A teenager?'

'She'd pretty much grown out of it all by then. She was normal enough, I suppose, but she was never any bother. She never stayed out late and always did what she was told—what we used to call a good girl.'

'Boyfriends?'

'One or two,' Roz nodded. 'I think Janice and Archie would have been more worried if there weren't any. She joined the chess club at school and got friendly with a boy called Clifford something. I can't remember his last name. Anyway, Marion went out with him for a year or two then it all fizzled out.'

'Did that bother her?'

'Losing Clifford?' Roz shook her head. 'No. It was Marion who finished it, I believe. Something about how boring he was and she wanted more out of life. You know what kids are like?'

'Mmm. I do. So what happened after that?'

'She got a job in Smith's, the newsagents, when she left school, and she met a boy called Robert Gill. She went out with him for about two years altogether and they seemed to get on all right, although I was never really struck on him. He had one of those horrible laughs that really grate on you after a while, but Marion seemed to like him.'

'Why did they split up?'

'He joined the RAF and they never saw each other from one week to the next. In the end it was easier to break up than carry on like they were.'

Charles drained his cup and stared at the ceiling thoughtfully, seeking a pattern or something out of the ordinary, but apart from the distractions and preoccupations of her early years, Marion appeared perfectly normal, no

140

more and no less so than a million other young girls struggling to cope with all that life had to offer, school, work and boyfriends forming an integral part of growing up and developing in a modern world.

'What happened after Robert Gill?' he asked, and Rosalind smiled.

'She met someone else ... Colin Ette. Janice and Archie had emigrated to Canada by then and Marion and me were quite close. She used to tell me everything.'

'Go on.

'Colin was the one who ... He was the first boy she went to bed with. She was eighteen, almost nineteen, and that was about the time I was diagnosed with MS. I lived in London then and she was always coming round to see me.'

'Marion and Colin ... were they happy together?'

'At first they got on like a house on fire, but he was what they call a control-freak and he tried to run her life for her. They ended up rowing about it and they split up.'

It was all pretty ordinary really, Charles thought to himself. A young girl growing up, in and out of casual relationships until the right man came along. No different to countless others, so what was it that set her apart? What was it that had triggered the reaction to warrant suicide?

'What about Terry?' he asked after a moment. 'How does Marion get on with him?'

'Terry's lovely,' Roz grinned. 'Marion thinks the world of him. They're getting married, you know?'

'Mmm. I heard ... So what went wrong? When did it all change? There she was, an attractive young woman on the verge of marriage to someone she loves, and it all suddenly changes and she wants to end it all. It doesn't make sense.'

'She was all right until she changed her job,' Roz murmured. 'She was fine until then, if you ask me.'

'But she loved her job,' Charles frowned. 'At least she did until ...'

141

'Until what?'

'She was going on a girl's night out with someone from work and they went to the girl's house first … then something happened and Marion changed her mind and went home. She was never quite the same after that.'

'So what happened at the friend's house?'

'I don't know.' Charles shook his head slowly. 'But I'm going to find out.'

Chapter 14

Charles postponed contacting Linda Beavis at Wembley Arena until he'd had a chance to speak to Marion, wanting to sound her out first before he blundered in with no thought to the direction his enquiries might take, and he played his part casually by making nothing of it and quietly slipping his questions in as though he was simply passing the time of day during his normal rounds on Monday.

'Morning, Marion,' he smiled, studying her chart. 'How you feeling today?'

'Bored, miserable, and fed up with lying in bed all the time. Can't I at least sit in the chair?'

'If you promise to be on your best behaviour,' he said lightly, and she grunted.

He examined the plaster casts on her leg and arm, feeling her toes and fingers, then he nodded, satisfied with her progress.

'Good. We'll have you up and about in no time. It's not as if you've been in a war, is it?'

'No.'

'That must be awful, don't you think?'

'What must?'

'To be in a war … you know … fighting and stuff?'

She stared at him openly then she blinked, her eyebrows coming together in a slow frown.

'Have you heard the tapes Macleod's been taking?' she asked softly, and he glanced at her.

'The hypnosis sessions? Mmm. Leon thought I should hear them.'

'You know about … about Babylon, then?'

'The fight at the palace? Yes. I know about that.'

'Well …' She sighed heavily. 'You could say I've had first-hand experience of … "fighting and stuff".'

'I suppose so.' He smiled, keeping it light. 'But it's not like modern warfare is it? Not like it is today with guns and explosives and things?'

'That depends on your point of view, doesn't it?' she murmured dryly. 'Would you rather be shot, or hacked to death with a sword? A gun can be pretty impersonal, shooting someone who's hundreds of yards away, but with a sword or a spear … well … it's up close and personal, isn't it?'

'I see what you mean,' he nodded sombrely, catching her mood. 'It can't be very pleasant, can it?'

She didn't answer him, her eyes fixed to the ceiling, and he tried again, drawing her out as he felt his way forward slowly.

'I suppose, if you think about it, one war's pretty much as awful as another, isn't it?'

She shrugged. 'I suppose so.'

'I mean … the First World War had more than its share of horrors, but who's to say it was any more terrifying than the Trojan War? You could still end up dead, couldn't you?'

'Only the method of dying was different,' she said absently, and he nodded.

'Exactly. Take the Falklands conflict, for instance. It wasn't a massive war, but it still must've been horrendous for the people taking part, wouldn't you agree?'

'I … I'd rather not talk about that war, if you don't mind.'

'Why not?' He frowned at her. 'Wars are wars, aren't they?'

'I just … the Falklands was different.'

'Was it? In what way?'

'I don't know … It just was.'

'You must have a reason for thinking that. How was it any different to other wars?'

'I told you, I don't know.'

'Marion?' he peered at her intently. 'Please answer me. What makes the Falklands War any different to a thousand other conflicts? We went to war and people died ... Isn't that what always happens?'

'Leave me alone,' she said irritably. 'I don't know why it was different, but it was. All right? Now just ... just leave me alone.'

'It might do you good to talk about it.'

'Can you tell the nurse I want a bedpan, please?' she said, ignoring him, then she glared at him meaningfully, leaving him in no doubt she wanted to be alone.

'Sure,' he murmured softly. 'I didn't mean for you to get agitated ... I'll leave you to it.'

'Thanks.'

'I'll er ... I'll send the nurse in,' he ended lamely, then stepped quietly from the room.

'Miss Beavis? Linda? It's Doctor Levington. I came to see you at work the other week.'

'About Marion?'

'That's right. I wonder if you could spare me some more of your time?'

'I told you all l know, Doctor. There's nothing else to add.'

He was aware of the hesitation in her voice and he pressed on gamely. 'Well ... I'd like to give it a try. It just might help Marion in some way.'

'We're rather busy, but I could meet you for lunch somewhere.'

'I'm tied up at the hospital until this evening.' He paused for effect. 'Perhaps I could see you at home?'

'I don't know, I ...'

'It really might help Marion, Linda. It could be very important for her recovery.'

145

'It's not very convenient. We're in the middle of decorating at the moment.'

'I really would appreciate it, Linda. Half an hour, that's all.'

'All right,' she relented reluctantly. 'What time?'

'Seven?'

'That should be okay. I live in Derwent Road. Number sixteen.'

'I'll find it.' He smiled into the phone. 'Thanks again. I'll see you later.'

Sixteen Derwent Road was a two-up, two-down mid-terrace house that had seen better days, the brickwork beginning to crumble and the window frames rotten with age, but it was pleasant enough inside, with bright colours and modern furniture seemingly out of character with the pre-war façade, as though a time-warp had placed the two eras in the same period in a tongue-in-cheek attempt at humour.

Linda opened the door to his knock and Charles was ushered into the sitting room, the walls devoid of paper and the smell of paint pervading the air, strewn sheets protecting the carpet and a naked light bulb hanging from the ceiling. He sat in an armchair facing the window and Linda curled on the couch opposite him, her legs tucked beneath her as she studied him carefully.

'Like I said on the phone, Doctor,' she began when they were settled, 'I don't know what else I can say to you about Marion.'

'I seem to remember you saying that you wondered if Marion became upset about the Falklands, but when you asked her about it, she couldn't really answer you.'

'That's right,' Linda nodded. 'I got the impression that it wasn't war in general that upset her, but the Falklands in particular.'

'I got the same impression when I spoke to Marion this

146

morning,' Charles murmured. 'She was okay when we discussed other wars, but she refused to talk about the Falklands, but she didn't know why.'

'She said that to me, too. Strange really.'

'And your brother died out there?'

'Tim? Mmm. He was in the Navy.'

'If this is too painful for you …'

'That's okay.' She smiled warmly. 'I was only five when he died so I was a bit young to know what was going on.'

'How old was he?'

'Seventeen.'

'Quite an age gap then?'

'Mmm.' She laughed softly. 'Mum said she wasn't having any more kids after Tim, then I came along. She said I was a result of the contraceptive that didn't work.'

'It happens,' Charles smiled. 'No contraception is absolutely guaranteed.'

The outer door opened and closed and Linda uncurled from the couch, casting Charles a quick glance as she crossed the room.

'That'll be Mum home from work,' she explained. 'I'll make a cuppa. Can I get you one?'

'Mmm, thanks,' he nodded.

She scurried into the kitchen and Charles peered about him, wondering if his visit had been worthwhile. He'd hoped to see a picture of Tim, something to explain Marion's change of behaviour, but the walls were bare, the photographs stowed out of harm's way, and he was no wiser than before, the evening wasted on a pointless exercise.

Linda returned with a tray and he helped himself to sugar, stirring his tea thoughtfully as he decided where to go from here, which avenues to take and which doors to unlock that might provide the answers he sought.

'Is your mother not joining us?' he asked for want of something to say, and Linda shook her head.

147

'She's having a bath. The smell of paint gets to her a bit so she keeps out of the way as much as she can.'

'I wondered if she might be able to tell me something.'

'Who? Mum? I doubt it. She only met Marion once and that was the night she came here with me.'

'Sorry.' Charles smiled apologetically. 'I meant about your brother.'

'What about him?'

'Well, something in this room upset Marion, didn't it? It's quite possible it was the photograph.'

'Oh, but that was a group thing, and I thought it was the Falklands War that affected her ... You think it was my brother that was the cause?'

'It's possible. Either that or something else in the room. I don't suppose you've got a picture of your brother somewhere, have you?'

'We should have,' she frowned. 'Everything's been moved for the decorating, but I think there are some photos upstairs. I'll have a look. Back in a tick.'

Charles heard her clumping up the stairs and the sound of footsteps overhead followed by drawers opening and closing and a moment of silence, then she came back down, passing him a little stack of photos before resuming her seat on the couch.

'Those were taken when Tim was home on leave before he sailed to the Falklands. They're the most up-to-date ones we have.'

Charles peered at them with interest, flipping through them as if expecting all the answers to leap out at him, but they were just pictures of a young man pottering in the garden or relaxing at home, filling in time before he went to war just as countless thousands had done before him. There was nothing particularly handsome about the face that stared back at Charles, no rugged features to set a young girl's heart on fire, no winning smile to start the pulses racing or

148

mischievous eyes to tempt with devilment and fun, but rather a solemn sadness as though he'd guessed his fate and had seen his future and knew he'd never see the age of eighteen or beyond.

There was nothing here, Charles thought glumly, nothing to disturb a mind or fill it with a driving need to commit suicide. There was just a bland face in an unremarkable body, so where was the power to unhinge and destroy? What was it about him that had sent Marion over the edge? Perhaps it wasn't Tim at all, but one of the others she saw in the picture or perhaps it was tied in with the Falklands and it was the war itself that was important, not one of its warriors.

Yet there was another possibility, and he was loath to leave without exploring all the avenues that might lead to an answer. Perhaps it wasn't Tim that had sent Marion tumbling into an abyss of depression, but someone else in the picture.

'The photo that was on the wall,' he said hopefully. 'The one Marion saw … Is there any chance I could look at that one?'

'Um …' She hesitated, her brow creased in a frown. 'Now where did we put all the stuff that was in here? We've been a bit upside down since we started decorating, Doctor … I think they're in a box in the hall. I'll take a look.'

She returned a few minutes later with a framed photograph which she dusted with the sleeve of her cardigan before handing it to him, and Charles studied it eagerly. It was a typical snapshot rather than a professionally posed photograph, depicting three companions standing shoulder to shoulder with toothy grins and sparkling eyes as they laughed at the person who held the camera, another shipmate, perhaps, sharing a joke that would never be retold. They wore round sailor caps with the ship's name emblazoned in gold around the rim, 'HMS Sheffield' displayed with pride, and it was a summer shot for they wore the white square-neck shirts edged in blue, pristine fresh and

149

crisp and dazzlingly bright in the sunshine. Charles examined each face minutely, feeling his heart sink with every passing second as nothing screamed at him to be recognised, nothing stood out from the ordinary, nothing to warrant depression and a desire for death, and he passed the picture back wordlessly, feeling deflated and suddenly tired.

'No clues there, I'm afraid,' he murmured, stepping to the door. 'I'm sorry to have put you to any trouble, Linda, but it was worth a try, I suppose.'

'It was no trouble, Doctor. If I think of anything, I'll let you know,' she said, and he nodded wearily.

'Thanks for everything.'

'I'm just sorry the photos didn't help.'

'Well, it was a long shot anyway.'

'I know you can't tell me about Marion's treatment, but … well, I'd like to know how she's getting on.'

'I'll keep you posted,' he promised with a smile, and turned away. ''Bye, Linda, and thanks again.'

The more he thought about it, the more Charles was convinced that there was something about the Falklands War that was the cause of Marion's condition, but what? That was the sixty-four-thousand-dollar question and he had no answers. Whatever else it was, though, the actual conflict wasn't one that she'd personally experienced in a past life because the mathematics of time and place put Marion as a two-year-old infant living in Farnborough, Hampshire, at the time the islands were being liberated. So, not another Babylon or Pompeii then, no recent catastrophes to unbalance an otherwise orderly mind, yet something had occurred twenty-three years ago in the troubled waters of the South Atlantic that had driven Marion to try and end her life.

War itself wasn't the deciding factor, he concluded, for Marion's first story of Egypt contained no battles and neither had the tale of Pompeii and the erupting Vesuvius. It was

150

fairly safe to assume then, that the common denominator wasn't conflict and war. What else did he have? A cat and a dog, Bastet and Anubis, personified and manifested in two people, a boy and a girl, linked for all time by an ancient ritual, an ancient prophecy, but ... but those were only facts if Marion's stories were to be believed ... and if they were to be believed, if Marion was Moona and Lindinia and Shera, then where was Nedemin? Where in this moment in time was the Darius of Babylon and the Parlian of Pompeii? Together for all time? Then where was he? Why weren't they united in this life just as they'd been in the past?

It didn't make sense. Charles sighed. Nothing made sense, and perhaps that's where Marion's problem lay. A confusing array of nonsense that was so twisted, so enmeshed and convoluted that it turned minds and brought about such a depressed state that suicide was the only solution. Dreams, memories, childhood experiences, the genes of timeless ancestors and an impressionable young mind all conspiring and acting in tandem to create a compulsive desire to simply lie down and die.

But the Falklands War was the trigger. Whatever else had gone before, it was that war and that war alone that had brought about Marion's present condition. *Find the link and you find the cause,* he thought. *Find the cause and you find the cure.*

'Morning, Marion,' Charles said breezily, casting her a smile. 'It's good to see you up and about. How's the leg?'

'Stiff and aching,' she muttered. 'My arm's bloody painful, as well ... and they won't let me walk far.'

'I should think not with the injuries you sustained! One step at a time, eh?' he cautioned. 'At least you're out of bed.'

'They're just afraid I'll do something stupid,' she said sullenly, and Charles shrugged.

'You have rather earned yourself a reputation for that,' he said affably. 'You can't blame them for taking precautions.'

'I expect they're just afraid they'll end up with a dead body on their hands,' she snorted. 'Think of all the bad publicity … not to mention the claims for compensation.'

'That's rather a pessimistic viewpoint, isn't it? Our job is to save lives, Marion, and that's all we're trying to do.'

'If you say so. Can you get me some crutches?'

'Possibly,' he said carefully. 'Not that you can use them effectively with your arm in plaster … but I suppose it sort of depends on you really. If you can convince me that you won't do anything daft, I'll see what I can do for you.'

'Convince you?' She blinked at him. 'I thought we had a deal. Isn't that why I'm letting Macleod into my head?'

'I suppose so, but humour me. Talk to me and if I like what you say, I'll get you some crutches.'

'What do you want to talk about?'

'The Falklands.'

'I told you, I … I'd rather not discuss that.'

'Why not?'

'I … I don't know,' she said in a small voice, and Charles nodded slowly.

'Okay … So let's try and find out why you'd rather not discuss it … That's the deal, Marion. You talk to me and I'll get your crutches … Okay?'

She stared at the wall for a long moment as though she were analysing her thoughts and feelings, examining them closely to see if they would hurt her, if there was pain hidden in their depths, then she shrugged lightly, giving a little toss of her head as she dismissed the demons inside her.

'All right, but you're not to get mad if … I *can't* answer you. I can only tell you what I know.'

'Fair enough.'

'Go on, then. Ask me.'

'What do you know about the war itself?'

'The facts?' She blinked at him. 'Not a lot really … I was

152

about two at the time, so I don't actually remember it. It's all stuff I've heard since.'

'What sort of stuff?'

'Margaret Thatcher was Prime Minister ... They were our islands ... belonging to Britain, and Argentina invaded ... A force was sent to kick them out, and that's what happened.'

'Is that it?'

'Oh ... bits and pieces ... General Galtieri ... Then there was Colonel H.—I can never remember his full name.'

'Jones.'

'Of course—Colonel H. Jones. Didn't he win the Victoria Cross or something? They sent the Gurkhas, too, didn't they? And that Welsh guardsman who was so terribly burnt ... Goose Green ... I always thought that was such a lovely name for a place, like Rose Cottage or Meadowsweet Way ... Brambleside.' She blinked up at him. 'It reminds me of sleepy villages in the heart of the countryside.'

'Let's get back to the Falklands.'

'Sorry ... That's about it really. I was never one for delving into past wars.'

'What about the battles themselves?'

'What about them?'

'Have you any thoughts on them? Any opinions?'

'I can't say I have. Battles are battles, aren't they? People get killed and you either win or lose. I once read somewhere that battles are never won ... battles are lost. We didn't win the battle for the Falklands, the Argentinians lost it.'

'An interesting theory. But those battles—they don't make you feel uncomfortable?'

'I don't think so.'

'What do you know of them?'

'Very little. Wasn't there a place called Tumbledown Ridge or something? That's another lovely village name.'

'Marion ...'

'I don't know,' she said, the exasperation plain in her voice. 'It's like I said … bits and pieces.'

'What about the naval battles?'

'What?'

'You mentioned the land battles, Marion, but what about the war at sea? What about the Royal Navy's part in the war?'

It was a stab in the dark, remembering Tim Beavis and his mates in the photograph, their naval uniforms or something equally explosive damming her to a downward spiral that was to culminate in her death, and Charles stared at her as she visibly paled, the scar on her temple a vivid swathe of crimson.

'Oh, Christ.' She barely got the words out. 'All those … all those poor sailors.'

'Marion?'

'On land you can … You've got a chance to dodge … to take cover … but on a ship … It's like a floating coffin, isn't it? Nowhere to run … nowhere to hide. You've just got to sit there and wait to be bombed. Christ, it … it must have been so awful.'

'So why wouldn't you discuss it?'

She seemed to shudder, an involuntary shaking of her body, then she sighed tremulously and shook her head, brows knitting together as she frowned.

'I wish I knew. It's just … I don't know … Something about it that makes me feel …'

'What? Makes you feel what, Marion?'

'Sad,' she whispered, her voice barely audible. 'So utterly, incredibly sad.'

'Sad enough to want to kill yourself?' he asked softly, and she forced a nod.

'Yes … But I don't know why.'

Charles took a long faltering breath, then he nodded slowly.

'I'll get the crutches sent up to you,' he murmured, and all she could do was look at him helplessly, tears streaming down her cheeks as the forlorn melancholy took her in its unrelenting grip.

Chapter 15

Charles increased Marion's medication over the following two days, fighting her deep depression with every means at his disposal, tranquillising and relaxing while taking care not to go too far and render her comatose and incapable. It was a delicate balance that he maintained with consummate skill, constantly monitoring her progress and adjusting the prescription accordingly, holding her steady on a plane of equilibrium that hovered between rational calm and weary acceptance, keeping the numbing despair at bay without sending her spiralling upward into the dubious world of lunatic fantasy, a world where the happy pills turned everything into a laughing matter and contact with reality was unattainable.

He looked forward to their daily chats, ten or fifteen minutes spent in idle conversation where he learned little but gained much, surpassing the usual doctor/patient relationship to achieve something higher, something more rewarding as he was drawn ever closer towards the very essence that was Marion Harting, personality and character emerging from the sullen girl who'd first caught his eye. He found himself making excuses to visit her, finding one pretext after another to share a moment, a word, a passing fancy, just to spend time with her, and she seemed to warm to his easy familiarity, even raising the occasional smile as he fussed around her like an overprotective mother hen.

'Haven't you got anything better to do than sit here

chatting to me?' she asked after his fourth visit that day, and he grinned as he felt her pulse, dutifully marking her chart before he answered her.

'All part of the service,' he said, his voice businesslike and brisk. 'Now lift up your nightdress so I can listen to the baby.'

'I'm getting fat,' she said, hoisting the nightdress above her lightly swollen belly. 'I'm definitely getting fat.'

'It's not fat, Marion,' he admonished gently, probing with the stethoscope and listening intently, his eyes carefully avoiding the little pair of briefs that covered her modesty. 'It's the growth of life inside you … Now, keep still for a second.'

She sat patiently until he'd finished then she straightened her clothing, peering up at him inquisitively as he put his things away.

'Well?' she murmured softly. 'Am I still pregnant?'

'Oh, yes,' he laughed. 'And doing very nicely, too.'

'It doesn't feel like it first thing in the morning.'

'Sickness?'

'Mmm.'

'That's to be expected,' he nodded. 'But you're in the best place to be looked after. Just take things easy and you'll be okay.'

'I can't do much else in here, can I?' she said with irrefutable logic. 'I can't even go to the toilet on my own.'

'All in good time. Besides, you'd find it a bit difficult with the plaster casts. Just let us look after you while you enjoy the nice rest.'

'Whatever.' She shrugged dismissively, tiring of the conversation. 'When does Macleod get back from holiday?'

'Monday week.' Charles studied her closely. 'Looking forward to more hypnotherapy sessions?'

'Not particularly … I just wondered.'

'Does it bother you?' he asked after a moment. 'Regressing back to the past, I mean?'

'Macleod doesn't think it is the past,' she said woodenly.

157

'He thinks it's just bits of information that I've picked up over the years and jumbled them all together.'

'And what do you think?'

'He makes it sound ... logical, I suppose ... It makes sense, doesn't it?'

'I don't know. Does it?'

'Well, what's the alternative? If he's wrong, what other explanation is there?'

Charles paused thoughtfully, a hundred possibilities churning through his head, then he shrugged, out of his depth when dealing with matters of the mind and all too aware of his own shortcomings.

'It's not for me to say, Marion. It's not my field, and anything I might suggest could be a million miles from the truth. But one or two things stand out as important. One is that you've been so depressed these past few months that suicide seems to hold an attraction for you.'

'And two?'

'Two is ... Two is the deep sadness that you associate with the Falklands War. That's two basic facts that we can't escape. Now, what their relationship is with Egypt, Babylon and Pompeii, Lord only knows, but that's what Professor Macleod and myself are trying to find out.'

'It's strange, isn't it?' she murmured dreamily, her voice far away and distant, and Charles frowned at her.

'What is?'

'How something that happened thousands of years ago— or something I read or heard about concerning that time— should be at the heart of my problem ... you wouldn't think that something as remote as that could affect me in such a way that I'd want to commit suicide, would you?'

'Well, it's hard to say. Like I said, it's not my field. I'm in no position to comment.'

'No, well ... He'll be back soon and maybe we can get to the bottom of this once and for all.'

'Yes.' Charles nodded positively. 'Once and for all.'

The week passed quite pleasantly for Charles, his days filled with the needs of his patients, especially Marion, who seemed to consume more and more of his time, and the evenings spent reading everything he could find on the Falklands War, going over it again and again in his search for clues, some pointer to the answers he sought. Nothing cried out to be recognised. Not one single fact demanded closer scrutiny and it was as Marion had said: Battles were fought and people died. It was ever the same since time began and the Falklands were no different ... but something made the difference, something in that conflict possessed the power to turn a stable young woman into a suicidal compulsive, and Charles had no idea what it was.

He spent the Sunday before Leon's return writing up his notes and putting all his thoughts and conjectures down on paper, assembling the facts and clearing his mind of all the loose ends and blind alleys that seemed to lead them in circles, going nowhere in the jumbled confusion of the past and the present, time and distance proving no barrier to a disturbed mind.

Monday morning was as busy as usual and it was twelve-thirty before he could see Leon Macleod, waving him into his office and ushering him to a seat with a friendly smile.

'Good to see you again, Leon,' he beamed. 'How was Malta?'

'Hot, dusty and crowded,' Leon muttered, stroking his beard. 'But I expected that. My wife enjoyed it so I suppose that made it worthwhile.'

'So, you're back in harness?'

'Aye. Apart from the mountain of paperwork on my desk, it's like I've never been away.'

'You'll soon catch up. Marion seems eager for you to continue the regression therapy.'

159

'Ah, yes. Marion. How is she?'

'Not too bad considering.'

'Good. I seem to remember you saying something about doing more research into her background. How'd you get on?'

'So-so.' Charles sighed, arranging his papers into some semblance of order and passing them to Leon. 'I made some notes. The first sheet is of a conversation I had with Marion's boyfriend, Terry.'

'I see.' He scanned them quickly. 'Not much here … Who's Rosalind Harting?'

'Marion's aunt. She lives in Cornwall.'

'You have been busy. She didn't have a lot to say.'

'Well … She said how Marion seemed preoccupied as a child … as though she were waiting for something.'

'Mmm.' Leon's eyes flicked over the pages, discounting the notes one by one. 'It seems to me that most lads and lassies are preoccupied these days. They've all got that vacant look about them.'

He read on, muttering to himself as he ran down the sheet.

'Boyfriends … employment … nothing unusual there … It's all rather ordinary really … What's this?'

Charles twisted to see.

'Oh. I saw Linda Beavis again. She worked with Marion when all this blew up.'

'She showed you photos of her brother?'

'Yes, but …' Charles shrugged. 'I couldn't find anything obvious there. Those last notes are of conversations I've had with Marion. I got her to open up a bit about the Falklands.'

'And found nothing?'

'Not really,' Charles admitted with a shake of his head. 'Apart from her distress when we talked about the Navy. I'm convinced there's a link, Leon.'

'Possibly … but it'll take more than general conversation to find it.'

'Regression?'

'Aye,' Leon nodded, passing the notes back. 'Everything helps, I suppose, but the truth is, we're no closer to a solution than we were when we started. It could be a long slog.'

'Are you seeing her today?'

'I thought I'd look in. Nothing too heavy, mind'

'Well—keep me informed.'

'Will do. See you later, Charles.'

'You're looking very well, Marion,' Leon beamed. 'If all my patients flourished in my absence as you seem to have done, I'd consider going on holiday more often.'

'Charles ... Doctor Levington has been looking after me.' She gave him a shy smile and his grin widened.

'Aye. So I hear ... how's the pregnancy?'

'All right ... I'm sick in the mornings.'

'And the leg?'

'That's okay ... itches like mad, but I've got a knitting needle.'

Leon wondered at the wisdom of allowing a compulsive suicide the use of a large needle, but he said nothing as he sat alongside her, surprised at how different she looked out of bed, the dressing gown a flattering replacement for sheets and blankets.

'Are you taking me back today?' she asked, and he blinked myopically at her, his hands absently smoothing the creases in his rumpled suit.

'Taking you back?'

'In time,' she murmured. 'Hypnotising me?'

'Did you want me to?'

'I'd like to know what's at the bottom of all this,' she said softly. 'The sooner we find out, the sooner I can go home.'

'And home is ...?'

'Fulham.' She frowned at him, eyebrows meeting in a knot over her nose. 'In the flat with Terry.'

161

'Of course.' Leon smiled, then came to an instant decision. 'Very well. I've everything here—tape recorder, note book. Are you ready?'

'Yes,' she whispered, closing her eyes and letting herself relax. 'I'm ready.'

Chapter 16

SOUTHERN ENGLAND, AD 500

The urgent blast of the horn brought Wenda up short and she straightened from the cooking pot, shielding her eyes from the sun as she gazed at the crest of the hill where a dozen or so men could be seen striding towards the encampment, a slain deer swinging from poles balanced on their shoulders. She recognised the unmistakable bulk of Lupus and she smiled with pleasure, her fingers automatically touching the scar on her left temple as she watched him approach, his long blond hair and magnificent beard stirred by the breeze like a halo of light, shimmering in the afternoon sunshine.

He was a big man in all respects, was Lupus, tall and broad with an easy gait and swinging shoulders, his powerful arms making light of the mighty battle-axe he carried, his constant companion and faithful friend that had served him well since they'd arrived on the shores of Kent from their homeland in northern Gemanica. They had come, like so many others, to swell the Saxon ranks that had forged a new home far from marauding Franks and Gauls, who had been too much to withstand after the ravaging years of an all-conquering Attila the Hun, and they came to settle in peaceful harmony on the gentle downlands of Britain where they could sow and plough and raise a family.

'Not that these Britons will allow us much peace,' Lupus

was prone to say. 'Wherever we go 'tis the same and we shall have to fight to hold onto a piece of land the size of a sackcloth.'

'Well, it *is* their land, Lupus,' Wenda reasoned. 'They fight for no more than you do.'

'We come in peace and they put us to the torch. How can they not see that we have much to offer this land of theirs? We grow crops and they tend pigs and cattle. Surely there is room enough for both?'

'The early settlers spoiled it for us all,' Wenda murmured solemnly. 'Instead of asking, they took, and now the Britons refuse to give.'

'So we have to take again, and take we shall. We have families also, Wenda, we have little ones who cry just as loudly when their bellies are empty. Would you have us ignore their cries and give in to the Britons? Would you have us take them back to face the Franks and the Gauls?'

'No, Lupus.' She shook her head, dark plaits caressing her shoulders. 'We have braved the sea crossing to be here, and here we shall stay.'

'So be it, then.' Lupus nodded his head like a lion displaying its golden mane. 'Engle land shall be our home and we will slay any who deny us the right to be here.'

Such was the conversation three months before, and since then they had trailed in the wake of their warrior leader, Cerdic, colonising the lands that he freed until his army of Saxons controlled a vast belt of prime ground to the south of Londinium while Aelle's Saxon hordes governed the north. Each week saw them edging slowly westward, their numbers increasing as boatload after boatload came from across the cold northern sea, a rising tide of humanity that clamoured for land and a place to settle far from the ravages of war.

It had been no different for Lupus and Wenda, and they had fled their village to the far north of the Rhine after one attack too many, gathering together their ox, their plough, their two children and a few scant possessions before joining the pilgrimage west, adding their numbers to the growing multitude that thronged the quayside in a bid to escape the horrors around them.

For them it had been a hard decision to make, leaving the land of their birth on a rumour and a promise of a better life across the sea, but the safety of the children came before all else, and they had made the journey reluctantly yet full of hope for the future, Wenda following wherever Lupus would lead. It had always been so from the moment they took their first faltering steps together as babes in the same communal hut, seeking each other out and finding a union of the spirit that would last them for all time, growing and maturing with the passing of the years until they joined hands in a ceremony of betrothal that would bind them for ever.

Lupus had been named after the sign of the dog-wolf he carried on his neck, a dark mole bearing the unmistakable features of narrow snout and pricked-up ears, crouching in the blond hairs as though waiting to strike from the undergrowth, ever alert, ever watchful, huge and powerful like the man himself. He seemed to derive great pleasure in his name and he had played the part well over the years, covering his upper body and legs with thick wolf skins and fixing a wolf tail to his battle-axe, the flying pennant the last sight many an enemy ever saw before they were dispatched to the netherworld where they must wait to serve their slayer when his turn came to depart the living earth. His bravery in battle was unquestioned, his courage never in doubt, witnessed by the iron warrior rings that adorned his chest that were fashioned from the treasures of those who had fallen victim to his flashing blade, too many to count, too numerous to guess at.

Such a skilled warrior, of course, could never be allowed to settle on the farmstead or at the fireside hearth, not when there were still conquests to seek, and all fighting men had been summoned to join Cerdic in his push westward, safeguarding the lands behind them as they stretched the frontiers further and further each day, valuable pasture land that would soon feel the metal of a Saxon plough.

'The Britons will oppose you, of course,' Wenda said, and Lupus laughed.

'And might succeed in throwing us back to Londinium,' he agreed affably, 'but they will never banish us from their shores. We are too numerous for them and they bicker and fight among themselves. As long as they are divided, we are here, Wenda, and we are here to stay.'

'I have heard that a leader has come to unite the Britons,' Wenda murmured, and Lupus studied her closely.

She was small and slight with narrow shoulders and delicate hands, but her hips were wide enough for childbirth and her slender frame had no trouble dispatching the two infants who slept in the makeshift shelter behind them, grown now to eight and ten summers and already begging their father to allow them to accompany him when he next fought with Cerdic. She had a plain, open face, only made interesting by the scar on her temple and the line of her brows that came together curiously on the bridge of her nose when she frowned, giving her the unmistakable appearance of a cat, an endearing feature that amused Lupus greatly, making him glow with a strange inner pride whenever he saw it.

Now it was his turn to frown and he gazed at her quizzically, blinking at her in the firelight.

'Leader?' he rumbled. 'What leader?'

'Arturis … He rides beneath the banner of the bear.'

'Arturis?' Lupus scoffed with a grin. 'Old wives' tales invented to frighten children. There is no Arturis, Wenda, or even Arthur if you would give him a Briton name.'

'Ruena says it's so, Lupus.'

'Ruena? What would she know? If they awarded honours

for idle gossip, Ruena would stand taller than Cerdic himself.'

'She spoke to a group who came from Cerdic's army. They have witnessed the bear banner.'

'Fox more like,' Lupus snorted. 'That's all these Britons do, Wenda. Slink and scamper like foxes.'

'Yet even foxes united pose a threat to Cerdic and his men.'

'They fight among themselves, I tell you. They could not unite to piss in a pot.'

'Cerdic has the measure of them, then? He will give us a victory?'

'Be sure of it, my little clucking hen. Would we gamble with the lives of our women and children? Our numbers swell by the day and the Britons forever retreat from our advances. They will be in the western sea before long. Just as soon as we can pin them down, we will fight and we will win.'

She scooped broth into a bowl and passed it to him, squatting on her haunches beside him in the gathering darkness, flickering flames from the dwindling fire reflected in her eyes.

'When do you propose to meet with Cerdic's men?' she asked after a moment, and Lupus shrugged.

'Three days, perhaps four. He moves quickly, does our noble lord, and while the Britons squabble and pick at each other's bones, our army grows mightier by the hour. I heard that twelve more longboats landed to the south yesterday.'

'A mighty army indeed,' Wenda smiled. 'And my Lupus is the mightiest warrior of them all. Cerdic will know his victory is assured when you stand beside him, my love.'

'Just as long as he does not stand too close.' Lupus grinned around a mouthful of broth. 'I need room to swing my death-maker.'

It was early when Wenda awoke the following morning and she curled against Lupus's naked body, snuggling into the

167

furs and skins as she hugged him tightly, her hand finding his manhood which she caressed lovingly, making him stir. He rolled onto his back and she touched the birthmark on his chest, her fingers lightly tracing its outline amid the faded scars of battle, and his eyes flicked open, peering at her sleepily as he struggled awake.

'Daybreak,' he murmured, and she nodded, slithering across to lay over him, naked flesh pressed to naked flesh.

'But early enough not to rush from your bed,' she said impishly, wriggling her body over him, and he grinned lazily.

'The fires will be out.'

'Then I shall relight them … when I have done here.'

'I have a hunger and a thirst, woman. Do they count for nothing?'

'I have a hunger, too, my love,' she countered. 'Satisfy my hunger and I shall satisfy yours.'

She slid down over him, gasping aloud as he entered her, and he held her lightly, kneading her breasts as she moved above him.

'Now would not be a good time for the Britons to launch an attack,' he said matter-of-factly, and she giggled delightedly.

'Quite the opposite, my love, for you would have two mighty weapons on hand to defeat your enemies—the one that impales me, and the axe by the door.'

'Ha! You think I would brandish both weapons with equal result?'

'I do not doubt it for a moment, for every time you penetrate me I die a little more … I am quite sure you could rut me to death.'

'Just as I could drown in the birth canal that receives me. Given the chance, Wenda, I would crawl inside you and lie there for all time.'

'Ha, ha. I would have to push food up inside me for you or you would surely starve.'

'Not so, my little hen—I would feast on your love.'

'Then you would grow fat and never be free to climb from your chamber, for my love is enough to feed you for eternity.'

A shadow passed over them and Wenda looked up into the eyes of her two sons, Vencil and Horst, standing patiently by the bed of furs and watching the events with bored interest, the older of the two, Vencil, giving them an exasperated scowl.

'It is time to eat, mother,' he pointed out, as if unable to comprehend what could be important enough to take precedence over food. 'The fire is cold and the broth is solid.'

'Then light the fire and take a stick to the broth,' she instructed, barely pausing in her movements. 'Are you incapable of such simple chores?'

'No, mother, but it is women's work.'

'And rutting is a man's,' Lupus challenged. 'So let me be about it while you do your mother's bidding before the stirring stick finds a better use on your hide ... Begone.'

Wenda laughed as they scampered away, resuming her thrusts with renewed vigour, and Lupus grunted beneath her.

'The boy was right to want food, Wenda,' he ventured. 'We have a long march today if we are to make ground on Cerdic.'

'And his father was wrong to say that rutting was a man's work,' she chuckled. 'It seems that I make all the effort while you simply wait to empty inside me.'

'And rightly so,' he laughed, twisting and tipping her onto her back and settling between her spread thighs. 'You catch me unawares while I still sleep and expect me to work for your pleasures! Well, I am awake enough now, woman, and joined to the battle. You will get work enough from me and quickly, too, for I am nearing the final outcome ... push up then … rise to meet me before we go and face the day … now, Wenda … do it now.'

It was three days before they saw Cerdic's campfires, the palls of smoke hanging in the air like a fog, a vast array of men and weapons, horses and wagons hugging the slopes of Mons Badonis, or Mount Badon as it was known to the Saxons, in an all-conquering tide, with Aelle's horde camped further west, filling the valley from horizon to horizon as if the whole world had gathered in this one place at this one time. The camp followers and women were housed to the rear with the supply train, makeshift shelters littering the trees, and Lupus saw his family settled before he hurried to the council of war, his battle-axe balanced on his shoulder as he strode away.

Wenda sorted through their belongings, keeping to hand the things she might need, then she prepared a supper, throwing hunks of venison into the stew and adding cornflower and maize to thicken it—women's work, as Vencil would say, that she attended to willingly. If her man had to fight, then he would do so with a full belly. Not that they would see fighting today, she thought as she added kindling to the fire. If the Britons were anywhere to hand the whole camp would be in uproar, and Cerdic would have his patrols ranging the hills far and wide to give them due warning of any attack. She fed Vencil and Horst, then settled down to wait for Lupus, counting the stars as they appeared in the darkening sky, pinpricks of light to match the flickering fires that littered the slopes and valley in great profusion.

A shadow came towards her and Lupus was illuminated in the flames, the iron warrior rings glinting in the wolf fur as he hunched by the fire, his calculating eyes staring into the embers as if to read his own fate in the glowing ashes. Wenda prepared two bowls of broth then sat beside him, sharing his warmth and his nearness as they ate in silence, the crackle of

170

burning wood and the breeze stirring the treetops the only sounds to interrupt their private world of togetherness.

'Well, then,' Wenda murmured after the last scraping of broth had been eaten, 'what has Cerdic to say of us, Lupus?'

'We are to fight, and we are to win,' he said simply, and she sighed softly.

'How will it be, this great battle that he plans? What will happen when the Britons come to our door?'

'The usual,' he snorted derisively. 'They will mass their army just as we mass ours, rank on rank. Shields locked to hold the wall—and they will stand facing each other for a time. You know, Wenda, it takes a tremendous amount of courage to attack a shield wall. All you can see is the line of shields with spears and swords bristling like the spines of a hedgehog. Many men will drink themselves into a stupor before they charge—it is the only way they can overcome the fear that grips them, the fear that renders them helpless. Our wizards and magicians will prance between the opposing armies, rattling their bones and casting their spells. Not that their spells and enchantments work in anyone's favour, but if the enemy believe we possess a magic greater than their own, it might discourage them a little, make them think the battle is lost before the first blood has been spilt. Their Druids will do the same, of course, but by then most of Cerdic's army will be too drunk to care, so it all comes to nothing. Druids are sacred, you know, so they are free to come and go where they will and none will harm them.'

'They do not fight?'

'Not the Druids. If they have any interest at all, they might watch from a convenient hill, but once they have cast their spells, their work is done and they leave the field.'

'Then what?'

'Oh, we shout and call our challenges, just as the enemy will, and if someone is foolhardy enough or drunk enough he will rush out and meet their champion in open combat.'

171

'Not you, Lupus?' Wenda said fearfully. 'You will not succumb to their challenges?'

'There is much honour to be gained by defeating their champion in open combat, Wenda,' he said softly. 'It also serves the purpose of disheartening their numbers to see their champion fall. But no, it will not be me. I will neither be drunk enough nor foolish enough to attempt it.'

'And after the champions have fought?'

'More shouting ... gathering our courage ... sword waving ... rattling our shields. Then our shield wall will advance slowly. The Britons will move forward, too, shield to shield, and the noise will be unbearable. When we are close, just before we charge, we will let loose the great war dogs. Gaps will appear in the enemy line as the dogs tear holes in the massed ranks, and in the confusion we charge them, pushing them back and fighting our way through the press of men and shields until the resistance crumbles and we are through.'

Wenda was thoughtful for a long moment, gazing into the fire with an unblinking stare; then she touched the birthmark on her temple, a dull throb making her head ache.

'And if ...' She licked dry lips and tried again, not daring to look at him as she asked the unthinkable. 'And if it is *our* line that breaks and crumbles ... if it is *they* who fight their way through?'

The question hung in the air, a chasm between them, and Lupus sighed softly.

'If they get among the wagons and the women ...'

He left the sentence unfinished, for no one was in any doubt as to the fate of the women if the Britons broke through.

'I suppose,' Wenda ventured carefully, 'that we can expect no more than their women might face if Cerdic wins the day.'

'Rutting was ever men's work,' Lupus murmured. ''Tis the spoils of war, Wenda, and ever shall be so.'

172

He gazed at her for an eternity as if he were memorising her features for all time, imprinting her face in his mind, then he shrugged wearily and pulled a knife from his belt.

'Take this,' he offered, and she blinked at him.

'I will slay few Britons with such a puny weapon as that,' she said disdainfully, and Lupus shook his head sadly.

'Not for the Britons, Wenda ... For the boys and ... and to spare you the rape that will surely follow if we are defeated.'

'I heard that Arthur was a kindly king,' she said, her voice neutral and devoid of all emotion. 'One who is fairly disposed to women and children.'

'Arthur is a myth,' Lupus said angrily. 'You will see no bear banner leading the field and even if I am wrong, do you think he can control thousands of blood-crazy troops in their moment of victory? Even Arthur is not king enough to deny them the plunder and spoils they will take by right. Do this, Wenda.' He softened, nodding at the knife still held between them. 'I will have enough to occupy my mind when the fighting begins without worrying about your honour.'

She hesitated for a moment, their eyes locked together, then she took the knife and tucked it in the folds of her tunic, forcing a smile and tossing her head with as much bravado as she could muster.

'It will not come to that,' she said with certainty. 'I will return it to you after ...' The smile broadened, her eyes twinkling merrily, 'after you have finished rutting with the spoils of Cerdic's victory.'

A grey mist hung over the valley at daybreak the following morning, the tops of trees emerging like spikes, and the summit of Mount Badon sat like an island on a sea of fog, isolated and adrift in a world of its own. Wenda yawned as she clambered from their makeshift shelter of skins draped between the trees, shivering in the early dawn as she squatted in the bushes and emptied her bladder, her mind on breakfast and the day ahead.

A blackbird squawked in the branches overhead and a squirrel scampered nearby, familiar sounds that she was used to, but there was something else, something far away and distant, and she strained to hear, every sense alert, poised and expectant. It came again, closer this time, a hunting horn, and closer still as the call was repeated, urgent appeal in the strident demand, then men were running and women and children were scurrying as the call to arms went out, the whole valley roused from slumber and galvanised into action.

Lupus thundered past her, the great battle-axe glinting in the early light, and Wenda dashed to the shelter, quelling the rise of panic inside her as she gathered their belongings and barked instructions to the two wide-eyed boys.

'Strike the camp, Horst … Vencil, the cooking pots. Hurry now. Assemble everything then take to the trees. Be quick for I fear the Britons are upon us.'

Everything seemed to happen in slow motion while at the same time moving with alarming speed, the valley filling with men as Cerdic harangued his army into a semblance of order, and as the sun cleared the trees and the last of the mist dissipated into nothing, the whole panorama was exposed to view and the awful truth was hammered home with devastating clarity.

There were no Druids or wizards rattling bones and beseeching the gods, no shouted challenges for champions to meet in open combat. No mustering of courage and slow advances, no snarling war-dogs to create gaps to be exploited. There was just a mighty clash of arms as men of Lothian and Gwent forged a wedge between the camps of Cerdic and Aelle, fighting on two fronts but barely breaking step as they hacked their way forward, light glistening on helmet and spear, sword and shield, banners held proudly aloft as they ploughed their way through the ranks of disorganised men still numb with sleep.

For a moment Wenda believed the Saxon host would win the day, a tremendous roar of victory rattling the trees around her, then the slopes of Mount Badon seemed to writhe like an ants' nest as the men of Powys and Cornwall charged into the fray, the banner of the bear at their head as they smashed into the flank of Cerdic's hard-pressed army and swept them from the field.

Still they came, slaughtering the wounded and those who tried to flee, who were caught in a vice of slashing steel that neither gave nor expected quarter, the army of Gwent linking with Powys and wheeling east to rake the sprawling encampment where isolated groups of men fought to stem the tide.

A searing pain lanced through Wenda's head and her hand flew to the scar at her temple—she knew without any shadow of doubt that Lupus had fallen, her beloved had battled his last and the cause was lost, then she turned quickly, grasping the knife in a resolute hand as she ran to her two sons, refusing to think of the rape and plunder to come in her haste to dispatch them mercifully to the netherworld of eternal darkness.

Footsteps crashed through the undergrowth and her way was barred by a troop from Powys, swords and spear-points bloodied as they shepherded women and children into a shrieking mass, and Wenda steeled herself for the horrors to come, unable to take her own life while her sons still drew breath. As if reading her thoughts, Vencil grabbed a fallen log and charged the soldiers, screaming vengeance as he wielded it like a club, shattering the kneecap of the nearest man and wailing a strident war cry as he turned to face the rest.

'VENCIL!' Wenda screeched, but it was too late and she stared in disbelief as a sword whirled with calm efficiency and

175

Vencil's head rolled lazily across the churned ground and came to a halt at her feet.

Without a thought, numb with shock, Wenda leapt to the attack, the knife flashing and stabbing in mindless fury, then Horst, her youngest, was there, clinging to her in abject terror, and she failed to see the spear that pierced the back of his neck and emerged at his throat, driving on to sink deep in her chest, the strength ebbing out of her and the knife dropping from lifeless fingers as she sank to the ground still clutching her son.

Treetops swirled above her, fading slowly as her eyes misted in death, and she felt the hot gush of Horst's blood soaking her, a sweet sickly smell pervading her senses, then she felt no more, her eyes glazing to seek Lupus in the netherworld as she gave up her fight and succumbed to the inevitable.

Arthur had had his day and the Saxons were broken.

Chapter 17

'I think the common factors in these stories are significant', said Charles when the tape had ground to a halt. 'Don't you?'

'Not if it's simply a case of fixation,' replied Leon. 'It's like a recurring dream where the salient facts are the same but the scenery changes ... Like trying to prove a point with repetition.'

'Even so ... I know you suggested Marion might have an overactive imagination, but these stories are too imaginative, don't you think? They're too real to be imagined.'

'Are they? How do you think an author writes his books? He churns out one best-seller after another and they're all figments of his fertile imagination. This is no different, Charles. Four short stories that anyone with an ounce of imagination could concoct in no time at all.'

'Without preparation? Without researching times and dates and places and people? I checked up on the Babylon story and it happened pretty much like Marion told it, with the king fleeing and Belshazzar left to face the Persians. They also entered the city via the watercourses which they'd redirected for that very purpose.'

'Quite,' Leon said shortly. 'I read about it, too ... And Marion could have read it just as easily as we did.'

'And Pompeii? And Mount Badon?'

'Vesuvius and Pompeii are very well documented, Charles, and quite honestly no one knows enough about King Arthur and the defeat of the Saxons to comment one way or the other with any degree of authority or accuracy. She could have invented the whole thing and we'd be none the wiser.'

'Did it sound like invention to you?'

'Anyone can make an unlikely story sound plausible. It's how the author sells his books.'

'I see,' Charles sighed. 'You're still keeping an open mind on all this, then?'

'Aye. I have to. I must remain objective. It's the only way forward.'

'I suppose so.' He made a note on his pad then looked up at Leon, a curious frown creasing his forehead. 'Tell me something ... off the record. Forget all the jargon and medical terminology. Forget your training and your vast experience in mental disorders. What's your gut instinct for all this? What do you honestly feel lies behind these stories Marion's telling you?'

'Honestly?' Leon blinked at him through his spectacles. 'In all honesty, Charles, I haven't got a clue ... but I've never heard anything so fascinating or absorbing in all my life. My gut instinct is to believe her. She tells these stories with all the conviction of someone who was there. When she got to the part where the Britons launched their attack, I could almost see them marching down the valley. I could hear the shouts and screams and I could feel the panic. At the end, when her sons were killed... ' He shook his head slowly. 'I don't know ... I *feel* that's what happened, that she was actually there, a part of it. And the fact they were born within days of each other and died on the same day—it's the priest's invocation, isn't it? His prophecy? Together in life, together in death ... Together in all things.'

'Until the sun god, Ra, is surpassed,' Charles finished for him. 'What do you suppose that means?'

'Lord knows,' Leon sighed. 'We may never know.'

'But it's already happened, hasn't it?' Charles said with sudden insight, and Leon blinked at him.

178

'What has?'

'The sun god being surpassed,' Charles pressed. 'If it hadn't, they'd be together now and they're not, are they?'

'Aye, I see what you're getting at,' Leon mused thoughtfully, stroking the goatee beard with delicate movements of his fingers. 'And the fact that they're not together could be cause enough to warrant the suicide attempts ... a subconscious desire to be with her soulmate.'

'You could be right.'

'It's a possibility.' He glanced at Charles and nodded. 'And you think the Falklands War has something to do with it?'

'There's a connection somewhere, I'm sure of it.'

'Well,' Leon came to his feet, gathering his things, 'no doubt we'll get to it in time. We're gradually working our way up through the ages. Marion can't hide in the past for ever.'

'When are you seeing her again?'

'Tomorrow afternoon.'

'Are you regressing her tomorrow?'

'No.' Leon shook his head. 'I want to give her a couple of days to settle down before I try again. Besides, I want to go over the last one with her first. I must admit though ...'

'Yes?'

'I'm quite looking forward to the next regression.' He smiled unexpectedly. 'It's become a journey into the unknown, and like I said, it's both fascinating and absorbing. I can't wait for the next instalment.'

'How much of the Saxon story can you remember, Marion?' Leon asked softly, and she shrugged.

'Most of it,' she murmured, her eyes far away and distant. 'All that I told you and ...'

'Yes?'

'Other bits, too. Our village far to the north of the Rhine— we knew it as Dansmaarg, which is probably an early form of Denmark, but it wasn't a safe place. The constant attacks from the Franks. The fear of the Gauls. The boat crossing to Kent.'

'You remember it clearly?'

'Not clearly, but ... it's like you remember your childhood ... Odd snippets ... A day or an event. It's not like a film you've seen where you can remember everything from beginning to end—it's too far in the past for that, but ... but if I think of cooking a rabbit I can remember the one Vencil caught when we were hurrying to catch up with Cerdic ... or I can think about sleeping rough and I'll remember the camp we made in the trees or the time we slept in a ditch.'

'And you think of them as actual memories?'

'As opposed to what?'

'Well ... if I was to think about sleeping rough, I could imagine being in a ditch, too, but it wouldn't be a memory, it'd simply be my mind imagining what it might be like to sleep in a ditch.'

'And there it would end.' She smiled gently. 'There you are sleeping in a ditch, for that's where your imagination has taken you ... but when you bring the picture to mind, can you imagine the ants crawling over you as you slept, or the beetles that infest your food? Can you imagine the lice that get into your clothing or the rats that bite your toes? Can you imagine rising in the morning soaking wet because the wind tore your shelter down and it poured with rain in the night? Can you imagine the mud or the choking dust or going hungry because the stoats and weasels have robbed you of your dinner or the rain has made the wood too wet to start a fire? Can you imagine any of that, Professor, or does your sterilised world forbid such clarity of thought?' She shook her head, her eyes boring in to him. 'No, Professor Macleod. When you imagine sleeping in a ditch, it's dry and warm and you rise to a perfect day where breakfast awaits at no trouble to yourself. You don't consider that you have to catch breakfast before you can eat it ... and that's the difference. The alternative to your imagined picture is too unpleasant to contemplate, isn't it? And your mind rejects it for that very reason.'

'What language did you speak?' Leon asked suddenly, and she blinked at him.

'I don't know … Saxon, I suppose … but here and now I think and speak in English and that's the only way I can translate it. It's a bit like the Pompeii thing. We must have spoken Latin, but it comes across as English.'

'You don't speak Latin?'

'No.'

'Curious.'

'Is it?' She shrugged again as though it were the simplest thing in the world. 'Tell me something, Professor. Do you ever dream?'

'Of course.'

'And in the dream is there dialogue? Do you speak?'

'Sometimes.'

'Yet, in a dream, not a word leaves your mouth, does it? Any speech that occurs is only in your head, isn't it?'

'Aye, that's right.'

'So … if the dialogue in your dream was in French or Latin or ancient Greek, you'd still understand it because your mind only works in English … unless you speak several languages, that is.'

'Go on.'

'Well, you've no way of knowing what language your dreams are in because you translate them all into English.' She nodded pointedly. 'This hypnosis thing is a bit like dreams. No matter what language I'm speaking, it all comes out in English because I can't interpret it any other way.'

'I see. Tell me,' he added, changing the subject, 'how did you feel about the death of your sons?'

'There wasn't much time for feelings,' she murmured. 'it was a time when life was cheap, but I felt so much for our boys. Vencil … His death was so quick … so sudden. I could only feel shock and a rising fury inside me. Horst? I didn't even know—it happened right at the end and I didn't even realise it ... or maybe I did. Maybe I knew what had happened when the spear point came through him into me, but ... but it was too late for thought, to late to understand that he was dead.'

The silence in the room was a palpable thing, thick and heavy with nostalgia and regret, and Leon cleared his throat softly, bringing her back to the here and now.

'I've been wondering about something,' he said cautiously. 'The people of the past ... the men who played an important part in your stories.'

'Yes?'

'Of them all ... Nedemin, Darius, Parlian, Lupus ... which one did you love the most?'

Marion blinked as if she didn't understand the question, her brows knitting together in a frown, and she shrugged helplessly, shaking her head as though the answer were obvious.

'I loved them all the same ... It was the same person. Not in looks ... not in outward appearances, but ... inside ... in the depths of their soul ... they were one and the same.'

'That's a hard concept to grasp,' Leon said objectively, and Marion shook her head.

'No, it isn't. It's like ... it's like a couple who meet and fall in love when they're sixteen and they stay together until they die in their nineties. They change over the years—looks. personality, character ... but the heart of the person doesn't necessarily change, the very essence of the person can remain the same as it was when they first met ... and that's how it is here.'

'But you didn't know that, did you?' he argued softly. 'I mean ... when you were with Lupus, you didn't think of Parlian or Darius, did you? You didn't know they were the same person?'

'No. It wasn't a knowing, not an awareness of the past like

182

that. It was a feeling … a feeling that we were so right together, that it was meant to be, that we … that we *belonged* together. That's the only way I can describe it … as a feeling.'

Leon studied her closely, sensing her words were totally genuine and heartfelt. Whatever the truth of the matter, Marion genuinely believed everything she said.

'Something else occurred to me,' he said by way of an afterthought. 'There seem to be large gaps in time between the periods of each story. Take the last two, for instance. There was a jump of four hundred and twenty-one years between seventy-nine AD and five hundred AD. It begs the question, were there times in between those dates when you and your soulmate were together, or was that it, just a blank, a nothingness between Vesuvius and your Saxon birth?'

'I have absolutely no idea,' she shrugged. 'I suppose the only way to find out is to regress me to a time between those dates and see what happens.'

'Well, that's something we can think about in the future perhaps, but for now I'd like to keep progressing forward until we get to the root of the problem. That's what we're here for, after all. To get you well enough to be released, then we can all go home.'

'Home,' Marion whispered solemnly. 'I used to think home was a flat in Fulham, but now I'm not so sure. Is it on the banks of the Nile or in Babylon? Is it in Pompeii or in some town in northern Germany? Or a field in southern England, perhaps? I just don't know any more.'

That's all we need, Leon thought bleakly, *an identity crisis on top of everything else!*

'We'll sort it all out,' he said positively, raising a bright smile. 'In the meantime, just relax and take it easy. I'll be back to see you on Thursday and we'll see if we can't bring you closer to the present. Besides, a cosy flat in Fulham must seem a welcome alternative to a wet ditch in southern England if it's anything like you described it.'

*

Charles read what he could on the Saxon defeat at Mount Badon, but just as Leon intimated, the facts were sketchy to say the least, conjecture and hypothesis seemingly forming the basis for any argument and leaving very little room for historical fact. Much of it was simply legend. Even the existence of Arthur was pure guesswork and Marion's tale did nothing to prove or disprove it one way or another. The closest she had come was to mention the banner of the bear, but that could have belonged to anyone and neither confirmed nor discredited the scholars of either persuasion, but rather left a blank, a huge question mark, over the whole episode.

If one were to accept Marion's accounts of Egypt, Babylon and Pompeii, then there was no cause to doubt the authenticity of the Saxon slaughter, and history tended to agree that they suffered a mighty setback around that time which effectively slowed their advance for many years to come. Nevertheless, to accept the story as a factual account was to accept it on faith alone because there was nothing else to substantiate it.

A vivid imagination, or a matter of fact? Those were the choices.

It was hard to conceive that Marion would be capable of such intricate invention, especially when subjected to a deep state of hypnosis, but it was equally possible that her mind could concoct a story of outlandish proportions and embellish it with infinite detail once freed from the shackles of conscious thought. It was an enigma wrapped in a conundrum and cloaked in mystery, and only patient perseverance and dogged persistence would unravel it entirely.

Charles Levington slept fitfully that night, his dreams filled with images of slashing blades and an unstoppable tide of advancing men, resolute in their determination to rid the land of Saxon vermin, be it man, woman or child, life's blood ebbing away in a forest clearing with the stench of death pervading the air and the rivers running crimson from the fallen host. He was irritable and short-tempered the next day, yet he felt his spirits rise when he entered Marion's room, his growing affection for her tinged with a sadness for the suffering she'd endured, whether in past lives or simply in the turmoil of her mind, equally tortuous and just as fraught. She watched him in silence as he checked the plaster casts and scanned her chart, then she smiled uncertainly, waiting for him to speak.

'Everything's fine,' he nodded. 'You're coming along nicely.'

'Is that what Professor Macleod says, too?'

'He's pleased with your progress.'

'I see. Did you hear the last tape?'

'Saxon England? Yes.'

'And?'

He blinked at her. 'And what?'

'Sorry.' She smiled sheepishly. 'I thought you were going to comment on it.'

'What can I say?'

'You could say whether you think it actually happened or if you think I made it up.'

He sighed softly and sat opposite her, gazing at her earnestly as he groped for the words.

'Do *you* think you made it up?'

'No, but … I think Macleod's still of the opinion that I'm just repeating stories I've heard before, weaving a tale from bits of information I've picked up along the way.'

'Well, that's still a possibility.'

'Not to me it isn't. It's so real, you know? I could feel the spear going into me. I could feel the weight of Horst on top of me and I could see the trees above me as I lay there dying.'

'I'm sure Professor Macleod has told you just how powerful the human mind can be, Marion. Even the most unlikely things can be made to feel frighteningly real.'

'Like people who say they can hear voices or believe they can see things that aren't there? Yes, he's told me all that. But this is more than just seeing things, it's feeling them, too. I've no doubt he can find explanations that make everything sound plausible, but … he'll never convince me they're not real.'

'Do you think it was King Arthur who led the attack on you that day?' Charles asked softly, remembering the comment she'd made to Terry about Arthur not being the hero he was made out to be, and she shrugged.

'Lord knows. I saw the banner of the bear and a man on a big chestnut horse, but it could have been anyone. Ruena believed it was Arturis.'

'Tell me about Ruena,' he asked suddenly, hoping perhaps to catch her unawares, but Marion neither paused nor took time to consider her answer, her voice as sure and strong as if she were speaking about Terry, a person as real as the doctor himself portrayed in her words.

'She was small and dumpy and she had rosy red cheeks. She had long blonde hair which she wore plaited down her back in a pigtail, and she had big breasts … huge brown nipples. Thorit, that was her husband, he used to laugh when we sat around the campfire at night. There was never any modesty like there is these days and he used to laugh like mad when he pulled her boobs out and played with them. He called her his little milk cow, his *Milchkuh*, and said she had the finest udders he'd ever seen.'

'Did they have any children?'

'Mmm. Three. Two girls and a boy. Morwen, Agnetha and Harvel. Harvel used to play with Vencil and Horst, and when they were older, they used to hunt together. Not big stuff. Just rabbits and things.'

186

'Can you skin a rabbit?'

'If you'd asked me that a few days ago, I'd have said no. But yes, I can skin a rabbit. Just the thought of it would have made me feel sick before, but now...' She shrugged simply. 'I'd give it no more thought than peeling a potato.'

'Strange,' Charles frowned. 'Anything else?'

'Anything else what?'

'Well, is there anything else you couldn't do before all this came up, but you can do now?'

'Mmm.' She nodded thoughtfully. 'I can make fire with sticks or from the spark of a flint ... I can make rope from animal sinew and I know how to crush a bone to get to the marrow inside ... I know which herbs ease toothache and which ones are best for indigestion ... I can sew with a bone needle and I know how to cure skins so you can wear them. I don't know how I know, I just do—it's like an awareness, a certainty, that if put to the test I could do all that and more.'

'Can you fight? With a sword, I mean?'

'Yes, but I'm not very good at it. I know what moves to make and how to parry a thrust, but I haven't the strength to block a downward swing. I'd have to rely on speed.'

'You did a pretty good job against the Persians in Babylon, I seem to remember,' he said lightly, and she smiled.

'Adrenaline ... It's surprising what you can do when you've nothing to lose.'

'You lost your life,' he pointed out logically. 'Was that nothing?'

'Without Darius, yes ... and all life comes to an end eventually, doesn't it? I sometimes think it's better when we have the choice of how and when we die.'

'Is that what's behind the suicide bid? Choosing when and how?'

'Maybe.' She shrugged. 'I don't know.'

'But we'll find out,' Charles said, coming to his feet. 'Professor Macleod will be in to see you again tomorrow.'

187

Chapter 18

FRANCE, AD 1348

Bridget Milais quite enjoyed haggling over prices with the market traders and she was more than satisfied with the few coins she'd exchanged for the turnips, marrow and parsnips that filled her basket, her attention turning to the poultry merchant who eyed her suspiciously, well aware of her ability to drive the hardest of bargains.

'Madame Milais,' he acknowledged with a curt nod. 'You wish to favour your customers with a fine chicken tonight? You have come to the right place. See for yourself, Madame. Are they not the finest chickens in all France?'

'What do you do, Hobier? Starve them to death? I have seen more meat on a toothpick. How much do you intend to rob me for that brown hen there?' She pointed with a bony finger, and he raised a smile.

'Ah, Madame, you choose the best of my stock. Such an eye you have for the finest hen money can buy. Your husband was well blessed when he sought you for a wife.'

'Forget the flattery, Hobier, and leave my husband at the inn where he belongs … How much?'

'For you, Madame … two ducats.'

'Two?' She stared incredulously. 'You would rob your own mother if you thought you saw a profit. What are you trying to do? Put me out of business? Would you see me begging on the streets?'

'Now, now, Madame Milais, you know full well that a sailing vessel is due in this afternoon and your inn will be full this evening. You will sell so many chicken dinners to a crew of hungry sailors that you need not open your doors for the rest of the week.'

'And you seek to retire from my gain? That scrawny creature would barely fill two platters. One ducat and no more.'

'Please, please … think of my family. Would you have them starve just so you can profit? Two ducats is more than fair.'

'Your family would surely starve if you tried to feed them on the chickens you sell,' she retorted sharply. 'One ducat and a flagon of ale when you next visit us. Or shall I feed the sailors with pork?'

Hobier threw up his hands and sighed, capitulating grudgingly before she changed her mind, and Bridget turned away with a grin, the plump hen securely tucked beneath her arm.

She was a tall, imposing woman in her mid-forties, her pointed features made morc severe by the way she tied her long auburn hair in a tight bun on the nape of her neck, exposing the angry birthmark on her left temple which she displayed with a certain arrogant pride as if she dared anyone to comment on it. It hadn't always been so and for many years in the town of Limoges where she grew up she had tried to conceal it, styling her hair to hide it from view.

'No half-decent man will look at you if he thinks you are tainted,' Bridget's mother constantly warned. 'He will believe you have been touched by the devil. Brush your hair to the side, girl. What have we done to deserve a child like you? Are we never to see you married and off our hands?'

It was true that suitors were few and far between, but who could blame them turning away from such a taciturn and shrewish creature as Bridget Garvois, whose acid tongue and barbed wit was enough to try the most patient of men? She was a loner, a recluse who seemed to live in her own private world and she had no time for her mother's matchmaking, content with her own company and seeking no other to share it.

No other, that was, until she met Claude Milais.

Not that Bridget lacked suitors. Her father owned a thriving, prosperous business and any man who won her hand would not lack bread on the table, but she spurned all the advances, informing one rather overweight young gentleman that he smelled like pig's offal, and telling another that she had received more passionate kisses from a long-dead flounder than she ever received from him.

'You will die an old maid, Bridget,' one thwarted suitor commented after a well-rebuffed foray beneath her petticoats. 'You will never know what it feels like to be possessed by a man.'

'But at least I shall die happy, Georges,' she replied with a certain venom, 'whereas you will die without ever lying between my thighs and knowing what pleasures might be found there. Your loss is the greater.'

Stout rebukes from a stout heart, yet deep inside that stout heart she knew she would not die happy, for she was alone and unfulfilled, a lost soul that desperately sought a companion. But not just anyone. It had to be the right one, the only one … or it would be no one.

Then she met Claude Milais.

She was twenty-eight that year and she had spent the summer and autumn working in her father's mill, grinding corn for the townsfolk from morning until night with barely a pause, unconcerned by the dust and flour that covered her and ignoring the distasteful glances she received from the few visitors who stopped to pass the time of day with her father. She saw the man when he was still some distance away, but something about him drew her eyes like magnets and she watched his approach with infinite care, her eyebrows knitting together on the bridge of her nose as she frowned into the setting sun.

'*Bonjour,*' he said softly, and she nodded silently, the bag of flour forgotten in her hands as she stared at him.

'You must be Bridget,' he went on, eyeing her curiously. 'My parents told me you worked up here.'

'Your parents?' She found her voice with difficulty and he smiled.

'The Milaises.'

'At the apothecary? I knew they had two daughters but did not know they had a son.'

'I was sent to live with an aunt in Lyon when I was five,' he explained quietly. 'She fled to Paris when the English invaded so I came back home.'

'Ah … that would account for it then.'

'Yes.'

'And you...'

'And I, what?'

She licked her lips as she broached a delicate subject, probing his circumstances with deliberate care which she found disconcerting. She was not usually as tactful or considerate in her dealings with people, but for some strange reason she found herself sensitive to his feelings and was careful not to cause offence.

'Are you simply visiting your parents, Monsieur Milais, or do you plan to stay here?'

'I have no intention of returning to Lyon.'

'You saw fit to uproot your family and bring them to Limoges from Lyon?'

'I have no family,' he murmured, and she blinked at him.

'Yet you are not a boy, Monsieur Milais. One would expect you to be wedded with children.'

'I am twenty-eight,' he smiled at her clumsy appraisal. 'I believe we share the same birth date.'

'We do?'

'So I am informed. My mother tells me that the midwife came to our house directly after bringing you into the world.'

'Goodness … such a coincidence!'

'My thoughts exactly.' He held her in the blue depths of his eyes, then without a word he reached out and brushed the hair aside from her temple with a delicate finger, wiping the dust and dried flour away to reveal a puckered scar, like a burn, that seared the flesh by her left eye.

Bridget couldn't move, rooted to the spot by his actions, and the world seemed to hold its breath, time standing still in an ageless moment that stretched into eternity.

'It would appear,' he murmured softly, 'that the midwife we shared left her mark on both of us.'

Then he opened his shirt to reveal the burn on his chest, tightened flesh that mirrored the blemish on her temple, and she stared at it as though mesmerised, too spellbound to move and too overcome for intelligent thought.

'What … why were you sent away when you were five?' she mumbled, and he turned his head, drawing her eyes to the mole on the side of his neck.

'People can be very superstitious,' he said lightly. 'An apothecary's son bearing the mark of a dog could be bad for business. When the customers started calling me *le petit chien*, my father thought it was time to get me out of the way.'

The little dog, Bridget thought. *Le petit chien.* It suited him somehow, as though he were born for the title, and she shook her head as if dismissing people's fears and superstitions out of hand, her left temple throbbing where he'd touched so gently.

'And you were never wed.' It was a statement, flatly given, and he smiled.

'I never met anyone I wanted to wed,' he told her seriously. 'Until now.'

She stared at him and she felt her heart melt, all the lonely unforgiving years falling away to nothing, and her acid tongue was silenced, sarcastic ripostes and cutting rejoinders forgotten as she fell under his spell, waiting for him to continue and ask the one question she knew she couldn't deny him.

'Will you wed me, Bridget?' He fulfilled the dream just as she knew he would, but old habits die hard and she couldn't resist a moment's stubbornness, sounding him out for reason and cause.

'You do not know me,' she protested mildly. 'We have barely met and already you ask for my hand. Am I not deserving of courtship and a time span when we might come to know each other?'

'I know all I need to know about you, Bridget, just as you are familiar with me. Hold my hand ... See?' He squeezed her fingers tenderly. 'Tell me you do not know me ... tell me you have not waited all your life for this moment ... tell me you do not love me.'

'I ...' She felt the colour rush to her cheeks and the blood pound in her veins, her heart racing with such fervour that she thought she might faint. 'I love you, Claude,' she whispered, never more certain of anything in her life before. 'It has always been so ... I have never met you, but I have loved you, sight unseen, since the day I was born. I will wed you, and willingly, for my heart is yours ... eternally yours.'

'Just as I am yours. Come then ... put away your flour sacks and take leave of your father. We have a matrimony to prepare.'

And it was as simple as that. They were married in the spring in the little church that sat in the centre of Limoges, the townsfolk filling the pews to see what manner of man would take such a harridan for a wife, but everyone had to admit they had never seen her so radiant or so happy as on that day, her auburn hair shining with a lustre that matched the sparkle in her eyes.

193

That night Claude took his virgin bride to bed where they consummated their marriage. He took her gently the first time and more urgently the second, surprised by her vigour and unquestioning surrender, denying him nothing as they sought the dizzy heights of release. She gave to him totally, unstinting in her desire to please him, and he wondered anew at the special woman in his arms, captivated and completely smitten with the love she showered upon him.

And love him she did. With all her heart and all her soul and all her mind and all her body, unreservedly and for always, forsaking everything and everyone in his favour, totally committed and basking in the certainty of his love.

When their first child died at birth, Claude held the sobbing Bridget tightly in his arms and soothed away her tears, comforting and calming and reassuring her that their love was strong enough to overcome the setback and other children would follow. But it wasn't to be and after a further two miscarriages Bridget resigned herself to a life without offspring and heaped all her devotion and love on the man she adored, settling down in a rural community and working the land on the outskirts of Limoges.

In 1339 the aunt with whom Claude had spent his youth died of the consumption and what wealth she had was passed to him. Spurred on by his good fortune and concerned for his wife's health, Claude persuaded Bridget to uproot and move to Brest on the Brittany coast where the sea air and fresh winds might bring the colour back to her cheeks, and like a dutiful wife she agreed, following her man wherever fate might direct them. They purchased an inn on the dockside and discovered a lifestyle that suited them both, Claude running the alehouse with surprising ability while Bridget saw to the kitchen and the comforts of the overnight guests, a profitable enterprise that saw their status rise in the rapidly expanding town. Claude thought to stand for mayor and Bridget's imposing frame and increasing wealth gave her a certain influence among the ladies, holding court when they met for sewing afternoons and airing her views with insight and clarity of purpose.

So it had been for nine years and Bridget felt a justified sense of satisfaction when she reviewed her life, her position and standing surpassing all her wildest dreams and a far cry indeed from the morose miller's daughter with few prospects and a doubtful future. Once considered unmarriageable and impossible to live with, she had proved a loyal and loving wife, aiding their fortunes in the kitchen, enhancing their position in the town and securing the eternal love and devotion of her husband by her feminine wiles in the privacy of their bedroom.

It was late morning when Bridget returned from the market with the struggling hen clutched beneath her arm, entering the inn by the rear door and depositing her basket on the wooden table before hanging the chicken over a bowl and slitting its throat, catching the blood, which she'd add to the stew later to thicken it. She set about cleaning the vegetables, scraping the flesh from the marrow and trimming the turnips, humming softly to herself as she worked, content and at peace with the world around her, and she smiled as Claude came to stand beside her, tilting her cheek for his kisses as he nuzzled her neck.

'A fine hen, Bridget,' he remarked conversationally. 'I trust Hobier was paid a fair price?'

'Fair enough,' Bridget grinned. 'We owe him a flagon of ale.'

'And when he has drunk it he will stay and pay for more. One ale was never enough for Hobier.'

'My thoughts exactly,' she laughed. 'But he is too slow-witted to see it. He believes he has a bargain so he hugs it all the tighter.'

'Did you buy any cheese?' Claude asked, stepping round

her to rummage in the basket. 'I found bread aplenty, but I had little else to offer our guests.'

'I left soup simmering on the grate, but I know how much the merchants like their cheese so I bought more today … Ah, you found it. Four varieties to tempt the most discerning of tongues.'

'Talking of tongues,' he said, unwrapping the cheese, 'I overheard the tongues wagging in the bar. It seems we are to expect a vessel from Genoa this afternoon.'

'I heard the same in the market,' she nodded. 'I will see to the beds when I have done here.'

'Perhaps …'

'Yes?'

'Perhaps we should discourage them from lodging with us.'

She had ripped the entrails from the chicken and had begun to pluck the feathers, but now she paused, blinking at him, her eyebrows forming a ridge over her nose as she frowned.

'Discourage them, Claude? Why would we do that?'

'Have you not heard of the plague that ravages Italy, Bridget? Would you have our customers die in our beds?'

'I am sure you concern yourself over nothing, my love,' she placated him, resuming her plucking. 'Italy is hundreds of miles from our shores and if the Genoese sailors bring the plague they would be dead before they even arrived here. There may well have been a plague in Italy, but I would wager it has long since moved on. You know how slow we are with the news here.'

'Well … perhaps you are right,' he conceded with a shrug. 'But I will heat water for the tub anyway, and ensure the sailors are clean before they lie between our sheets.'

'You cannot *make* them bathe, Claude.' She shook her head with exasperation. 'You will drive them away with your demands. Now, as soon as you have taken the cheese to our

196

visitors, take yourself along to Monique and Celeste and make sure they are available tonight. They will not want to pass up an opportunity of earning a few ducats from foreign sailors, plague or not ... and the prospect of sharing a bed with a maid of the town might sway our guests to jump in the tub first. Now, where did I put that sack? Ah, there it is. I have enough feathers here to make another pillow ... Come along, Claude. Our visitors await.'

The Genoese vessel duly docked in mid-afternoon, bringing bolts of cloth and silks, salt and dyes, and a crew of land-starved sailors that took the town by storm, drinking in the taverns and pleasuring the local girls with the willingness of their bodies and the dispensation of their purses, a liberal generosity that was difficult to resist. The vessel also brought something else although the cargo went unnoticed—the rats scurrying from the ship to the dock unseen and unheeded by townsfolk immersed in frivolity—and the rats brought the fleas and the fleas brought the Black Death to Brest, that same plague which had reduced Cairo to a ghost city and taken seven thousand lives every day until the plague had run its course.

No one noticed anything untoward at first, then gaps began to appear in the market as trader after trader fell sick, and custom at the inn fell to an alarming level, the once-thriving meeting place now deserted and bereft of life as the townspeople took to their beds, fighting the fever and vomiting blood as the initial symptoms made themselves known.

Claude was the first to show signs of the plague's fearsome grip, and Bridget tended him lovingly, mopping his fevered brow with a cool cloth and clearing away the vomit as she prayed for his recovery, despairing of his weakened state as he fought his lonely battle, staring death in the face with no hope of salvation save for the intervention of a merciful God.

197

'Bri…Bridget,' he moaned, teeth chattering even though he was sweating profusely. 'You must … you must go away from here … take yourself to safety … My sisters in Limoges will take you in.'

'Hush now, Claude,' she soothed softly. 'Would *you* take someone in who came from a plague-ridden town?'

'We did, remember?' he managed with effort. 'We took in the Genoese sailors.'

'And I scoffed at your concerns … How I wish I had listened to you, my love.'

'It … it would have made little difference … Nowhere is safe from this curse.'

'You must rest, Claude. Try to sleep … I will bring you a little soup later.'

She never told him of the fever that wracked her own body, nor of the copious amounts of blood she vomited in the backyard, nor of the suppurating boils that littered her flesh, finding instead a hidden strength from somewhere to tend him as he thrashed feverishly on the soaked bed, living a continual nightmare that seemed to have no end, a constant daily struggle to stand and move and draw breath.

Claude's fever worsened over the following days, angry pustules forming in his groin and beneath his arms as the Black Death took hold, tightening its grip with relentless persistence and sweeping all before it as it rampaged through France and Germany before crossing the channel to England.

Bridget could barely move by then, but she fought to ignore the agonising lumps that appeared in her groin as she stumbled and lurched about the inn, dizzy with fever and hallucinating badly while she tended her man, bestowing on him all her love and attention just as she always had, just as she always would.

On the fourth day, Claude's pustules grew to an enormous size and finally burst, pus and mucus staining the sheets in a foul mess, and he writhed in agony, beseeching God and all His angels and saints to end the misery that had afflicted them all, for no one seemed to have been spared the pestilence that had laid the country to waste, decimating the populace like a scythe through a cornfield.

In the early hours of the fifth day, Claude died, gasping his last and seeking a peace from the torment, and for all her pain and torture, Bridget still found the tears to mourn him, feeling his loss like a knife through her heart. She refused to leave the bed they shared, hugging his still form as she shrieked her agony when the oversized boils in her armpits and groin burst in an explosion of yellow matter and blood, and she surrendered to the pain and accepted it as just reward for the conceit of wealth, God's judgement dispensed and received with stoic forbearance.

As the day turned to evening and dusk turned to night, Bridget finally gave up her valiant fight for life and the death rattle from her throat echoed round an empty inn, reverberating from timbers that once rang with laughter and song, the stiffening body of Claude by her side, together in death just as they had been together in life.

Chapter 19

Charles said nothing as the tape hissed on into silence, all the poignancy and pathos of fourteenth-century Europe gripping him in its melancholy conclusion, the same inevitable fate shared by countless millions from Asia to Britain. He remembered studying the bubonic plague for a thesis when he was a medical student, but back then it was simply symptoms and statistics with no real people to bring the horrors to life. But this? Marion's story was a touching reminder of the swathe of disaster the plague had caused, a microscopic view of a catastrophe that reduced the world by a third of its entire population. Two people who experienced firsthand the deadly result of infected fleas, made real and given character and personality by a story so poignant, so heartbreakingly sad, that he wanted to bury his head in his hands and weep. To think that whole communities went through that nightmare, towns and cities wiped out in a matter of days, mothers watching their children die before succumbing to the same agonising fate or, worse perhaps, surviving the horrors and picking up the shattered pieces afterwards, burning the dead in a funeral pyre that stretched from China to Bristol.

Leon's voice brought him back to the present with a start, the words hanging in the air and ringing in his ears, but he seemed not to hear them, shaking his head as if to clear it and blinking as if waking from a dream.

'Sorry? What did you say, Leon?'

'I said, "It presents us with another problem".'

'What does? What other problem?'

Leon smiled indulgently and shifted in his seat, all too aware how personal tragedy and trauma can cloud the issue and obscure the facts, the most obvious distortion passing unnoticed by Charles in his absorption with the people concerned.

'Bridget,' he murmured thoughtfully. 'She was twenty-eight when she met Claude. If we're working on the assumption that they're following the high priest's invocation and prophecy for them to be "together in life, together in death, together in all things" then how is it they spent the first twenty-eight years of their lives apart?'

'I see what you mean.' Charles frowned, coming to grips with a twenty-first century problem when his mind was still locked in a time warp that existed six hundred and fifty-odd years in the past, and he shook his head to clear it. 'But perhaps...'

'What?'

'Well ... perhaps that's all it was, an invocation, a plea ... But a plea is more of a hope, isn't it? It's not cast in stone ... And you can make all the pleas you like, but when fate steps in and takes a hand you just have to go with the flow until you can get back to where you want to be.'

'So fate steps in and sends Claude to Lyon when he's five and they have to wait another twenty-three years before they can get together?'

'Something like that,' Charles nodded. 'Remember they didn't get together until they were five in the Pompeii story, so it's not as if they were together from birth, is it?'

'But they lived in the same house.'

'And in this case they lived in the same town.'

'Until fate separated them.'

'Yes.'

Leon waited for the most obvious fact to sink in, but

Charles gave no sign it had registered and he sighed heavily, pausing before he spelled it out.

'And that's where our problem lies,' he said after a moment, and Charles blinked at him.

'How is that a problem?'

'Because you used the "Together in life" theory as a basis to link the Falklands War with the fact that Marion's not with her soulmate. You said they were not together so something must have happened to separate them … but Marion's only twenty-five and Bridget was twenty-eight before she got together with Claude.'

'So you think there's still time for them to meet and fulfil the prophecy?'

'If there ever was a prophecy and if it was ever ordained that they should spend every life together.' Leon nodded, then shrugged lightly. 'It rather makes a mockery of all our previous deductions, does it not?'

'I don't know that it does … We have to start somewhere.'

'But not with assumptions.' Leon shook his head. 'We should only concern ourselves with the facts.'

'And the facts are?'

Leon steepled his fingers and looked at the ceiling as he gathered his thoughts, fully aware that an untrained mind could not be made conversant with all the intricacies of phobias and schisms of a troubled brain in a single sentence, but simplicity was all he had.

'Simply put, Charles, the facts are that Marion has tried to take her own life four times in as many months and when regressed to find a possible reason she came out with some rather intricate yarns that have taken us through periods of history that might or might not be total figments of her imagination.'

'Yarns?' Charles stared at him. 'Is that what you call them? Yarns?'

'Tales, stories, yarns.' Leon shrugged. 'What else would you call them?'

'Detailed accounts of previous lives?' Charles ventured warily, and Leon smiled.

'And when you can prove it I'll agree with you. The stories are interesting to say the least, but we can't assume they are anything more than that—stories.'

Charles sighed wearily and came to his feet, thrusting his hands deep into his pockets as he turned to stare out of the window, knowing in his mind that Leon was right and they had no just cause to assume anything, but feeling in his heart that Marion's accounts were the real truth. The problem was, he *wanted* to believe Marion's stories, he *wanted* them to be factual accounts, but wanting and proving were two different things and until they had more to go on he had to accept them for what they were.

'When are you seeing her again?' he asked woodenly, still facing the window, and he heard Leon stir behind him.

'Tomorrow. I want to go through the plague thing with her.'

'Well ...' Charles turned and forced a smile. 'I'll look in on her this afternoon ... see how she's coping.'

'Right. I'll see you tomorrow, Charles.' Leon collected his things and moved to the door. 'Just be careful what you say to her. 'Bye.'

Marion was very pensive that afternoon, saying nothing as Charles studied her chart and checked the healing lesions and plaster casts on her arm and leg, and he wondered if she was thinking of the plague's awful toll, the suffering and torment of those struck down with its unforgiving blight, or whether it was simply the same depression that had dogged her from the outset, reducing her to a forlorn melancholy that she couldn't shake free from. Small talk was wasted on her, his every effort to draw her out ignored or dismissed with a sullen sniff that made him think of Bridget before she met Claude, moody and morose and seeking no favour. Was it a hangover from the last regression, or merely a mood swing to unco-operative silence?

'I heard the last tape,' he said conversationally, and she blinked at the ceiling, the only indication she'd heard him.

'It must have been a terrible thing,' he went on quietly, watching for any response, however slight. 'The fever ... vomiting blood ... the huge boils that gradually got bigger until they burst ... The ...'

'Shut up,' she hissed vehemently. 'What the fuck do you know about it anyway? Were you there?'

'Of course not ... were you?'

Her eyes flicked to his and held, boring into him with all the certainty of someone who knew, someone who'd seen it and felt it and breathed its very essence, and he had to look away, cowed by her sure knowledge that reduced all his ramblings to nothing.

'I'm sorry,' he murmured. 'That was a silly thing to say.'

'Yes, it was. Maybe I wasn't there, Doctor. Maybe it was just a figment of my wild imagination, but it sure as hell *felt* like I was there—I could feel the heat of the fever ... taste the blood when I vomited ... feel the absolute agony of the boils in my armpits and my groin. Christ, I could hardly walk ... and ... and most of all ... most of all, Doctor, I felt the loss of Claude. The pain of his death was twice the pain of the plague.'

'Marion, I ... I'm sorry.'

The fire left her eyes and she emitted a long, faltering sigh, resting her head on the back of the chair as she returned her gaze to the ceiling, her body losing the rigid tenseness as she softened.

'When I think of the way it was before,' she whispered, her voice barely audible in the stillness, 'before the plague came—the town alive and buzzing with activity ... ships in the harbour ... merchants in the market ... Hobier and René Albois ... Célon, the baker, and Victor Dupont who made candles ... Monique and Céleste who lifted their skirts and dropped their drawers for a ducat and a goblet of wine ... Claude haggling with the brew-master over the price of a barrel of ale. I can't ... I can't even begin to explain it to you, Doctor ... How normal it all was. Then it all changed ... so swiftly and without warning ... I don't know. Someone described it once—what what it they said?' She knitted her eyebrows in a frown of concentration. '"Death coming on silent wings like a thief in the night" ... and that's what it was—a thief, stealing our lives ... taking away our loves ... robbing us of our future. And if ... if I wasn't there, if it didn't really happen to me, then why do I remember so much more than I revealed on the tape?'

She turned her head to appeal to him with beseeching eyes, searching for answers when the question itself defied all explanation.

'Why, Doctor? Why do I remember that Yvette Charmont made posies of flowers and her eldest son was called Etienne? Why do I remember the fire at Monsieur Duval's house so clearly? How do you account for that, Doctor? How is it that I remember the time when Pépé La Compte sold us some bad mushrooms and Claude was sick for a week? A million untold facts and figures that swirl around my head like they belong there? How, Doctor? You tell me how.'

What could he say to her? How could he even begin to find the words that explained the impossible? He had no pearls of wisdom to offer her, no easy answers and simple solutions because the whole issue was so complicated, so complex, as to defy imagination itself, and he had no crumbs of comfort to ease a perplexed mind, no ready-made standard reply, no glib and trite remarks to pacify a troubled soul.

'Marion, I ... I don't know,' he murmured lamely. 'In all honesty, I just don't know ... I mend bones. I stitch cuts and I heal wounds, but this?' He shrugged helplessly. 'It's beyond me ... beyond anything I've ever dealt with before. I just can't answer you.'

She held his gaze for a long moment as if she were reading the contents of his heart, then she nodded slowly, a glimmer of a smile touching her lips.

'I'm sorry I swore at you a minute ago,' she said softly. 'You didn't deserve that.'

'Yes, I did,' he admitted, returning the smile. 'I was being rather patronising ... pompous, and nothing deflates pomposity faster than some well-directed scorn.'

'I know you're doing your best for me. It's just ... just so confusing. My head's in a permanent spin these days.'

'I can understand that,' he nodded. 'After the revelations of the past few weeks, it's a wonder you're not climbing the walls.'

'Broken leg.' Her smile broadened. 'Otherwise I might be.'

He was glad he'd lifted her gloom, pleased that she could make weak jokes and treat the whole affair lightly, shrugging off the slough of despondency with a resilience that surprised him, making him grin with delight.

'I've got to go,' he explained, edging toward the door. 'Patients to see ... I'll ask the nurse to make you a cup of tea.'

'Doctor? Charles ... thank you.'

'You're welcome,' he murmured, and stepped into the corridor.

Charles found himself discussing the case more and more with his wife, Rosemary, in the hope that she could give him a woman's perspective into the mind of another woman. He mentioned no names, simply outlining the facts and using Rosemary as a sounding board for his ideas and conjectures, testing his theories against the solid practicality of her well-ordered mind.

'It seems to me,' she said thoughtfully, 'that you need to look closer at the Royal Navy connection.'

'Why?'

'Because it was a photograph of sailors that started it all off and when you were talking to this girl about the Falklands War, it was the death of sailors that had reduced her to tears. Whether she knows why or not is irrelevant. If it makes her cry, Charles, then it has a hidden significance.'

That made sense. He remembered the conversation he'd had with Marion on the subject and it hadn't upset her until he'd mentioned the Navy's role in the war, and it had reduced her to tears. Had Marion avoided the subject on purpose? Bearing in mind that it was a possibility it had been a photograph of uniformed sailors that had started her on the downward spiral into numbing depression, Charles reasoned that she'd deliberately evaded the issue of the Navy's involvement. Either it was too painful to recount or she'd blotted it from her mind, erasing all trace of the catalyst that had triggered her desperate need to commit suicide.

It was an interesting concept that might ultimately lead them to solving Marion's problems, but just how far were he and Leon prepared go in their efforts to test the theory? Charles firmly believed it was important, perhaps even critical, to broach the subject again with Marion, but to do so clumsily might tip her over the edge of the narrow precipice she walked between despair and acceptance, the fragile balance upset with possibly calamitous results.

He mentioned to Leon the following day the possibility that it wasn't the Falklands War in particular that Marion found difficult to discuss, but the Royal Navy's involvement in it.

'It might have some significance,' Leon conceded grudgingly, 'but quite frankly, Charles, I think you're clutching at straws. Just because Marion didn't talk about the Navy's role doesn't mean she views it any differently. She was two years old when the war took place, and it could simply be a case that she doesn't know enough about it, rather than deliberately avoiding it. I still think the best way forward is to regress her slowly to the present and see what develops. Something's bound to emerge sooner or later.'

'If you ask me, Leon, it's emerged already and you've chosen to ignore it.'

'Reincarnation? Same people, different lives? We've gone over this time and time again and we always arrive at the same conclusion: only when we can prove it will we have sufficient data to effect a treatment. Until then we're just groping in the dark.'

'But surely you've come across this sort of thing before?' Charles persisted stubbornly. 'There must be hundreds of instances where reincarnation was a distinct possibility.'

'Oh, aye,' Leon nodded. 'There are several well-documented cases that indicate a past existence, but it can't be proved one way or another. They attribute it to reincarnation simply because they have no other logical explanation.'

'You don't think it's worth following up, then?' Charles went on. 'Put it to Marion and see what she says?'

'Good Lord, no.' Leon shook his head adamantly. 'Making her face up to it out of the blue like that could be the worst possible thing to do. No, if and when I decide to use this information, rest assured it will be under strict control. Only when I'm absolutely sure it won't send her tumbling over the edge will I be even tempted to bring the subject up with her … And you mustn't, either.' He almost glared at Charles, his Scottish burr becoming more pronounced as his agitation grew. 'The whole topic is taboo. Understand?'

'Yes,' Charles nodded meekly. 'I understand.'

'Good.' Leon came to his feet, collecting his papers together as he prepared to leave. 'I'll go and see her now.'

'Do you want to take a bet on where she takes you?'

'What?' Leon paused, turning to stare at Charles. 'What do you mean?'

208

'The date.' He shrugged easily. 'Choose one this side of thirteen forty-eight—one where they would have died together. Where do you think today's regression will take her, Leon?'

Macleod eyed him in thoughtful silence then he gave a dismissive shake of his head, fully aware how fruitless the whole exercise would be.

'Pointless,' he snapped. 'Trying to select one date from six hundred and fifty would be like trying to find a pebble on a beach. It would be a pure stab in the dark. Besides, my history's not that brilliant.' He hesitated, frowning suspiciously. 'Why, Charles? Have you got a particular date in mind?'

'I've thought of several possibilities,' Charles admitted with a wry smile, 'but like you say, it's a case of picking one from hundreds. There are limitations, though.'

'Oh?'

'Well, if we're to assume they die together and we ignore the possibility of it happening in a car crash or something, then we're faced with three scenarios: natural disasters, like Vesuvius, common sickness, like the plague, or war. Now wars are plenty, but in usual circumstances it's the man who goes off to fight while the woman stays at home, so for them to die together they have to be in the same place at the same time—which means we can forget isolated battles like Agincourt, Waterloo and Trafalgar, and just concentrate on wars or battles that affected whole communities.'

'Like Vietnam?'

'Well, that's a bit recent, but, yes, that sort of thing.'

'What did you come up with?'

'Like I said, a few possibilities spring to mind—I had a trawl through the history books at the weekend. There was the persecution of the Protestants by Bloody Mary in 1557, or the earthquake in China that killed eight-hundred thousand in fifteen fifty-six. There's the Fire of London, of course, in sixteen sixty-six, or the French Revolution of seventeen eighty-nine.'

'Anything else?'

'The potato famine in Ireland took its toll in eighteen forty-five, or the San Francisco earthquake in nineteen oh-six could be a safe bet ... but when you get right down to it, there are just too many options. They could have been in all those places or none of them.'

'Aye, well.' Leon gave an "I-could-have-told-you-that" shake of his head. 'I'll go and find out, shall I?'

Chapter 20

COLORADO, AD 1864

Black Kettle was a tired man. Despite all his efforts to broker a peace between the white settlers and his Cheyenne tribe, a war between them seemed inevitable. No matter what treatise he signed, it was never enough, and he despaired for the future of his people. The Fort Laramie treaty of 1851 guaranteed the Cheyenne nation the vast territory of western Kansas and eastern Colorado, but the Pike's Peak gold rush of 1859 had sparked a population boom in Colorado and this had led to extensive white encroachment on Cheyenne land. Even the US Indian Commissioner had been forced to admit, 'We have substantially taken possession of the country and deprived the Indians of their accustomed means of support,' and Black Kettle could only agree with him.

Rather than evict the white settlers, the government sought to resolve the situation by demanding that the Southern Cheyenne sign a new treaty ceding all their lands save the small Sand Creek reservation in south-eastern Colorado, and Black Kettle had been faced with an impossible situation. Fearing that overwhelming US military power might result in an even less favourable settlement, he had signed the new treaty in 1861 and did all he could to see that the Cheyenne obeyed its provisions.

All in all he was a great leader with an almost unique vision of the possible coexistence between white society and the culture of the plains tribes, but the Sand Creek reservation could barely sustain the Indians who were forced to live there, as the land was unfit for cultivation and the nearest buffalo herd was over two hundred miles away. Many of Black Kettle's young warriors had begun to leave the reservation to prey on the livestock and goods of nearby settlers and wagon trains, and he could hardly blame them when faced with the choice of stealing from the rich whites or starving to death. Such a raid in the spring of that year had so angered the settlers that they dispatched their militia, who opened fire on the first band of Cheyenne they happened to meet. That the band had played no part in the raids, or the fact that the leader was actually approaching the militia for a parley, seemed to be incidental, and the shooting began in earnest, decimating the little band before they'd covered fifty yards.

The whole incident touched off an unco-ordinated Indian uprising across the Great Plains as Indian peoples from the Comanche in the south, to the Lakota in the north took advantage of the army's involvement in the civil war by striking back at those who had encroached upon their lands. Black Kettle, however, understood the white supremacy too well to support the cause of war and had decided to secure a promise of safety for his people by brokering a treaty with the military commander at Fort Weld.

Eleven moons had come and gone when Black Kettle's people erected a makeshift camp outside the fort's stockade, scraping away twelve inches of snow to set up their tipis and light their fires as they waited for their chief to parley with the white leader, the wind howling down from the plains and rattling the dream-catchers like the dry bones of the dead.

Beneath the fluttering buffalo hide of a tipi on the western edge of the camp, Hutenay, whose name meant She-Lion, worked diligently in one corner, busily fashioning a birthing robe for the unborn child inside her that swelled her belly to immense proportions and stretched taut the calico shift that covered her sparse frame. She was small and slight with evenly spaced almond brown eyes and jet black hair tied back with a leather band decorated with coloured beads, her aristocratic features only marred by the scar on her left temple that many said was the claw-print of the lion whose name she'd taken at birth, twenty winters before. Others said she'd derived her name from the mewing and growling she'd emitted from the moment she entered the world, a constant snuffling that had only ceased three days later after the birth of Wotenon, known as Crouching Wolf because of the sign on his neck. Not only had Hutenay ceased her growls of displeasure, but she seemed to thrive whenever Wotenon was near, her eyes taking on an animation never seen before, perking up with interest and delighting those around her.

So it had been during the years that followed, Hutenay and Wotenon sharing everything together as they grew and prospered, and when the time came for Wotenon to undergo the rituals of manhood, it was Hutenay who had prayed to the Cheyenne prophet, Sweet Medicine, for his success, none more proud than she when he passed the tests and was accepted as a warrior.

It was only natural that he take her as his bride and he had spent four days ranging far and wide for the pelts and hides demanded for her dowry, and during the ceremony he presented her with the skin of the she-lion he'd killed in the hills to the north, a fitting tribute to the woman who had stolen his heart.

Wotenon had wanted to join the young braves who had ridden away to raid the white farmsteads, and only Hutenay's love and the child she carried inside her had prevented him from going, his loyalty and devotion to her never in question. So they had come with the rest of the tribe to Fort Weld, Colorado, in the hope that their chief, Black Kettle, could bargain a treaty for their safety, a safety that would ensure not only their child's future, but the future of the whole Cheyenne nation.

She glanced up as Wotenon entered the tipi, shaking snow from his shoulders as he shrugged free of the mantle of fox fur, his dark eyes lighting up as he took in the kneeling figure of Hutenay, his lips spreading in a wide grin.

'You do not have to kneel when I enter, wife,' he teased. 'A low bow and a kiss of welcome will suffice to greet me.'

'So considerate you are,' she countered with a smile. 'If I could easily rise to my feet I would accord you all the honours you are due. As it is, you will have to stoop to me if you wish my kisses.'

He did so with a laugh, touching her cheek lightly with his fingertips as he kissed her, then he settled beside her, watching her work the beaver fur with small strong hands, the birthing robe taking shape beneath her fingers.

'How goes the parley?' she enquired softly. 'Have you news from Black Kettle?'

'No.' Wotenon shook his head, black locks shimmering about his shoulders. 'He still seeks counsel with the white leader. We will know the outcome soon enough.'

'Then we can go home,' she murmured, and Wotenon gave a derisive snort.

'Home? The Sand Creek reservation? That is not home, Hutenay. It is a blight given to us simply because the white settlers have no need of it. What will we do there other than starve?'

'We will see our child born in safety.'

'Only to die of starvation when your milk runs dry. I should have gone with Hawk Nose and brought food from the whites.'

'Brought a bullet from their guns, more like,' she said equably. 'Or brought their wrath down upon us just as Hawk Nose does. Only Black Kettle can pacify the whites and guarantee us free from attack.'

'All the tribes are united against the whites, Hutenay. They all fight for our rights and our freedom. Only Black Kettle holds back—only he seeks peaceful settlement when we should be taking back what is rightfully ours.'

'We cannot overcome the whites, Wotenon. Black Kettle knows this, just as you do. They are too many and too powerful. Our only hope is to live side by side in peace with the settlers.'

'The peace is already broken,' he pointed out logically. 'The white military massacred a friendly band of Cheyenne and now the nations are joined as one against them.'

'Friendly band of Cheyenne they might have been, Wotenon, but the raids Hawk Nose makes on the settlers are reason enough to stir their anger. We cannot hope to win any fight against them, no matter how many nations rise to our side.'

'I would rather die fighting like a true warrior than starve in my tipi like an old woman afraid of shadows,' he said hotly, and Hutenay touched his arm lightly, soothing his frustration with a calming hand.

'I know you would, Wotenon,' she murmured softly, 'but I would rather you live by my side than die for a lost cause at the hands of a white settler. I would rather you see your child grow. I would rather we live long enough to share grey hairs and see the birth of our grandchildren.'

'You would rather we live in shamed poverty than die proudly,' he stated flatly, and she sighed.

'And when you have ridden away to join Hawk Nose, what becomes of us you leave behind? When you die, all alone and in pain from the guns of the whites, who will see to your Hutenay and your newborn child? When you lie so proudly in death, who looks to the comfort of your family? Who will take your place in the hunting lodge and bring meat to our fires? There is no pride in dying a useless death, Wotenon. There is no pride in leaving behind misery and desolation.

There is no pride in creating a widow and a fatherless child for a pointless cause.'

'Is it pointless?'

'You know it is. Any cause that cannot be won is pointless. You die for the sake of pride and that is all you will die for.'

'Well ... I hear the truth of your words, Hutenay,' he conceded grudgingly, 'but it does not make the bearing of it any lighter.'

'No. Truth was ever a burden to carry. Just like the burden I carry inside me. Help me to my feet, Wotenon, and we shall go to the shaman's lodge and pray to the prophet, Sweet Medicine. Let us ask for the strength to carry the burden of truth, for when truth fails us we are surely lost for all time.'

So they prayed to Sweet Medicine, the great prophet who had given their nation the laws of government and the laws that spoke against lying and cheating, and supplied them with a comprehensive value system that dealt with such things as love, respect and co-operation with others. Sweet Medicine had also given them the central belief in the four sacred persons who are the representatives both of the four directions of the wind and of the different stages of life, safeguarding the people from famine and hardship, the arrows of these persons given to the Cheyenne by Sweet Medicine to be protected or the nation would not prosper.

Such was the story of creation that the Cheyenne guarded and kept sacred, told only at night by the spiritual leaders of the tribe, the beliefs and legendary tales handed down verbally through the generations so that all the history and perspective of the Cheyenne might be preserved for ever.

Three days passed before Black Kettle secured the guarantee of safety for his people, gathering his tribe together and leading them back through the drifting snow of the plains to the sanctuary of Sand Creek, the harsh weather impeding them every step of the way. Wotenon made a litter to carry

216

Hutenay in the wake of his horse, his woman heavily muffled and wrapped in furs against the bitter wind, and each night he made a camp and a fire to warm her, rubbing her hands and feet and feeding her oatmeal crumbs and strips of dried meat from their carry-sack.

'Tomorrow, Hutenay,' he soothed. 'We will reach Sand Creek tomorrow and the shaman's woman will tend to you.'

'It is but a birth, Crouching Wolf.' She smiled at his concern, calling him by his full name for effect. 'I am sure I shall manage without her.'

'All the same … I fear the jolting you have endured on the journey might bring the child before it is due.'

'Another moon at least.' She nodded with all the certainty of a pregnant woman. 'There is little movement within me so I feel sure the child does not hurry for release.'

'It will be a son,' Wotenon decided, gently stroking her distended belly. 'I shall teach him how to hunt and ride a horse … and teach him to love his mother as much as his father does.'

'And if it is a daughter?'

'She will be as beautiful as her mother and she will break the hearts of a thousand warriors when she marries.'

'Such a daughter would demand a heavy dowry.'

'A dozen horses at least,' Wotenon grinned, scooping snow into a pot and melting it over the fire. 'Only a chief's son or a mighty warrior will have the means to pay the price.'

The firelight flickered over his features, bringing the mole on the side of his neck to life, the outline of the wolf shifting as though it stirred and stretched, and Hutenay touched it lightly, her frown of deep fascination bringing her eyebrows together on the bridge of her nose.

'So good you are to me, Wotenon,' she whispered, her warm breath causing vapour to form in the cold air. 'It is no wonder I love you so.'

'They say you felt the claw of a mountain lion at your birth,

217

Hutenay,' he murmured, turning to peer at the scar on her temple. 'But I say it was the arrow tip of Sweet Medicine … He marked you out for me, for do I not carry the same mark on my chest? The prophet had spoken and set us aside for each other. Love joined us from the moment we dropped from the bellies of our mothers.'

'Yes.' She nodded sombrely. 'It has always been so, Wotenon. Even the shaman's magic could not keep us apart.'

'When the magic of Sweet Medicine is cast, She-Lion, all the shamen in the land could not overrule it.'

She knew he was right, of course. No shaman, however powerful, was a match for the power of Sweet Medicine, the great prophet of the Cheyenne nation, and he had made the sign on Hutenay's head and Wotenon's chest, his sacred sign that bound them together for all time.

She watched as Wotenon sprinkled herbs in the pot of melted snow that had begun to bubble and boil, the rich aroma of basil and thyme filling the tipi as he stirred it with his knife, then he brought the pot to her lips, supporting her with a strong arm as she sipped slowly.

'Drink your fill and then you must rest,' he said firmly. 'Black Kettle has decreed we break camp early tomorrow. He intends to be in Sand Creek by nightfall.'

'Who else is wintering there?' she asked between sips, and Wotenon shrugged.

'Kiowas and Apaches … possibly some Comanche. We will join Chief White Antelope and his Cheyenne by the bend in the river. Now, sleep, Hutenay. We have a long journey tomorrow.'

They made slow progress through the drifting snow, the open plains a barren white wilderness that froze exposed flesh and dazzled the eyes. Hutenay was jostled along behind Wotenon's mare, the litter carving deep runnels amid the hoof prints of a nation on the move, returning to the dubious sanctuary of the reservation. The weak sun had all but disappeared by the time they reached Sand Creek, the smoke from the Kiowa fires hanging like shrouds in the bare trees. White Antelope's people came to help them, unloading the horses and erecting the tipis along the river bank, heaping wood for the fires and sharing their meagre rations with Black Kettle's weary tribe.

Crouching Wolf saw Hutenay settled in their tipi, snuggled in furs by the fire, then he made his way to the river, his moccasins leaving deep imprints in the snow as he checked for signs of beaver and bear or fallow deer who came to the water at twilight to drink, an arrow already nocked in the bowstring in case he chanced upon an unsuspecting creature, any meat welcome to an empty cooking pot and a rumbling belly. It was fully dark by the time he heard the rustling in the undergrowth and the little splash as something entered the water, and he followed the trail of ripples reflected in the moonlight, eyes narrowed in concentration as he stalked his prey.

A sleek wet body emerged on the far bank, a dark shape silhouetted against the snow, and the faint twang of the bowstring was followed by a whisper of the streaking arrow, then Wotenon was up and running, splashing through the icy water to retrieve the stricken creature. It was a muskrat, neatly impaled by the arrow and lying still on the bank, not the best of meats but it would make a welcome addition to the cooking pot and they could use the fur, any contribution, however slight, thankfully received in times of hardship.

Hutenay was feeding logs to the fire when he returned to their tipi, the damp wood causing the shelter to fill with smoke and making their eyes water, but she looked up and smiled when he entered, immediately skinning the muskrat and dropping it in the pot with the sweet potatoes, beet and a handful of dried maize before adding herbs for flavour.

'You did well, Wotenon,' she nodded appreciatively. 'I

thought the Kiowas and Apaches would have stripped the river bare of game by now.'

'They camp further downstream,' he grunted, 'but I was fortunate tonight. Tomorrow I will go the hills to hunt with Crooked Finger and Rising Moon. Twisted Horn of White Antelope's Cheyenne has spoken of goats in the Valley of Snakes.'

'Settlers' goats?'

'What other kind are there? Twisted Horn said they are strays from the wintering flock at Fort Lyon.'

'You will bring their militia down upon us, Crouching Wolf,' Hutenay warned prophetically, and Wotenon grinned.

'The goats are strays, Hutenay, and the whites have not even begun to search for them. Even if they did, they would not think of searching the hills. They have no reason to suspect our people of taking their animals and will simply blame the timber wolves.'

'Well, take a care. If they should find you with a goat …'

She let the warning hang in the air and Wotenon shrugged.

'Black Kettle flies the flag of the settlers and the white flag of peace over his tipi. We have a guarantee of safety from the militia.'

'Even so, Wotenon, it takes only one spark to set a forest ablaze.'

'We have to eat. What kind of warrior would I be if I did not provide for my woman?'

'Better a hungry warrior than a dead one,' she pointed out, stirring the pot with a cooking stick, and he studied her closely.

'And will you say the same when the child in your belly cries out with hunger? Will you warn me of the dangers in hunting the settlers' flock when he lies dying for the want of goat meat?'

'Yes, Wotenon, I will,' she said adamantly. 'You are hunter

enough to provide for us without the need to chase stray goats and cattle that belong to the white settlers. They have given us the poorest land and we share the reservation with Kiowas, Apache and Comanche, yet you always fill our cooking pot. But were it not so, Crouching Wolf, were we to have to gnaw the bark from the trees, I tell you this—I would rather lose our child to hunger, and a hundred more children besides, than to lose you to the white man's guns.'

He saw the fire in her eyes and heard the determination in her voice, determination borne out of love for him, and he softened, reaching out to take her hand and squeezing her fingers gently.

'Hutenay … She-Lion who is my very spirit, I hear you … I know where your words come from and the reasons that placed them inside you. Is it not the same for me? You are my very life and I would forego anything to have you remain a part of it. We share a love that drives all before it … yet it is because of my love for you and the child you carry that forces me to bring meat to our fires. Would I watch you starve? I would fight the bear and the lion with nothing but a throwing stick if it gave you life. Fear and danger are nothing when compared with the value I place in having you by my side.'

'Then do not squander it for the sake of a goat, Wotenon. Search for the den of a bear or the lair of a lion if you seek danger to prove your love for me. I do not doubt your skill as a hunter and am sure that any creature you encounter will find its way to our food store, but goat meat carries a terrible price, and one that I am not prepared to pay.'

'I will speak with Crooked Finger at daybreak,' Wotenon sighed resignedly. 'He will know where the bears have gone to ground.'

'And if the kill is yours, Crouching Wolf,' she promised with a smile, 'I will make you a sleeping robe from the fur … which is more than I could fashion from goat hide.'

'And the extra meat will see us to the new moon,' he conceded with a grin. 'It will not be just the child she carries that turns my Hutenay into a little fat Cheyenne squaw.'

The three hunters found no trace of bear, but Rising Moon discovered the track of a deer and they followed the imprints into the forest, fanning out and creeping forward silently as they stalked their prey. It was late afternoon by the time they cornered their quarry in a thicket of bracken, and Crooked Finger edged closer from the north, his advancing scent driving the beast to break cover into the path of Wotenon. Too late, the deer saw him and veered away to the left, nostrils flaring and frightened eyes rolling as the startled creature impaled itself on Rising Moon's spear, spraying blood and kicking up the snow as it tumbled to the ground.

Crooked Finger cut its throat and they divided the meat into three portions, the hide going to Rising Moon who had made the kill, and they each filled their carry-sacks with the precious cargo before making their way back to the reservation, justly proud of their day's work and hungrily anticipating the taste of fresh venison. Hutenay was delighted and she roasted a leg there and then on a spit over the fire, the succulent aroma making their mouths water and bringing the children from neighbouring tipis to watch wide-eyed as the meat sizzled and spat deliciously.

'Bring a knife, little Shooting Star,' Hutenay encouraged, beckoning the gaping children. 'And you, Six Toes. Cut yourselves a strip … all of you. Sweet Medicine has heard your prayers and you will sleep with hot meat in your bellies tonight. Come, children. Be careful of the heat. Hold the spit, Dog's Tail—one at a time or you will dislodge our supper into the fire … There now. Tell your fathers of Crouching Wolf's skill as a hunter.'

Wotenon watched grudgingly as the children cut hunks of meat from the joint, and he shook his head despairingly as the last of them scurried away back to their tipis, the deer leg sadly depleted and ravaged over the crackling fire.

'It is a wonder you do not throw what is left of the bone to the dogs,' he muttered, and she laughed at him, crouching at his side and kissing his cheek.

'Would you begrudge the children a little food when we have so much of it, Wotenon?' she chided gently, and he snorted.

'*Had* so much of it,' he emphasised. 'There is barely enough left to fill one belly, let alone two.'

'Now you stretch the truth wide enough to put the storyteller to shame. See? There is plenty for us both with a breakfast there besides … *and* a good bone to add to the cooking pot. Not to mention the hind quarters and treats we have buried in the snow for safekeeping. We will feast for a week on today's hunt, and well you know it, Wotenon.'

'Aiee,' he laughed. 'I have stirred a viper's nest and Hutenay strikes with all the venom of a disturbed snake. How easily you rise to mild rebukes.'

'Tease me, would you?' she giggled, tipping a handful of snow down the back of his doeskin. 'And there was I thinking Crouching Wolf had turned callous towards starving children. I should have known better than to listen to him.'

'Indeed you should,' he laughed, holding her at bay as she tried to fill his leather breeches with snow. 'Now calm yourself woman, before you cause harm to the child in that big belly of yours.'

'Calm me with kisses,' she bargained, the snow melting between her fingers, 'or I shall place my cold hand where it might best cool your passion for teasing.'

'And other passions, too … enough to thwart a She-Lion on heat.'

'Well,' she relented, settling back on her haunches with a rueful grin. 'I have to admit to a heat for Crouching Wolf … Eat your fill, warrior brave and mighty hunter of mine and we shall see how you stalk the game between my thighs.'

'I will pierce you with my spear, Hutenay, until you cry out in surrender.'

'Tenderly, Wotenon,' she whispered lovingly. 'Tenderly from behind so we cause no hurt to the child in my belly.'

'Tenderly it shall be,' he agreed with a resolute nod. 'Never would I be the cause of hurt to you or the one you carry.'

'Eat then, and let us to our furs ... then we shall see how well you wield your spear.'

It was at dawn the following morning that the white troopers charged through the sleeping encampment, ignoring the American flag and the white flag of peace that flew so proudly from Black Kettle's tipi, their horses stampeding through the packed shelters as they fired at everything that moved, gunshots echoing through the trees in a never-ending cacophony of sound.

Wotenon did not bother with breeches as he stormed from the tipi, shock and disbelief inuring him to the icy cold. The first bullet caught him in the shoulder, spinning him round, and he dropped to his knees, searching for the knife that had slipped from nerveless fingers. Hutenay appeared at the flap, eyes wide with fear, and Wotenon shoved her back out of sight as he scrambled to his feet, oblivious to the pain in his shoulder as he tried to make sense of the mayhem around him.

He saw the receding troopers wheel and turn for another charge and he braced himself for the onslaught, the vapour from the horses' nostrils like the fires of hell as they bore down on him, the very earth trembling beneath his feet to the thunder of their hooves. Crooked Finger leapt into their path and Wotenon saw him cut down, half his head blown away and gaping holes where his chest should be, then there was no more time for thought for the horses were up to him

224

and he hurled his knife at the nearest rider before diving to one side and curling into a protective ball.

A flying hoof caught his thigh, cutting the flesh to the bone, and he heard Hutenay scream somewhere behind him, a high-pitched wail of despair, then there was nothing except a deepening numbness and a mild surprise as his body jerked once, twice, three times in response to the bullets that slammed into him in quick succession.

Hutenay couldn't believe how much blood there was, staining the snow in crimson streaks and turning the river red with the life-pulse of her people, so many shattered bodies down and broken like rag dolls tossed aside by a wayward child.

Rising Moon with a hole neatly between his eyes and his brains oozing in a grey slime. Little Shooting Star with a gaping wound in his chest you could put your hand through, and the twisted body of Dog's Tail with no outward signs of hurt but an ever-widening pool of blood seeping from his spine. So many dead and dying. Two Spoons and his wife, Dancing Swan. Falling Rock and his eldest son, Brown Beaver, who would have been made a warrior in the spring. Blunt Knife and Rain Cloud, Running Fox and Falling Leaf, and tiny Six Toes, sightless eyes staring at the lightening sky.

Hutenay held her swollen belly as she ran, lurching through the undergrowth in blind panic as she fled the awful guns, side-stepping the terribly wounded wife of Black Kettle in a desperate bid to escape the mindless slaughter of the innocents. The air was sucked from her body and she found herself sitting on the ground, one shattered hand still covering the bloodied hole where her child had been only seconds before, and she stared in disbelief at the entrails seeping between her fingers, holding on to the moment before shock gave way to pain and she shrieked her agony.

Something heavy thumped her in the chest and she flopped back in the snow, feeling nothing now, totally numb and detached as the swirling mists descended before her eyes, the shouts and screams, gunshots and pounding hooves fading into an unearthly silence that went on and on for all eternity.

Chapter 21

'Tell me what you know of that time, Marion,' Charles said softly, and she blinked at him.

'Know? I only know what I told you.'

'It was winter, yes?'

'Not really,' she shook her head. 'Eleven moons—that would mean November, wouldn't it?'

'If you say so. Can you remember it?'

Her eyes glazed and she seemed to look deep within herself as if she were examining some inner thought processes that required concentration and effort, raking through the ashes of the past with a trowel of perception and insight that defied all logic or reasonable explanation.

'It was cold,' she murmured distantly. 'The snow was thick that year and food was scarce. I remember we went back to the reservation so full of hope—Black Kettle had a guarantee of peace from the militia and we thought we were safe for the winter at least.'

'Do you know who attacked you that morning?'

'No ... just ... it was just troopers ... white men on horses charging back and forth through the camp ... shooting everything in sight ... the women ... the children ... everyone ... my poor Wotenon ... He was so brave, you know ... so very, very brave.'

'He had a mole on his neck like all the others? And a birthmark on his chest?'

Marion absently touched her left temple, her fingers

almost caressing the scar, and she nodded, all the pain and trauma of that day at Sand Creek reflected in her eyes.

'Yes … just like Darius and Parlian … just like Lupus and Claude … the same.'

'Professor Macleod thinks it might be an appearance fixation,' Charles said carefully. 'That's why all the characters have the same traits. Would you agree with that?'

'I don't know,' she murmured wearily, her eyes coming back into focus, and she seemed to shake herself as if breaking free of a terrible dream. 'You're the expert. You tell me.'

But Charles could tell her nothing, for there were no ready answers to explain the unexplainable. He could tell her he thought the stories were actual accounts, but what would that achieve? He might be doing irreparable harm to her fragile state of mind if he led her to think he believed her tales to be true and factual and experienced by Marion herself … and the bottom line was, he was only guessing. He had no proof, no concrete evidence to suggest she actually lived those past lives. It was all conjecture, and until they had more to go on it would be foolish to lead her along a path that might be so far removed from the truth that it would do her more harm than good.

'It's curious, though,' he said slowly, and she turned to peer at him.

'What is?'

'Well … your tribe of Cheyenne had just returned from a meeting at Fort Weld where your chief, Black Kettle, had secured a guarantee of safety, but you no sooner get settled back on the reservation when you're attacked. Doesn't that seem strange to you?'

'Not really. The whites were always breaking treaties— nothing was sacred to them. They had no respect for the land or the people who roamed it. They had no respect for truth or honour. They had no respect for our culture or our ways.

They were so greedy, so … insensitive. What they did …' She shrugged expressively. 'It was to be expected, really.'

'And they attacked at dawn, you say?'

'It was so warm wrapped in our furs like that … so snuggly warm. We were both naked. Wotenon was cuddled into my back, his arms around me, holding my belly. … our child. I remember waking up after the first gunfire and thinking it was thunder … Then Wotenon was up and out of the tent before I could stop him. I heard the gunshots then and I just threw my buckskin over me and went to the flap. I could hear the galloping horses … the shooting … the shouts and screams. I called for Wotenon to come back so I could attend to the wound in his shoulder, but he shoved me inside out of the way and when I looked again he … he was dead.'

'So you ran.'

'Nowhere was safe,' she said woodenly. 'It was pointless even trying to hide, but … but at times like that you don't think logically, you just feel this driving need to get away … to escape the carnage.'

'Do you remember being shot?'

'Not really. Even at the time I couldn't understand it. One minute I was running, and the next I was sitting in the snow with a hole in my stomach. The … the bullet that hit me went through my hand first … right through the knuckle, and it took my middle finger clean away. When I looked, I … remember thinking, "That's odd. I'm sure I had five fingers a moment ago." Then I saw the mess of my belly and all I could think about was the baby … dead before it had even had a chance of life. I was thinking about that when … when, I suppose, the next bullet hit me. Instead of sitting up, I was suddenly on my back. Then everything went grey and quiet and I thought, "Thank Sweet Medicine the awful noise has stopped at last," and that was it.'

'Sweet Medicine was your god?'

'Manito was our god, Doctor,' she said firmly. 'Sweet Medicine was our prophet ... our link with our god.'

'And was he the same prophet for all the tribes?'

'The prophet was different, but the concept was the same. The Cheyenne had Sweet Medicine and the Arapahoe had Erect Horns ... same principle, different prophet.'

Charles sighed at the complexity and intricacy of the whole story, every facet detailed beyond belief, beyond the bounds of an active imagination, and he knew Marion hadn't simply made it up, for no invention could withstand such probing questions or provide such knowledgeable answers.

'Well,' he said, coming to his feet: 'I'll leave you to get some rest.'

'Are you seeing Professor Macleod today?'

'This afternoon ... I expect he'll be in to see you later.'

'Another regression?'

'I doubt it.' Charles shook his head. 'It's too soon after the last one. Tomorrow perhaps.'

'It's getting close, isn't it?' she murmured, blinking at him helplessly. 'Getting closer to the modern day ... closer to the moment of truth.'

'Don't worry about it,' he placated softly, raising a warm smile. 'The closer we get, the closer you are to being cured and released from here.'

'Cured?' She gave a derisive shrug of her shoulders. 'I don't know which is better ... Carrying all this ... this history around in my head like this, or ... or the not-knowing, the ignorance of before ... the time when I was just plain Marion Harting with a suicidal tendency. Now I don't know who I am any more.'

'We'll get there, Marion,' Charles nodded decisively. 'I promise we'll get there.'

Charles spent his lunch break in the library, reading everything he could find on a tribe of Cheyenne Indians

230

under the leadership of a chief called Black Kettle who were massacred in a place called Sand Creek in November 1864. What he read startled him beyond reason and he was pensive and thoughtful as he waited for Leon Macleod, launching into his theory as soon as the psychiatrist had sat down.

'Tell me, Leon, are you still of the belief that Marion is simply recounting stories that her mind has picked up over the years?'

'I haven't entirely thrown out that possibility, Charles. Why do you ask?'

'I read about it in the library today—Black Kettle's Cheyenne tribe.'

'It's well documented then?' Leon shrugged. 'That could explain how Marion picked up the information.'

'I don't think so.'

'Why not?'

'Because ... because the information carries the whole story, not just bits of it. If someone were to read about it, Leon, they'd know that when Black Kettle led his people back to Sand Creek after the parley at Fort Weld, there was a certain Colonel John Chivington of the Third Colorado Volunteers who had no intention of honouring any agreement made at the Fort. He took his troop out looking for bands of Cheyenne to fight, but he couldn't find any. When he learned that Black Kettle had returned to Sand Creek, he attacked the unsuspecting encampment at dawn on November the twenty-ninth—just like Marion told it.'

'But that doesn't ...'

'Oh, yes it does, Leon,' Charles insisted, 'because when I asked Marion who attacked the camp, she didn't know. If she'd read it like I did, she'd have known it was Chivington, but she didn't have a clue.'

'And the dead and injured?' Leon snapped. 'Did she get that right, too?'

'Oh, yes. She could have just said a lot of people were

killed, but she was more specific than that. It's true that Black Kettle's wife was terribly wounded, but he survived. He came back for his wife later. It's also true that Black Kettle flew the American flag and a white flag of peace above his tent. More than two hundred Cheyenne died that morning, Leon, many of them women and children, and after the slaughter, Chivington's men sexually mutilated and scalped many of the dead, then exhibited their trophies later to cheering crowds in Denver.'

'I see.'

'Marion didn't mention any of that, Leon, because she didn't know of it, she *couldn't* have known of it, because as Hutenay she was dead by then. She didn't read about it, and more to the point, you *know* she didn't.'

'You can't prove ...'

'I don't have to prove it.' Charles shook his head angrily. 'It's as plain as the nose on your face, only you won't admit it. You're so busy searching for fixations and psychoses that you can't see the obvious when it's staring you in the face. Marion knows too much for her to be inventing these stories, and she doesn't know enough to have read about them.'

'That's an oversimplification, Charles,' Leon protested, and Charles snorted with derision.

'No, it isn't. She knew too much about Babylon to have made it all up, but she didn't know that Belshazzar died during the fighting. If she'd read about it, she'd have known it, but the truth is she didn't know because as Lindinia she died before the news ever got out. The same goes for this last episode in Colorado. She didn't know who attacked the encampment for the simple reason she died in the slaughter. It's as simple as that, Leon.'

'Well, I'm afraid you're wrong, Charles,' Leon said with quiet authority. 'Minds like Marion's can totally convince themselves that what they're saying is the utter truth and minds like yours can totally convince themselves that they believe it wholeheartedly, but that is the nature of the beast. In all honesty, and for what it's worth, I'm inclined to believe it, too ... but believing it and proving it are two separate issues and my "professional integrity", as you call it, demands that I deal only in facts. I can't cure a belief. I can't treat reincarnation and I can't recommend a therapy for a dose of history. So, prove your theory, and if you're right that's all well and good, but we still have to find the cause of Marion's suicidal compulsion. Because that's the bottom line here, Charles.' He nodded emphatically. 'Marion wants to kill herself and we don't know why. Forget the stories from the past. Forget Babylon and Pompeii and Colorado, and concentrate on here and now, because something in the present is the root cause of the problem, Charles, no matter how much you dress it up with the pages of history. It doesn't matter if they're true or not. It doesn't matter if they're real or imagined. The only thing that matters is why Marion wants to commit suicide ... and that's what I intend to find out.'

Charles felt himself deflate, all the passion and fire subsiding inside him beneath the quenching water of Leon's quiet logic. He was right, of course. It didn't matter if Hutenay really existed in the dim recesses of the past if that existence failed to provide answers to the questions in the present. It wasn't the validity of history they had to prove, not the truth of yesterday, but the truth of today. That's what was important. Marion's sanity and future depended on it.

'I'm sorry,' he murmured apologetically. 'I didn't mean to sound off like that.'

'Quite all right,' Leon smiled. 'I understand the emotive nature of these stories and it's easy to get caught up in them. Take a break from it. Enjoy the weekend, and I'll see you on Monday.'

Charles spent Friday evening at home in his study, working his way through the pile of notes he'd made on Marion's case, searching for clues to account for her present state of mind. Something in the stack of handwritten jottings held the answer, but it eluded him like a forgotten dream, chasing shadows and will-o'-the-wisps as he leapt from one half-baked theory to another. As midnight approached he forced himself to return to the basics, the fundamental facts that had first convinced him there was a connection between the Marion of today and the characters of the past.

He tore a clean sheet from the notebook and wrote down the salient points, taking his mind back to the very beginning where it all started, Linda Beavis and a house in Derwent Road, and an ornament or a photograph of a group of sailors that was enough to send a young girl over the edge into suicidal despair.

He wrote the name 'Tim Beavis' on the page followed by 'Royal Navy' and 'Falklands War', definite links that were beyond question, and he stared at them as if he expected the answer to jump out at him, but things were never that simple and there had to be another link in the chain, one that held them all together. Tim was in the Navy and the Navy was an integral part of the conflict, so was that the link? If so, what was it about the Navy that held the key?

Was Tim himself the link? Charles had seen photographs taken of the man before he sailed away to his death, but there had been nothing untoward there, no telltale signs that he had any connection with Marion in any shape or form, so what had Marion seen that he had so blatantly missed?

Perhaps, he thought, it wasn't Tim Beavis, but someone else in the photograph who had been the catalyst. Perhaps it wasn't the photograph at all that had sent Marion on a downward spiral into suicidal depression, but something else in the room, something that had been absent when Charles had visited, when the room was stripped bare for decorating. It may have been something entirely different and Marion had simply mentioned the photograph absently, talking about the first thing that came into her head in an effort to avoid the horror that had numbed her to the core. Charles needed to see the room again, see it as it had been on the day Marion was there, all the ornaments and pictures and knickknacks returned to their regular places and the room restored to its familiar state.

Something in that room held the key and Charles was determined to find it.

Derwent Road hadn't changed and number sixteen was just as dilapidated as ever, but at least the doorbell worked and Charles heard the chimes echoing through the house as he waited on the doorstep, sheltering from the rain beneath the overhanging porch. He caught a movement in the hall and the door was opened by an older woman, grey-haired and thin-faced, and he smiled warmly as she frowned at him, assuming her to be Linda's mother.

'Mrs Beavis?'

'Yes?'

'Sorry to trouble you on a Saturday morning ... Is Linda there, please?'

'She's gone shopping uptown with some friends. Was she expecting you?'

'No.' Charles shook his head. 'I should have phoned first. I just expected her to be in.'

'Was it important?' The woman peered at him quizzically. 'Can I take a message?'

'Perhaps you can help me. I'm Doctor Levington, I came here a few weeks ago and spoke to Linda about a work colleague of hers.'

'Marion Harting?'

Charles blinked at her.

'Linda told you about that?'

'Oh, yes. I was feeling a bit off colour when you called before.'

'You should have popped your head round the door.' Charles smiled. 'I am a doctor, after all.'

'I didn't think of that,' she laughed, then frowned, deep furrows lining her brow. 'I don't know how I can help you, though. I only ever met Marion once.'

'Actually … I came today in the hope of discussing Linda's brother … Your son, Tim.'

'Tim?' The smile left her face. 'Why would you want to discuss Tim? Linda was just a toddler when he died.'

'Yes, l know … I'm sorry if this is painful to you, Mrs Beavis, but Marion mentioned a picture she'd seen of your son when she came here and it might have been that photograph that affected her. It could hold the clue to her present problems.'

'The photo of Tim?' She stared at him. 'Are you sure?'

'Not entirely,' Charles admitted with a shrug. 'I'm clutching at straws, really. But either that picture or something else in the room sparked the whole thing off. I wonder … Would it be at all possible for me to see the room now that you've finished decorating?'

'Oh … right.' She opened the door wider and moved to one side. 'If you think it would help, Doctor. You'd better come in.'

'Thank you.' He stepped into the hall with a grateful nod. 'I was a bit presumptuous there. I assume you *have* finished decorating?'

'Downstairs is all done,' she told him, ushering him into the sitting room. 'Just the bedrooms to do now. Cup of tea, Doctor?'

'That would be lovely, thank you. White with one sugar, please.'

'That's the photo Marion saw.' She nodded at the picture on the wall. 'Make yourself at home. I won't be a minute.'

Everything had been returned to its rightful place following the disruption of redecorating, and left alone,

236

Charles studied everything with minute care, searching for a connection, for the one thing that Marion had instantly recognised as a link between this life and the past. His eyes came to rest on the photograph, seen now from a distance and not close-up like before, and he looked at it as a whole and not as he had previously done, when he'd simply inspected the three central characters. He could see the superstructure of the warship in the background, the sweep of a metal deck trailing away to the left, and Charles's eyes were drawn like magnets to a fourth figure sitting on the deck, a lonely figure bearing all the mournful sorrow of a lost soul.

Charles leaned closer, screwing up his eyes as he concentrated on the character, dressed as the others but minus the cap, his white front pulled askew by something cradled in his arms. It was a cat, a little kitten, and the man was stroking it lovingly as if he were heaping all his love and devotion on the simple creature nestled so tenderly against his chest.

Charles straightened, a puzzled frown creasing his brow as he tried to fathom what it was about the man that held his interest. Then he saw it, as plain as the nose on his face, and he stared as though mesmerised, his heart pounding fearfully in his chest and a rushing like the wind in his ears. There, on the side of the unknown sailor's neck, was a large mole, its shape unmistakably that of a crouching dog with pricked-up ears, a replica of Anubis, the Egyptian god of mummification.

It seemed as if the world held its breath, poised and still for countless aeons as Charles fought to absorb the impossible before him, his eyes gaping incredulously at the same sight witnessed and recognised by Marion, a simple blemish imbued with all the mighty power and prophecy of an ancient high priest and charged with the ability to reach across the span of centuries and turn minds.

237

'Did you find what you were looking for, Doctor?' Mrs Beavis said at his elbow, and he jumped like a startled rabbit. He nodded quickly, finding his voice with the greatest difficulty.

'Do you ... do you know all the men in the picture?' he managed at last, his heart pounding fitfully, and the woman smiled.

'That's my Tim in the middle and the other two are Sam Westbrook and Trevor Singleton. They were great mates, those three. Did everything together.'

'What about the other man?' Charles nodded at the photograph. 'The one holding the cat?'

'Glen something.' She passed Charles a brimming cup of tea and settled herself on the couch. 'Do sit down, Doctor.'

'Thank you.' He found a seat then peered at her intently. 'I don't suppose you can remember his last name, Mrs Beavis?'

'It was a funny name ... Botchey ... Potchey ... Something like that. He was a very quiet boy, I seem to remember.'

'You met him?'

'Mmm. Tim brought him home one weekend. I don't think he said half a dozen words all the time he was here—a moody sort of lad, but he was polite enough.'

'Did he—I don't suppose you'd know, but ... was he ...'

'Was he killed when the *Sheffield* was hit?' she finished for him. 'Yes, he was. Sam was the only survivor out of the four in the photo.'

'Did Linda know that?'

'Of course.'

And Linda told Marion and Marion knew she'd lost her soulmate. Perhaps "knew" was the wrong word. Sensed it maybe, a subconscious awareness that triggered a desperate need to join him, unknowingly guiding her along a path of self-destruction, a path she couldn't see and couldn't control, but all-consuming in its compulsive intensity.

'Would you know where I might find Sam Westbrook?' Charles asked after a moment, not really holding out much hope that she'd know, but to his surprised delight she nodded, smiling at him over the rim of her cup.

'He left the Navy some years ago and runs a pub in Portsmouth. He wrote to me about Tim after he came back from the Falklands and he keeps in touch—you know, Christmas cards and suchlike. He keeps inviting me down there for a drink, but I've never been.'

'Which pub?'

'It was called the Bayside when he took over, but he changed its name to the Shiny Sheff—that's what they called *HMS Sheffield*, you know—the Shiny Sheff.'

'Mrs Beavis … thank you.'

It was nearly over, but not quite. Together in life, together in death, together in all things, Ki-Un-Rah had prophesied, but something had driven them apart, breaking the pact with the gods, and that would account for why they weren't together now. The sun god had been surpassed and their eternal duty to protect the pharaoh Ramesses was done.

He just had to find out when and how and why.

Chapter 22

Charles and Rosemary drove down to Portsmouth that afternoon, enjoying the last of the summer sunshine, and they took a room overlooking the beach in the Queen's Hotel in Southsea, taking their time to change before going down to dinner.

'I can't think why we had to traipse all the way to Portsmouth,' Rosemary said around a mouthful of prawn cocktail. 'This Sam Westbrook didn't even know your patient, did he?'

'No, but I'm hoping he can throw some light on Glen Botchey, or Potchey, or whatever his name was. It just gives me a fuller picture … fills in some of the blanks. Anyway, it does us good to get away now and then.'

'I can see where all this is leading.'

'Can you?'

'Yes.' Rosemary smiled. 'Sam Westbrook is going to tell you that Glen Botchey came from the Outer Hebrides or somewhere, and you'll be dragging me up there tomorrow.'

'Probably.' Charles laughed. 'Do you mind?'

'Not really,' she shrugged. 'Like you say, it does us good to have a few days away. I was only going to mow the lawn this weekend.' She paused, fork poised halfway to her mouth. 'Do you really think Sam can tell you anything useful?'

'Well, he can tell me something about Glen, and when you get right down to it, he's the other half of the equation. It all revolves around him and Marion, whichever piece of history you look at. Glen is the key to the whole thing.'

'When were you planning on seeing Sam?'

'I thought we'd go along this evening,' Charles said, pushing his plate away and sitting back in his seat. 'I checked in the phone book before we came down to dinner. The Shiny Sheff isn't far from here. We could catch a taxi.'

'I see. And if Sam tells you Glen came from Glasgow or somewhere?'

'How do you fancy a run up to Scotland tomorrow?' Charles suggested with a grin, and she shook her head despairingly.

Sam Westbrook was a stocky man, twenty years or so older than the young man who had stood alongside Tim Beavis and Trevor Singleton for a photograph on the quarterdeck of *HMS Sheffield*, but for all that, Charles recognised him straight away and he ushered Rosemary to the end of the bar where Sam was working, jiggling the change in his pocket as he waited to be served.

'Yes, sir,' Sam smiled. 'What can I get you?'

'Pint of bitter and a white wine, please,' Charles nodded. 'And take one for yourself.'

'I'll have a half, thanks.'

'My pleasure ... perhaps you could join us for five minutes when you're free.'

Sam frowned at him and Charles gave him a hasty smile.

'Just for a chat. It seems we've got something in common.'

'Oh?'

'Mrs Beavis ... Lives in Wembley.'

'Dora?' Sam's eyes lit up. 'Lovely old girl. I keep inviting her down here, but I think she's glued to London.'

'She told us about your pub.'

'The Shiny Sheff'? I've been here six years come February. There you go, pint of bitter and a white wine—on the house.'

241

'That's very kind of you.'

'Any friend of Dora's ... How long are you down here for?'

'Just tonight. That's why I'd like the opportunity of talking to you while I've got the chance.'

'What did you want to talk about?'

'Glen.'

Sam blinked at him over the bar. 'Glen?'

'Glen Botchey? Potchey? Served on the *Sheffield* with you in the Falklands?'

'Oh, you mean Glen Kotchley. Did you know him?'

'No ... that's what I'd like to talk about.'

Sam seemed to consider for a moment then he shrugged, casting a practised eye around the half empty bar.

'Give me a couple of minutes and I'll be over.'

Charles nodded and guided Rosemary to a table in the corner. When Sam joined them, he raised his glass in a salute as he slid onto the bench seat opposite them.

'Now then, Mr...?'

'Levington, but call me Charles.'

'Charles ... you wanted to talk about Glen.'

'Yes. How well did you know him?'

'As well as anyone, I suppose. We were in the same mess on the *Sheffield*. He was a bit younger than me, but we went ashore together a few times.'

'You were friends with Tim Beavis and Trevor Singleton?'

'Inseparable we were.' Sam smiled nostalgically. 'Great mates—they used to call us Freeman, Hardy and Willis, you know, after the High Street chain—either that or the Three Stooges. Always together we were.'

'And Glen used to tag along sometimes?'

'Rover Kotchley we used to call him. He had a mole on his neck like a big black dog.' Sam nodded. 'Yeah ... he came ashore with us a few times. When you're in the same mess, you know, shipmates like, you share things ... all muck in together. Like I say, he was a bit younger than us and he wasn't

242

the best company in the world, but he was likeable enough.'

'When you say he wasn't the best company …?'

Sam took a swig from the glass and shrugged.

'He was very quiet. Most times, matelots are pretty friendly, you know? Fun-loving, party animals—get ashore and have a few wets. Have a singsong and get legless on Saturday nights, that sort of thing, but Rover? He hardly ever smiled and I don't think I ever heard him say more than four words in one go. He always had this hangdog expression. He was always very polite, but he was a loner … Seemed to prefer his own company. That and cats.'

'Cats?' Charles blinked at him, and Sam nodded.

'Loved them, he did. I can't say I'm all that enamoured with them myself, but Rover thrived on them.'

'Did he have a cat on board?'

'Not officially,' Sam grinned. 'Our captain wasn't that keen on keeping pets on the ship, but Rover used to come back on board with any stray he picked up along the way. That was the only time he seemed to come alive, you know, when he had a cat to fuss over.'

Bastet, Charles thought, *the cat goddess of ancient Egypt made an eternal companion of the dog god, Anubis, by a powerful priest in a ceremony as old as time itself, made one by a burning ember that joined hearts and minds for three thousand years.*

'Tell me …' Charles ventured. 'Did Glen have a scar, here, on his chest?'

He tapped beneath the top pocket of his jacket, and Sam nodded.

'Mmm, he did … But if you didn't know him, how did you know about the scar?'

'It's a long, long story and medical confidentiality prevents me from saying too much.'

'Oh? I'm intrigued now.'

'I'm a doctor, and the patient I'm treating had a long association with your friend, Glen.'

'I see. Well, as far as I remember, Glen had no real friends apart from the blokes on board. Tim took pity on him one weekend and took him home with him, but he never even had a girlfriend. He was a loner. Too morose and sad-faced to attract any interest from girls. Maybe that's why he lavished all his affection on cats.'

'Maybe,' Charles sighed, sipping his beer, and Rosemary leaned forward in her seat.

'Do you know where Glen came from, Sam?' she asked softly. 'Where was his home?'

'Somewhere in Hampshire or Surrey, I think.' Sam frowned. 'Guildford? Farnham? Aldershot? Somewhere around there.'

'Farnborough,' Charles whispered, knowing without a shadow of a doubt that he was right. It was where Marion was born, the little girl who'd studied every strange face with eager interest, but her soulmate was long gone, departed to join the Navy where he cast his fate in a battle eight thousand miles away in the South Atlantic.

'Well…' Rosemary murmured after a long silence. 'It looks like we're going home via Farnborough tomorrow.'

There were three Kotchleys listed in the Farnborough telephone directory and Charles found the one he wanted at the second attempt, the voice of a woman echoing back at him through the receiver.

'Hello?'

'Mrs Kotchley?'

'Speaking.'

'Sorry to disturb you on a Sunday morning, but I'm trying to trace the family of Glen Kotchley who served in the Royal Navy during the Falklands War.'

'That would be my son. What was it you wanted?'

'My name's Charles Levington and I'm a doctor from London,' he explained slowly. 'I'm dealing with a patient who seems to have had some connection with your son.'

'I doubt it.' Charles could almost see her shaking her head. 'I don't think Glen knew anyone from London, unless it was someone he knew in the Navy ... Oh! There was someone who lived in Wembley, I think ... Tim something ... Beaty? But he died with Glen.'

'Tim Beavis,' Charles supplied. 'No ... My patient is a woman ... and she's twenty-five years old.'

The pregnant pause seemed to go on and on and Charles guessed what she was thinking, anticipating the obvious and prepared for it when it came.

'Are you saying she's Glen's daughter?'

'No, Mrs Kotchley. My patient isn't related to your son at all.'

'I don't see ...'

'It's rather complicated. I wonder if I might come and see you.'

'Is that necessary?'

'It might help my patient if I can fill in some of the missing blanks.'

'Well ... I suppose so. When were you planning to call in?'

'I'm in Farnborough today, Mrs Kotchley. Would it be possible to see you this afternoon?'

'This afternoon? This is a bit ...'

'A bit sudden,' he finished for her. 'If it's inconvenient ...'

'No. I've got nothing planned for today. What time?'

'Two o'clock?'

'That'll be all right, I suppose ... Two o'clock, then.'

'Fine. Thank you, Mrs Kotchley. I'll see you at two.'

It was a neat house in a terraced row of similar dwellings, the front lawn manicured and tidy with well-maintained borders, the rose bushes deadheaded conscientiously and the lone fruit tree pruned and ready for next spring. Rosemary waited in the car when Charles went inside, leaving him to deal with

245

lengthy explanations and reasons for interrupting a quiet Sunday while she caught up with the newspapers, relying on his tact and diplomacy in what could prove to be a delicate situation.

Mrs Kotchley was small and round with tired eyes and deeply lined features that gave her a world-weary expression as though she'd experienced it all in her life and wanted no more of it, a dejected look that spoke of long-sufferance and pain. Her grey hair was pinned to the back of her neck in a bun and the carpet slippers she wore were a little on the large side, making her shuffle as she walked, a rolling gait not unlike that of a sailor compensating for the pitch and toss of a ship at sea. She was softly spoken and peered at Charles without blinking, as if she was studying him minutely like an insect under a microscope, but her polite smile had a degree of warmth that made him feel welcome and he relaxed a little as he was ushered to an armchair in the sitting room. She made a pot of tea then settled opposite him, her soulful eyes staring at him over the rim of her cup as she waited for him to explain his visit, wondering just how she might be of help to a patient she'd never even met.

'I'm sorry to barge in on you like this,' he began hesitantly. 'It must all appear rather strange to you.'

'I must admit your phone call intrigued me a bit,' she nodded. 'If my son had nothing to do with your patient I can't quite see what this is all about.'

'It's a long and complicated story, Mrs Kotchley.'

'Edith,' she murmured. 'Please call me Edith. So, do I get to hear the story?'

'The patient we're treating is somewhat disturbed and our resident psychiatrist has been regressing her to enable him to get to the root of her problem.'

'Regressing? That's hypnosis, isn't it?'

'Basically, yes,' he nodded. 'The idea is to take her mind back in time until we find the cause of the disturbance.'

246

'So, what's this got to do with my son?'

'It seems they shared a past together.'

She blinked for the first time, her eyelids flickering in quick succession as she absorbed Charles's words, then she frowned, cocking her head to one side in quizzical appraisal.

'Shared a past? What's that supposed to mean?'

'We've regressed our patient six times, each time to a different period as far back as twelve twenty-three BC ... and every period features our patient with your son.'

'My son? How? How do you know it's Glen? It could be anyone.'

'We know it's your son because of two distinguishing marks that appear every time ... a mole on the neck in the shape of a dog, and a birthmark on the chest. Every time we regressed our patient, it was the same ... Born in the same place and bearing the same marks.'

'Born in the same place?'

'That's how I traced you, Edith. Our patient was born in Farnborough, too.'

She was silent for a long moment, sifting through the nonsense in her head, then her frown deepened as if something had occurred to her, and she looked at Charles directly. 'Are you allowed to tell me your patient's name? I might know her.'

'I doubt it. The family moved to Middlesex when she was four.'

'Harting,' Edith murmured softly, and it was Charles's turn to blink, his mouth dropping open as he stared at her incredulously.

'You knew them?'

'The Hartings? Oh, yes. My younger sister used to go out with Archie at one time. When Archie married Janice they moved into a house round the corner.'

'I see.'

'We were quite close friends at one time and we kept in

touch for a while after they moved, but I haven't heard from them since they emigrated to Canada.'

She didn't need to give it much thought. Charles's patient was a woman and the only woman left in England from the Harting family was Marion.

'She was a lovely little girl, I seem to remember,' Edith said, and Charles peered at her over the rim of his cup.

'Sorry?'

'Marion Harting. She was a bonny little babe, but there was something strange about her eyebrows, I recall.'

'Did Glen ever meet her?'

'No.' Edith shook her head. 'He joined the Navy about a year before she was even born. She must've been about two years old when he went to the Falklands.'

'I spoke to someone who was on the *Sheffield* with him … Sam Westbrook.'

'I didn't know him,' Edith shrugged. 'I knew so few of Glen's mates.'

'Would you mind telling me about Glen? I'd understand if it was too painful for you.'

'It was a long time ago,' she smiled sadly. 'What do you want to know?'

'Sam told me Glen was the quiet type. A man of few words. Is that how you'd describe him?'

Edith took a deep breath as if she were composing her thoughts, then she shrugged lightly.

'I suppose so. He wasn't like other kids. We wondered if it was anything to do with the mole on his neck, you know, if it made him feel self-conscious or something because he had very few friends at school and he wasn't into team games and stuff like that … He seemed to prefer his own company, but he did quite well in the classroom … especially history. That boy really loved history. He was always reading something … his father called him a bookworm … reading or walking. Every weekend he'd be out and about somewhere on his own

248

'… itchy feet. That's why he joined the Navy. He wanted to travel and see the world.'

'Any place in particular?'

'He wanted to see the pyramids and he had this thing about Rome. It was the history, you see. I think he was hoping to go there on a Navy ship, but he never did. He was saving up for a holiday in Italy that year when the Falklands War broke out.'

'Sam said he liked cats.'

'"Liked" isn't the word for it,' Edith smiled fondly. 'He adored them … He called them free spirits. When he was eight, a little kitten followed him home from school and he kept it. I think it had been in a fight because it had a patch of fur missing by its left eye. It never did grow back. Like a permanent scar, it was. We didn't mind him having the cat. He was an only child and we thought it'd be company for him.'

'What name did he give the cat?'

'Moona … We thought that was a strange name for a cat, and when we asked him where he got the name from, Glen said the cat told him to call it that, which was rather extraordinary because Glen wasn't a very imaginative boy. He wasn't inventive like other kids. You know, he wasn't one for making things up. The cat died when Glen was sixteen, and soon after that he joined the Navy.'

And if the cat had somehow carried the spirit of the real Moona, Charles thought, it would need to die in order for its soul to pass to the foetus in Mrs Harting's womb, the foetus that would become Marion.

'Tell me about the cat,' he asked softly, and Edith gave a little laugh.

'Almost human that thing. She used to sit on the window-sill all day when Glen was at school. Wouldn't budge an inch until he came home, then she'd follow him around the house like a shadow. I remember one summer we were in the

249

garden and Glen had his shirt off. As soon as he lay on the grass, Moona came up and licked the birthmark on his chest and sort of cuddled up against him. She was always doing things like that. That birthmark seemed to fascinate her. When Glen went for his walks at the weekend, Moona used to sit on his shoulders and he'd take her with him. I think he loved that cat more than he loved people.'

Charles drained his cup and sighed. There was nothing else he needed to know.

'I'd better make a move,' he said, rising to his feet. 'I've taken up enough of your Sunday as it is.'

'Well, I had nothing else to do,' Edith smiled. 'Since my husband died there's just me to think about these days.'

Charles paused by the door, a sudden thought crossing his mind, an idea that just might help to stave off the loneliness of growing old alone.

'Tell me something, Edith … Did you know Archie's sister, Rosalind?'

'Roz?' She grinned. 'We used to go to school together. We used to see a lot of each other when Archie moved in round the corner, but we lost touch years ago.'

'I know where she lives. I'll get her to give you a call.'

'Would you?' Her eyes lit up excitedly. 'That would be marvellous.'

'No problem. Thanks for everything—you've been more than helpful. No, sit still, I'll see myself out.'

'A most productive weekend, Charles.' Leon nodded pensively. 'It looks as if you've found the root cause of Marion's problems. It would appear that your detective work has paid dividends.'

'You're in agreement, then?' Charles found it hard to believe that Leon had accepted his theory so readily. 'You think she's pining for a lost love?'

'It certainly looks that way. When she saw the photograph

and learned the man in it was dead, something in her subconscious was triggered and it sent her off on a downward spiral. She had no idea why she wanted to commit suicide, but it became compulsive … a driving need to join her soulmate.'

'So …' Charles sighed softly. 'Is that the end of it? No more regression therapy?'

'I think we still need to get the whole picture, don't you?'

'The last piece of the puzzle?'

'Aye. Once Marion's aware of it, it'll make treatment that much easier. Close the door on the past and enable her to cope with the future.'

'A future without the love of her life,' Charles said bleakly, and Leon shrugged.

'It's how most people conduct their lives, Charles. Who's to say we all marry the right person?'

'I suppose so. It'll be difficult for her, though.'

'Aye, well, that's what we're here for, isn't it? Once we can get Marion to accept all that's gone before, she'll be better prepared to face up to her life ahead.'

'If you say so. When are you seeing her again?'

'I'm going along now—just for a quiet chat.'

'You're not regressing her today?'

'I don't think so.' Leon shook his head. 'I want to give some thought to what you told me this morning before I go any further with this.'

'All right … I'll go and see her later. I've got some news that might cheer her up.'

'You won't mention anything, will you?' Leon said abruptly. 'I want to feel my way carefully on this one.'

'What? Oh, no.' Charles grinned. 'It's nothing to do with that—her plaster's coming off tomorrow.'

Chapter 23

Leon found Marion sitting in the chair at her usual place by the window, her fractured leg propped on a stool, a cup of cold tea forgotten on the side as she stared absently at the outside world, her eyes far away and distant. She made no move when Leon entered the room, her head turned away from him, and he approached her quietly, wondering if she was asleep.

'Marion? Are you awake, Marion?'

She seemed to shake herself as she became aware of him, taking a deep breath and blinking her eyes rapidly as if she were coming back to the here and now from some faraway place, holding on to some half-forgotten image with difficulty as she struggled to reconcile the past with the present, too many lives and too many emotions clouding the issue and blurring the edges of a history long gone.

'I'm sorry.' Leon perched against the windowsill and peered down at her. 'Did I wake you?'

'No ... I wasn't asleep. Just ... Just miles away.'

'Anywhere in particular?'

'I was thinking ... If ... if they were all to walk in here now ... Nedemin, Darius, Parlian, Lupus, Claude, Wotenon ... If they were all standing together in this room ... if I had to choose ... Which one would it be.'

'And?'

'Impossible,' she whispered. 'They were all so very different and yet ... they were all the same ... Here.' She touched her heart. 'And here.' Her fingers caressed her temple. 'It was true, wasn't it?'

'What was?'

'What the high priest said? The prophecy ... One heart, one mind ... That's exactly how it was, wasn't it?'

'I do believe it was,' Leon said carefully, and she turned to look at him, wondering what had brought about the sudden change of heart.

'Not an appearance fixation?'

'No.'

She sighed wearily and closed her eyes, giving a little shake of her head as she absorbed his certainty.

'Up until I came in here," she murmured, 'I never believed in ... in reincarnation. Now I don't know what to believe. I mean ... is it just Nedemin and me because of the ceremony in ancient Egypt? Or does everyone get reincarnated after every time they die?'

'Marion ...' He groped helplessly in the dark, wanting to answer her, but unable to find a truth, a solid foundation in the quicksand of uncertainty that surrounded a subject too perverse and ethereal to prove conclusive one way or another. 'I just don't know.'

She turned her sorrowful eyes to him in a beseeching gesture, craving definite answers to which she could anchor her beliefs, and she frowned, eyebrows coming together on the bridge of her nose just as they had done for three thousand years.

'But surely ... surely people have been regressed before?'

'Of course.'

'And what did they say?'

'Most people are regressed to their childhood or some earlier part of their lives, not into the dim recesses of the past, Marion.'

'But I've read about people who were regressed to the Napoleonic war or something. What about them?'

'It's difficult,' Leon conceded with a shrug. 'It's a difficult thing to prove and it's a difficult area to pin down precisely. Anyone can read about something and then relate to it under hypnosis. Another school of thought is that it's simply memory carried in the genes. Yet another theory is that it's just a fantasy coming to the fore when the mind's in a relaxed state. Someone else has suggested that the magnetic field surrounding the brain can become susceptible to other magnetic fields and absorbs outside information that way. There could be a hundred explanations why someone tells a plausible story about the past when they're regressed, and not one of them can be proved one way or the other ... It's all guesswork and theory and not enough research has been carried out to make a substantial case for or against. At the other end of the scale you've got the mediums, "flat-earthers", psychics, paranormal whiz-kids and the "alternative" brigade clouding the issue until no one knows which way is up anymore. Basically, Marion, the whole subject is a minefield and all we're left with is conjecture and speculation.'

'And yet ...'

'Yes?'

'Yet for all that, you're convinced I've lived before. You believe the things I've told you actually happened and I haven't been making them up.'

'That seems to be the case,' he nodded. 'I've no doubt that others in my position would see things differently, but I'm of the opinion we've been hearing factual accounts rather than figments of your imagination.'

'So what changed your mind?' she whispered, her eyes locking on to his. 'What's happened to make you suddenly believe me?'

'It's not a sudden thing,' he said lightly. 'I think it's a slow process and over a period of time I've become convinced of the validity of your accounts.'

254

She eyed him suspiciously, thinking it through, then she shook her head slowly. Something had happened to change his opinion so dramatically. Something beyond her control had occurred in the recent past to bring about this reversal, and she was determined to discover what it was.

'Are you going to tell me, then?' she murmured, and Leon blinked myopically at her over his spectacles, smoothing the rumpled creases in his suit as he played for time.

'Tell you what?'

'You've found out something, haven't you? Something has come to light in the last few days to make you change your mind about me. Are you going to tell me what it is?'

'Not for the moment.' Leon smiled brightly. 'It could be something or nothing, and until we're absolutely sure I'd rather put it to the back of my mind and concentrate on your progress.'

'More regression? I thought that once you found the reason for my behaviour we could forget all that hypnosis stuff and get on with the treatment … and you *have* found the reason, haven't you?'

'It's a possibility,' Leon conceded graciously. 'But that's all it is, a possibility. I'd like to make doubly certain before we even think about treatment.'

'It seems pointless to me. Carrying on when you could finish it right here and now.'

'It's not as simple as that, Marion. Successful treatment depends on the patient coming to terms with the cause of the compulsion. Once we can get you to recognise it and accept it, you'll be well on the way to a full recovery. Besides, aren't you in the least curious as to the final chapters in this epic of yours? Do you not want to know the outcome of all those past lives?'

'I already know the outcome,' she murmured softly. 'I'm the outcome, Doctor. Me. Marion Harting … It doesn't stretch any further than this.'

'Well … There's a gap between eighteen sixty-four when you were Hutenay and nineteen eighty when you became Marion. Maybe only one or two more regressions should see it through.'

'If you say so.' She shrugged wearily, past the point of caring. 'Let's get on with it, then.'

'Not today.' He came to his feet. 'You could do with a break and I've got other cases to attend to. I'll see you again on Friday.'

She was neither disappointed nor heartened by the news there would be no regression that day, and she sat expressionless and immobile as Leon stepped from the room, her hands limply folded over the growing swell of her stomach.

Charles looked in on Marion later that afternoon, smiling brightly as he studied her chart and checked her notes, but she gave no outward sign she was aware of him, her eyes cast to the outside world from her seat by the window, her body relaxed and still. He pulled a chair opposite her and sat down, watching her closely, and after a moment she sighed softly, her eyes fixed on something beyond his line of sight, holding her interest with magnetic fascination.

'You lose track of time in here,' she murmured softly. 'I didn't realise it was autumn already … I've been watching the leaves falling.' Her eyes returned to the window and she nodded slowly. 'A leaf comes, lives for a summer, then dies. Over the winter there's nothing, then another leaf appears in spring. All those leaves coming and going like that, one after the other—it's a bit like reincarnation—a life, then nothing, then a life again. And just as the leaves aren't the same ones each time, so each life produces a different person … yet deep inside we're the same because like the leaves, we come from the same tree … we have the same soul.'

She turned to peer at him, blinking as though she'd

discovered some basic truth, some fundamental fact of life that had escaped her until now, a revelation made in the quiet tranquillity of a dying summer.

'Do you think, Charles, that it's the same for every living thing? A life, then death, followed by another life again?'

He remembered having the same conversation with Leon and thoughts of Buddhism flitted through his mind, thoughts that held no answers because when you dealt with the spiritual you were dealing with beliefs and there were as many beliefs as there were people on the planet. No two beliefs were ever exactly identical, and without concrete proof it all came down to faith … and that was all that religion was in the final analysis, faith in the unknown. Faith in a superior being. Faith in a life after death.

'Marion …' He groped for the words, knowing that whatever he said would never be enough because he wasn't a sage with the wisdom of the world to impart. He was simply a doctor trying his best to cure the sick and he had no ready answers to the meaning of life. 'When I was at university I got talking to a science professor and he told me about energy. It seems that you can't get rid of energy entirely, all you can do is transfer it into another form of energy. So the energy produced by a generator is turned into electricity which is another form of energy. Put that energy into a light bulb and you create heat and light which are energy sources in themselves … Do you see? If the life-force within a person is an energy then you can't destroy it with death, it just goes on to become something else—a spirit … a soul … You can't kill a soul, Marion. You can't destroy a spirit … now, who governs that spirit, who directs it and controls it, I have absolutely no idea, but I have no doubt that the spirit lives on somewhere.'

'Does it have to be controlled?' she asked quietly, and he shrugged.

'I don't know, but … well, take the souls of Darius and Lindinia. When they died their souls had to go somewhere

257

before they came back as Shera and Parlian. So, what happened in the meantime?'

'I don't ...' She frowned, shaking her head, and Charles warmed to his theme, leaning towards her earnestly.

'Okay ... The next time their spirits appear is over five hundred years later, but the timescale doesn't matter because the concept is the same, their souls are in the afterlife and are about to come back as Shera and Parlian. All right?'

'Yes.'

'Right ... So who controls it? Were those two souls asked if they *wanted* to come back? Were they given the choice? Let's assume they *were* given the choice and they both decided to give life another try. Who decided where they were going to live this new life they'd both volunteered for? Who made the decision that one was going to be the daughter of a slave and the other was to be the son of a rich merchant? Do you see what I'm getting at? If you had the choice, why would you choose to be a slave?'

'I see what you mean.' She nodded slowly. 'So it looks like you aren't given a choice ... Whoever controls it doesn't ask ... they tell.'

'It would appear so,' Charles murmured sombrely, then he smiled, making light of a melancholy subject. 'I can imagine going up to heaven and asking one of the angels what their job was, and he turns round and says, "I'm a Soul Controller First Class, Europe Division." It would make you think a bit, wouldn't it?'

'It would.' She returned the smile, her mood lifted by his easy manner, and Charles sat back, pleased to have drawn her out a little.

'I've some news for you, Marion.' His smile widened. 'Something to cheer you up a bit.'

'That'll make a nice change, then. It's all doom and gloom in here.'

'Not quite … We're removing the plaster casts before dinner. You'll still need the sticks for a few days, but you'll be able to get about easier.'

'Are you sure I can be trusted?' She gave him a rueful smile. 'I might do a runner once I'm mobile … Jump under a bus, or something.'

'Do you still feel suicidal?' he asked with solemn interest, and she gave a curt nod.

'It's … it's a permanent thing … Like a continuous nagging in the back of my mind. Constant. It hasn't been too bad in here and I've managed to cope with it, but I don't know whether it's because there's always been someone on hand here, or if it's my dodgy leg that's stopped me doing anything stupid. That's why it's a bit frightening to think the plaster's coming off … I might jump out the window.'

'And harm the baby?' he said softly, and she rubbed her tummy absently as if she were caressing the child in her womb.

'I don't want to hurt the baby, but…' She sighed heavily. 'I don't want to live, either. For all that Macleod thinks he can cure me, I can't see an end to all this. I think this feeling of wanting to do away with myself will just keep getting stronger until I finally succeed in doing it … After the baby's born if I can hold out till then.'

'I thought you'd got over all that, Marion,' Charles said bleakly. 'I thought those kinds of notions were well and truly behind you.'

'They're always lurking just under the surface,' she admitted candidly. 'That's what makes it so terrifying.'

'Well …' He came to his feet and returned the chair to its place by the bed. 'We'll be keeping a close eye on you, making sure you don't do anything silly. Ah, here's the nurse come to take you down to have the plaster removed. Take it easy and we'll get you started on some light physio in the morning. Goodnight, Marion.'

259

She didn't answer and he watched in silence as she hobbled away, the clunk of the sticks fading with distance, then he turned and quietly left the room.

It was the following morning when Charles saw Marion again. He waited until the physiotherapist had finished before he knocked lightly on the door and stepped into the room, finding it strange to see her sitting normally without the incumbent plaster cast protruding between them like an accusing finger. She was panting heavily from her exertions and her leg shook spasmodically from the unaccustomed effort, but there was a glint of triumph in her eyes and a self-satisfied look on her face as she glanced up at him, as if to say she'd overcome another hurdle, conquered another mountain.

'It suits you,' he smiled, and she blinked at him.

'What does?'

'Having two normal legs and two normal arms. It makes you look more human.'

'That was bloody hard work this morning,' she muttered. 'I'm sure it wasn't this difficult when I first learned to walk.'

'Less weight to carry when you're a toddler,' he explained. 'The muscles will soon get used to working again.'

'I'll take your word for that. In the meantime, I'll not be volunteering for the London marathon.'

'You seem a bit brighter today,' he nodded, perching on the window sill and peering down at her. 'Not quite as pessimistic as you were yesterday.'

'I'm a fatalist,' she shrugged. 'If it's going to happen, it'll happen, whatever you or Professor Macleod might do to try and thwart it.'

'Well, we'd both disagree with you on that score. Things are progressing nicely and we'll have you out of here in no time.'

'Mmm ... Macleod told me the reason behind my

260

compulsion,' she said matter-of-factly, and Charles studied her closely, a slight frown creasing his brow.

She was probing, he thought, playing one against the other in the hope of learning something about the cause of her condition, and he shook his head slowly, not for one second falling into the clumsy trap she'd set for him.

'No, he didn't, Marion,' Charles murmured. 'Leon said no such thing, and you know it.'

'Well, as good as,' she insisted. 'He hinted that he knows.'

'Did he?'

'Yes ... so you might as well tell me.'

'I don't think so,' he said carefully. 'Like I told you before, psychiatry isn't my field and I'd probably be doing more harm than good.'

'You do know, then?'

'I've discussed it with Leon, yes.'

'Thought so.' She smiled thinly. 'Everyone knows except me.'

'Well, you'll know soon enough when Leon regresses you again. You couldn't have lived that many lives in a period of one hundred and sixteen years. We must be getting close to the end now.'

'That's what he said ... I'll just be glad when it's all over.'

'So will we.' He straightened and crossed to the door. 'Not long now and you'll be well enough to go home ... and stable enough to enjoy it.'

'Well, then, Marion,' Leon murmured, switching on the tape recorder and settling back in his chair. 'Are you ready for this?'

Chapter 24

OKINAWA, JAPAN, AD 1930

Gushikawa is a coastal town that sits comfortably along the middle of the eastern seaboard of Okinawa, approximately twenty-five kilometres north from the capital Naha. In the unusually hot spring of 1930, the inhabitants of Gushikawa bore witness when Masako Mitsuru married her love, Kuribayashi Tadamichi, in the Sogen temple that had been the burial place of the rulers of the Okinawa kingdom since time immemorial. The townsfolk had waited a long time for this wedding, keeping a close eye on developments for the past twenty years, but Kuri's patience had finally been rewarded and at long last he was marrying the girl he had courted for two decades. It was way back in 1910 when Kuri had first seen the sweet young girl he learned was called Masako, and he was smitten from that first sighting, knowing without a doubt that one day he would take this girl into the temple and make her his wife. Masako was a loner, a young girl not given to making friends easily and well-used to her own company. She was totally ignorant of Kuri's affections, and she had no idea that he followed her home from school or sat beneath the cherry tree at the front of her house and dreamed of the day when she would be his for ever. So it wasn't unusual on that summer day in 1910 that Kuri had escaped his father's scrutiny and ran up the hill from the wharf to sit by the rice-threshers and wait for the school to empty, his eyes on the door as he idly twirled the boathook that he always carried, as much a part of him as the loose tunic and sandals that denoted his craft. He stiffened as the first pupils emerged into the sunlight, the boathook now stilled in his hands, and he smiled a secret smile of longing as Masako swung her satchel over her shoulder and took the path through the field where Hideki Oyama grew sweet potatoes and kept his bee hives, the scent of honeysuckle and jasmine pervading the air in a rich aroma, and the hum of bees a fitting accompaniment to the squabbling chaffinches that flitted among the peach trees.

Masako gave no thought to finches or honey bees as she followed the path that would lead to her father's factory and her home that nestled between the kilns, her mind full of a grave yearning that she couldn't understand, a certain disquiet that all was not as it should be in her life, that something was missing, and she didn't know what it was. She was ten years old, yet her big brown eyes seemed to gaze out at the world with an ageless wisdom, a timeless quality that suggested she'd seen it all before and little had changed.

Three boys, not much older than Masako, stepped from the trees and barred the path, intent on mischief, and Masako slowed, taking a tight grip on her satchel as she eyed the boys warily.

'Ah. Masako Mitsuru,' one of the boys said as if he'd just recognised her. 'What a pleasant surprise. Got any food in your satchel, Masako?'

'I have nothing for you, Nogi.' She tossed her head disdainfully at him. 'Let me pass or my father will be having words with your father before the day is out.'

'Don't threaten us, Miss Clever-boots Mitsuru,' another boy jeered, his hand grabbing the strap of her satchel before she could pull away. 'Nogi asked you politely if you had any food in there.'

'Only books,' she said, tugging on the strap. 'If you want

263

food go and search for scraps in the dustbins and the gutters where you belong.'

'She spits venom like a viperish snake,' the third boy snarled, stung by her words, 'but you'll not slither away from us so easily. Look in the satchel, Akira.'

A boathook thumped on Akira's ankle before he could react, and Kuri turned in one graceful movement and rammed the blunt end into Nogi's midriff, the breath knocked out of him in an agonised gasp, then Kuri spun on his heel and jabbed the lethal hook at the third boy, who stepped back in alarm. Kuri swung a protective arm at Masako, motioning her behind him as he faced the boys levelly, the boathook swaying with hypnotic menace, but the boys thought better of it and drifted away into the trees: a boy armed and dangerous was a more daunting prospect than the easy bullying they'd planned for a defenceless girl.

'They're gone,' Kuri smiled, turning to face a wide-eyed Masako, 'but I'll walk the rest of the way with you in case they come back.'

His eyes strayed to the scar by her left eye and she raised a hand to cover it, conscious of the one blemish that marred a flawless complexion, and Kuri shook his head at the futile gesture, his smile softening as he loosened the top of his tunic.

'There is no need to hide it, Masako,' he said gently. 'We are marked by the same brand, you and I ... See ...'

He bared his chest and her eyes dipped to the similar scar that puckered the flesh like an old wound to the heart, a twin to the one on her temple that she'd been at pains to conceal for as long as she could remember.

'I know you, Masako Mitsuru,' Kuri said with a certain sureness, and she shook her head as if denying him his certainty, her whole world suddenly turned upside down by a boy she'd never met before.

264

'You know nothing of me,' she whispered, failing to keep the tremor from her voice, and he laughed softly.

'You seek something and you don't know what it is you seek,' Kuri said assuredly. 'You look and you search, but you don't know why and you don't know what you're searching for. You sit at your window at night and gaze up at the stars as if they might provide you with answers, but they never do. You are not sad, but neither are you happy ... not completely happy, but today, now, now you are happy.'

'How ...' She swallowed hard and tried again. 'How do you know all this? Have you been spying on me?'

'It is true that I sometimes sit beneath the cherry tree in your garden, but I seldom catch sight of you. I sit there merely to be near you.'

'But ... but why?' Her voice was a hoarse whisper, and he smiled a secret smile.

'Because it is like I said. We have been marked by the same brand. We are kindred spirits, Masako. I knew it as soon as I saw the scar on your temple five months ago in the market.'

'But how ... how do you know I do the things you said?'

'Because I do them too,' he said simply. 'I have been searching for something, too, Masako, but I found it that day in the market when I first saw you.'

'How did you know my name?'

'Ah!' Kuri laughed. 'I have an older brother and he knows your older sister. That's how I found out that I was born two days before you in the same hospital in Naha.'

'I don't know your name,' she murmured, as if it mattered that she should. 'I know nothing about you.'

'You know the important things,' he said seriously, placing a hand over his heart. 'The things in here. You know them because you share them ... just as we share a scar.'

'I would still like to know your name,' she said gravely. 'I think I would like to know everything about you.'

'Kuribayashi Tadamichi,' he said with a mock bow, 'but

you can call me Kuri. My father's name is Ushijima and he owns a fishing boat in the harbour. He catches tuna and I help him.'

'You should go to school,' Masako admonished gently, and Kuri shook his head.

'My brother, Koiso, went to school. He is the brainy one and my father has high hopes for him. I would rather catch tuna and my father is happy for me to go with him.'

'Happy,' she murmured softly. 'You said I wasn't completely happy.'

'But you are now,' he said confidently, then turned abruptly, a frown creasing his forehead as he looked at her. 'You *are* happy now, aren't you? Now you've met me?'

'Yes,' she said incredulously, examining her feelings and realising he was right. She had never felt so absurdly happy in all her life.

'Come on,' Kuri nodded at the path ahead. 'We should get home before your father comes looking for you.'

'Kuri … my father …'

'Makes very fine porcelain,' Kuri finished for her. 'He is a very important man with money and status and he would not take kindly to his favourite daughter being seen about with the son of a fisherman.'

'He can be difficult.' She frowned, her eyebrows knitting together on the bridge of her nose, and Kuri's heart seemed to soar at the gesture, a carefree abandon that melted all his reservations and made him feel lighter than air.

'Which is why I will walk with you as far as the factory and leave you to walk the rest of the way on your own,' he told her, and the frown eased.

'But I will see you again?'

'Oh, yes,' he nodded emphatically. 'Not every day because when the tides are right and the winds are right and the tuna are shoaling I must go out with my father, but whenever I can, I shall be here to walk you home from school.'

'I would like that,' she said almost absently, her eyes suddenly mesmerised by a dog-shaped mole on his neck that held her fascinated, spellbound as if she'd finally found the one thing she'd been searching for without ever knowing it. 'I would like that very, very much.'

True to his word, Kuri escorted Masako home from school whenever the opportunity presented itself, only the call of the tuna and his father's wishes preventing further time spent together. Later, after the passing of the years and when they were both fully grown, he contrived to meet her at her father's factory, where she helped with the paperwork, calling only on the days when her father was away on business or out making deliveries so that nothing could come between the precious moments they secretly shared.

Not as secret as they would have liked, though, for when the subject of Masako's marriage was raised, her father was adamant that she would not wed beneath her station.

'Kuniaki's son, Tomiichi, would be a good match,' he pointed out forcibly, ignoring Masako's protests. 'He has a good position at the bank and is tipped to be a manager one day.'

'Tomiichi Kuniaki?' Masako scoffed. 'I would not marry him if he *owned* the bank!'

'You would rather the owner of a fishing boat, then, Masako?' her father sneered knowingly. 'You prefer your husband to reek of fish, is that it?'

'Kuri does not own the boat,' she said, wondering how he'd found out about the illicit meetings. 'It belongs to his father.'

'The only man stupid enough to employ the boy, I expect. He never went to school, so I hear. Is that who you would see yourself married to, Masako?'

'He loves me, Father,' she said earnestly. 'He loves me like no other … and I love him.'

'Love? You think love will put food on your table and clothes on your back? You will not marry the tuna fisherman, Masako, and I don't want to hear his name mentioned in this house again.'

'If I cannot marry Kuri, Father,' she cried defiantly, 'then I shall marry no one.'

'How dare you defy me and speak his name when I have forbidden it! You will marry where you are directed and not on some whim or a fancy of your choosing. Never have I heard a woman speak so openly. Would you go against my wishes and see me dishonoured?'

'Would you dishonour me then, Father, and see me in a loveless marriage? And how am I to honour my husband if I feel nothing for him?'

'Your mother and I didn't know love when we were first married, Masako. It is the way of things. Love comes over a period of time, which is what you will discover when we have found a suitable husband for you.'

'Father ... you talk of love, and you have told me often enough that you love me. If ... if that is true, Father, and you love me as you said you do, then I beg you not to force me into a marriage that I want no part of. You talk of honour, Father, but I have honour, too, and I will not be dishonoured by a man I feel nothing for. You might arrange a marriage, Father, but I will not live long enough to see it through ... and I promise you that on the sacred tombs of our ancestors.'

The implied threat that Masako would rather die than marry a man not of her choosing was enough to dissuade her father from forcing an unsuitable marriage on her and he consoled himself with the bittersweet certainty that just as she might refuse those he thought worthy of her hand, so he refused the one man she would gladly seek a betrothal with, the tuna fisherman Kuribayashi Tadamichi.

They still met, of course, secret assignations where they might steal a kiss and plan a dubious future, and despite

268

Masako's father's adamant stance, Kuri remained convinced that one day they would be married and at last free to consummate their love.

Their good fortune came out of tragedy when Masako's father died unexpectedly in 1929, and eight months later, during the hot spring of 1930, Kuri led his bride through the Shurei Gate of the Sogen temple and they were finally married.

OKINAWA, 1945

The people of Okinawa, as in most of mainland Japan, embraced two religions: Shinto to oversee the values and culture in their everyday lives, and Buddhism to take care of the afterlife. Both religions were relied on heavily but never more so than in those early months of 1945, for the war was going badly and Okinawa had suffered constant air attacks since October the previous year. Prayer and humility were all that the people had left and the shrines and temples were forever ablaze with votive candles, the pungent aroma of incense mingling with the smell of cordite and the wood smoke of burning buildings. Kuri had avoided the war, his important role as a tuna fisherman making him too valuable an asset to squander in the Imperial Army, and he had a letter of authorisation signed by Emperor Hirohito himself, allowing him freedom of movement so that he might ply his trade unhindered and bring much-needed food to the beleaguered islands.

Kuri's father had died just before the onset of war and the fishing boat was his alone now, leaving him to expertly seek out the shoals of tuna as he had been taught since before he could walk. Masako had made a good home for them on the quayside of Gushikawa and they wanted for little, requiring no more than the basic needs to satisfy their simple lifestyle.

They never had children. Masako miscarried once in 1934 and had never been pregnant since, a harsh fact that they both bore with stoic fatalism, their love for each other more than enough to make them fulfilled and complete. Now, with the winter finally gone and a watery spring sun warming the air, it was time to think ahead to the future.

'We must go, Masako,' Kuri said one evening in early March, and she looked at him in the firelight, a curious frown drawing her eyebrows together as she cocked her head at him. 'Go, my love? Go where?'

'Away ... My brother told me the Americans are coming.'

'Koiso? What does he know of the Americans' intentions?'

'He works in the Ministry, Masako. He hears of these things.'

Masako's eyes were drawn to the dog-mole on his neck, the flickering flames and dancing shadows seeming to cause the dog's outline to shift and leap as if it were a live creature writhing on his flesh, and she felt a throb of anguish in her left temple, her fingers absently touching the scar by her eye, an automatic gesture born of habit whenever she was tired or distressed.

'What did Koiso tell you?' she asked, and Kuri sighed wearily.

'There are signs, Masako, that the Americans are gathering to launch an attack ... a landing with thousands of troops. They will overrun us like vermin, butcher the children, slaughter the men ... and rape the women. We must go.'

'Where would we go? If what you say is true, nowhere is safe on Okinawa. We cannot take to the hills and hide until they have gone. It's a madness, Kuri, and you speak no sense.'

'The mainland, Masako,' Kuri said, his eyes glowing in the firelight as he turned to gaze at her. 'I have an aunt ... We can stay there.'

'And when the Americans come to the mainland, Kuri? Where would you have us go then?'

'They will not come to the mainland, Masako,' he said assuredly. 'The Prime Minister, Tojo, is mobilising the whole population to rise up and stand against an invasion. The Americans could not hope for a victory against so many ranged against them. Just imagine, Masako, the whole population armed and ready to defeat them as soon as they step onto our shores. It will be magnificent, and we can be a part of it if we go to the mainland.'

'But how. Kuri? How are we to get there? All travel permits have been withdrawn.'

'The fishing boat,' he said simply. 'I've looked at the maps. We sail up past Amami-O-Shima, through the straits at Osumi Shoto and up the east coast of Kyosho. It's pretty straightforward from there.'

'It sounds a long way.'

'About six hundred miles. I worked it out that if we can maintain fifteen knots we should be there in less than two days.'

'And you think we'll be safer there?'

'Of course we will, Masako,' Kuri laughed at her fears. 'The Americans won't invade the mainland. Once the war's over and things have settled down, we can come back. It'll just be for a month or two. Once the Americans have been defeated everything will return to normal.'

'I see,' Masako sighed. 'Well … If you think it's for the best, Kuri.'

'I do. Now, tomorrow you must gather all the food and water you can find and we'll load the boat with all our things on Friday. The tides are good for an early start on Saturday morning. Don't look so worried, Masako. We'll be relaxing at my aunt's house on Monday.'

So, in fear of the Americans, they fled.

Kuri steered his fishing boat out of Gushikawa's harbour at first light on Saturday, 17th March, and two weeks later, on Sunday, 1st April, the Americans invaded Okinawa.

271

Masako and Kuri found a new peace in Aunt Sato's quiet residence on the edge of town, a deep contentment now Kuri was no longer spending his days fishing for tuna, and they spent long lazy days together, rediscovering the love that had been forged in a field of sweet potatoes, peach trees and honey bees thirty-five years before. They had to attend the civil rallies, where officers from the army base told them what part of the city they were to defend, and although they were given no weapons to repel the invaders, they armed themselves with a garden fork and a hoe and diligently practised, bringing back memories of a ten-year-old boy with a boathook who'd fought with speed and courage to safeguard a young girl's honour.

Summer came slowly, hot June days spent in the cool of the water gardens, and balmy July evenings when they strolled arm in arm through the park or along the waterfront of the port, laughing at silly things when all about them was sombre with the realities of war. But it was a distant war, a war that barely touched them, and they longed for the day when they might return to their home in Okinawa and the friendly harbour of Gushikawa where the gulls wheeled and screeched and sea salt was blown on the wind, where the tuna fishermen haggled prices on the quayside and the women gossiped in the market. They'd heard of the firebombs the Americans had rained down on Tokyo, but the capital was 450 miles to the northeast and they were safe enough in their little corner of Japan. But war, modern war, has a habit of striking where it is least expected. They didn't know it, but the distant war was coming ever closer, and on 6th August it was to come with a terrifying vengeance and shatter the world of peace they'd found in Aunt Sato's quiet house in the leafy suburbs of downtown Hiroshima.

'Come on, sleepy bones,' Masako laughed, tugging at Kuri's foot that protruded from the sheet at the bottom of the futon. 'You promised to work on Sato's water garden this morning. Do you plan to sleep all day?'

'What time is it?' Kuri yawned, his fingers touching the scar over his heart as he scratched his chest, and Masako smiled as she opened the screens at the window to let daylight flood into the room.

'It is past nine o'clock and time you were up and working.'

'Am I allowed to bathe and eat first?'

'Breakfast has been ready for an hour,' she told him with a nod, 'but I have made fresh tea. Be quick now and I shall eat with you before I go to the market.'

'I can hear an aeroplane,' Kuri murmured absently as he searched for his sandals, and Masako cocked her head to listen.

'Mmm. Must be one of ours on morning patrol. Five minutes, Kuri,' she warned, stepping through the rice-paper door. 'If you're any longer I shall feed your breakfast to the carp.'

Far above them in a brightening sky, Colonel Paul W. Tibbets made the final adjustments to bring the B-29 Superfortress, *Enola Gay*, onto the correct heading for the port town of Hiroshima, and at precisely 9:15 on Monday, 6th August, he released the first atomic bomb to be dropped in warfare. Within seconds of the resulting explosion, 66,000 people were dead and upwards of 100,000 were wounded.

Two of the dead, in a flimsy house in the suburbs, were Kuri and Masako, instantly vaporised in the intense heat. A black cloud rose over Hiroshima to a height of 40,000 feet and the flash of the explosion was seen by a reconnaissance plane 170 miles away, a giant flash that seared and burned and scorched and obliterated and blinded and maimed. It was a burst of light so brilliant, so intensely white, that for a brief moment of time it outshone the sun, and the sun god, Ra, was surpassed, and the two souls who had shared every life and every death for 3,168 years were torn asunder, their duty to the Pharaoh God, Ramesses, finally done and a long-ago prophecy duly fulfilled.

Chapter 25

'So when I went round to Linda's,' Marion murmured softly, 'and saw the photo with Glen Kotchley in the background ...'

'Something inside you recognised the mole on his neck,' Leon finished for her. 'Linda told you that everyone in the photo except Sam Westbrook had died in the Falklands and the dormant part of your brain told you that your soulmate was dead ... and if he was dead, then you should be, too. Your subconscious took over then, silently nagging away at you and driving you to commit suicide, to rejoin your lost love, but you didn't know why because the conscious part of your brain was unaware of it.'

'It was a vicious circle,' Charles added. 'Driven to suicide, but not knowing why, made you depressed, and the more depressed you became, the more you sought suicide as a way out from your despair.'

'From an academic point of view,' Leon mused thoughtfully, 'I have to admit I found this case most interesting. The concept of time and reincarnation has never been adequately explored. It opens up a whole new world of possibilities, too.'

'It does?' Charles frowned, and Leon nodded.

'Aye, it does. Take for instance the last two regressions. Our main characters supposedly died in Colorado in eighteen sixty-four, but were born again in Okinawa in nineteen hundred, which gives a period of inactivity of a mere thirty-six years. You yourself, Marion, died again in

275

nineteen forty-five and were back on this earth in nineteen eighty, a period of thirty-five years, which was even less for your soulmate because he was a grown man and fighting the Falklands War in nineteen eighty-two. Now, if we suggest an average life-span of forty years with a dormant period of thirty-five years it raises the possibility that you experienced approximately forty-two lives in the three-thousand-year term of the prophecy ... and we touched on just seven of them. One wonders what we missed, what fascinating insights into the past that weren't brought to light during regression. I might have to write a thesis on the subject.'

'I'll look forward to reading it,' Charles said dryly, making Marion smile. 'So what happens now?'

'The hardest part is over, Marion,' Leon said with authority. 'We've established the root cause of your compulsion and you understand it. You can relate to it and you can admit to it. There's no reason for you to die now, Marion. The cycle has been broken, you see. Way back in the time of the pharaohs you were dispatched with a purpose that you've carried out for over three thousand years. You've served your purpose now, Marion, and the prophecy has run its course. It's over. Finished and done with. You're free to get on with the rest of your life.'

'Is that it?' She blinked up at him, a frown bringing her eyebrows together on the bridge of her nose. Are you saying I'm cured and can just walk out of here?'

'Not quite,' Charles told her softly, and Leon cleared his throat.

'I think you'd benefit with a few sessions of therapy,' he said with a decisive nod, 'and perhaps some counselling wouldn't go amiss. It's just a matter of tying up the loose ends and making sure you're completely adjusted before we send you back out into the world. We don't want you to suffer a relapse, do we?'

'Is that likely?'

'It's a possibility,' Leon admitted with a shrug. 'The human mind is an extremely powerful force and we can never master it completely. Basically, all we can do is counter it with a greater force of autosuggestion. Now you know where your problem lies, that shouldn't prove difficult at all.'

'I see.' She nodded thoughtfully. 'How long before I'm well enough to leave?'

'That depends on the therapy sessions,' Leon smiled. 'Two weeks? Possibly three.'

'Time enough for more physio on your leg,' Charles added with a grin. 'By the time you're ready to leave here we'll have you skipping through the door.'

It was late February when the first heavy snow came, covering London in a thick white mantle, and Charles shivered as he entered the hospital and loosened his coat, peeling off his gloves and stuffing them in his pocket.

'You're early this morning, doctor,' Sister Barrett said as she picked up her overnight bag. 'I'm just going off duty.'

'Mr Russell's broken tibia,' Charles said with a wry smile. 'I want to read through the notes before we get him into theatre today.'

'Tough at the top,' she grinned. 'I'm off home to bed.'

'It's all right for some! I took one look at the snow when I got up and could have crawled back into bed quite easily. It's bitter out there.'

'I'll think of you slaving away while I'm all snuggled up nice and cosy.'

'Yeah, you do that,' he laughed, then gave her a goodbye wave as he crossed the foyer.

'Oh, Doctor Levington?'

He stopped and turned and Sister Barrett took a half-step towards him.

'We had an old friend of yours admitted during the night … Marion Harting?'

'Oh?'

'Tried to throw herself under a bus.'

'Good God!'

'She's all right,' Sister Barrett said quickly, allaying his fears with a nod of her head. 'The bus skidded in the snow and missed her. Just one or two cuts and bruises, but the shock sent her into labour. She had the baby at five o'clock this morning.'

'She wasn't due for another ...' He mentally totted up the months. 'Four weeks? Five?'

'Well ... It didn't seem to do the baby any harm. I'm told he's a bit underweight, but healthy enough and none the worse for arriving early.'

'Is Marion still in the labour ward?'

'As far as I know, yes.'

Charles nodded as he changed direction and headed for maternity.

'Thanks, Sister. See you later.'

Charles knocked on the door of the staff nurse's office and stepped inside, letting her get a good look at the badge pinned to his lapel as he studied her name-tag, a warm smile of reassurance lighting his features.

'Staff Nurse Gray,' he said pleasantly. 'Doctor Levington, Orthopaedics. You've got one of my old patients in here, so I believe.'

'Have we?'

'Mmm. Miss Harting.'

'Oh, her.'

'Is there a problem, Staff Nurse?' Charles asked warily, a hint of unease creeping into his voice, and she nodded.

'Marion doesn't want anything to do with the baby. She won't even hold him. I took him in to her earlier and she just shut her eyes and turned away. We wanted to express some breast milk to feed him, but she won't even let us do that. I've known women reject their babies before now, doctor, but

278

this one's adamant she wants nothing to do with it.'

Charles sighed wearily and wondered what new upset had caused this present crisis. The last time he'd seen Marion she was looking forward to a future with Terry and the baby and now it had all fallen apart at the seams.

'Has her boyfriend, Terry Newell, been in to see her?' he asked, and the staff nurse shook her head.

'We asked her last night if there was anyone we could contact and she said her boyfriend was away on business. She said something about him finally trusting her to leave her on her own … He obviously couldn't, could he?'

'Is the baby okay?'

'The baby's fine. You want to see him?'

'Mmm, I will.' Charles nodded. 'Then I'll go in and see Marion if that's all right?'

'Sure. No problem. She's in Ward B.'

'Thanks.'

Charles stood for a long time looking at the infant sleeping peacefully, blissfully unaware of the furore he'd caused by coming into the world so suddenly, and Charles wondered if things might have turned out differently if Terry hadn't had to go away at such a crucial time. It seemed that once she was left alone, all the old fears and phobias had come back to haunt Marion and she'd succumbed once again to the magnetic lure of death, not even the precious cargo developing inside her enough to dissuade her from a fifth attempt on her life. He sighed sadly and turned away, retracing his steps to the office before carrying on through to the wards, where he spotted Marion alone and pitifully forlorn in a far corner by the window, her eyes riveted to the leaden skies, comparing them, perhaps, to the bleak grey heaviness in her heart. He stepped up to the bed, certain that she was aware of him, but she neither turned nor acknowledged him, the scar on her temple a pink flush on the pale texture of her flesh.

'Marion,' he said softly, and her lips twitched in the barest

279

smile of recognition as if she'd been expecting him and he hadn't disappointed her.

'I thought you'd come,' she murmured, her eyes still focused on the snow-filled clouds. 'I wondered how long it'd be before you came snooping down here to find out what was going on.'

'So, what has been going on?' he asked quietly. 'You want to tell me about it?'

'Not really,' she shrugged. 'There's not a lot to tell, anyway.'

'Then it won't take you long to tell me then, will it?' he said dryly, and she sighed deeply.

'I got fed up living a lie, and that's what I was doing, Doctor, living a lie.'

'Go on.'

'I'd convinced myself that I could make it alone, you know? Without … without my "soulmate" as Macleod called him. I told myself … I told myself that even if we'd been together for three thousand years, it was time for me to move on … live a life without him … but the truth is, Doctor … the awful truth is … I can't.'

'Marion, you can. You know you can.'

'I thought I could,' she admitted tearfully. 'I really did, Charles. I thought everything was going to be fine and I'd make a wonderful life with Terry and the baby, and when Terry was around I almost convinced myself that it was all going to work. Then he had to go away for a few days and all the old doubts crept back in … all the old yearnings to end it all … the compulsion to join my soulmate. I resisted it as best I could, but I woke up in the night and I knew I just had to do it … just had to finish it once and for all.'

'And botched it for the fifth time,' he said airily, trying to lighten her mood, but it had the opposite effect and she broke down completely.

'Oh, Christ,' she sobbed helplessly. 'I can't even do that right, can I?'

'Marion ... You've got to stop torturing yourself like this.'

'I just ...' She waved her hand pathetically in front of her face as if she could magic away her tears, and Charles took her hand in his own, squeezing her fingers gently as he tried to soothe her.

'Marion don't ... don't keep laying the blame squarely on your own shoulders. You heard what Professor Macleod said. The mind is an extremely powerful force and you'd have to be superhuman to conquer it all on your own. Why didn't you contact someone? They must have given you helplines to phone if you needed them.'

'Oh, yes!' she sniffed derisively. 'Carmel Bloody Douglas from social services. Fat lot of good she is.'

'That's pretty funny considering how, um, slightly obese Miss Douglas is,' Charles remarked glibly, and Marion's sob choked into a despairing laugh. She wiped her eyes with a tissue and finally turned to look at him, all the pain and sorrow mirrored in the brown depths of her tormented eyes as she took a deep breath and calmed herself with effort.

'I'm sorry,' she whispered, and Charles shook his head.

'There's nothing to apologise for.'

'Listen to me, Charles,' she pleaded, her soulful eyes begging his understanding. 'I've been lying here thinking ... Since I had the baby in the early hours that's all I've done ... just lay here thinking. Nothing is going to change, I know that now. I'll keep trying to commit suicide and one day I'll succeed. I know it. I've accepted it. Terry can't watch me like a hawk for twenty-four hours a day every day. He's got a business to run, a life to live, and all I'm doing is ruining it for him. The sooner I'm out of it the better.'

'That's not true, Marion. If you ...'

'It's going to happen, Charles,' she interrupted abruptly. 'One day I'll be feeling a bit down and I'll succeed when all the other attempts failed. The law of averages are on my side. I'm going to do it, so I might as well get it over and done with.'

'Is that why you rejected your baby?'

Marion closed her eyes and Charles thought she'd gone to sleep, then they flickered open and she shook her head sadly.

'My life is in enough mess, Charles, without adding to it. Here I am, just waiting for an opportunity to pop my clogs, the last thing I want is the added misery of leaving my baby. I thought … I thought, if I don't bond with it … if I can maybe get it adopted or something, then it'll be easier when I … It'll be less of a wrench. It's only a baby, Charles. It doesn't know me … no ties have been made. I thought that would be better rather than wait until he's older … when he'd miss me.'

'Terry might have something to say about that,' he said softly, and she shook her head as if it didn't matter anymore.

'If Terry wants his son, Charles, then he can have him. As far as I'm concerned it's all over … finished.'

Charles looked down at the pitiful figure lying in the hospital bed, a seemingly shrunken creature, cowed by events and driven by a will not of her choosing, and his heart went out to her, knowing that all the therapy and all the psychiatrists in the world couldn't help her … but perhaps he could.

'All right, Marion,' he said gently. 'I've listened to you and now it's your turn to listen to me... I want you to do me a favour.'

She cocked her head at him as if she suspected a trap, and he ploughed on.

'It's a small favour, simple to do, and will only take two minutes of your time.' He waited and she had to ask, just as he knew she would.

'What favour?'

'I want you to hold your baby.'

'No!'

'Marion … two minutes, that's all.'

'No!'

Charles sighed and looked at her long and hard, then he

nodded as if he'd come to a decision, a make-or-break final plea that was all he had left to give.

'Marion … I'll make a deal with you, okay? Listen to me, Marion, because I'm putting my job on the line here.'

She looked at him levelly, then she shrugged.

'All right,' she conceded grudgingly. 'I'm listening.'

'Hold your baby for two minutes, Marion, and if you don't want him after that, if you still want to commit suicide … then I'll give you the injection myself.'

'What?' She stared at him as if he'd gone mad, and he forced a weak smile.

'That's the deal You hold your son for two minutes and if you're still determined to end it all I'll do it for you.'

'You've taken leave of your bleeding senses.'

'Probably.' He shrugged matter-of-factly. 'But that's still the deal.'

'You'd …'

'Give you a lethal injection, yes.' He nodded, mute emphasis to his words. 'It's quick, painless and guaranteed to work in less than two minutes. Have we got a deal here, or what?'

Time seemed to stand still as she stared up at him, all her doubts and uncertainties, all her misgivings and suspicions reflected in her eyes, then she rose to the challenge, bearing herself up determinedly as she looked him squarely in the eye and nodded.

'All right, Doctor Charles Bloody Levington … We've got a deal.'

Charles wheeled the newborn baby in in the little trolley, seeing the way Marion steeled herself as he entered the ward, but he didn't hesitate, pulling up alongside her bed and lifting the infant from the folds of blankets and dumping him unceremoniously, but tenderly, into Marion's unwilling arms. He waited, breath held as the moment stretched on and on, then she finally lowered her eyes and looked at her son.

Just to the left of centre of his tiny chest, about where the heart would be, was a little birthmark, a discoloured smudge that was plainly visible, yet not unsightly, on the pink softness of his flesh. It would fade with time, Charles knew, but at this moment, at this most critical of moments, it stood out like a beacon of hope in Marion's hopeless world. On the side of the baby's neck was a little mole, blurred and fuzzy round the edges, but if Charles was to screw up his eyes and squint a bit he could almost convince himself that the mole was shaped like a small dog with a pointed snout and pricked-up ears. Marion's eyes weren't screwed up, nor were they squinting, for they were brimming over with tears, but the effect was the same, a blurred image of Anubis, the ancient Egyptian god of mummification. The prophecy had been fulfilled and the brands that had carried them for three thousand years had begun to fade and die.

'You see, Marion,' Charles said softly. 'There's no need to kill yourself to be with your soulmate … he's come back to you as your son.'

'H…how can this be?' she managed through her tears, and Charles shrugged lightly.

'Well … if I was a religious person I'd say that the God of Moses, the Hebrew God … our God, is a darn sight more powerful than old Ramesses ever gave him credit for. Beat him in the end, didn't he? And maybe, just maybe, the God of Moses thought you'd suffered enough over three thousand years and deserved a little peace … a final farewell, Marion. You've loved him as a husband and as a lover … now love him as your son. Nurture him and watch him grow. See him married and give you grandchildren. For when the time comes to let him go, you've got to swallow that love and release him, because that's what love is all about. A final farewell, Marion. Enjoy him as a child, as your son, then let him go to make a life of his own just as you've got to.'

284

The baby began to fret, tiny arms flailing and little lungs protesting, and Charles smiled.

'Poor little beggar's hungry. Don't mind me, Marion. I'm a doctor, remember.'

She laughed through her tears as she scooped a full breast free of her nightdress and fed a nipple to the hungry mouth, and Charles turned away, knowing it was finally over and Marion was destined to live.

'By the way,' he said at the door, turning to peer at her over his shoulder. 'Have you thought of a name for him yet?'

It was a moot question, a host of possible names springing up from the past, and she shook her head, her hands gently soothing the babe cradled so lovingly in her arms.

'I think I'll let Terry decide,' she said, then her face creased into the biggest grin he'd ever seen. 'Perhaps we'll call him after this doctor we know ... Perhaps we'll call him Charlie.'

And Charles's delighted laughter could be heard ringing through the corridors as he turned and walked away.

The Face in the Stone

Ex-Warrant Officer Class I Edward Mather died in his luxury Cyprus villa from asthma. That had also been the medical reason for his army discharge two years before. But his wasn't a serious case and some thought he shouldn't have died. Two months later an exhumation and post-mortem laid suspicion of murder on his widow.

An efficient Signalman, he was also a rogue adventurer with an eye to making his fortune. So where was this fortune, who were his associates and what had he been involved in?

Police investigation takes time, and the mystery man from Athens looked likely to get the answers first—until the widow took an active interest and the case blew wide open.

CLARE CURZON

The Face in the Stone

COLLINS, 8 GRAFTON STREET, LONDON W1

William Collins Sons & Co. Ltd
London · Glasgow · Sydney · Auckland
Toronto · Johannesburg

First published 1989
© Clare Curzon 1989

British Library Cataloguing in Publication Data

Curzon, Clare
The face in the stone.—(Crime Club)
I. Title
823′.914 [F]

ISBN 0 00 232239 0

Photoset in Linotron Baskerville by
Rowland Phototypesetting Ltd
Bury St Edmunds, Suffolk
Printed in Great Britain by
William Collins Sons & Co. Ltd, Glasgow

CHAPTER 1

'*Whore!*' the man mumbled, lurching over the counter as he untangled his sandals from the bar stool.

His breath reached her and she turned away from the fumes of secondhand *ouzo*. His eyes, small and fierce as a boar's, were unfocused. Sweat clung in the grooves of his weathered skin, beaded the roots of his dark, springing hair. His body gave off a male, bitter smell.

'Just like a whore,' he muttered again thickly. '*Anybody's!*' In English, but she knew it wasn't meant for her. His complaint was of some woman whose personal infidelity scoured him acidly inside. He struck the counter with a calloused fist. 'Kill him!' The words were breathed through clenched teeth. 'I—will—*kill*—the bastard!'

He twisted away, dragging the fist until it swung heavily against his paint-stained jeans. He stood a moment uncertain, then hunched his powerful shoulders and made off without a word or a backward glance.

'There's no real harm in him,' Spiros allowed from his vantage point among the bottles, 'or I would have shifted him when you came in.'

Jean Mather upturned the small mixer bottle over her empty glass, sadly swirled the tonic to pick up any late clinging of gin, and downed it reflectively. 'I played fair by my man,' she murmured to herself. 'Headache though he was in some ways.'

Spiros caught the low words and came along the deserted bar towards her, hands busy polishing a tumbler. She considered him. He knew the way it had been, had respected Ted enough to change his free day and follow the hearse all its stony way to the cemetery, on foot and carrying his token bunch of wilting herbs, just as though Ted had been Cypriot too, and family. He was nodding, watchful eyes on the

departing man as he limped past the dusty oleanders border-
ing the road. 'But that one has no woman. The sea is his
wife.'

Silently Jean denied this. Everyone had someone: the
First Law of Amodynamics. It's what hit so hard when you
were a monog and your partner died. You went on with pretence life, made social gestures, showed synthetic interest.

She rearranged her heels on the stool crossbar. 'Who is
he, then? A regular? I haven't seen him before.'

'Not in here, no. He drinks down at Limassol harbour.
Stelios Baroutis. He runs a small boatyard. It was his
father's before him. I was at school with his younger brother.
Everybody liked Kostas. Sad that he was drowned last
winter. This one is different, a surly man who walks alone.
I have never before seen him so—' He seemed to run out
of words.

'Aggressive?' she asked helpfully.

'So desperate.' Spiro's dark eyes blinked once and then the
tan, square face resumed its Olympian detachment. 'Will
you have another drink, Mrs Mather? On the house?'

'Thank you, Spiros, but tomorrow perhaps.' It would be
too easy to slither into the habit. She made and kept rules
now, keeping only table wine at home, drove down to
Spiros's Bar at a slack time for the modest gin or brandy
she prescribed for herself.

'I have to get back.' Back to what, though? Nodding to
him, she stepped down from the high stool, wriggling her
skirt straight as she glanced into the reflecting glass doors
of the gifts showcase. Almost short enough to be dumpy,
unritzy, widowed, what was there for her to hurry off to?
Functionless, with no prospects unless *Dallas* ever needed a
younger Miss Ellie. Grinning, she acknowledged that that
was her type, and she'd have enjoyed the challenge of a
large, complicated family. Ted and she had never produced
a child, and neither had openly complained of it. Even now
she wouldn't admit to any shortfall, but she missed having
someone to be more than an acquaintance. Spiros was as

near a friend as she could boast, and he made no demands. A barman, that was all.

'Goodbye, Spiros.'

'Goodbye, Mrs Mather.' As ever, they kept to English. He knew the woman had a fair command of Greek, but she properly recognized his professional standing; that since English was an important qualification of his calling, he insisted on using it. He nodded. Maybe that was why Baroutis too had spoken in English, spitting out that disgusting word in front of her, half soused as he was.

Whore. Strange, that. Why should Stelios Baroutis concern himself over such a type? It was out of character. The man's mood had disturbed Spiros. If the boatman came a second time up to the hotel, he would ask him to leave: residents only. There were other, cheaper places for a local man to get legless.

He looked after the Englishwoman's small figure as it went black in the doorway against the late afternoon light. 'Uh-uh—' but when she turned back he had already thought better of the warning. 'Uh, mind how you go,' he said without emphasis, as though it were just part of a customary farewell. She smiled. 'You too.' Raised a hand and was gone.

He stared after her, mouth puckered. He had meant to ask, 'There's been no trouble?' but in the event he'd chickened out. If she wasn't worried already, why start it up? Empty talk, perhaps; but if not, who had the poor lady to protect her now? If the rumours didn't die away, if they hardened into official suspicion, there would be trouble enough for her. And she so unaware, working so bravely at not giving in to grief.

Driving with open windows back through the sparse afternoon traffic—mainly coachloads of early-season tourists 'doing' the antiquities, and the abominable taxis hooting their demands for the centre of the road, Jean Mather relished the breeze reducing the oven-heat of the car. Her fine, fair hair, worn straight to her shoulders, whipped about her head. She half-closed her eyes against gritty sand blowing up from the beaches between the white apartment blocks. She turned left along Makarios Avenue and then into the secondary road towards the village, to the house she thought of as asylum.

She recalled her first sight of it, when Ted had driven her up a few weeks before his discharge. It was old, faintly peach and its weathered stones bore the stains of decades. Squarish at the centre, with two modest attachments stepped back from the main part so that there were shaded corners at any time of day. There was a formal portico with columns. Two immense, stout palm trees stood on sentry duty at the front.

There hadn't been any grass strip then between building and dirt road. The house looked part of the rock it stood on, like an ancient temple. Constructed of pale stone, the cracks down its flaked rendering were like fine roots holding it firm to the earth. Fancifully she'd said as much to Ted, and screwing up his practical eyes he'd replied, 'More like the veins in a woman's legs. We'll have it fixed. You'll see.'

And she had seen, because next time she came builders had already gutted it. She had thought all he'd meant was a cosmetic fix plus updating of plumbing and electrics, there being no way Ted could settle to retirement without mod. cons. In fact it had amazed her that he'd gone for such a traditional property, and she'd felt guilty at having under-rated his sensibility to her own preferences. Or, because the house was old, perhaps it was going cheap?

That suspicion was killed stone dead on her second visit. Clearly Ted wasn't bothered by consideration of costs. The alterations were going to run his service pension heavily into the red, and there remained only a few thousand from what Dad had left her.

She'd dared to voice her misgivings and instead of blowing his top Ted had chuckled. 'Digging in, aren't we? Might as well make a good job of it. Don't worry. Property's cheap out here, so's labour. *Dirt* cheap.' She had wondered then if his sudden discharge from Signals had turned Ted's head. All along she'd agreed with him that retirement out here would offer a better standard of living than back in England, but such grandiose schemes . . .

Since then she'd had plenty of time to realize that it wasn't retirement at all: not a gradual, relaxed approach to the evening years. Ted was at his burning noonday, meant it to be a permanent state. Engorged by his own powers, only slightly incommoded by the asthma that had bought his release from the Service, he expected—*intended*—an eternity of sunshine and plenty. They went short of nothing, unless it was some significant occupation for Jean herself. For Ted there was an endless string of calls for unspecified employment. 'A little job for the lads,' he would say, and be gone for three, four days, coming back smugly satisfied and certainly well rewarded. But that had been private business and there'd been no part in it for her.

Ted had considered that the house should provide occupation enough, especially after she'd insisted on sacking the daily cook-maid who'd bussed up from Limassol. She managed well enough with old Elpida from the village who came in three times a week ostensibly to clean and who would frequently pause in mid-task to throw up her hands and exclaim ecstatically at the opulence of their existence and possessions.

She was in her middle fifties, squat, undeniably greasy with her badly hennaed greying hair and shiny black cotton dress, but neat for all that. A prima donna *manquée*, she still believed herself to be the doelike, dark-eyed beauty she must once certainly have been. When she caught anyone's eye on her she made a great production of whatever small detail she was about. She practised an ostentatious piety and made it known that she regularly prayed for the unenlightened souls of her foreign employers. It had exasperated Ted, but since Jean had found her mildly amusing he'd only once sent the woman packing and then overlooked her wheedling her way back when Jean had been at the house on her own.

She would be there now, Jean guessed. Thick little thighs straining at her skimped black skirt, she would be seated on the terrace wall, heavy face lifted to the evening breeze, ready to be found by any passing artist/employer/archangel and pressed into overwilling service. And her pretty confusion on being discovered, however unsuited to the lumpy body it found itself trapped in, would be played through for Jean's benefit before the inevitable outpouring of sorrow over the widowed state they both now shared. That, Jean could do without. She had made it clear that nothing would persuade her to adopt the lifelong mourning that Elpida had embraced with such relish.

She thought the message had at last got across, and possibly that was why the village woman made such an assiduous chaperon of herself whenever anyone vaguely male appeared in the offing. Doubtless she considered Jean's shocking pinks and vivid blues, suntops and briefs signalled an eagerness to throw herself into the arms of any possible —or improbable—successor to the late Ted Mather . . . If only she knew!

'I dress to please myself,' Jean defended herself half aloud, 'just as Elpida does although she'd never admit it. True, Ted's gone, but I'm still here. I won't commit mental suttee, however morbid I feel at times.' Talking to herself was a habit that had crept up on Jean in the past few weeks. Although she was aware of it, it didn't trouble her. She had long had a dreamy way of halting in the middle of an action to think out some interruptive idea and it seemed that this new habit was at least consoling in that she knew she still had a voice. It was a pleasant voice, deep for a woman, but sometimes with a hint of uncertainty in its flow. Recently she had noticed that when making a positive statement she'd tended to weaken it with, 'don't you agree?' or 'unless perhaps . . .' Now she practised a tone of certainty, apology-free, and quite often ended on a low chuckle.

Yes, Elpida was still there, overseeing the hosing of the paths. Georgios was perfectly capable of doing it, but the woman liked to assume seniority, scolding him for the faintest trace of blown sand on the terrace furniture or on the blue tiles at the bottom of the pool. She came out for the shopping from the car and when Jean had garaged it behind the house Elpida was still busy fussing it all into its right places in fridge and freezer.

Georgios nodded silently, coiling his hose. The whole garden was blessedly cool from its drenching. He lingered, his eyes on the wet path before him. 'There is a stranger in the village. All afternoon he has sat at the taberna, watching.'

'A tourist perhaps.' Again there sounded that tone of uncertainty. 'Kalidrofi is a village worth visiting.' A definite statement now, with a hint of defiance.

Georgios lifted the coiled hose and swung it on to one shoulder. It left damp weals across his pale blue shirt. 'He waits,' he said, and began to walk away.

Jean looked after him. Waits for what? Watches what? It had nothing to do with her. But Georgios was a man of very few words and never wasted them. So he meant her to take some action on there being a stranger in the village. Forewarning. Well, a stranger to him might well be someone familiar to herself, or some connection of Ted's from his duty years at Episkopi or since. She'd better not go straight into the pool this evening. Entertaining a fully dressed visitor while in a dripping swimsuit could be embarrassing. She mixed herself a jug of crushed orange, threw in ice cubes and settled down to wait.

The stranger at the taberna spread a handful of coins over the table, helped himself to another ripe mespila, spitting the stones into the street outside, and rose to his feet. He was tall and spare, lean-faced and hawkish, as dark of eyes as the local men but his complexion was a faded bronze as though he had recently worked indoors, his finger ends unscarred, his dress casual but expensive.

'The man from Athens is leaving,' said Yannakis's little

son, running indoors to rouse him from the pages of his newspaper, but his father's scowl told him to hold his tongue.

Nobody came out from the shadowed interior to wish the man well as he left. He pocketed a few more mespilas, tapped the breast of his jacket where the instamatic camera lay hidden and stepped down into the dusty street. As he passed the onetime schoolhouse he thought he heard music but it was drowned in the clatter of a fruiterer's van accelerating up from the main road. He gave a final quick glance at the sentinel palms, the fresh colour-washed columns, immaculate pantiles, scrolled ironwork, shuttered windows, and smiled grimly.

Never on a soldier's salary could one live in such a palace; still less on only a pension. What was it Papa Loutsios had said last week over their game of backgammon: that you could see how the Almighty despised money when you considered those he'd inflicted it on? Not that the good priest was indifferent to wealth himself: indeed, who was? Certainly not I, not Nikolaos Clerides. Time enough to despise it when it became too familiar; perhaps when he had pulled off the present project?

He patted his inner breast pocket again and smiled grimly, walking more jauntily down the dirt track to where he'd earlier parked the hire car under a carob tree.

It had been a fruitful day. He had sighted the woman, would know her again, had decided against confronting her alone at the villa. It must be elsewhere, perhaps when next she went shopping. The photographs he'd taken, once enlarged, would reveal addresses printed on the carrier bags she'd brought her purchases home in. In one of those shops she would eventually find him waiting.

Patience, Nikolaos. Sooner or later the unsuspecting mouse must venture from its hole. Then would be the moment for the game to begin, first with pat of soft paw, claws sheathed. Later, the pounce. Finally, the kill.

*

As the taped Vivaldi ran to its end, Jean Mather noted that
the garden was in darkness and all the ice was now melted
in the jug. She consulted her wristwatch and rose from her
chair on the terrace. It seemed that her first intuition had
been right: the stranger at Yannakis's bar was no visitor for
her. She was aware of slight disappointment, regret that
because of what old Georgios had said she'd delayed her
swim to no purpose.

Standing by the side of the floodlit pool she felt the
winking water enticing her to its depths. It was too much
bother to go indoors for her swimsuit. She stepped out of
her crocus-yellow skirt, dropped blouse and briefs beside
her sandals, stood poised an instant on her toes and dived
naked into the silky water.

CHAPTER 2

Next day she was to lunch with Lance and Marjorie Rowley
—the Rowley-Powleys as Ted snidely dubbed them. They
were established residents, expatriate Brits almost twenty
years older than he was, and thirty-five more than Jean.
Lance had once served in the RAF at Akrotiri between tours
of duty in Malta and West Germany. Commissioned from
the ranks, he was a rotund, fussy little man with a wife
grown so like him that they might have been twins. They
had never been close friends of the Mathers although circumstances had sometimes pushed them into a foursome.
Jean suspected that it was their very ordinariness that Ted
had appreciated, because it showed him up as the dynamic
leader.

Retirement had negatived the distance between the two
services and two levels of messing: Ted had always kept
the threat of a commission at bay, recognizing there were
financial advantages that way, and bragging that every
soldier in the British army knew it was run by the senior

technical NCOs. As far as the despised subalterns had been concerned, he must have been right, Jean thought, and even up to the level of Corps majors there was a distinct wariness displayed towards Warrant Officer First Class Mather E. J. Until the new CO had started making changes.

His arrival had coincided with Ted's first really serious asthma attack and he'd been seven weeks in hospital before mention was made of discharge on health grounds.

That hadn't worried him. It was she who worried, Jean acknowledged. She had—rightly as it turned out—felt that Ted's health was in a far worse state than he would accept, and she had been slow to give full support to what then seemed his hare-brained scheme to settle permanently in Cyprus on his army pension. Back in England he could have found undemanding part-time work as a Communications consultant. She herself could have gone back to teaching Junior Science. They would have found friends among neighbours of similar interests and the same age groups. And then there was the National Health Service.

But he'd decided on it this way, she'd fallen in with it, and now—whether by inertia or from matured preference —she no longer thought of England as home. Home was their gracious old house in the Tróodos foothills, surrounded by orchards, vineyards and scenery that stirred the heart. Home meant never feeling really cold again, and knowing that when it rained there was a date by which it would surely be over.

On principle she made herself go down to Limassol for shopping, regularly toured the whole island in her little renovated Morris Minor, right up to the Green Line that marked the Turkish illegal occupation. And more than half the pleasure in these sorties was the coming back, even when it was to an empty house. 'Empty, but not necessarily silent,' she reminded herself. Elpida was given to moving in as custodian in her absence and would welcome her return with noisy greetings. Some people kept dogs for that very purpose.

She didn't want to go out today: there were a dozen things she'd promised herself to get on with. But she still felt under an obligation to the Rowleys, specifically because Marjorie had been there on that awful evening when Ted died. She had shared Jean's panic, run round in much the same kind of circles, been equally helpless and appalled when they realized it was all over.

Seeing her again always brought the agony back for Jean, but she felt that by struggling on with the relationship she must eventually wear it thin enough to snap, as though the unwanted contact were a penance set for her that could at last outweigh the situation that earned it.

To be fair to her, Marjorie never referred to that occasion, just squeezing Jean's arm with a plump, moist hand at such times as she imagined Jean's feelings were welling into misery. She didn't understand that Jean liked to speak of Ted still, Ted making things work, taking over others' problems, digging into difficulties, finding solutions; Ted very much alive.

It was Lance, away in Nicosia during Ted's last week, who went back time and again to that evening, asked questions, wanted details, somehow seemed so disturbed that he couldn't leave the subject alone. Jean felt like telling him to get a check on his own health and let the dead lie peacefully, but she knew such outspokenness would have shocked the older couple.

They had a pretty, modern bungalow out at Coral Bay west of Paphos. It was in an upmarket development and they kept themselves busy entertaining neighbours—mainly other retired British officers and their wives—playing bridge and sailing their twenty-four-footer. Unlike those of the houses round them, their garden was unmade, with wild flowers settled in the crannies of golden rock. Instead they had built on the roof a loggia which trailed purple bougain-villaea, and had set pots with geraniums and lilies along the low roof wall. When she had been there a few hours Jean always longed for the shade of her own trees and the cool, upland air. By the end of May the breeze off the sea was itself hot and dry. Keen swimmer that she was, she was disturbed by the intense blueness out there, unchanging under the sun. Later she was to wonder whether some deep animal level within her had warned her she should fear it.

On arrival she found that the Rowleys had bought a new canopy for the roof which she was required to exclaim on, and then there was the pristine Lefkara lace cloth on which their place settings were arranged. Marjorie was excited about a recipe she'd found in an English magazine and was trying out for the first time. At the meal's end, 'I expect you want to go for a walk,' Lance prompted as usual. 'Mustn't hold young people back, eh?'

Jean fell in with the suggestion, assuring Marjorie that no, she wouldn't dream of swimming for at least an hour, to let her lunch settle; and then she was free to wander round the far end of the bay, follow a track diagonally up the cliff and find herself a green hollow strong with the scent of sagebrush where she could lie and let sleep creep slowly over her like water lapping at the edge of the sands below.

Her mind adrift, she was listening to Ted explaining some new moneyspinning plan, all muddled in with Lance's conversation over lunch. Suddenly she was awake in the full afternoon glare, with the baked earth, hard against one hip, ticking with small insects. Alone, on the cliffside.

Down in the cove there were raised voices, men in dispute over a sailing-boat that was being beached on wooden rollers. Jean peered between stems of wild scabious to watch how it went. One of the men was Lance (supposedly at home with his feet up) and the boat looked very much like his *Zoë*. The other man, threatening him, was vaguely familiar; heavily built, dark, certainly a Cypriot, possibly had been crewing for Lance. A boatman—that made the connection. This was surely the man she'd seen in Spiros's Bar yesterday. Stelios something—Barakis? No; Baroutis.

He'd gone drinking to forget a woman who'd let him down. Spiros had once been at school with his younger brother Kostas who'd been lost at sea.

She glanced at her watch. Only an hour since she had set out on her walk. Lance had stayed on at the house and there was no one else in sight now, so Baroutis must have sailed the boat in single-handed to the cove. From Limassol? From his boatyard? Or, more likely, he'd just taken it out to check some minor fault. If so, what were they fighting over—surely not the cost of repairs? That would be bad customer relations. The man really was an aggressive type.

The quarrel seemed to have been settled, Lance subsiding, the other man still with bunched fists stiffly at his sides as they made their way together along the waterline. Lance was wearing sandshoes, plodding flatly so that with each step he splashed water up on his rolled trouser legs. Jean watched them disappear round the head of the cove and turned again on her back, reflecting that today she'd found Lance particularly disagreeable when Marjorie was out of the room fussing up the dessert.

It had been almost as if he was waiting for his wife to go. He'd come round the table with the wine to refill her glass and stood behind her with his face hidden. 'Went over to watch the polo on Sunday. Splendid game. You ought to have come, Jean. Ran into old Stanley Moffat. Remember him?'

She could hardly forget. Moffat had been the MO when Ted first went down badly with his asthma, said it had been due to a virus but from then on he'd have to take precautions. Moffat and the CO between them had been responsible for Ted's discharge, although he'd been having little wheezy spells off and on for a year or so. After all those weeks in hospital having tests, Ted had been in no condition to argue, had even seemed complaisant. It was as if, with the Medical Board's decision, he suddenly changed course, gave up his career, instantly picked up the *dolce vita*. And the asthma, which two years later was to kill him, he regarded almost as a joke, a means towards exchanging his grub life for the butterfly one.

'How was Mr Moffat?' she asked.

'Seemed fit enough; pasty, of course. Back in Camberley; routine desk job checking the cadet intakes. Pretty boring, I gathered. Wangled a flight out for a week of sun. Asked after you. And Ted.'

'He hadn't heard, then?'

'No, and it rocked him back somewhat, I can tell you.'

'I didn't think they were all that close.'

'No, well. What I mean is, he couldn't believe it. Said old Ted was fit as a flea when he left here.'

'He surely couldn't have forgotten! Or is he getting senile? It was Moffat who made such a song and dance about the asthma, swayed the Medical Board. Nobody thought anything of it till then. Certainly Ted was up to fulfilling his responsibilities, more than capable. There was never any idea of discharge for health reasons until Moffat took over.'

'That's what I thought too, at the time. Seems I was wrong. Asked him why all the weeks in hospital if Ted was basically OK.'

'Did he remember that much?'

'Oh yes. Said Ted needed to be out of service for a while. The CO's way of avoiding some bad publicity. So Moffat whipped him into sick bay, ran a lot of tests for allergies. Some got a positive result, but they weren't substances he'd be much likely to come across in quantity. Saw it as more in the nature of a medical experiment.'

'But I remember how Ted was at that time. He was really ill.'

'Moffat says not. Bit of malingering, he seemed to suggest.'

'But Lance, Moffat *fixed* Ted. He and the new CO together. If it hadn't been for them Ted would still have . . . Well, perhaps not. But I do think it's very odd that *now* he chooses to deny everything he said before.'

Lance was still standing behind her, silent. She twisted to look up at him and he dropped his eyes. 'So what else did the remarkable doctor say?'

Rowley carried the wine bottle back to his own place and refilled his glass. Abruptly he made up his mind and faced her. 'He said Ted was in on the plan all along. He wanted out, fancied swapping the Service for an early pension.'

It hit her between the eyes. 'Do you mean that Moffat actually admitted collusion—with the CO and Ted himself —to *wangle* the discharge?'

'Not the CO, no. He wanted Ted out for other reasons; thought his extended service had been a mistake. Been here too long, had a bit too much influence with the locals one way and another. Sensitive area of work he was employed on, you know. There had been enough security alarms in the Corps already.'

'My God! You had a real good gossip, the two of you. Well, either Moffat was right the first time or right the second. And Ted was the final arbiter, wasn't he? Maybe you're going to tell me he didn't die after all, because he was far too healthy?' Her voice rose as she felt her face flushing. She had a wild desire to fling the glass of wine in the pompous little bastard's face.

He had coloured up too. His whole round head looked swollen. 'Kindly keep your voice down. I don't want Marjorie unnecessarily alarmed.'

Jean was speechless.

He took a gulp of the wine, steadied his voice and said barely above a tense whisper, 'He doesn't *deny* Ted died. He just said he shouldn't have. There was no real *reason*.'

She went on staring at the man, incredulous.

Lance decided she needed it made plainer. 'He said— there was something—*fishy* about the death.'

'Fishy,' she repeated weakly, afraid she was going to laugh in his face.

'He wanted to know what medical treatment Ted was taking. Drugs, you know; things to inhale. All that.'

'Oh, did he.' It wasn't a question.

'Well then, what *was* he taking? Marjorie said he had two inhalers, one blue-grey and the other cream.'

'Lance, I just can't believe this. You know what happened. God knows, you've made me go over this time and time again until I'm sick to the back teeth . . . Ted must have overdone things, or he ate something that brought on a severe attack. We were there, Marjorie and I. She'll tell you. She *has* told you. He used his emergency spray, properly, and it had no effect. He was choking. The noise he made was terrible. I stayed with him while Marjorie went to phone, but she hadn't brought her reading glasses and I had never memorized the emergency number. So we changed places. She stayed with Ted, and when I got back to them he'd collapsed. After a few minutes I couldn't find a pulse. I tried to resuscitate him, mouth-to-mouth, but nothing happened. He was going blue. When the doctor got there he said we couldn't have done anything. The coroner said the same. Who is this man Moffat, to come back all these months later and make such monstrous suggestions?'

'Jean, I know this is upsetting, but don't you see, we can't hide our heads in the sand . . .'

'There—isn't—any—sand.'

And that was when Marjorie had come bustling in, creaking in her shiny blue dress, carrying her triumph of the hour, some abominable confection laced with liqueur and swagged with cream grotesqueries.

Jean picked fragments of dried grass off her skirt and stood up. Implacable as ever, the dark sea stretched up to the skyline, full and seemingly unmoving. Such power, dormant. She had always felt awed by great volumes of water. Once as a child in Wales, standing above a new dam, she had experienced the vision of its latent force suddenly unleashed. When the vertigo had passed she opened her eyes and could no longer trust the calm of its unruffled surface. Whenever she swam, cleanly cutting through the water, she never forgot how puny the strength of her own limbs and how limitless the element she moved against. It was almost a phobia with her, a fearful fascination.

'*Thalassa!*' she murmured now in respectful salutation and turned back towards the Rowleys' model bungalow.

She found Marjorie alone there, setting out tea-things and apologetic because Lance had suddenly been called away. 'Running someone over to Limassol,' she said breathlessly. 'Such a nuisance, but he could hardly avoid offering a lift.'

'I could have done it for him, if he'd cared to wait,' Jean told her. 'A neighbour, was it?'

'No. *Yes*; a neighbour. A sudden emergency. Well, you'd rather go with someone you know in that case, wouldn't you?'

Jean looked away from the flustered woman to save her further embarrassment. There was no obvious reason that she could see for Marjorie lying, but if she wanted to cover up the surly boatman's existence, why not? It would seem that having beached *Zoë* he'd bullied Lance into providing transport back by road. Jean was glad she hadn't been asked to offer him a seat in her own little car. And even more grateful that she hadn't to face Lance again this day. He'd been so disagreeable that she wouldn't ever want to come here again, but she supposed that staying away would cause real offence.

'Take it,' she said to herself aloud. 'Don't give it.' An old precept of her grandmother's. She smiled wryly.

'What's that, dear?' Marjorie asked, but Jean shook her head and reached for a home-made scone.

Lance couldn't possibly get back within the next hour. By then she should be safely on her way home.

CHAPTER 3

The coastal route eastward from Paphos never failed to thrill her with its finale of deep green tunnels of trees between vineyards, after sunbaked golden cliffs with a roller-coaster track of good, metalled road. Holding the bends at speed gave her a physical pleasure, and by the time she neared Episkopi her resentment was less scalding.

For all that, she found it hard to credit Lance's insensitive mischief-making, and even more the old MO's willingness to gossip. Surely he couldn't have been so indiscreet about his own part in Ted's discharge? Lance had almost certainly misunderstood the implications, just as he'd misjudged the true gravity of Ted's illness. She had been falsely lulled herself during the two years when regular use of inhalers had kept the asthma totally at bay, assuming that freedom from the pressures of a Service career had cured him.

But there was no disputing what had killed him. The local doctor, who always prescribed for the dormant condition, had been certain. There had been no hesitation in providing a death certificate. Even the insurance company had paid up without demur.

Why, then, should Colonel Moffat, on short leave from England, voice any astonishment that Ted had gone under from the very disease he'd earlier signed him off with? Moffat should have seen it as confirmation of his own prognosis, and not set up a hare so that Lance could turn its pursuit into a full-scale scandal. Because if the death wasn't natural, what was it? Dammit, she'd ask him herself just what he was after. She could stop off at the base, where someone would help her to contact Moffat.

She slowed towards the brow of the hill, but there were trucks drawn up in the checkpoint bay; the MPs examining them were unfamiliar faces.

'Drop it,' she told herself. It was only Lance's pompous interference. He was a silly old woman without enough to occupy his woolly mind. If he'd exaggerated, added a few decorative touches to the original conversation, Moffat would think she was out of her mind to come checking on it. Morbid, even.

Too late now, anyway. She was over the summit and already rolling down the eastern slope past married quarters. She put her foot down firmly on the accelerator, shot past a taxi and zoomed along the straight. Whatever Ted had put in to replace the original engine, it certainly made the bird fly.

At Kourion, on a whim, she swung right into the track leading down to the mosaics and amphitheatre; parked in the shade and took a ticket for thirty-penceworth of strolling over the ancient past. The site was partially excavated, minimally reconstructed; dominating the sea and hard-baked by sun, as it must have been when thousands of the long-dead thronged it. It fascinated her and horrified the student still in her that at every step she took she risked crushing disregarded fragments of artefacts mixed among the natural rocks; the broken rim of a giant pithoi, a chip of worked cornice, a polished tile.

Stones themselves were to her more beautiful than fine wood grains, partly because of what they suggested to her mind, each natural lump of quartz or limestone having affinity with a living form that her growing skill could bring out of the unorganized mass.

The first object she had created from stone was a head. She had sat watching the workmen gouging out their hole for the pool and it had lain on top of the pile thrown up from their excavation; a squarish, irregular block of sandstone, like a man's profile, deep-browed, long of nose, thrown back, with its beard jutting up at the sky. But when she bent over it the sardonic features were gone. Just knobs and nodules remained that had no significance.

So she had whittled at it, first with a plasterer's miniature

trowel and later with a skewer, rubbing at the surface to
recover what she'd earlier glimpsed, feeling for the hollows
under cheekbones, caverns to hold the eyes.

'Zeus,' Elpida had pronounced, the first time she ever
saw the finished head (village Cypriots, like Greeks, saw
Zeus in everything old, which perhaps explained his reputation for changing his shape so often). But to Jean the face
was more likely that of some vanished schoolmaster
who had once lived at the house and left something of
himself behind. She felt too an affinity with it, as though
it had some influence over her life, and almost a sense of
déjà-vu.

After the head, a fat, golden lizard; a tortoise from some
darker, more shiny stone; then a human baby, curled on its
side asleep. Each time she had seen the finished creature
there in the unworked rock before she began. It was simply
a case of letting the living thing out.

Yannakis at the taberna begged some of her work to set
out on his terrace, and she knew he had sold two figures
last summer to passing tourists, but she wouldn't take
money herself for fear it somehow infringed her conditions
of residence. It was her private pleasure to make things,
and walking the stony mountain tracks had a new excitement when anywhere she might find some rock that had a
life form inside.

This evening she was eager to get back and look again at
a block of limestone that suggested a kneeling woman. By
now, having read up on techniques of sculpture, she had
acquired the proper tools. They were laid out and ready for
her return on the balcony that overlooked the side garden.
As soon as she was back she would make coffee and work
on the stone until the natural light was gone.

Next afternoon, just after two, the man from Athens caught
up with her. Like Jean he didn't keep siesta, merely reducing
physical effort during the hottest hours of the day. Thorough
as ever in pursuit of his devious ends, he was cruising in the

area, map on the seat alongside, familiarizing himself with
routes and dead ends. You never knew when it might be
vital to give chase or lie up concealed. And then, on a 7%
uphill gradient behind Korphi he spotted her grey Morris
parked on the dirt frontage of a low building that advertised
'Ceramics'.

There was little that could interest her farther uphill.
Beyond Limnátos the road ran out; if she took the right fork
for Kapilió she would be taxing the car's suspension. It
was reasonable to suppose that having completed whatever
business or pleasure took her to the pottery, she would head
downhill again.

Accordingly Clerides drove past, turned his hired car and
ran it into a clump of olive trees. Clambering over a tangle
of thistles and rock he found a point that commanded the
building below and a crescent of secondary road beyond it.
After a wait of some twenty minutes the woman appeared
in the open with a short, dark man, his grey shirt bloused
over mottled navy slacks. Clerides raised his field-glasses to
take in the detail. Not a lover: they walked side by side but
apart. This was a business meeting with the potter. Mottling
on his clothes was produced by splotches of grey and red
clay.

They moved together out of sight and Clerides heard the
distant sound of a car engine starting up. The man walked
back into the lee of the building, and a few seconds later
the roof of a small grey car swept round the downhill bend.
The watcher grunted, returned to his white Toyota, rattled
it back on to the road. He should easily catch her up before
the turn off to her own village.

Jean Mather settled her shoulders firmly back against the
driving seat and enjoyed the breeze of her descent. She had
long intended to take up the invitation to try her hand at
throwing pots. Tomorrow they would be busy firing, but on
Friday she'd be welcome to take her first lesson. Perhaps
not so satisfying as carving at rock, but a new interest, a

fresh denial of the void she refused to be sucked into. When people failed you, turn to things, even if it implied turning in on yourself to create those things.

God, she was never so introspective before! Keep busy; go and mix with strangers; window-shop; at least run down to Limassol for the mail she'd forgotten to pick up on Monday.

She frowned into the sunlight ahead, unaware of the white car following a hundred yards behind.

It could not have worked out better. He actually watched her open the letter. Seated at a table back against the wall, he could see her profile as she removed the elastic band and pushed the bundle of papers apart with one finger, scanning the stamps and postmarks. The first she opened was on blue paper from a blue envelope, something personal, probably from England. Then one with a transparent window, possibly a bill. Third time lucky.

She turned the envelope in her hands, curious about the postmark Athens. On the reverse side was printed the logo and address of a Greek assurance society. It was one she had heard of, in connection with marine losses. She unfolded the letter and laid it down beside her cooling coffee. Dated a week earlier, it ran:

Dear Madam,
We are only recently acquainted with the sad news of the decease of your husband Edward Joseph Mather on March 15th of this year, and we write to express our condolences on your bereavement.

In view of the cover of his Life Policy XP 30572-01 executed with this company July 27th 1986, our Inspector at present visiting the Nicosia agency will shortly call upon you to discuss its implementation.

We assure you, as ever, of our sympathetic concern and willingness to be of service as required. We are, yours faithfully, etc . . .

'But I've had the insurance money,' Jean murmured. 'They've paid up already.' She went through the letter again. It dawned on her then that there had been two companies: Ted had taken out more than one policy on his life.

Good, he thought. Plenty for her to think about there. He watched her reactions, the careful perusal of every word, her checking of the dateline. She would notice how many days ago it was written, be expecting someone to get in touch at any time now.

She gathered the post into her capacious shoulder-bag, extracted a purse and came right into the bar to pay her bill. Leaving, she glanced incuriously down on the man slumped at the back table of the terrace. He seemed asleep, panama hat tilted over his face, allowing only a glimpse of a figured silk cravat threaded through a wide gold ring over a dazzling white shirt.

Immediately on her departure he went inside and pointed a long finger at the phone on the bar counter. He received a nod of consent, lifted the receiver and dialled the number he had memorized.

Elpida, refreshed after her catnap on Jean's cushioned lounger, was interrupted in her contemplation of the marinating apricots. She padded to the instrument, flashed an ingratiating smile and shouted the number printed on its base.

The caller spoke in Greek and she carefully wrote down the message he gave after expressing his disappointment that madam was not available herself to speak with him.

'A *gentleman*,' she insisted when Jean came in and heard her out. 'Concerning, he said, some correspondence you had received in the past week from his head office in Athens.'

'Ah,' Jean said.

'I have written down his phone number here. He is staying at the Miramare in Limassol. Mr Nikolaos Clerides, with a beautiful voice. He wishes to call tomorrow morning at eleven, but you should ring him if it is not convenient.'

'So it says here,' Jean pointed out with gentle sarcasm.

'Such a good hotel too. But it would not be proper for you to go down there yourself. If you wish, I am prepared to come and serve . . .'

'Thank you, Elpida, but he won't be coming here tomorrow, and certainly not for a meal. As it happens, I have a previous engagement. It will be better if he tells me what he wants by letter.'

It dashed the poor old thing, but she should know better by now than to try acting marriage-broker. Time enough to ring the man after supper tonight, put him off until she could lay hands on the policy the letter quoted. As the bank hadn't turned it in, who would know where it was?

She did leave it until after nine to return his call, but curiosity and a vague unease modified her resolve to put him off. That and his voice, which Elpida had been right about. It was a level baritone and he spoke perfect English, quite unaccented. He must surely have spent his early professional years at the company's West London branch. He was persuasive, with a hint of steel behind the politeness. Sensing her initial reluctance, he assured her, 'If it is inconvenient, I am sure my office can spare me to stay on longer. Particularly in view of the importance of the claim.'

Something caught in her throat. 'Importance? You mean, quite a large amount is involved?'

'A considerable sum, yes. Even for us.'

Oh God, what had Ted been up to? Considerable claims must mean considerable premiums. Where on earth had be found such money?

'And then there is this question of a rebate. Two monthly payments made since the date of decease.'

From what account? Paid in by whom? Somebody who didn't then know he'd died? 'I see. An adjustment, yes.'

'It would be a good thing, you must agree, to have it all cleared up.'

He couldn't be more right. Nothing was clear at the

moment. It was like walking through blown sand along the seashore. It obscured the outlines of everything. If she closed her eyes she couldn't see Ted distinctly any more; just changing shapes which threatened to assemble themselves into a stranger. She wanted the screen of doubt removed, but feared what might be found behind.

'Oh, very well. I can perhaps rearrange my programme. Eleven, I think you said originally. We will make it that, out here at my house. If you take the secondary road from—'

'Thank you, I know where you live, Mrs Mather. Until tomorrow morning, then. Goodbye.'

She put down the receiver, finding no comfort in his last words. He knew where she lived, and it was pretty inaccessible for a stranger. Stranger—that was the clue. There had been a stranger in the village on Monday, while she was away.

Jean went out into the garden, where fresh scents came off the blossom from the drenching Georgios had given them. It was Georgios who had told her about the stranger, *warned* her.

On an impulse she went back through the house and down the road to the taberna. They were all men there, sitting together in companionable silence over scarcely touched drinks. Yannakis was busy opening bottles, but his son, a serious little lad of nine or ten, was seated on the side steps to the house. 'Gregoris,' she called.

'Kyría?' He came over, smiling. 'I have found a stone for you, a green one. Look.' He pulled it from his pocket. Striated sandstone partly covered in copper leaf. 'Could you make me a creature, Kyría? All for myself?'

'I could try, Gregoris.' She turned it critically. 'Perhaps a frog?' The layers were brittle. Much interference could chip away the copper deposit. 'Some of the green may come off,' she warned him.

'I should like a frog.'

'That's decided, then. Gregoris, were you here on Monday, right after school?'

'Yes, Kyría. Helping Papa.'

'Did you see a stranger come in?'

'The man from Athens. He was on the terrace. He drank a Metaxa, and after that mineral water.'

She drew a deeper breath. 'Did he *say* he was from Athens?'

'No, but I knew. He spoke good Greek, but he was not used to our coins. He had to look at them to see what value they were. I think he is used to drachmas.'

And, of course, he would have worn sophisticated clothes. The boy was well capable of putting facts together. 'Thank you, Gregoris. Will you keep your stone for now? When I am not quite so busy I will ask you for it. All right?'

'*Endakhsi, Kyría. Efkharistó polí!*'

There had been no need to ask him what the man was like. She would see for herself soon enough. And she already knew something: he was intelligent, patient, watchful, firm. And also a little frightening. If there had been anything—what was Lance's word?—*fishy* about Ted's life or death, this man was going to seek it out. And then what would follow?

It was a shorter, more formal interview than she had anticipated. He appeared courteous and respectful, waiting for her to be seated before he took his own chair; depositing his panama hat on the ground beside him; offering his credentials for her inspection.

She fetched for him the death certificate and he merely nodded. Well, he would have obtained a copy for himself by now.

'I need to satisfy my office about the actual circumstances of the death,' he said, 'and I regret the necessity to cause you fresh pain.'

'It has to be done, I suppose.' She sat bolt upright and waited while Elpida made a houri entrance with the coffee tray, flashing the gold caps of her canines at the stranger.

'Thank you. No milk, a little sugar,' he said, accepting the cup Jean poured. 'The medication your husband regularly took, the emergency measures and so on . . .'

'He used two inhalers, one in a blue-grey container and the other cream-coloured. I'm sorry, I've forgotten their names. It's not much more than two months ago and I can't re—'

Clerides supplied the names of the two sprays. 'Is that correct?'

'Yes. Yes, they were British-made.'

'I understand the UK leads the world market in this type of product.' Coolly factual.

'He used them regularly, night and morning, as a precaution. Two puffs of each, four in all. Eight for the day. Normally he didn't need anything more. Just occasionally, if he did something very strenuous or there was heavy pollen or sand blowing.'

'Then he would use the blue-grey one again?'

'That's right.'

'Had he previously done so on the day in question?'

No one had asked her this before. She tried to think back. 'I'm not sure. We'd begun by shopping together, down in Limassol. Yes, I remember now.'

On the way down their road had been blocked by a flock of sheep crossing from higher ground to lower, their herd-boy going on ahead.

'There was a sheep,' she said, 'got its horns caught up in a fallen olive tree by the side of the road. It was struggling to get free. Ted went over and wrestled it out. It was quite a tussle. When he came back his hands stank of some chemical the animal had been treated with. He swore a bit and started to wheeze. So he took a couple of puffs of the Ventolin and his breathing became normal again. It worked almost instantly.'

'So he carried an emergency inhaler on him?'

'Always.'

'Was it the same one he used night and morning?'

'No. That pair always stayed in the bedside cabinet.'

'Have you still got them?'

Had she? The cabinet had been cleared out. If Elpida hadn't thrown the stuff away it would be in the bathroom medicine-chest. She was almost sure she had seen the two inhalers in there recently, still in their boxes with dates marked on the outside to indicate how much had been used. 'I'll go and look.'

It was just a formality: nothing to alarm her.

He checked them as she handed them over. He smiled. 'And the other?'

She stared into his dark eyes. He was like a hawk. 'That's all. The emergency one must have been thrown away. Perhaps it was almost empty. Or the undertaker . . .'

'Nothing is retained. And there would have been a list of the contents of your husband's pockets.'

'I don't recall any Ventolin on it.'

'So we appear to be short of one inhaler.'

'The one he'd used after the sheep incident. It worked perfectly well then. But later on . . .'

'Or perhaps we are missing the other one from the bedside cabinet, exchanged so that he used it for the next emergency. Which happened later on the same day, and then he did not respond to treatment.'

'Exchanged?' The repetition sounded hollow.

'By Mr Mather for some reason. Or an unknown person.'

An inhaler made faulty in some way? With murder in mind? That was surely what he was implying. Despite the noonday heat, she felt a chill stirring of fear. She looked back at the lean, keen face, deep-grooved from nostrils to hard mouth, and she cursed him silently. Nothing was coming clearer. With every word he stirred up more sand. It was gritty in her throat, making her eyes water. The memory of Ted's face had disappeared. In its place recurred the distorted mask of agony and anger as he fought to stay alive, while she ran to the phone after Marjorie's futile fumblings for the number.

'I am truly sorry,' the man said softly. 'I have distressed

you. I can come again. Tomorrow perhaps, if you will telephone me with a convenient hour.'

He put his cup back on the tray, stood, bowed gravely and went away, panama hat in hand.

'I told you,' Elpida said, bouncing in with enthusiasm. 'He is very handsome, and has beautiful manners.'

Jean stood apart, arms folded tightly across her chest, refusing to hear. Her own wakening fears and some indomitable quality about the man had provoked an untypical spite in her. 'Mr Clerides is far too sure of himself. He behaves like a Hollywood gangster!'

CHAPTER 4

Bought time was of little use when she had no clue to work on, no one to turn to for advice. It was obvious where the man's next questions would be directed and all she could hope to answer was, 'I don't know.'

She stared again with dismay at the insurance letter from Athens. The date of acceptance for the proposal had been July '86, before Ted had been officially declared an asthmatic. So they couldn't quibble over his having concealed a known disability. The man Clerides had carefully checked the circumstances of the death and was conversant with the treatment given. He had made no criticism of that, apart from a wild hypothesis that Ted's inhaler might have been exchanged for a faulty one. But he hadn't seemed put off by the outside chance. In fact, the claim seemed in order, and as far as she could see there was no reason for its being refused.

So next he would demand to see the policy, confirm that she was Ted's sole beneficiary and agree to make payment.

Except that she didn't have the policy and had never heard a whisper of it. Nothing in the statements of their joint account showed regular payments of a large sum.

The English policy, signed a week after their wedding in Catterick, had been covered by the bank on a standing order, and although it had strained their resources at first, it was nothing like the premium that would be required for a 'considerable sum'.

So if she didn't know of it, and there was no source for the payments, surely it didn't exist. Some other Edward Mather—that wasn't impossible: someone of that name, having connections with Athens—had made provision for after his death, and the company had confused the two accounts. She had simply to tell Clerides that there had been a clerical error over identity; she was making no claim.

And he probably wasn't going to believe it, just as she didn't herself deep down. Because there *was* something fishy about where Ted got his money from, even if not about his dying. It *would* have been like the new Ted who was emerging posthumously to have set up some private fund with rather shady resources and, assuming he'd go on for ever, prepare to net a nest-egg later on. Clerides had murmured something about Endowment/Life.

Well, Ted, this time you've been too clever, too much the Fixer; and your precious savings will be going begging. Because she had no intention of claiming. She hadn't been counting on an extra sum and she could manage—just— as things were, if she went carefully. There was a nasty smell coming off the whole business and she didn't want to be covered in it. Sorry, Mr Clerides, your mistake. Goodbye; nice knowing you.

And it would be best to get it over quickly. Then the tall man with the haunting hatchet face could return to Athens. She could resume coming to terms with her widowing, without any more disturbing doubts about wool pulled over her eyes, or sand thrown into them.

She picked up his visiting card, on which he had written the Miramare's telephone number, and dialled reception. Within minutes they had traced him and she heard his voice, speaking Greek on a questioning note.

'Mr Clerides, it's Jean Mather. I thought it would be better to get this matter settled quickly, particularly as I'm sure there is some mistake.'

'Shall I come back, Mrs Mather?'

'Please don't trouble. I'm coming down to Limassol myself this evening. I could drop by.'

'Thank you. Perhaps we could discuss it after dinner. May I suggest eight o'clock, so there is time for an apéritif together first?'

She found she had fallen in with his offer. It had been slightly ambiguous whether she was to dine alone before meeting him, but the word apéritif could only mean that what she'd let herself in for was the entire shooting match, Miramare four-course *haute cuisine* and all.

She found him in the lounge, slightly embarrassed by a small, plump Japanese child who was running in circles round his chair, making big eyes at him and swinging her two ribboned bundles of dark hair. He rose at once on seeing Jean and came forward ruefully, followed by the child.

'You appear to have an admirer.' It was out before she could stop it. His embarrassment made him so much more human.

'Alas, so young.'

They had begun on quite the wrong note, Jean realized. He was eyeing her admiringly, might well have taken her opening as provocative.

'Go to your mother, child,' he commanded in English.

The little girl put her doll-like head on one side and giggled with a hand over mouth and chin. He made an unmistakable gesture of waving away a persistent insect. From behind a screen of shiny vegetation a woman appeared and dragged the child away by its hand.

'I thought we might go somewhere else for dinner. At the Park Beach Hotel it is *Meze* night. I am told it is very good. Perhaps you would like that?'

Had he made the suggestion from discretion, so that she

couldn't be accused of pursuing him to his hotel; was it to avoid the Japanese child's attentions; or was he deliberately choosing a less formal background for their discussion?

'I really don't mind,' she said, and then since that sounded offhand, 'I like a Cypriot *Meze*.'

'Also there is a very pleasant garden there, where we can sit afterwards and talk.'

Talk business, he meant, because certainly they wouldn't be eating in silence. During the meal all conversation would be on a personal level. For the first time she felt curious about him, ready to ask questions as well as suffer answering his. She looked back at where the Japanese couple were lecturing their forward offspring. 'Have you children of your own?'

He pulled a comic face. 'Oh no, I am not a family man. I was married once, but it was not a happy experience. I think you have no children yourself?'

She wondered how he knew. Perhaps from Ted, when he filled out his application for the insurance. 'That's right. And my husband had none from his earlier marriage, which was dissolved. His first wife was later killed in a light aircraft crash a few years back. She was a very adventurous person, not a bit like me.'

They were walking along the busy street, thronged with evening pleasure-seekers. 'So you do not like adventures.' It was a statement and he seemed to find it mildly entertaining. 'But you are not timid, I think.'

She considered this. 'Not really. I can stand on my own feet, but I don't go looking for excitement.'

'That is because you have a centre of contentment. You have calm, which is a rare attribute. You are a person adventurers turn to at the end of the day.'

He had reached an intensely personal level, but she could not take offence. What he said was true in a way. She'd been anchorage for the buccaneer in Ted. Shrewd of Clerides to reach that opinion on such short acquaintance. She looked up at him now, thoughtful in profile, and he seemed for the first time strangely familiar. 'We haven't met before, have we?' she blurted out.

He seemed to think about it, considering her gravely. 'Not in this life, I'm almost certain.'

'What other life is there?'

'Ah, that is worth speculating on, don't you think? So many planets, so many galaxies. So much time inside eternity.' Smiling, he held out one arm, in an almost Arab gesture of invitation. 'Shall we stop here for something to drink?'

They went up a step off the roadway into a little latticed space where a dozen small tables were already lit by candles inside crimson glass globes. It was a hot night and she chose white wine, nibbling sparingly at the olives for fear their brine should make her drink too much. She needed to keep her head clear for later on when they must talk insurance. But for the meanwhile she could surely relax, enjoy herself as she hadn't done for so long.

He was good company, this Nikolaos Clerides; entertaining and not pushy. Behind the businessman lay unexpected depths. A man who was shrewd about people, and could talk of eternity in the next breath.

'You've quickly become familiar with the hotels and tabernas round here,' Jean commented. 'This can't be your first visit to Cyprus.'

'My first since I was a child. My parents brought me once when I was about eight. I loved the island; so familiarly Greek and yet so admirably different. It is a part of your British Commonwealth, of course, and that has had an influence.'

'Not a universally popular one.' And then they were on to politics. At a little after nine they moved a short distance to where they would have dinner. The *Meze* was a magnificent spread of salads, dips, fish and meat delicacies displayed all along one wall of the dining-room where they served themselves.

'There is only one wine to drink tonight,' Clerides declared. 'We will have the Claret 62. Tell me if you like it.'

She did. It was one of those red wines that tasted as ruby as it looked, not fruity-sweet but simply satisfying. More than satisfying, because it gave her a lift she had not been looking for.

'Ted was a beer man,' she recollected out loud. 'Most noncommissioned soldiers are. And usually when we had dinner with friends they served white wine, chilled. I'm really quite ignorant about what to drink. This is lovely.'

'You didn't drink wine at home, in England?'

'Before I was married? Yes, I did. I affected all the current snobbish notions. I was a schoolmistress, you know.'

'And you married a soldier. Had you always known him? Was he a family friend?'

'Anything but. My father couldn't stand him, possibly because underneath they were so similar, claimed the same ground to stand on.'

'They were both possessive about you.'

She stared at him in surprise. 'I suppose you're right. I hadn't seen it from that angle. Ted more or less swept me off my feet. We met during one of his leaves from Northern Ireland. I was rather a loner, but I never realized until then that I didn't want to be. After a rather damped-down childhood I just felt apart from the others.'

'Until the right man appeared.'

'Yes. And he was the right man, everything that I wasn't. We—completed one another.'

'Something rare,' he murmured, and she remembered that his own marriage had been 'not a happy experience'.

'I would never have wanted anyone else,' she said with conviction. 'Never shall.' The words hung in the air between them.

'And your father?' he asked after a moment.

'Died after we came out here. It was quite sudden and I wasn't able to get to him in time.'

'Which makes you feel guilty. And so now once more you are alone.'

'Completely, yes.' And it's awful, *awful!* she wanted to shout.

He must have heard the silent cry, because he put a long, dry hand over hers on the table and gently squeezed. 'But now you are different, more experienced, with good memories to help you get through the bad times.'

He was right about the good memories. But there were disturbing ones too. Recently, over the past few weeks, as the portrait of her dead husband crystallized in her mind, there had come doubts denied or held at bay while he was alive, because of her habit of not questioning his actions. The acting-lance-corporal syndrome, plus an early-implanted notion that men were a different breed, if not superior at least better left to believe that they were.

'You have a beautiful smile,' he said. 'A little sad, but beautiful.'

Afterwards she didn't remember what dessert they had or whether they stayed on for coffee, but they walked together through the dark gardens while the long hotel sailed above, all windows alight like some fabulous ship bound for the Spice Islands. It didn't matter being a little off guard because she would never see this man again after she disputed the insurance policy tonight.

She had been a little muddled in her mind but it didn't prevent her admitting to him, silent beside her, that if Ted were the man the policy named she had no way of checking this. Surely some other person was concerned. It would all be so much easier that way.

He found two loungers under the pines and while she lay back staring at the stars he sat across the middle of the other, hands clasped between his knees, solemn in thought. 'There is no doubt we have the right man. He was in the army when he made the application. We have his rank and number. We also have his signature.' There was a short silence and then he added, 'Strangely enough, it is the same one as on the covering notes with the last two payments dated after his death.'

'So it *couldn't* be the same Ted Mather!'

'It could, if he had prepared a number of these notes in advance for someone else to send on to us, and that person didn't know of his death.'

'But the cheques! You can identify him through the bank, surely?'

'There never were any cheques. It was always treasury notes made up into a package and sent by registered mail. An awkwardness for us, but he was a valuable customer and had insisted on that manner of payment from the beginning. Sometimes our clients are a little eccentric and we have to humour them.'

'So you are determined to find this unknown person you think was entrusted with my husband's secret funds!' She meant it to sound scathing, but it came out breathless and uncertain.

In the half-dark she could see his stern profile as he considered all the implications. 'Whatever we discover, it need not be a public matter. It is certainly not part of our duty to cause unnecessary distress. But you must understand that a large sum of money has been paid into our company and we have no right to keep it. It cannot be left in limbo. It is physically there, invested and gaining more interest all the time. The simplest, most publicity-free solution is for you to find whoever holds the policy, have it forwarded to me and let me deal with the matter discreetly. I think you do trust me enough for that?'

She heard the wounded pride in the voice, and saw it suddenly from his viewpoint. What a witless creature he must think her, knowing so little of her husband's private affairs, appreciating nothing of the efforts being made now on her behalf.

'I'm sorry. I haven't been seeing things very clearly.'

'Because you are willing what is there to become invisible.' His voice was harder and he seemed to have withdrawn behind a front of dignity.

'Mr Clerides, I have said I am sorry. I am very grateful

to you for your patience. But if I am to accept all you say, I still don't know how to go about finding this friend of Ted's who holds the policy.'

'Will you let me help you, then? Make out a list of everyone you know who had any dealings at all with him, army, civilian, business or pleasure. And, please, if we are to work together on this, my name is Nikolaos. Nikos, perhaps. And may I too call you Jean?'

At the end of the evening he sent her home by taxi. 'You are tired,' he insisted. 'Leave the car where it is. Give me the keys and I will drive it up tomorrow.'

Tired, perhaps. Not quite herself, in any case. Just a little affected by the wine and the occasion. More than a little off-balance about the man Nikos was turning out to be. And amazed at her own reactions, that she could have been enjoying his company, responding to his (undoubtedly practised) charm, so soon after Ted. This was a disquieting aspect of being widowed that she hadn't anticipated.

Befuddled, certainly—or she would have seen at once that if he returned her car next day, she must then drive him back to Limassol. They could end by seeing each other home *ad infinitum*. She laughed in the dark of the taxi's interior, and the driver said, 'Eh?' turning his head to listen to her while he kept one eye on the road.

'Nothing. Just it's a beautiful night,' she sang back.

He looked up as though he hadn't known the sky was there. 'Yeah,' he said. 'It's OK.'

She began at breakfast next morning, with a writing-pad alongside her grapefruit: a list of all Ted's acquaintances, right from their arrival on Cyprus. First, his fellow NCOs still in service on the island; civilian contacts among the British expatriates; Cypriot associates; tradesmen he'd dealt with; people unfamiliar to herself who had come up to the villa to see him. Quite a list, covering the six years since they'd left England, but there was nobody on it she recognized as an intimate. Ted had stood head and shoulders above them all, using them as occasion required, but never depending on them for anything. The sort of person she looked for just wasn't there.

But there were those occasions when Ted had been called away, doing his 'little jobs for the lads'. Now they had taken on a new significance. Jean wondered who would have known where he went off to, who he had been with. Perhaps if she asked the Rowley-Powleys—but she'd need to be very circumspect. Although in retirement he'd become a pompous old dodo, Lance had been in the Services himself, understood quite a bit about the confidential nature of Ted's special work. Intercepting was a sensitive area of Signals operations. There had been scandals already, security investigation of suspected leaks to the Russians. Men had been charged, and although they'd got off, resultant tremors were still felt at the Cyprus bases.

If Lance ever got wind of Ted's having undisclosed resources he could easily jump to the conclusion that Ted too had been involved in selling information; or, for a price, doing the reverse—suppressing vital information acquired on intercept.

So she would need to introduce the subject with seeming casualness, without mentioning the high rate of the insurance or the mystery of its funding. Simply say: did he have any idea who might be holding the second policy on Ted's life?

And if the whole thing turned out to be news to Lance, would be blather about it all over the island, get people putting two and two together to create scandal to the nth?

The cold sober truth was that she still didn't want the policy found, unless the matter could be settled with a guaranteed clamp-down on publicity. But if the Athens company paid up, how could she keep dark a large influx of capital? It would have to go through probate, be reinvested, and the interest declared for taxation. Some nosey official was certain to want to know more about its provenance.

She decided to put off contacting Nikos. He could wait for his list. This morning she was due at the pottery for her first lesson. It would be a welcome escape from the worries of the past two days. Elpida's nephew could drive her down in his ramshackle Panda. He was only sixteen, handsome and carefree. His aunt was forever scolding, predicting he'd turn into a good-for-nothing. 'No, I shall drive my own taxi,' he'd counter.

'You see? That's what I said—a good-for-nothing!'

Jean left her list on the marble table in the hall weighted down with a brass bowl. As she walked to Elpida's sister's she passed little Gregoris on his way to catch the school bus. He looked up brightly and half-reached into his pocket.

Ah yes. The green stone. 'Not today, Gregoris,' she called. 'Tomorrow, perhaps?'

'Thank you, Kyría.'

Damn, Jean thought. Too much on my mind at once. Now I've disappointed him. But it shall be tomorrow, come hell or high water.

Her session at the potter's wheel went well. The clay had felt good between her fingers. She let herself into the house in a happier frame of mind than she'd known for days. On the marble table lay her car keys for the little Morris. The list of names which she had made had disappeared.

Starry-eyed on her behalf, Elpida swooped in from the kitchen. 'The nice gentleman from Athens called. He has put your car in the garage and gone away in a taxi which drove up behind him. He was so sad to find you not at home.'

So now it was 'nice gentleman'. Clerides had made progress. Well, to herself he was already 'Nikos', wasn't he? Perhaps she had been too ready to let him get close. In a purely business sense he was even the opposition. What was he likely to do with that list of names? Not badger the people on it, she hoped.

Should she give the Rowleys a ring this evening, in case he rushed at them? She would thank them for their hospitality of three days back, explain she was under pressure over clearing up Ted's affairs, and then mention it appeared there was a second policy on his life somewhere. Could they suggest anyone he might have left it with? Then round off the call with an invitation to them both for lunch one day soon.

It was Lance who answered, and her inquiry drew no response. He sounded offhand in a rather dudgeony way and she was clearly meant to remember she'd been ill-mannered with him last time they met. He would relay her message to Marjorie who was out somewhere playing bridge, and she'd ring Jean tomorrow to say which day was best for them to come over.

Marjorie, informed on her late return of the gist of Jean's message, looked thoughtful. 'Funny, that,' she said with regard to the second life policy. 'You haven't got it, Lance, have you? No? Well, I wonder if I should mention it to—'

'Keep your nose out of it,' Lance snapped tetchily. 'You don't want to go stirring up trouble. What she doesn't know can't harm her. And nothing we can do is going to help Ted where he's gone. *Kismet*, Marjorie. *Kismet*.'

That was all very well, she decided crossly. *Kismet* could be taken both ways: what-will-be-will-be if you do act, and what-will-be-will-be if you don't.

While Lance was in the bathroom just before bed, she used the kitchen telephone to dial a local number.

CHAPTER 5

She must have overslept. Light was pouring into the room aslant the bed. '—'morning, Elpida,' she managed, and floundered among the pillows.

It wasn't daylight and it wasn't Elpida moving towards her. Against the dazzle of the neon tube through in Ted's dressing-room the indistinguishable figure was growing bigger, looming over her. Fear rose in her throat like bile.

'Don't move,' a low voice hissed. 'Keep quiet and I shan't have to hurt you.'

Jean sank back, only her eyes swivelling to follow the intruder's retreat across the thick carpet. She could make out the squat shape in the silhouetted hand which must be a gun. He was making for the door to the balcony. If he meant to leave by that way there must be a ladder. Can you shin down a ladder and aim a hand gun with any accuracy at the same time? She wasn't the one to find out.

She let the man get away, lay frozen and silent as he'd demanded. There was no sound of footsteps outside. It could have been a sham retreat and he was still crouching under the wall, waiting for her to show herself. She stayed still a few minutes longer, and then distantly a car started up. The sound of its engine grew fainter as it turned away down the rough track beside the orchard, heading for the road.

Jean flung herself out of bed and ran to the corner room that overlooked the downhill route. She was in time to see a single headlight sweep round the bend and disappear below the band of pines that grew between. It was only half an hour or so to sunrise, but she couldn't have told what colour the car was or what size.

She was shivering and went through to the kitchen to start up the coffee-maker. She had never been burgled before. It wasn't what you expected up here in the hills. Kalidrofi was a fruit-growing village, not a rich men's playground.

So perhaps it wasn't a burglar, but a more personal incursion. And at once she thought of Nikolaos Clerides.

She ran back to her bedroom and into the dressing-room next to it. The light was still on. It must have been the ticking of the neon tube as it started to fire that had disturbed her. Enough to make some waking noise and warn the intruder that escape was cut off. The single window to Ted's room was shuttered and padlocked.

Everything there was in confusion, with clothes spilled from open drawers. The contents of his tallboy were scattered over the floor. The bed had been taken apart and the mattress slashed. A hand torch rattled at her feet as she walked forward to gaze into the opened seams. She picked it up and found it faulty. So that explained the need for the overhead light. And now she had probably destroyed whatever fingerprints were on the torch.

Not that the police were ever going to be invited in on this one. She could see now that it was less an attempted burglary than a search. For something of value which Ted had supposedly kept hidden. But surely anyone who knew him, or knew her, would realize he wasn't that simple. And she wasn't such a poor housewife that she didn't check drawers and cupboards regularly.

Clerides, she thought again. Maybe he thought I was lying about the policy being missing, though God knows what good that would do.

Four in the morning or not, she had to know. She looked up his number and dialled the Miramare at Limassol. A night porter seemed unsurprised at her request and agreed to ring through to Mr Clerides's room. After a short pause a sleepy voice answered in Greek.

She could have replaced the receiver, but he would surely question the porter and conclude that the woman who called was herself. 'Nikos?' she said uncertainly. 'This is Jean.'

'My dear, what is it?' More concerned than alarmed.

'There's been a break-in. I don't think he took anything, and he's gone now, but—'

'He frightened you.' There was no mistaking his outrage. 'Jean, make sure he's right off the premises, then bolt the doors if you can, and lock all the windows. Ring the man who runs the taberna in the village. Tell him I'm on my way and I'll pick him up as I come in. But don't allow anyone, anyone at all, in the house before I reach you. Understood?'

'Yes,' she said faintly, thinking: it could be Ted over

again. He issues orders in just the same way. But she felt better for knowing he would be with her shortly; infinitely better for knowing that he'd been in bed fast asleep while the break-in occurred.

Of course, that didn't guarantee he hadn't set it up for someone else to do.

It was just over half an hour before she heard his car slather to a halt outside, and by then there were at least four other men circling the house armed with shotguns. Their low voices mingled as she stood ready to unbolt the front door. 'You made good time,' she greeted him as he strode up the steps, dark-browed. He hadn't shaved on the way up. His speed on the mountain road would have ruled that out.

He disregarded her and strode straight past. 'Your husband's room?'

She pointed upwards and followed to watch him make a quick survey of the disorder. 'Does anything seem to be missing? Have you checked again?'

'Nothing that I know of. He left behind that torch. I'm afraid I've handled it.'

Clerides went across to examine it, bending close. 'Wretched little thing. He can't have been a pro.' He was running a hand along the uncut seam on the far side of the mattress. 'You say you actually saw him. Can you give a description?'

'No. I was in bed. He came into my room with the light behind him. He had a hand gun which he threatened me with. He looked enormous.'

'His voice?'

'Between a hiss and a whisper. He spoke English, not enough for me to judge if he spoke it very well. Just told me not to move or call out. Then he eased out of the door on to the balcony. I always leave it open for the air. He must have come in that way; Ted's room is more or less shut up.'

'My poor Jean.' At last he was letting concern for her

override his nose for investigation. Then, 'Let us take a look at how he climbed up.'

The ladder was still there, an old wooden one from the orchard, which had previously been propped up against a large carob tree. Yannakis came forward from the group of villagers and ticked his disapproval of the way things went from bad to worse. Elpida's nephew was there happily nursing a loaded shotgun and looking, Jean was sure, for a valid reason to discharge it in anger. 'That ladder's not all that heavy,' he boasted, 'but the burglar had to drag it all the way. You can see its marks on the ground.'

Clerides went down again to inspect the evidence. He came back looking thoughtful. 'If there is enough coffee left, you could offer it to the men and then they could go home. It will soon be time for them to get up and be about their work.'

But at this suggestion they all made excuses and began to drift away. Except Elpida's nephew who, with a meaning glance at Clerides, cheekily demanded whether he should summon his aunt. 'She was snoring when I left,' he added.

'Then I don't think there is any call to disturb her,' Jean told him icily.

In the kitchen she poured coffee for Clerides—somehow she couldn't think of him as Nikos just now—and refilled her own cup. 'It was very good of you to come at once,' she said. (And quick-witted to have her rouse the village men to witness that he wasn't there with her himself!)

'You say this "intruder" looked enormous as he bent over the bed. But he caused no damage to the wall on his way out. Not so much as a scratch. And he made a poor showing of carrying the ladder, as the young man pointed out. So perhaps he was not such a strong person as you first thought. Smaller, daintier. Handling the ladder much as a woman would.'

'I suppose it could have been a woman. Whoever it was wore trousers. I saw a white triangle of light between his legs as he ran out.' She looked up to see Clerides frowning at her severely. For an instant they outstared each other and she was suddenly aware that just as she had suspected him he had doubts about her.

'You think that *I* . . . That's preposterous! Why should I pretend that someone broke in? Nikos, I was *terrified*! Oh, what swine you men are!'

He pounced on her and almost shook her. 'Take that back! Oh, don't cry now. I didn't mean to make you unhappy. Of course you didn't set it up yourself, but I had to make sure. It would have been so convenient, you see. It wouldn't be the first time someone claimed falsely that a policy had been stolen or destroyed. They do it with wills too, to obscure the issue and cast doubt on the standing document being the last one. Jean, I am a suspicious man because I have had cause to be. Will you forgive me?'

It is hard to refuse when you are crushed against a man's chest, with his unshaven chin hovering over your nose and his heart crashing away in your ears. Even more so when he is kissing you. And you kiss him back, liking it.

It took them both a little while to get over the shock of what had happened. Jean's prescription for a return to sanity was the offer of a meal, which Nikos accepted instantly, himself taking over the making of toast while she saw to the scrambled eggs.

'English breakfast,' he said happily as they sat down opposite each other on the terrace. 'That is what I most missed when I returned from London. That and the gentleness of the rain.'

'The permanence of the rain,' she corrected. 'You know, I don't normally eat like this in the mornings. Something must have given me an appetite.'

He caught the smile in her eyes and reached over for her wrist. 'Jean, you can't stay on here alone. I want you to book into a hotel down at Limassol. Will you do that for me?'

'I don't know. I don't feel frightened any more at the

moment, but maybe in the middle of the night, if some
strange noise wakes me . . .'

'That is what I mean. Nothing is likely to happen here
after this, particularly now that the village men are aware
there was an intruder, but I can't think of you lying here
afraid. It isn't necessary. Just for a few days, my dear.'

'Won't it be worse coming back if I run away now?' But
she was thinking of his words, 'a few days'. A few days
earlier she had never heard of Nikolaos Clerides or Ted's
second insurance.

'What are we going to do about this break-in?' she demanded abruptly. 'I say "we" because you do think it's
connected with the missing policy, don't you?'

'That is something we shall have to consider very carefully; which will be so much easier if you are near at hand
for me to consult. In addition to any personal advantages
it offers. So will you please pack a bag and come?'

It wasn't until she was well on the way, her little grey
Morris following the white Toyota on the tight bends down
towards the sea, that she considered how she'd left the house
untenanted, for any second invasion to be made unobserved.
And this had been on Nikos's suggestion, providing plausible reasons why she should abandon the place, including
the fact that they were undeniably drawn towards each
other. On this last score was he a very good actor, as well
as being a diligent investigator?

There was no spare accommodation immediately available at the Miramare. If she would wait until a room
could be serviced after a departure for the early flight from
Larnaca, Madam could use it for half a day, but the next
booking would arrive on the night flight and the room must
be cleaned again in between.

'We will discuss it over coffee,' Clerides told the desk
clerk, took Jean's elbow and steered her towards the restaurant. When they were seated and refreshments had arrived he looked long at her. The dark eyes seemed to burn
in the stony face. 'I suppose it is no use saying that mine is

a double room and you are more than welcome to share it with me.'

Not when he put it like that. Under different circumstances, who knows where her inclinations might have led her. She shook her head. 'I do need to get my head down, after I've had a shower. So when it's ready perhaps I will take the room that the hotel is offering. Until the afternoon. After that I must get back to Kalidrofi. There are things I've left unfinished there. Above all, I've commitments to a small boy.' She told him about Gregoris and the green stone.

'You are fond of children?'

'Of some more than others. I was a teacher before I was married, so I've suffered at their hands more than once. But Gregoris is a thoroughly nice village boy. I couldn't break my word to him.'

Nikos was smiling as if at some private joke. 'So you return good behaviour for good behaviour. What would you do to someone you found offensive?'

It didn't seem just an academic question. His eyebrows had gone up into sharp angles. He lifted his chin and looked down his long nose at her, still smiling.

'I usually walk away. There's no point in wasting good anger. I'm not a teacher any more.'

'So I shall be very careful not to cause you any offence. And perhaps, if I am *very* good to you, you will someday be good to me.'

She wasn't going to encourage him, on the other hand she couldn't slap him down. He had been very considerate and concerned, beyond the course of duty as an insurance investigator.

'Meanwhile, I will give you my key. Please make use of my bathroom, anything you require. I have business to attend to which will occupy me until midday. By then you will have your own room. If you are awake at one, phone my room and you may care to join me down here for lunch. Will that suit you?'

It seemed perfect, leaving her free to make up for the

sleep she had lost, and free from too much obligation to him. She took the key, thanked him and went up to luxuriate in a shower and shampoo.

She had barely finished when there was a rap at the door and a woman's voice called, 'Mrs Mather, your room is number 307. I have the key here.'

She let in the chambermaid who started to remake Nikos's rumpled bed. His pyjamas, pants only, were of brown silk and lay where he had flung them on receiving her message. Jean looked guiltily away from them and went back to the bathroom to clear up.

Dropped at the back of the box-stool was a black sweat-shirt. She pulled it out and started to fold it, but the thing was wet, smelled of salt water. And of something else: diesel and tar. It brought back a memory of long days spent at sea with Ted, fishing and scuba-diving off an old vessel which the Sergeants' Mess had clubbed together for. They had gone to sea a lot together in those early days out here, both strong swimmers, although she hadn't joined in the spear-fishing, never considering the catch was worth the effort the men put into it. Instead, she had taken up dinghy-sailing and Ted had found the little craft too cramping for his big frame. If she had known their time together was to be so short, she would have set a greater value on it. But it was too late now for regrets.

She laid the damp sweatshirt over the side of the bath, collected her things and headed for bed in the room allocated.

When she awoke just after 2.0 p.m. she rang through to Nikos, ready with apologies, but there was no answer. A second call to Reception brought another negative. Mr Clerides's key was still on its hook and he was not in the lounge or the restaurant.

Jean dressed, repacked her overnight bag and went down to pay her bill. Fortunately she was in time to beat Nikos to that! She left a note of thanks for him with the front desk and collected her car.

All the way up to Kalidrofi she congratulated herself on having escaped him without commitment. She felt a strong attraction, but it was too soon. Unsuitable, given the circumstances of his coming into her life. And she wasn't a woman to give herself freely. There had to be commitment in return, and she wasn't really sure . . . So many reasons why she was right to cut and run.

And yet . . ! '*A consummation most devoutly to be wish'd*: Shakespeare, wasn't it? But—God!—that was Hamlet talking about *death*!

Elpida was at the villa, queening it as she sometimes did when Jean was away. She had a new black cotton dress on which crackled slightly as she moved, blown out as she seemed with news for the homecomer.

Mrs Rowley had phoned twice, and the second time left a message: they would like to come for lunch tomorrow. And also, Kyría, a young lady had come visiting. That was her motor-scooter down beside the wall. Elpida had given her a chair out by the pool.

'What made you think I would be back soon?' Jean demanded.

Elpida displayed the gold caps of her canines. 'Because Mr Clerides rang from the hotel to say you were on your way. He wanted to be sure someone was here to look after you.'

CHAPTER 6

The woman who looked up as Jean stepped out on to the terrace was small and fine with a narrow head in which the dark eyes seemed unfairly large in the creamy face. Her hair, russet-brown and smooth, was parted in the centre and looped back into a silver clasp on the crown, then falling in a close cap to chin level. It gave her an elfin look and probably reduced her apparent age by three or four years.

She would be, Jean guessed, about her own age. Thirty, or possibly a little less. She was undeniably attractive; and she had been crying.

As Jean came towards her she stood up, pushing her chair back and grasping at its arms as if she needed support.

'I understand from Elpida that you wish to see me,' Jean said. 'She should have offered you some refreshment. Have you been waiting long?'

'Yes. I mean she offered me coffee, but I felt I . . . No, I haven't been here long. About ten minutes, I think.'

'Perhaps you would rather have something cool. I know I would. Elpida, would you bring some crushed orange, please, and the apricot cake.'

The visitor was still standing, uncertain of her welcome despite Jean's greeting. 'I should tell you, Kyría, that my name is Kakouris.' She waited for Jean's reaction. '*Maritsa Kakouris.*'

'And I am Jean Mather. Please sit down, Miss Kakouris. Or is it Mrs?'

The girl stared at her, speechless. 'But surely you have heard of me? Your husband—he must have—he swore he had told you . . .'

'Oh no!' Jean said aloud. Not that awful old cliché situation: the broken triangle, and two mourning women. She didn't think she could cope with that just now. She waited for her voice to steady and then said levelly, 'No, I'm afraid I haven't heard of you. Why don't you tell me all about yourself?'

Maritsa Kakouris sat drawn up tightly, head bowed. I won't feel sorry for her, Jean vowed. I don't have to make it easy for her. How did she think *I* would feel, coming to confront me like this, in my own home, *Ted's* home? If it's hard on her, who made it that way? Not I. I owe her nothing.

All the same, the girl was suffering. 'Do you—do you come from round here?' Jean asked, to get her started.

'I—I have a boutique in Paphos. Lace and silver,

things like that, for the tourists. My family came from Famagusta . . .'

Ah, refugees from the Turkish invasion. She had done better than many of them if she could set up a shop on her own. It was pitiable how they had lost everything, and so little notice taken by the rest of the world.

'You were more fortunate than some.'

'Yes, I wouldn't deny that. I had cousins at Lefkara. I went to work for them in their shop.'

'Which is where you learnt all about lace and jewellery.'

'That is right. And who not to buy from and how much to pay when the retail prices are standardized. I was there for nearly two years. That is where I met your husband.'

'He came into the shop?'

'To buy something for your birthday.'

It was ironic. She remembered the day he had given her the set of silver bracelet and ear-rings. What had he given to the shopgirl? 'I have the jewellery still,' she said to fill the pause. 'If he said it was for his wife, you knew he was a married man.'

'I had no excuse, yes. But at that time there was no intention to—'

'Supplant me? Seduce him?'

'Oh, he needed no seducing, believe me.'

There it was, out in the open, the latent passion that Ted had recognized, but now it was showing as anger. Because I am not reacting as she wishes, Jean told herself. Does she hate me for being in her way, for not having been disposed of while Ted was still alive?

'The second time he came he made no pretence of buying anything. He stayed on in the shop while I served several customers, and when a traveller came in from a silversmith in Nicosia he fiddled with some lace cloths while he listened to every word of our bargaining. What he proposed to me was purely a business arrangement.'

'Go on.' Jean was inclined to believe her. That was how Ted would have made the approach, getting her interested in a career opportunity until she was obliged to give in to him as a man so that the chance shouldn't slip away. He did manipulate people, even if he hadn't in her own case.

'So to seal the deal you slept with him?' To her own ears it sounded crude enough. This girl would think her a hard case.

'Not then. He told me he had capital to invest. I knew he was a soldier because he wore uniform when he first came. He was with a British truck that had troops in and he seemed to be in command. I knew a lot of officers had put money into businesses on Cyprus when they retired here. He said he wanted to do the same. He was willing to rent a shop for me and pay me a salary. I was to buy the stock with money he would supply, and I should keep strict accounts of all transactions. I wasn't sure about it but he had figures to show me it would work. I promised to go over the proposition and think about it.'

'*Ted* set you up in the shop you say you have at Paphos?' It was the first time they had spoken his name between them, and to cover it up she hurried on. 'Why Paphos?'

'I couldn't set up in opposition to my cousins. There are more than enough shops selling lace and silver in Lefkara. But people go there because it is the recognized centre. Your husband had a different idea. He said Paphos was going to be developed as a principal tourist centre. It would be popular with the British and Scandinavians who always bought gifts to take home. I should aim at stocking the sort of things they liked best, keep on my suppliers for silverwork and lace, but add some ceramics and fine glassware.'

'And you took his advice. You let him set you up in your own shop over on the west of the island.'

'For me it was a gamble, because it upset my relatives. If it had turned into a disaster, they would not have wanted me back.'

'But you enjoy a gamble.' Yes, she could see they had little in common. It wasn't a case of a man going for the same type of woman over and over again. He had one Jean and that was enough. Next time he went for something quite different. Bored with me, Jean wounded herself. He set up the business because he was bored with security and his successful army career, but he went to bed with her because he was bored with me.

'I like a gamble, yes; a little risk.'

'When was this?'

'Three years ago. I think he may have had a partner for the finance, but I only saw him once. Well, the shop was a success. When I gave him the figures for the first year's profits, we had a celebration. It was then that we—we became lovers.'

A year after he had entered into such close, secret dealings with this attractive girl. Perhaps I was wrong, Jean reflected. Perhaps he wasn't so bored with me after all. Seducing Maritsa Kakouris was just the gilt on the gingerbread. And it cemented their partnership with a contract a woman would be less likely to break. Clever old Ted. The bastard.

'Then he fell ill,' Maritsa said. 'That is when I glimpsed his partner. He was just leaving the hospital as I arrived to see him. I saw you once too, through a glass door.' She sighed. 'The money went on coming in for the rent and my wages. I was well paid, and he had given me the apartment over the shop. Very modern and convenient. But now, you see, he is dead and I have to meet expenses for which I have no money. I am using the sales money to buy new stock but I have not paid myself for a month. All the time I was expecting him to come and hand over more but he did not come. I did not know, you see, until last week, that he was dead.'

She put her hands over her face, still new to grief. Jean looked away, her own eyes pricking. But somewhere in her mind a new excitement was stirring. Maritsa had not known about Ted's death. Nor had the person sending insurance payments to Athens accompanied by pre-signed cover notes. Maritsa had access to reasonably large sums of money. Hadn't Ted set her up to provide a new fund for his endowment/life policy? Everything was coming perfectly together!

'So you went on paying in for his insurance after he had died? It was you, then.'

The woman looked up with red-rimmed eyes, uncomprehending. 'What insurance?'

'And whatever you have come to find today, you also came to find during the night. You were my intruder of the early hours. It was only my fear and the unusual angle in the dark that made you look so big. But you did have a hand gun. You found a ladder in the orchard, dragged it to my balcony, broke in and went through Ted's belongings in the dressing-room. It was a motor-scooter I heard start up later, not a car. And that's why I saw only one headlight going down the hill.'

The other woman was frowning intently. It made her narrow face look strong as well as keen. 'I did not *break* in,' she said angrily. 'I climbed in. The balcony door was open. And what I pretended was a gun was really that little bud vase from the landing table.

'Yes, it was me, because I was desperate. I had nothing —*nothing*—to prove who was financing the business, and insufficient money left to pay my suppliers after I'd met the wages and the shop insurance. I was not even allowed to keep the ledgers, and although he was generous to me, the business was still a young one, so there was never any spare capital not reinvested.'

Clever old Ted, Jean thought again. Clever, mean old bastard.

'Well, I must disappoint you,' she said aloud. 'There is nothing of that kind here. I know everything that is in the house, and there is nothing in any way connected with a shop or with you. The truth is that my husband covered up his life too well, and he had no idea that he'd arrived at the end of it all. Your only hope is to find that policy you were looking for. It sounds as though it will be quite rewarding for you, and it is no concern at all of mine.'

'Policy?'

'His life insurance. It isn't here because I'm not the beneficiary. I knew nothing about it until the company in Athens wrote.'

'Athens?' This time she seemed to come more alert.

'Yes. And I suppose you are going to say you know nothing of any Nikolaos Clerides either.'

'Clerides? Is he the partner your husband brought in? He, if anyone, should be able to help about business matters. Will you tell me, please, how I can reach him?'

Jean stared back at her, amazed. No one could act that well. It really did appear that Maritsa was telling the truth. Ted's mistress she might have been, and last night's intruder, but she seemed honestly to know nothing about the missing policy that had brought Clerides to Cyprus.

'Is he?' Maritsa insisted. 'Can you put me in touch with him? I know I have behaved badly and there is no reason why you should help me, but truly I never meant to hurt you. I believed that you knew all about me and did not mind. There are women like that; I have met them. Once they have their comfortable home and their children, it does not matter any more about their husbands. I can see now you are different, and I am sorry that you had to know. He was right to say nothing.'

Sorry I had to know, Jean thought wryly. Not sorry she was Ted's mistress in the first place. Well, at least she was being honest.

And this notion of hers about Clerides: wild, but not impossible. She herself kept having doubts about him even while he attracted her. Suppose his story about an insurance policy was complete fiction and really he was trying to get access to details of the business he'd shared with Ted; or a double share in its profits through the inheriting widow? That last was a chilling thought.

'I would help you if I could,' she said, 'but I don't know any more than you do. Less, in fact. But if this man Clerides is the one you saw when he visited Ted in hospital, there is

a good way of finding out. I will arrange to see him tomorrow
or next day and you can be somewhere close with a good
view of our meeting. Let me have a number where I can
reach you by phone and I'll send you details of where and
when.'

They rose and Jean saw her to where the scooter was
parked. There were a lot of questions she could still ask, but
there would be other occasions. Whether the paperwork
turned up or not, some owner would have to be recognized
for the business. She supposed that, as Ted's sole beneficiary
in his will, she would be drawn in on any claim. She wanted
no part in a payout, but if the shop was a good proposition
there was no need to take away the girl's means of livelihood.
Jean could continue to cover it as an extra interest. It did
look, after all, as though Maritsa was little more than a
small fly caught up in Ted's money-making web. And even
if she had been the grand passion of a lifetime, did she,
Jean, mind so very much? Not any more; not since the
blown sand had started to settle and she could see Ted's
features emerging with a new, hard clarity.

The sound of the scooter receded. Yes, that was what she
had mistaken for a car in the night, amplified by darkness
and the surrounding silence.

Jean took the uncut apricot cake back to the fridge. 'We
didn't feel like eating after all,' she told Elpida. 'Please go
home now. I can manage on my own, and I don't need
anyone from Athens taking over my household arrangements. I'm going across to see little Gregoris, if he's back
from school.'

'He is at home,' Elpida reminded her, 'because it
is Saturday. Do you wish me to come in tonight? Or to
help with lunch tomorrow, when Mr and Mrs Rowley
come?'

Oh Lord, the Rowleys! 'I haven't decided yet what to
give them,' Jean admitted. 'I'll have a look in the freezer
and let you know. If I keep it simple I may not need you.'

'I come anyway, to bring in the coffee and clear away,'

Elpida said smugly. 'It does not spoil my Sunday. The good Lord will forgive it if I serve you in your need.'

'Yes, well. Thank you, Elpida.'

Gregoris was sorting empty bottles in the backyard of the taberna. He seldom seemed to have time for play like other boys. 'It is in the house,' he told Jean when she asked him for the green stone. 'I will run and get it but, Kyría, do not waste your time on it now when there is so much to trouble you.'

'I shall enjoy doing it, Gregoris. Truly. It helps to take my mind off other things.' Like what to cook for the Rowleys, and how to arrange a meeting with Nikos (which Maritsa could witness) without making herself appear over-eager for his company.

She returned to the villa and set up her table on the balcony off her bedroom. Now that she knew the identity of the intruder she had no more fears about spending other nights here alone. By the law of averages, Kalidrofi wasn't due for another turn-out with shotguns for at least fifteen years!

The outer layers of the green stone were as brittle as she had expected. From one angle the frog was clearly there already, but at ninety degrees there was no suggestion at all. It was the same as her first sculpture, the Zeus head. She screwed up her eyes and with a chinagraph pencil lightly sketched in the outline of its side view. Then she set the stone, wrapped in a layer of felt, in her vice to steady it while she made her first marks with the chisel.

The concentrated work had the desired effect. It left part of her mind relaxed, to orbit on its own. By the time she covered over the half-emerged frog for the night, she had a ready-made menu and a good idea of how to tackle Nikolaos Clerides.

She had taken the receiver off the phone when she came in earlier, and fortunately Elpida hadn't noticed and re-placed it. Now Jean did so and went off to move provisions from freezer to fridge. By the time she had mixed pastry to a fine crumble the phone started ringing again. It sounded eight times while she dusted off her hands and wrapped them in a tea-towel.

'Mather residence.'

'Jean, I've reached you at last. You must have had a conversational marathon. Every time I rang the line was engaged.'

'Nikos, hullo. I'm afraid the receiver hadn't been put back properly. I noticed the buzzing when I went past it just now. I'm sorry. Was there something urgent?'

The short pause indicated that he was hurt. 'But I'm so glad you rang. You've beaten me to it. I wanted to thank you for your good care of me in the early hours. I hope it didn't hold you back from your sailing.'

Another obvious pause, then he said warily, 'Are you quite sure you want to stay up at the villa tonight? I'm not at all happy about it, after the break-in.'

'Don't worry. The village is alerted. I think the men are looking forward to a repetition—not that there is likely to be one. Such an oiling of guns and swapping of stories about the good old days of the fight for freedom!'

'Ah. You mentioned sailing. Of course, you found my old sweatshirt in the bathroom. Please forgive the way I left the place. I am not normally so untidy.'

'You dropped everything to come to my rescue. I'm really grateful. Did you find the note I left for you at Reception?'

'Yes, thank you. And again I must apologize that I was away when you awoke. Another matter of business came up during the morning. I expected to be back sooner than I was.'

'I realize you have other cases to check on besides my own. It was good of you to give me so much of your time.'

'Jean, surely you know how I—When shall I see you again? Tomorrow? Perhaps we could have lunch somewhere special, or take a hamper to Fig Tree Bay. I'm told it is very pleasant there, and the sand is silvery-yellow, not like the grey grit about here. Do say you will come.'

'That sounds lovely, but I'm afraid it's out of the question. I have friends of my husband's coming to lunch here. It's an engagement made way back. They're rather a dull old couple or I could include you, but it would be a disaster. How about Monday, or is that a workday for you?'

'Wonderful! And since you mentioned sailing, would you be interested in a trip by sea? There is a boat I can hire locally, and I will bribe the chef here to surpass himself with a picnic ice-box. Bring your costume and we can swim at anchor. There are fins, masks and snorkels, if you care to go spearing fish.'

She suppressed a shudder at the thought. 'Swimming sounds a good idea; sailing too, provided you don't expect a lot of energetic crewing. I tend to lie in the shade of a sail and practise *après-swim*.'

'What a delicious prospect. At what time can I expect you on Monday morning?'

'Shall we say half past ten, in the lounge of the Miramare?'

'Perfect. I look forward to it. Meanwhile, take good care of yourself.'

Perfect from my viewpoint too, Jean decided; with Maritsa lurking behind the tropical greenery to identify him as Ted's secret business partner.

CHAPTER 7

All the while she kept busy with preparations for next day's entertaining, Jean was able to forget the visit she had received from her dead husband's mistress. She said the word aloud as she confronted herself in the bathroom mirror, toothbrush in hand. It sounded melodramatic, nothing to do with everyday Ted, certainly nothing in connection with her own life. All the same she found herself brushing with unaccustomed vigour and glowering from the reflection above a spot of blood welling on her lip.

She went to bed in the room they had shared, with his dressing-room door wide open, giving a view of the things he had handled every day.

So he had slept with Maritsa, she reflected. There's nothing in that which I couldn't have pictured myself doing with Nikolaos Clerides, if I'm to be really truthful about it. But the situations are different. Ted was married. I'm widowed. He actually did. I managed not to.

And then she buried her head in the pillow while the tears came again because Ted *was* dead and so many, many opportunities had been missed, it being too late now to put anything right.

I wouldn't have minded too much, she told herself miserably. I would have bitched a bit when he told me, but I'd have forgiven him if he'd wanted it, just so that he'd still be here, and alive. But the time for bargaining and contracts was gone too. She was no longer a child promising God she'd be good.

Sleep was a long time coming, and she awoke with the awareness of frustration. In a dream she had been working on a flat stone, trying to bring out the face that was concealed in it, but the more she rubbed and chipped the more hollow the stone became until it was shallow like a saucer and she began to see through it to her own hands holding it on the far side.

She got up, put on a swimsuit and went out on the patio, but before sliding into the pool she walked to the far end of the garden where a shoulder-high white column stood under the jacaranda tree. On it was set the first head she had ever made, the sandstone 'Zeus'. She was almost afraid to look now because of what she feared to see.

She had been right. Strange that Elpida had not realized too. The sense of *déjà-vu* that had haunted Jean these past few days was now partly explained. The stone face, so full of majestic authority, was the face of Nikolaos Clerides. More than two years back, when she had first sat here and looked across to what seemed a naturally formed profile in the rock, the man's features had materialized in her mind and she had recorded the image, perhaps for all time. It had outlived Ted, perhaps it would outlive her too. She was afraid of it as if it had some occult power, yet it was just something she had caused to be: her crude first attempt at sculpting; but also something that crept out of the recesses of her subconscious.

What was it Clerides had said when she asked abruptly whether they'd met before? '*Not in this life.*' Wasn't that it? As though he knew something she didn't. As though he recognized some extra-temporal link that exerted influence over her still.

'I don't believe in Destiny,' she said aloud. It sounded fine in English, but she knew she wouldn't dare say it in Greek. There was too much ancient magic in the language. In this landscape, under this cloudless sky, there could come an instant thunderbolt. 'I'm not superstitious either,' she added defiantly. But she wasn't fool enough to take risks.

'Swim,' she told herself briefly, turned her back on the pedestal and the head, and went to the pcol. When she emerged from the water and was drying herself she found that she would rather think now about Maritsa than Nicolaos; there was less threat to herself in that.

Even less would there be any menace from the Rowleys. Today would be mainly devoted to them. How much of her own affairs was she prepared to mention to them, at their typical gossipy level? It would surely depend on what sort of mood they were in, and how things progressed conversationally. Play it by ear, then.

Marjorie seemed a little more relaxed than in her own home, possibly because now she hadn't the pressure of hostessing. She was following each of Jean's movements with a bright, birdlike stare, and seemed satisfied that in catering she wasn't to be dramatically upstaged. At the same time she appeared to be engrossed in some private calculation. Lance's mood was almost one of tetchy resentment.

It was quite new for Jean to consider the Rowleys as two separate entities. Ted's lumping them together as the Rowley-Powleys, a minor comedy duo, must have influenced her more than she was aware of at the time. True, they were a couple as few married pairs were nowadays, even physically similar due to their lavish intake of calories, almost Siamese in their attachment to one another.

Perhaps their shared seniority and the decades they had spent in harness had welded them together. Certainly Marjorie must have been an ideal officer's wife, always yielding priority to the Mess, conducting a correct shadow existence under the Service umbrella. But there must have been interminable periods when she was left on her own, had to find substitute companionship, alternative interests. This could explain her frenetic enthusiasms for trivialities. Perhaps since his retirement Lance too had been categorized as one of these! Jean watched their double act with a new interest, curious to see where the seams of the partnership showed up, whether there were tell-tale stress marks.

'I don't suppose,' she threw into the conversation, 'that you heard about my intruder?'

They hadn't heard, and professed alarm.

'The night before last,' Jean told them, testing the heat of a dish against her knuckle and then cutting into the quiche set out on it.

'That would be Friday night,' Marjorie said pedantically.

'Early Saturday morning, to be precise. I was asleep, with the door to my balcony open.'

'And someone actually got in? Did he wake you?' Lance demanded fiercely. 'My God, what are things coming to? You must have been scared out of your wits.'

Jean considered what he'd said. 'Yes. Yes, I was at the time.'

'And did he take anything?' Marjorie asked, mindful of the many little treasures in her own home which she just couldn't face living without.

'Not that I've discovered yet. He'd gone past me into

Ted's dressing-room and my waking startled him.' Call the intruder 'him' for the moment, she decided. After all, Maritsa and herself were the only ones to know otherwise.

'You mean you wouldn't know what Ted kept in there?' Lance inquired cautiously.

'Oh, I know everything that was there, but I haven't really checked since. There didn't seem much point in it. The intruder had got away by the time I felt bold enough to give chase. The village men turned out ready for a manhunt, but by then it was too late. They've armed themselves to the teeth in the hope that there will be a replay. Nothing so exciting has happened in Kalidrofi, it seems, for a long time.'

'You must come and stay down with us, Jean. Mustn't she, Marjorie? It's quite out of the question for you to go on living up here alone. Not a single English person to talk to for miles. Why don't you let us look for a little bungalow for you down at Coral Beach? Not so very much cheaper, I'm afraid, because the idea's catching on fast. We're getting to be a very desirable neighbourhood, as the estate johnnies say. But if you could find the right buyer this place ought to bring in a packet. Some rich old Greek who wants a haven outside his own country.'

Poor Lance, seeing everything from the viewpoint of a British tax exile, as if this were the Cayman Islands or Guernsey! You couldn't miss the unconscious disapproval in 'some rich old Greek'; innate racism of the sort that ought to have gone out with the Raj and Empire-flinger shorts. The more recent Brit expatriates didn't seem as narrow as Lance, but she would never settle among them and risk finding out.

'I'd never leave here,' she said comfortably. 'This is just what I need.'

'You mean you won't be going *home*?' Marjorie demanded, shocked.

Jean looked back at her with understanding. There, if

anywhere, were the stress marks she had idly wondered about. Settling here was Lance's choice, Marjorie falling in dutifully behind him. But left to her own devices—if she had been widowed herself, say—the day couldn't come soon enough for Marjorie to pack her bags and book her final flight. Back to Cooden Beach or Pershore or Midsummer Norton or whatever.

'This is home.' Jean collected the dishes and balanced them up her arm. 'It's kind of you, Lance, to make the offer, but I don't see any reason to come away from here.'

Dropping the crockery in hot suds for Elpida to retrieve, she realized something more about Marjorie. Lance had made the offer spontaneously and called for her to second it. Which she hadn't done. Marjorie didn't want Jean staying with them. Marjorie didn't share Lance's anxiety over Jean's safety. Does she dislike me, then? Jean asked herself. Or is there something else I've missed?

Inside the fridge the dish with the *charlotte russe* had become perilously wedged between encroaching tubs of butter. As she wriggled it free, Jean considered another of Marjorie's statements: that the night before last had been Friday night. Muttered calculatingly, as if there was something significant about when the break-in occurred. Why should that be, unless something special happened just previously? Even something that caused the break-in to be made?

That was ridiculous. What had happened on Friday?— she couldn't remember. So much had been happening in a few days. But anyway Marjorie wouldn't have access to Jean's comings and goings, except where it overlapped with her own. She pushed the fridge door shut with one knee, flicked on the percolator switch in passing and went back cheerfully to change the subject.

'How's *Zoë* since you had her serviced?' she asked Lance.

He looked mystified. 'Serviced? She's a sailing-boat, Jean, not a ruddy car.'

'Lance, dear; language.'

'Oh, I must have misunderstood. I thought she'd been
over to Limassol for refitting or something.'

There was no disguising the man's discomfort. 'You must
be clairvoyant. She's going sometime today. The man's
going out to the bay to fetch her. Be away a week or so, I
guess. Sprung a—a board, he says. Below the waterline.'
He was mumbling into his dessert. Jean looked about her
furtively for a fresh topic that would bring no one embarrassment. Her gaze lit on the silver napkin ring Marjorie was
fiddling with. It reminded her of Maritsa and the filigree
clasp in her hair.

'You shop quite a lot in Paphos, Marjorie, don't you?'

'I get most of my regular stuff there, yes. Why?'

'Because yesterday I met someone from Paphos who deals
in lace and silverware. She worked for relatives in Lefkara,
then set up in a shop of her own.'

Jean was aware that this as a subject was going down
better. Now she had the complete attention of them both.
Marjorie at least was hanging on her words. Even before
she mentioned the name, Jean had an intuitive flash of the
likely reaction.

'Maritsa Kakouris.'

'Oh my God, this is too much!' Lance had pushed back
his chair and was standing up. Trying to stand, but his legs
were somehow entangled in the long edge of the tablecloth.
Jean went round to help extricate him and looked up to see
Marjorie's deathly pallor.

Lance gave up struggling and sank back on his seat. 'So
you know? We were almost sure you hadn't any idea.'

Jean felt a strong pulse start up in her throat. 'That she
was Ted's mistress? Yes, I knew,' she admitted quietly, not
letting on how recent the news had been. 'What I didn't
know was that you were both in on it. Don't tell me there
was collusion. Did you help him find a local shop to set her
up in?'

'We didn't approve at all,' Marjorie said with a tight
mouth, and Jean could well believe her. 'It didn't seem

right, with you tucked away up at this village, and that girl flaunting herself with him all over Limassol and Paphos.'

'It started as a business venture,' Jean said mildly, 'so I imagine they would have to go about together to a certain extent. Then later I suppose they realized they were both attractive people and . . . You know how it is.'

Marjorie's expression said clearly that she did not know.

'Is she making trouble now?' Lance demanded. 'She's not going to contest the will, surely? I know that in America mistresses have almost equal rights, and it's on its way in England, but here the family still matters.'

'I think she's in some difficulty at present,' Jean said thoughtfully, 'because Ted didn't finance her very far ahead. Of course, dying was the last thing he thought of doing, so what need was there?'

'Well, she's made her bed and now she must lie on it,' Marjorie pronounced with satisfaction. 'That's what I told her when . . .'

The other two turned and looked at her, Lance speechless.

'Go on, Marjorie,' Jean prompted. 'That's what you told her when you broke the news of Ted's death, less than a week ago. She didn't know until then. Somebody had to tell her and you were practically on the spot. It was you, wasn't it?'

'For God's sake, why did you have to interfere, woman?' Lance was flushed now with more than the light wine he'd drunk with his lunch. He bunched his fist and banged the table under his wife's nose.

It seemed more than time that she suggested they move out under the canopy for coffee, but there was something else niggling away in the back of Jean's memory. 'Friday. Friday was the day I went to the pottery for my first lesson. And in the evening I rang you, Lance, to ask if you knew anything about Ted's second insurance, because I couldn't lay hands on the policy. Marjorie was out playing bridge, you said. So whom else did you tell that I'd rung?'

'No one at all,' Lance declared, 'though you never said

anything about it being confidential. Anyway, I'm not one to go gossiping about such things.'

'No, I believe that. *You* aren't. And at that time Marjorie didn't know. What time did you get back from your bridge, Marjorie?'

'It was after half past ten,' Lance said, defending. 'Molly Bax dropped her off, and she didn't go out again. You must be out of your mind, Jean, if you're implying that Marjorie or I broke in here to go through Ted's things, interested though we've always tried to be in your and his affairs.'

'No,' Jean said simply, 'I don't think that. I know exactly who did break in, and now I know how the word was passed on. You made a phone call, Marjorie, didn't you? You thought Maritsa might be making some claim on Ted's money through the second insurance, and you couldn't bear that. But she was equally astounded to hear about the missing policy, so your attempt to spike her guns must have fallen flat. But she knew this address and she decided to come herself and hunt for the policy among things she supposed the stricken widow would have had no heart to search through.

'Yesterday was the first time I met Maritsa, and the first time I knew anything at all about her.'

'You couldn't say,' Jean remarked drily to Elpida later, 'that my entertaining went very well today. Every time I meet that pair I get steamed up about something and I put my foot in my manners. In fact, it's not just with them that I'm off-key. My entire social life is a mess.'

Elpida wrinkled her broad brow under the cotton scarf she used to cover her hair when working. Her English wasn't good enough for her to follow all Jean said, but she caught the words 'life' and 'mess', nor could she mistake the wanness of the other woman's smile. Impulsively she clasped Jean to her warm ampleness and murmured comfort in Greek, ending, 'What you need is a good man to take care of you.'

Gently Jean extracted herself. 'I thought at one time that I had one, but I wonder if perhaps I was mistaken.'

Certainly there was more to Ted than she had ever guessed in the seven years they had been together. And yet, was that true? She had known what he basically was—a strong, determined winner—and that it was his best facet he always turned towards her. That was surely something to be grateful for. He could be harsh with the men he controlled; he drove hard bargains; he couldn't resist making money on the side if there was half a chance. There were a lot like him in the army and they seemed to reach levels of responsibility. She had always thought of him as a good example of a buttoned-up senior NCO. And, underlying all that, not too high-principled in some things; even a bit of a rogue. Without discussing it, each had recognized in the other an attraction of opposites. And, undeniably, it had worked. Or so she had thought for the best part of her married life. The best part of her whole life.

CHAPTER 8

Monday was a working day for Maritsa, but as Jean gave her good warning on the day before, she was able to call Aris in to take charge of the shop. He was glad enough to exchange his overall for the smart suit he'd been married in eight months earlier, and a cramped workbench for the elegant shop it supplied. He had a pleasant, un-pushy way with customers which he felt was wasted on his fellow silversmith in the back room.

Maritsa dressed carefully in a navy cotton dress with an emerald green scarf at the neck, fashionable enough not to seem out of place in a hotel lounge but not chic enough to attract attention. All she had to do was sit quietly reading until Mrs Mather arrived and greeted the man Maritsa would recognize from visiting Ted at the hospital before his release from the army. He would then be identified as the partner Ted had told her about, the man who must hold the missing insurance policy, and who knew—if anyone did —where the money was deposited for paying the rent and suppliers' accounts.

She booked her taxi for the single journey to Limassol, noting it down as a legitimate expense recoverable from the man when they had everything sorted out. She wasn't sure what Mrs Mather intended her to do once she'd identified him, but presumably she would find some way of contacting Maritsa and cueing her in.

She was twenty minutes early, and Mrs Mather arrived dead on time. As she came towards the glass swing doors, a tall man in casual dress put out a cigarette and rose from a settee opposite to bow and take from her hand the canvas grip she was carrying.

Maritsa stared at him. It was over two years since she had visited Ted in hospital, but no one could change that much in so little time. This man was one she had never set eyes on before this morning. She had had a good opportunity to study him as he sat waiting like herself. A lean, strong face, the nose aquiline with deep lines from nostrils to corners of the wide, sardonic mouth. A hard face, perhaps at times an arrogant one. She was glad now that he wasn't the man she would have to talk business with.

She put down her magazine and started across towards the reception desk, as if to make some inquiry. She passed close to the chatting couple and from behind the man's back shook her head sadly at Mrs Mather. While she bought postage stamps at the counter the two moved away out through the door towards the car park.

She might have pretended I was a friend and spoken to me, Maritsa thought. She could have given me a lift if she is going out towards Paphos, or at least offered to pay for my taxi. Now I am more out of pocket and no farther forward. These rich women have no idea how hard it is to work for one's living!

But there was no need to go back at once. Aris would be content to bill and coo to the customers until closing time if necessary, once he was dressed for the part. She could make the most of a free day, window-shopping and taking coffee in one of those cafés fronting the formal gardens and the sea. But first she would check on the lace shops, see what the opposition was here in Limassol, perhaps even pick up some new ideas.

She took a bus bound for the centre and dropped off it at the corner of Ayias Zonis Street. Waiting to cross, she idly scanned the cars slowly infiltrating into Makarios Avenue. It was then, utterly unexpectedly, that she recognized the man she had hoped to identify with Mrs Mather this morning. The saloon, a medium-sized green Nissan bearing the red licence-plate of a hire car, stood stationary a moment only five metres from her, and the driver turned his head to look curiously in her direction.

There was no mistaking him. He had aged and lost colour in the face but it was the same man. And if he didn't recognize her, that was not to be wondered at. Ted had never brought them together. It was by accident that she'd glimpsed him leaving the ward when she was coming to visit. 'Ah, you just missed meeting my business partner,' Ted had said, smiling as if it was a joke. She had asked what he meant and then he had clammed up, talking vaguely about other things until he fell alseep, stupefied by some antihistamine drug they were trying out on him.

Maritsa stepped forward into the road, her arm lifted to try and detain the car. Immediately she was seized from behind and lifted bodily back on to the pavement, deposited and soundly scolded by a fierce-looking policeman with enormous moustaches. When she had mumbled her apologies and broken loose, the man in the Nissan was gone. She could have wept, to have been so close to him and then for him to have got away. Perhaps the chance would never come again, and if he knew as little of her as she did of him, how were they ever to find each other and get the business sorted out?

Jean's mind had had plenty to bite on as she came through the swing glass doors of the Miramare. First there was the disconcerting leap of her heart as Nikos moved towards her, then, almost before she had steadied herself to think, Maritsa was there behind his back sadly signalling with a shake of the head. Already Nikos was swinging her grip up, ready to be on his way. Maritsa moved off towards the reception desk and seemed to have business there.

A pity, Jean thought. It would have made things so much easier to settle if Nikos had turned out to be the secret business partner come to Cyprus to check on his investments.

On the other hand, it was gratifying that his story of the elusive insurance claim hadn't yet been disproved, although she had begun to suspect that his interest in Ted's affairs smacked more of a policeman's, and the policy was an invented excuse to make inquiries.

She must go along with his story a little longer until she felt on firmer ground. Everything that had happened in the past few days had been increasingly disturbing, as though some sinister happening in the past—Ted's past?—were rising up to enmesh her. It even seemed, as she looked back, that Spiros, when she called in at the bar, had had some premonition and been on the brink of issuing a specific warning to watch her step. How many more were a party to this secret of which only she had been totally unaware? It left her unsure of who was to be trusted. Were the familiar faces any more reliable than this stony-faced stranger alongside now?

They drove eastward to the Sheraton marina where *Zephyr II* was tied up, her mast stepped and sails ready to hoist. Nikos transferred an ice-box from car to galley, slung their grips into the saloon and went up again to inspect the rigging. 'Since you object to energetic crewing,' he called down, 'we'll clear harbour on the motor.'

Jean nodded, threading her arms into a life-jacket. It wasn't an entirely calm sea. There were irregular patches like pieces in a jigsaw puzzle, where the surface was feathered by wind, and far out, without any apparent reason, a single horizontal would curl a white lip and then go blue again. The sleeping beast, Jean thought, always aware of the fathoms below.

Once free of the harbour, Nikos cut the engine, removed his T-shirt and treated her to a display of unexpected muscle as he ran the jib and Bermudan mainsail up, then settled at the tiller, turning *Zephyr* to reach at eighty degrees across wind. She heeled over beautifully and Jean ran amidships, slipped her bare feet into the grips, throwing her weight back to windward, almost horizontal above the hissing water. The sail was straining as they made speed towards where sea and sky met.

Nikos came over and threw his weight beside hers. 'This is the life,' he shouted above the sound of their whipping progress. Exhilarated, like a boy.

She thought he would bring the boat about and show off his nautical skills with complicated tacking along the coast, but he was content to stay beside her, eyes half-closed against sun and wind, until with a grunt he looked back in the direction they'd come from and grinned. 'Lost it. Anybody think to bring a compass?' The sort of reckless humour she had heard so often from Ted.

She squinted at the sun which was almost overhead. 'You'd better set a starboard watch before we hit Port Said.'

'Sometime on Thursday,' he agreed. 'Meanwhile there's lunch, with champagne. So we'll change to an even keel.' He readjusted the mainsail sheet in its cleats, took over the tiller and set *Zephyr* on a steadier course.

'I'll see to the galley,' she offered, and swung below.

Zephyr was neat and well equipped. 'If you've seen one you've seen the lot,' she said aloud, hands automatically going out to familiar positions of oven, cupboards, fridge.

When she lifted down the plates it seemed to her that the degree of familiarity was quite uncanny. Could this white-dots-on-blue crockery be standard issue with this class of sailing craft? And the chipped sugar basin too?

She stood, hands on hips, and made a three hundred and sixty degree turn surveying the cabin. Different curtains, but then the ones she remembered had been distinctly tatty. There was one way she could check for certain. She opened the fridge, lifted out the plastic ice tray and turned it upside down. There across the bottom was the brown stain of a cigarette burn. She remembered the occasion well; one of Lance's lady guests washing up when half-seas-over, dropping a lighted cigarette among the draining articles and too fuddled to get it out quickly.

But that was on *Zoë*. This boat was *Zephyr II*. Quite different, apart from the first letter. Ah, but the new name was longer, so it would cover the first one and a little beyond. There was no reason why it shouldn't be the same boat, except that formalities had to be observed in re-registering a name. And *Zoë* belonged to Lance. He had definitely said it had gone to have a sprung board repaired. So far as Jean could see, there appeared to be nothing wrong with either the deck or hull of *Zephyr II*.

Her hands went on unwrapping the delicacies from the ice-box Nikos had provided, while she considered the position. Would Nikos be aware that they were aboard a boat with an alias? That seemed more likely than that someone was leading him by the nose. He didn't look the type to be made a gull of.

If Lance was trying to make money by having *Zoë* hired out, presumably through Baroutis, had he authorized the (probably irregular) change of name? And why should it be necessary? If anyone commented on its use by strangers he could always save face by saying it was on loan to friends. No, Lance was rather a stickler for doing things by the book. The change of name must have taken place in Baroutis's boatyard. At Nikos's insistence? Why, if this was a purely straightforward pleasure trip?

It should have alarmed her to be out of sight of land, heading roughly south-east (or would it be due south now that Nikos had changed course?) in a boat with a definitely questionable background and a skipper who could be much the same.

When Nikos came silently down she suppressed a start and looked up with a challenging grin. 'How long have you been a white slave trader?'

'Ah, I have you frightened now; is that it? Alone with me on the high seas, bound for the African coast, no less! Shall I have my wicked way with you now, then sell you later for two bags of dates and a blind camel?'

'I think you might value me higher than that.'

His lean face became serious. The wolf grin disappeared. 'Indeed I do. Above the price of rubies. A virtuous woman.' He looked at her gravely. 'That is one of the few quotations I remember from childhood.'

She looked back at him evenly. 'Shall we eat on deck? Somebody ought to keep lookout. Will you carry the champagne? I'll follow with a tray.'

'To prove my good faith,' he said with mock piety when she had joined him, 'I shall let you set course for wherever you wish.'

'That's optimistic of you. Suppose I can't handle the navigation.'

'I am quite sure you can. Take me to some magic bay only you know of.'

'I sail on the hit-or-miss principle,' she warned him. 'Crew for me, will you?' and she went back to free the tiller. It was already past one-thirty. 'Coming about,' she shouted and turned the boat with the sun over her left shoulder. 'How's that, then?'

He gave her a look of comic despair. 'Do you really want us to fetch up at Beirut? Or Gibraltar?'

'We shall see,' she promised. 'If you tighten sail we could have our lunch now. I'm famished.'

They ate as they sailed downwind on a port tack, and there was no need to break the companionable silence until Nikos pointed ahead and said, 'Look, New York harbour!'

Jean scanned the coastline anxiously. The height of the undulating cliffs indicated the central southern shore of Cyprus, and as they came closer she recognized the corniche route she knew so well. She went off and sat by the tiller, set the course two degrees more westerly, and Nikos trimmed the sails to give more speed. 'Find us somewhere good for swimming,' he ordered. She was already heading for her favourite cove.

He had brought scuba gear on board. She would have preferred her own equipment but he seemed proficient in handling the bottles of air, testing them carefully before he set the valves. 'Do you want a spear gun?'

She shook her head: the fish were there before her; she was the outsider. 'Just snorkelling for me; no bottles, thanks. *Now*, drop anchor,' she ordered.

They went overboard together, falling to the water backwards, flippers last. Here the water was a strange transparent green. Below it the seabed, at eighty feet, was a mixture of sand and rock flowing with silvery weed, but from it rose irregular walls of darker rocks which they finned between. There were green fronds like a woman's long hair streaming in a slow-motion wind, small fishes and all manner of pink life from palest shell to the dark puce of rock-clinging predators. Three clear white jelly-fish squirted themselves by and sand billowed up cloudily where a reluctant squid buried itself in a secret cranny.

They swam slowly, hand in hand, using the sign language of divers to suggest their next moves. She signalled she was at the end of her held air and he passed her his mouthpiece. She drew on it twice and returned it to him. Their view constricted by the rims of their goggles, they turned outwards from each other and their legs tangled. Nikos pulled out his mouthpiece and reached for hers. Underwater, holding their breath for an eternity, they kissed, rolled together in a weightless state. Nikos gave her the air supply first, then took it back.

He was crazy, Jean told herself, but she hadn't resisted. She broke loose now, bit on her snorkel mouthpiece, pointed her right thumb upwards and began to ascend.

She waited at the rope-ladder until be broke surface beside her, took the weight-belt he unbuckled, and flung it on deck. Then he helped her to climb up, and in turn she gave him a hand over the side.

He held out an upturned fist to her. 'Open my fingers.'

She pulled them apart and peered in at what he held.

'It's for you.'

'What is it—a coin?'

'Something of the sort, I imagine. It was lying on a sandy rock.'

'You mean you went right down? Wasn't that rather deep?'

'Just a quick flash to touch the seabed and up again. And I happened on that. I wonder if it's the only one or—'

'Oh, not sunken wrecks! You aren't going to start up that old story!'

'You mean people do think there's something down here?'

'There must have been wrecks off the coast all round Cyprus. They've been a seafaring nation since the beginning of time. And a trading post for the Cretans, the Ancient Greeks, the Egyptians, Phœnicians, Romans . . .'

'You think there could be rich pickings down there, then?' He sounded boyishly enthusiastic.

Jean looked at him sceptically. 'Of course. That's probably why you can't go after the wrecks without a licence from the Department of Marine Archæology. If they didn't put an embargo on it, everything would be looted and lost, for the value of the treasure on the black market in ancient artefacts. The best thing you can do is throw that back, whatever it is, and forget where it came from.'

'But I found it. It isn't anybody's. And I want you to have it.' Again he sounded like an earnest ten-year-old.

'If you give it to me I shall have to offer it back to the fishes.'

'Do that, then. The only gift I have ever offered you.'

She inspected the encrusted and deformed little lump of stone or metal. It didn't look as if it had any value; possibly some small, badly worn engine part chucked overboard from a power boat. When he had gone back to Athens it would be all that was left to her of this exhilarating day. There seemed no harm in keeping it, purely as a memento.

He was watching her face closely, and now he folded her fingers over it.

Jean smiled, dropped it into her grip and started towelling her hair. She dabbed at the water beading her limbs and rummaged among her belongings for sun-protection cream. Nikos lay alongside on his back, hands clasped behind his head, still as a lizard. Very soon, Jean thought, she would have to bring it all to an end, repeat that she hadn't the insurance policy. Then he must either express regrets and return slightly puzzled to his office in Athens, or confess there was no second insurance and come clean about what his game actually was. Soon—but not just yet. She would prolong as far as possible this precious time before she had to send him away.

He sat up and held out his hand for the tube of cream, circling a finger end to make her turn her back to him. His fingers gently explored every hollow and hillock exposed, but he remained respectful, left her to lift the shoulder straps while he creamed the flesh underneath.

'Such fair skin. You need to be careful with it. It goes a lovely shade of copper.' Whereas his body was weathered teak. Already he had lost the indoor look he had when he first arrived. 'You swim underwater a lot?'

'I used to. Less of late.'

'Ah yes. You and your husband. He taught you?'

'No. I joined Sub-Aqua while I was still at college. Ted had begun with the Forces on Malta.'

'So you often went out together?'

'Sometimes, but more often he made up parties with some of his men. They had their own compressor to service their air bottles, and they used to harpoon fish. It was too professional for me. An all-male show. I took to sailing. Dinghies, very small-time.'

'On your own.' He considered this, staring at the sky. 'And this cove is one of the places you used to sail to? So where did your husband and his merry men make for?'

'Farther west, I think, and they'd sneak up into Turkish waters if there weren't any patrol boats in the offing.'

'Did he ever say where?'

'I did overhear him mention names, but they meant nothing to me. I wasn't here before the Turkish invasion, so I've never gone north of the Green Line. You can go over, but the difficulty is getting the Greek Cypriots to let you back. They won't accept the illegal stamping on your passport.'

Nikos began to recite Greek-sounding place-names which on his tongue had the alluring magic of 'Chimborazo, Cotapaxi . . .' Only half-listening, Jean checked him. 'Say that again,' and when he did, 'Kato Pyrgos?' Yes, that's one I heard him mention to his sergeant. Of course, they didn't spend any time ashore. They dived in quite deep water. I know that because of his decompression charts. They were folded open at a certain page, from a hundred and thirty feet onwards. I used to worry sometimes because of the risks he'd take, being an asthmatic too.'

'A man's life,' Nikos said simply.

'It was what he wanted.' There was a short silence. Jean sighed. 'Nikos, this insurance business—'

'M'm.'

'I don't have any policy on Ted's life with your company. And there's no reference to it anywhere among his papers.'

'Perhaps someone else holds it, a close friend.'

'We've discussed this before. You had that list I made out. There was one more person I questioned, the closest of all, and I drew a blank there too. It seems he had a mistress. If she didn't have it and I didn't, we have to accept that it isn't going to turn up. I'm afraid your journey here has been completely wasted.'

He opened one eye. 'Not wasted.' He reached for her hand. 'I am not such a single-minded insurance man.'

'No, but your quest has been fruitless.' Jean sat up, businesslike and schoolmistressy in her detachment. 'So now you must call it a day and go back to Athens.'

He was watching her with something like uncertainty. It struck her as quite untypical. He seemed almost fearful of going on, as though her coming reaction must be unwelcome. 'Not just yet, Jean. There is something I must wait for.'

'Nikos, something is wrong, isn't it? What must you wait for?'

'Perhaps it is better that I tell you before the official notice comes. The authorities intend to exhume your husband's body. Someone has been querying the cause of death.'

CHAPTER 9

When she left Nikolaos Clerides, refusing his offer to accompany her home, she went straight to Spiros's bar. Not for the drink, but his company. The place had filled up and two assistants were helping out, all busy with customers, but Spiros saw her at the door and came across. 'Mrs Mather, can I help you?'

'Spiros, something's happened. Something awful.'

'One moment, please.' He held her elbow while he signalled to someone behind, then, 'We will go into the front office. It is time Andreas went home anyway.'

He guided her into the lounge and across to a louvred

door in one corner. They went through into a square room
with strip lighting and modern office equipment. A man
seated at the computer looked up startled, then at a flick
of Spiros's head started shutting down the programme.
Without a word he made the final switch-off, nodded and
went out, dragging his jacket from the back of a chair.

'Spiros, you can't—'

'I can. I own the place. I only tend bar because there are
others better at the hard jobs. Sit down and tell me what
has worried you.'

She poured it out: about Clerides and his inquiries; about
Lance's earlier doubts over how Ted died; about the intruder
and how she turned out to be Ted's mistress and the girl who
ran a shop for him in Paphos; finally, about the terrible news
that Ted's grave was to be reopened and a full post-mortem
performed. What she omitted was the fascination Clerides
had for her, and their sailing trip together that very day.

'This is bad,' Spiros said, absently holding her hand in
his large paw. 'To reopen a grave. To trouble you with
questions when you are grieving. What do they suspect,
then?'

'That his death wasn't from natural causes. Spiros, I
was there, I saw! I suppose they will accuse me of doing
something to make his asthma come on so badly. You know
I wouldn't. Me, kill Ted? They always look for the nearest
in these cases, the wife or husband. But I loved him, I
wouldn't have done anything to hurt him. And if it ever
comes out that he had a mistress—although I swear I knew
nothing of it then—they will say I did it from spite or
jealousy. A *crime passionnel*!'

'Who is stirring up this trouble?' Spiros asked darkly.
'Your husband died two months ago and there was no hint
of scandal then.'

'I don't know. Clerides merely said someone started
asking questions. And only last week, when I was having
lunch with friends over at Paphos, a man who is usually
quite sympathetic was—awkward. He kept asking for de-

tails of what happened before Ted collapsed, as though it was worrying him. He was more Ted's friend than mine, so it's possible he thinks . . .'

'He must be stupid.' Spiros sat hunched, hands loosely clasped between his knees still absently holding her captive. '*If* there was any truth in what someone seems to suspect, and your husband's death was—hastened, there are two things you should consider. Who might want to do it, and how it was done. Whichever question you tackle first, it could lead you to answering the second. You have an advantage over any other inquirer because you can at least eliminate yourself as a suspect.'

Jean smiled in spite of her unease. 'You're very practical. Yes, I ought to start thinking positively instead of worrying. It was a shock at first. And then—if all sorts of questions are going to be asked, some of them may have unpleasant answers. I didn't know an awful lot about some of Ted's interests. I'm beginning to think I was always afraid of knowing too much in case it burst my bubble.'

'Bubble?'

'We were very happy together. He was always good to me. Protective.'

'And you think there are some he was less good to?' There was a sardonic edge to his voice.

'You knew him, Spiros. You saw him sometimes with his men. He was tough, a hard fighter and a sure winner. People like that can make enemies. If he did, they would have belonged to a world he kept me out of.'

'So it will not be easy for you to work out who might want him dead. In that case you should try to find out how it could have been done, if at all. And that is what a post-mortem is intended to do. Perhaps the doctor who signed the death certificate was less than thorough, because he knew your husband was asthmatic and the body's appearance was consistent with that cause. Now it will be properly looked into and the truth will come out. You have nothing to be afraid of.'

'I hope you're right, but there are so many mysteries coming to light that I'm scared of where it will all end.'

'In case your husband was involved in some dubious affair?'

'He had too much money, Spiros. I see that now. I don't know where it came from and I believe there must be a cache somewhere that he drew it from. And then Maritsa spoke of a business partner. I arranged for her to see Clerides because I had a wild idea he might be the one, but he wasn't. Only she can identify him. If he held money in common with Ted, he might have had him removed to keep all the money himself. It's strange that there is no cache, and no accounts or bank statements that I can find to explain the source of extra money.'

'Have you any other suggestions who this partner might be?'

She hesitated. 'No real suspicion, not enough to tell you about. Was there anyone you saw him with in here who fits the bill?'

'I will certainly think about it. It is true he came into the bar on several occasions with men I did not recognize as being British army friends.'

'Everybody fetches up in here eventually,' she said, trying to lighten the conversation. 'Do you remember the last time I was in? There was a man who had a boatyard, and you'd been to school with his young brother.'

'Baroutis. Yes.' Spiros smiled. 'There was a rude word he used in front of you. I found out later he was not speaking of a woman at all, but a boat. I believe I told you he was married to the sea.'

'A *boat*?'

'He has a caïque which he used to take tourists out in for a day's fishing, but would never allow it to be skippered by anyone but himself. Now some foreigners have hired it and gone off without him and he does nothing but sulk and drink.'

'Why doesn't he take legal action?'

'Baroutis is no lover of lawyers, and you can depend on it that he has been very well paid to allow it to happen. Otherwise how can he suddenly afford to drink to excess?'

'Maybe I should work in a bar for a while,' Jean commented wistfully. 'It might give me the wit to work out my own problems. You're quite the philosopher, Spiros. I'm glad I came in here tonight. I feel much better about things; less panicky anyway. Thank you.'

'I'm a poor barman. I haven't asked what you would like to drink. You said I could offer you one on the house next time you came in.'

'I'd like coffee, then, and a cognac. Will you have one too?'

'I'll bring a pot for us both. And the Grand Marnier bottle.'

While he was gone she combed her hair and repaired her make-up. The sun had brought out freckles down the side of her nose and flushed her cheeks. As Clerides had remarked, she went a nice copper colour.

Clerides. What was he? Not Ted's mystery partner, it seemed. So who was? The next man she would have to consider was Lance Rowley. He lived quite near Paphos and could have kept a discreet eye on the business without revealing his identity. Nor need Maritsa ever have met him face to face, because Marjorie was the one who went shopping, and Lance let her do it alone. Also he might well have visited Ted in hospital. He was one of the small number of British contacts who had stayed on for the two years and a bit since then.

It had grown dark long before she left Spiros, but her mind was too preoccupied for her to enjoy fully the moonless starlight journey back to Kalidrofi. When she drove round to garage her car she found all the garden lights were on. In the house too there was evidence of Elpida's being in charge.

Jean frowned. It was good to have support in the village,

but weren't they getting in on her a little too much? Elpida almost taking over? Even old Georgios was there tonight having drenched the evergreens, and now he was pottering about in the garden shed under the bougainvillaeas. He came out when he heard her arrival, rubbing machine oil off his wrinkled hands. '—'*Spera, Kyría.*' And then, almost in the same breath, pettishly, 'There is a stranger on Yannakis's terrace—again.'

It was nearly a replay of the time he had warned her of Clerides's arrival. Elpida came out of the house wearing an embroidered apron and clearly prepared for visitors. Her expression was anxiously watchful.

'Not the same stranger surely?' A stupid question, she knew as she asked it; Clerides wasn't a stranger any more. In Elpida's estimation he was half way to belonging here.

'English,' Elpida said shortly. Well, that explained why both of them connected his coming with her. She and Ted had been the only foreigners to settle in the village.

'Old or young?'

'Not the one nor the other. He waits for you to come home.'

He wouldn't have needed to explain the fact. The whole village would have been aware of him, particularly since her intruder. If he had asked where she lived, someone would have said she was not at home and her household vigilantes would have been alerted to take up their positions.

'Thank you, Elpida. It was good of you both to come. I can smell coffee. Perhaps we could all have some while he makes up his mind whether to call here. But first I have to make a phone call.' Let the stranger wait a little longer if he arrived before she had finished.

She watched Elpida pour and then took her cup up to the extension telephone in her bedroom. Maybe the stranger would see the light go on up there, decide she had retired for the night and discreetly go away. She dialled the Rowleys' number and impatiently counted the rings at the far end of the line. Were they out socializing, or refusing to be interrupted during some television show? Surely not already in bed? Normally they were late risers and late to call it a day.

At last Lance answered, reciting his number.

'Lance, it's Jean.' Now that they were face to face, or voice to voice, she wasn't sure how to tackle him. What exactly did she expect of him? She couldn't demand outright, 'Were you involved in some funny business with Ted, making money on the side to finance Maritsa Kakouris's lace shop, and are you keeping quiet about it so that I'd never know and ask for some of the proceeds?' That approach was impossible; she and Lance had clashed sufficiently at their last two meetings.

'Could I speak to Marjorie, do you think?'

'I'll get her.' Curt and on his dignity.

'Jean?' Marjorie sounded over-enthusiastic, possibly a trifle drunk. 'Lovely of you to call up. What a delightful lunch you gave us! I tried ringing you twice today, but you're such a butterfly . . .' Tinkling laughter. Decidedly merry. Whatever had loosened her up must have had the opposite effect on her husband.

'Am I interrupting a party or anything?'

'Lord, no! Just our dull old selves, you know. Nice to hear a cheerful voice. I like a little chat and Lance isn't the world's best conversashal—conversationist. Trouble is, when you've been married as long as we have, and live in each other's pocket, there's nothing new left to talk about.'

'Except people,' Jean suggested.

'Ye-es. But then men and women never agree about them.'

Jean skated delicately round the apparent problem of Lance's deficiencies. 'I was going to ask you, actually, about that Kakouris girl. Ted's friend we mentioned yesterday.'

'Oh, *Maritsa*. Well, I must say I thought you took that pretty well, Jean. I mean, us blurting out . . . I don't care for the girl myself, you understand. I can't think what Ted was thinking about, getting involved with a scheming little hussy like that. Of course, you can see she had everything to gain, a refugee from the invasion, and not having two pence to rub together. I said to Lance, that first evening when she came here looking for Ted because she recognized his car standing outside . . .'

'She actually came to your house? You didn't mention that.'

'Well, as I remember, we dropped the subject sharpish yesterday, didn't we? But yes, this would be a year ago. Lance was annoyed at first, but then she fluttered her lashes at him—you know what big, dark eyes the girl has—and there he was opening a fresh bottle of gin for her and making a fool of himself over was she quite comfortable—in *my* favourite chair, too. Oh, men are so gullible, don't you think?'

'And what was Ted doing all this while?'

'Oh goodness, he wasn't there. He'd just left his car and gone off. Fishing or something. Was away a couple of days or more. He used to do that now and again. You must have known.'

'Yes, of course. I just never wondered where he left his car on those occasions.'

Downstairs there had been a ring at the front door and a murmur of voices as Elpida let in the visitor. Jean could visualize Georgios standing behind the half-opened door of the dining-room with a reaping-hook or equivalent in his hands, just in case.

'Marjorie, it's been lovely chatting to you, but I'm afraid I've got callers dropping in. Must go.'

'Lucky old you. Living it up, eh? Can't say I blame you. I'd probably do the same in your place.'

'Well, good night, then.'

''night, Jean. Keep in touch.'

That was interesting, Jean admitted, bending to the mirror to check on her face. She shook her head and her sunbleached hair flew out, then hung demurely straight. There was no time to go into the depths of what Marjorie had told her. (Marjorie's conversation deep?—that was a droll thought!) She smoothed the creases out of her skirt and went down to face her visitor.

Elpida had put on every light there was in the lounge, and the unaccustomed brilliance gave the man an added theatricality. As he rose to greet her she recognized at once the pasty, coffin-shaped head topped by scant, carroty hair; small, light eyes underlined by a series of wrinkles; tight little drawstring mouth. She felt a sudden dart of fear. 'Major Moffat? What a surprise!'

He gave a humourless smile. 'Not an unpleasant one, I hope. In fact it's Colonel, as it was already before I left Cyprus.'

'Yes, of course. I'm sorry. It's just that you were Major when—when we had most to do with . . .' She was talking too much and too fast. As if demoting him wasn't Freudian slip enough, revealing that her mind went instantly back to Ted's discharge. About which Lance had said there was 'something fishy'. No, he'd said the suddenness of his death was fishy. He'd implied that the discharge had been something of a put-up job between Moffat and the CO, Ted not being seriously enough affected by his asthma to warrant it.

The fluttering in her breast was making her mind wobble too. She had to get a grip on herself. This was her opportunity to sort these puzzles out—if she really wanted to know. And did she?

'Please forgive my calling so late, but I haven't much longer on the island. Demands of the Service, you know.'

'Had you heard that they're exhuming Ted's body?' It came out of her in a rush, and she was caught off balance by it as much as he was.

'I—there was some mention of it, yes.' He looked uncomfortable, and she knew he'd been behind the order, probing and not approving of what he'd heard.

'He died here, you know. At the house. I was with him. It was a very bad attack. He used his emergency inhaler, but it had no effect at all.'

'That can happen with a severe attack, but what brought it on? There must have been something special, unless his condition had deteriorated very rapidly in the past two years.'

'I wouldn't know what he'd been doing for most of the day. We went down to Limassol together early in the morning, called in at a couple of shops and then he was going off somewhere for a few days. It was quite windy, gale force expected, so perhaps he'd been intending to sail and called it off. I hadn't expected him back that evening.'

'So he might have been exerting himself more than usual. And windy, so there would have been a lot of sand blowing?'

'Yes, but not round here. They're good in the village about watering it down. And Georgios had drenched the garden. I remember the wistaria scent; it was very strong, gusting in whenever we opened the windows. That may have excited the asthma too.'

'M'm. May I ask how you came to hear of the exhumation order? Was it an official announcement?'

'A friend warned me.' That was all she would tell him. Such a rigid, calculating man might instantly suspect she was closer to Clerides than was true.

'Normally it is carried out at night.'

'Secretly?'

'To cause the least disturbance.'

He must know that nothing but a few birds ever disturbed the village cemetery. Few mourners left flowers there after funeral day, because on the open hillside the sun withered them at once. All the remembrancing was done in the little church, with candles.

'Tonight?' She shivered.

'Quite soon, I think. But you will probably be informed first.' He looked at her, bloodless and unpitying.

'I can't understand,' she burst out, 'why it should be necessary with a natural death. You, if anybody, must be able to assure the authorities how serious his health was; at least when he left the army. That was the finding of the Medical Board when he was granted his discharge.'

Moffat shifted uncomfortably in the chair he had resumed when she indicated it. 'There was a little more to it than that. The new CO—'

'Didn't get on with Ted.'

'Wasn't happy about some aspects of his activities— outside his instructed duties. He spoke to your husband and could get no assurance that matters would improve.'

'So he determined to get rid of him by any means available, and you fell in with his wishes!'

'It wasn't like that at all. Your husband was prepared to quit the Service provided no inquiry was started. In view of previous scandals in the Corps the CO was anxious to avoid further publicity, so it was agreed—'

'To fabricate a health record that would get him his *honourable* discharge. And you carried the rest of the Medical Board with you. That is what Lance Rowley hinted at. He said too that when Ted was in hospital you were only running tests; he wasn't seriously ill.'

'He was producing marked symptoms of asthma. You must have observed them yourself. This was due to certain substances ingested with his food. But he reacted only mildly to particles of dust and pollen. It was an interesting study of allergies. I kept detailed notes at the time because I once had some idea of writing a paper on the subject.'

'And now you have used those notes to imply that my husband shouldn't have died when he did, couldn't have died naturally, therefore somebody deliberately killed him! I'm surprised that you care to have it known how you bent the rules in fixing his discharge. I suppose that is what is known as a gentlemen's agreement? To me it's a singularly dishonourable way to rig an "honourable" discharge.'

'Mrs Mather, I had hoped you would show more understanding. It was in his best interests, I can assure you.'

'In everybody's, it seems. Well, I don't know what it was that offended the Colonel's fine feelings, and I'm not particularly interested now. Whatever Ted did, above and beyond his Service duties—which had never been called in question—was his concern only, unless it did anyone any harm. I don't see the point in dragging it into the open now, presumably to find someone who could be accused of a murder that never happened!' She was trembling and her rising voice had brought Elpida to the door.

'Madam,' she inquired, looking daggers at the visitor, 'do you wish me to serve coffee?'

'No! Oh wait, perhaps you'd better. We must remain civilized. Colonel, please sit down. There are things I still need to know, and we shall be better for some refreshment. Perhaps you would tell me why you have come this evening.'

He waited for Elpida to withdraw, then sucked in his wan cheeks and explained, 'I was unsure how much you knew of your husband's circumstances on discharge. It seemed you could be distressed if discreditable things came out suddenly of which you were quite unaware until then.'

She looked at him assessingly. 'As an officer you were in a position to keep back matters that concerned yourself. You wanted to be sure that I wouldn't demand to know too much about your assessment of my husband's health.'

'All that it was necessary to point out is that two years ago your husband was a fit man with a tendency to bronchial asthma and that natural death from asthma would not normally be expected so short a time after. Surely if there was something sinister about the manner of his dying you would wish to know who was behind it?'

Jean didn't know how to answer. Fortunately the need was obscured by Elpida's return with a large tray of coffee things which she set out on a low table between them. When she had withdrawn Jean poured out, and as she handed Moffat his cup demanded, 'Did you ever meet Maritsa Kakouris?'

'Not to my knowledge. I take it this is a lady?' His pale eyes never wavered. He looked intelligently curious.

Jean nodded. 'And did you ever go to see my husband in hospital when you were in civilian dress?'

Again he was puzzled. 'Several times. May I ask why?'

'Because I believe Maritsa Kakouris passed you leaving when she once went in to visit my husband. He said she had just missed meeting *his partner*. We both took it he meant his partner in some business he'd undertaken. But I think now he was referring to something else: your being partners in the deception that was to get him his discharge.'

'I assure you, madam, there was no impropriety in the arrangement at all.'

'Whatever you say, that is how Ted would have seen it. Partners in crime. That would have amused him. I suppose you would have preferred to think you were obliging the new CO?'

Moffat put down his coffee untasted and stood up. 'I am afraid you have completely misconstrued my intention in coming here, which was to avoid unnecessary distress to you when matters were raised in any future inquiry.'

'Oh, I quite understand that, Colonel.' Her distress, his own, what difference? He was singularly selective in his objections to cover-ups. 'Let me see you to the door.'

He went stiffly out and recovered his car from farther down the lane. this necessitated his driving past again on his way out of the village. Jean, watching from the doorway, noted that the car, a green Nissan, had a hire firm's red licence-plate.

CHAPTER 10

Back in the kitchen Jean interrupted a council of war. Elpida had thrust a tea-towel into Georgios's empty hands while she held forth on recent events, her forearms plunged in soapsuds and crockery.

'I threw away the cold coffee,' she called over her shoulder more loudly as she heard Jean come in.

'Yes, it would only keep me awake now. But save some milk for the hedgehogs.' Jean slumped at the breakfast bar. 'I suppose you heard what he came to tell me? Colonel Moffat was Medical Officer at Episkopi when my husband was there. He wants Ted's grave reopened, for a post-mortem examination.'

She saw by the silent glance exchanged by the other two that they had already gathered this. Her own raised voice would have told them as much as the unfamiliar English words. Protective eavesdropping.

Elpida presented a tragic profile. 'It is irreligious.'

Never mind irreligious, was Jean's silent protest; what about the mud-slinging, the pointed fingers? If there's talk of murder, who will be the first suspect, the only one with opportunity to cause his death? What are they going to make of it in the village? If they turn against me I could never stay on here.

'These meddlers will do themselves no good by it,' Elpida condemned the opposition. At least she still stood defensive, reducing the crisis to the level of Them-and-Us, Jean appreciated. Elpida's conviction that right must ultimately prevail, no matter how deeply disguised, was painfully familiar. 'Well, never mind,' she said again wearily, to close the subject.

Georgios took this as his dismissal, mumbled his good nights and departed, the crockery undried. Jean took over the tea-towel. She watched through the open door as Elpida took out a cracked bowl of milk to the patio now bathed in moonlight. Even this task she had to perform as a solemn ritual, pausing with the bowl uplifted before laying it, two-handed, at her feet. 'Is that all, Kyría?'

'Thank you, Elpida. Yes. It was good of you to come.'

'You will bolt the door, Kyría, because no one can see the back of the house.'

'I will. Good night.'

She sat on in the kitchen, silent now but for the quiet tick of the clock and the humming fridge. Her day bag was still on the floor where she had dumped it on coming in. Elpida would not have presumed to open it and take out her damp swimming things.

She did that herself now, running cold water in the sink to leave them soaking overnight. They smelled of the sea and the boat, and also of Clerides's cigars. As she shook out the towel something fell to the tiles with a clatter. It was the small, misshapen pebble or piece of metal which he'd given her as a memento. She swished it absently through the water and set it on the window-sill. Then she bolted the door, switched off the lights and went through to the drawing-room.

Elpida had plumped up the cushions and beaten from the seats any evidence of the disagreeable interview with Moffat, leaving only one table lamp alight. Jean went across, selected a record and put it on the turntable. Bruch's First Violin Concerto stole into the room, poignant with memories of Ted sitting here with her, hand-in-hand as it unwound its tale of longing and satisfaction. She reached out and held on to the corner of a cushion, squeezing until it hurt, while jumbled echoes of the day flitted mothlike through her mind: Ted's car left outside the Rowleys' while he went off sailing; her own body stretched out on *Zoë-Zephyr*'s deck as she dried in the sun; the dive; the dangerous underwater embrace; Clerides, the man from Athens, the face in the stone; and then abruptly, as the music cut off, Ted's agony as he fought for his last breath, dying on the garden room floor.

Jean turned her face into the cushions and wept until her eyes burned.

Next morning she started to sort things out.

As early as 8.30 there was a visit from the Coroner's Officer with questions and official forms. She wiped it all from her mind when Maritsa's telephone call came through.

'I have seen him, Mrs Mather! Yesterday, less than half

an hour after the other one you showed me. I am sure it is
he, the man your husband said was his partner!'

'I think I have guessed the man you mean,' and Jean
described Colonel Moffat for her benefit.

'Yes, it is the same man. He drove a hire car through
the centre of Limassol. I was almost close enough to touch
him.'

'He came to see me last night,' Jean told her. 'You
misunderstood what my husband said about him. They
were connected in some quite different way, not any business
deal. Ted was making a sour joke which he didn't expect
you to understand. I'm afraid we're no farther forward in
tracing the man you need.'

As she laid down the receiver it came to her quite clearly.
Perhaps this 'business partner' was not to be found because
he didn't exist. Ted wasn't the sort to share responsibility.
He led, with the others well behind him. He would have
taken charge of his own affairs, certainly his own money.
It was less a case of finding a cashier than of finding a
cache.

She would need to consider every inch of this house as a
potential hiding-place for valuables, and think back to the
stages of its reconstruction, to work out where he would
have had a safe put in, or had a space left in which he could
set one himself when all the builders had left. More clearly
than ever in his lifetime she could see his mind at work, the
total man of whom she had been permitted to glimpse only
a few facets. She knew now there had been much more to
him, like the dark side of the moon.

This morning she was due to go down to the pottery for
her second lesson. Because it intruded on more essential
matters, she was tempted to cancel, but once there, with
her hands in the wet, slippery clay, she found that she was
also working on herself, firming and shaping. Definitely
therapeutic. At the end of the session she felt more capable
of the search for clues, perhaps even of predicting in which
direction they might lead her.

She tidied herself in the primitive little washroom the potters used, then set her car downhill, making for Limassol harbour. It might be irrelevant to Ted's mainline interest, but the enigma of Lance's boat still itched in her mind. After all, if Ted used to leave his car at the Rowleys' when he went off on his private missions, it was more than likely he'd gone in Lance's boat. Coral Bay wasn't a terminus for anywhere important inland.

So if Clerides had hired *Zephyr II* from Baroutis and it was really *Zoë* incognito, it would be interesting to see what name was on the bow today. A visit to the boatyard during siesta, with a precautionary disguise of headscarf and dark glasses, might cast fresh light on Clerides or Lance, or even both.

She parked the Morris on the sea-front, ordered a Greek salad and yoghurt at the Spider's Web and sat watching the passers-by until they thinned out and the afternoon torpor took over. Then she drove through the town centre and left the car near the Customs Building, going the rest of the way on foot.

It was hot and the quaysides dusty. She found the shed at last, set among several of the same kind, possibly more valuable today as a site than as a going concern. She identified it from a printed notice pinned to a board just inside the sliding gates above the slipway. 'G. Baroutis and Sons' advertised boat repairs, stripping and painting; hire of small craft. The initial G presumably referred to the father from whom Stelios had inherited, he and the drowned Kostas being the sons. Inside, the building was total silence and an empty space where she had hoped to find a sailing-boat undergoing transformation. Disappointed, Jean went in, her eyes adapting to the shadowed interior.

Stelios Baroutis was not a tidy man. Tools were left about in a surprisingly trustful way, but there had been an attempt to organize larger equipment. To one side fishing nets had been hung along the walls and there was an open bin containing bright plastic floats. Farther in she noticed a deep chest with a new padlock attached. No problem there, since there had been a bunch of keys hanging from a hook on the notice-board. Jean tried three before the right one opened the padlock.

Whatever revelation she had expected, this was further disappointment. There seemed to be no reason why Baroutis should take special care of its contents. The deep wicker baskets—like the old-fashioned ones British housewives once took on wheels to go shopping—were not much different from the fish skips stacked over by the nets, except that although they smelled of the sea, there was no stench of fish about them. The rest of the space was taken up with diving-gear: air bottles, harness, wet suits, goggles. Jean turned them over carefully, uncertain what she was looking for. And suddenly froze.

What lay in her hand was the lower half of a black neoprene suit, red-lined. Stuck to the inside of the waistband and above the maker's label was a name-tape with the initials EJM. She lifted it out and it hung hollow with Ted's past shape still in it.

She sat down on the edge of the chest and closed her eyes. Then she laid the suit aside and checked on the other equipment. Everything had his initials, some taped and some in ballpoint in his familiar hand. This chest, then, had belonged to Ted. He had kept a complete set of diving-gear here, apart from the one at home. Which meant he could go off spear-fishing at any time without her knowing. Why the secrecy? She had never objected to the sport. He was a man who had to be active, take risks, keep a part of himself apart.

She closed the lid and the hasp, replaced the keys, poked around a little longer. There were the sort of things one would expect in such a workshop: carpentry tools, spare electrical and motor parts, cans of marine paint, stencils for lettering boat names and identity marks (or for altering existing names!). Nothing here of special note, except that she had looked for links between Baroutis and Lance, or

Baroutis and Clerides, and instead she'd discovered that the only clear evidence here led back to Ted.

She stood outside in the hot, gritty sunshine and felt the urge to swim. In the town there were plenty of shops selling bikinis. She chose one in patterned black and white, then drove to the shore behind the Park Beach Hotel, swam out to the new breakwater and climbed up on the rocks. The sea, she thought: for all that I choose to live inland and swim in my own pool every day, I still need the sea and my love-hate relationship with it. Love-*fear*.

That's what I felt for Ted really. And that's what lies behind the fascination Clerides has for me. Fear which is an exaggerated form of respect. It is something I need, to complete me.

She slid into the water and swam farther out, until when she looked back the pine-green shoreline and white buildings beyond seemed almost alarmingly distant.

I could drown out here, she thought suddenly, and nobody would know. If I drowned I wouldn't feel alone any more, or have to worry about what enemies Ted had. But then some people would think it deliberate because I was guilt-ridden. They'd see it as a confession that I had something to do with Ted's death. And I'm damned if I'll let anyone pin that on me!

She turned and struck out for the shore, intensely alive, loving the movement of her own body slicing through the water, the salt taste on her lips, the dancing lights on the tilting surfaces ahead. Not now the menace and the morbid fancies. In an instant she and the sea were at one.

When she waded through the shallows and with pleasant weariness made for her clothes on the sand, the brief euphoria shook off with the loose drops of water. The worries returned. She was still alone and the puzzles remained.

She suppressed a wish to call at the Miramare to see if Nikolaos Clerides had been trying to get in touch with her. Yesterday he had broken the news of the exhumation only a few hours before Moffat had come to devastate her, both ahead of the official notification this morning. If Moffat had been a party to raising queries on Ted's death he might well have been informed of the intended move. But how had Clerides got to know, unless he too was in some way an official; or a complainant? Would an insurance investigator have the right to be present at the graveside when the body was recovered? She shuddered.

His actual standing still troubled her, his apparent friendliness to herself alongside his nose for something being amiss. But was the suspicion of murder sufficient to keep him here so long, at a luxury hotel, with so much time on his hands and money in his pocket?

She had a distinct feeling that he sought her company for more than the pleasure he implied it gave him. He could be waiting to pick up information he thought she possessed, or for her to make some slip that would reveal she had killed her husband. Then would he phone Athens that the job was done, the policy invalidated?

Would there actually be a clause which disallowed murder by person or persons unknown as a death on which they would pay out? Surely not. But a criminal would not be permitted to benefit from the results of a crime. So if she was the beneficiary it was in the insurers' interests to prove that she was the killer. What would then happen to the 'considerable sum' due on Ted's life? Would the assurance company make part payment to the state and retain the rest? It had to go somewhere.

She sat on the sand staring with glazed eyes out to sea while she turned it all in her mind. The best sense was still what Spiros had said. She alone could eliminate herself as the suspect, which left her free to find the true one. And because she was present at the moment when Ted died, she was in the best position to discover how it had been engineered. If indeed it had, which more and more she was coming round to believing.

Marjorie had been there too. It seemed unlikely that

she would have noticed anything which Jean had missed, but there would be no harm in going over it all with her in detail, at least to check that their stories were the same.

And she must find out where Ted had been earlier on that last day. A gale had blown up and he had come back in the evening unexpectedly. From what she had learned recently—his habit of leaving the car at the Rowleys' and 'going off'—it seemed quite likely that he'd been sailing or fishing from Lance's boat *Zoë* and curtailed the trip because of the weather.

So would Lance have been with him? Marjorie had thought that he'd gone to Nicosia but no one had checked with him about it. On the contrary he had been the one to shower Jean with questions. Disagreeable as she found it, there was a definite need to seek out the Rowleys again and get a few things straight.

Her new swimsuit had half-dried on her. She peeled it off and put on her sun dress, combed her hair through and checked her handbag. She was almost out of money, but there was a bank just fifty yards along the road which stayed open for tourists during siesta. She was just approaching it when she recognized a tall figure leaving. He was wearing a khaki safari suit and had his left forearm bandaged.

Of course, this was the nearest bank to the Miramare too, so naturally Clerides would use it. She wondered what he had done to injure himself.

She could have turned aside into a nearby shop and avoided the encounter, but she was in no mood for evasion. If Clerides was out to pin the blame for Ted's death on her she'd achieve nothing by pretending the danger didn't exist. 'Nikos,' she called, and raised a hand in greeting.

Poised on the edge of the pavement he swivelled to take her in. 'Why, Jean! How fortunate to meet you. I have tried several times to reach you by phone today.'

'I had business to attend to in Limassol. In fact I'm just

going in for some money now, then I'll be free. If you would care to wait—'

'Of course. Then we can perhaps go somewhere for a drink. I need to talk to you.'

Not as badly as *I* need you to talk to me, she thought. I must learn what the man knows or what he thinks he has against me. She smiled. 'It won't take long. Just cashing a cheque.'

When she had her money he steered her by the elbow across the traffic flow. Siesta was almost over and the streets beginning to fill again. He looked down on her hair. 'You've been swimming. I too. That's how I did this.' He indicated the bandage.

'Is it serious? What happened?'

'Only a graze, but salt water doesn't help heal it. It was my own clumsy fault. I was trying to aquaplane. Have you done any?'

'No. Isn't it like skiing underwater?'

'Something of the sort. More like hang-gliding at depth. You have a board with handgrips which is attached by reins to a hundred-foot rope connected to a power-boat. When you tilt the board down, the boat's speed pulls you underwater. You can control your depth by angling the board. It's quite fun. You should try it.'

'It sounds rather dangerous. Weren't you wearing a wet-suit top?'

'Yes, I always do with an aqualung. But I met a little defile with sharp rocks on the sides and the boat dragged me in before I could rise. It scored the back of my hand and tore my sleeve back. I was lucky.'

'What speed were you doing?'

'Not more than three knots, but the driver can't tell exactly what's below him when the sand gets stirred up. The idea is to cover ground much more quickly than by finning along the bottom. It's a restricted depth thing, of course. You can always let go of the grips if the going gets rough.'

'As you say, fun—for some—but it doesn't sound my kind of sport.' She wouldn't have imagined it was his either. He was a competent diver, as she had had the opportunity to observe, but he still struck her as an indoor breed of gangster, the godfather in his lair.

She looked up at him. 'You seem to be enjoying your time on Cyprus.'

Clerides pushed open a vine-hung gate and they entered a small taberna garden close-packed with round tables already laid for the evening meal. He smiled wolfishly. 'I detect disapproval. Is it because I mix business and pleasure?'

'It's not my place to approve or otherwise. I'm a little amazed at your professional patience, though—when I'm taking so long to unearth the policy you came for. That is your reason for being here, isn't it?'

'Primarily, but since it *is* taking so long, I have arranged to use up some of my due holiday here. I find it a pleasant place to be, and some of the company delightful. As for the policy, I realize it is not always a simple matter to sort through a dead person's affairs.'

'Particularly one who had had no intention of dying for a considerable time, if at all.' She was pushing him, because she was sure he was already protesting too much and therefore on the defensive.

'That can complicate things, I agree.' His voice was lightly ironical.

'The more so if doubts are voiced about the manner of his dying and the financial advantages to a surviving spouse?'

He gave her a hard look, took in the straight back and challenging eyes. She went on speaking with a cold anger. 'You need to know who, if anyone, was responsible for Ted's dying. Well, so do I. So I am proposing we trade information and work together on this. I'm getting tired of all these implied mysteries about my husband's lifestyle, and *very* tired of others' innuendoes about the way it ended. I know nothing about his death, but I'm damn well going to. And the more we find out, the more certain it will be that I'm entirely innocent in this.'

Clerides nodded slowly and sadly. 'You want me to tell you why you seem to come under suspicion?'

'That to begin with. And why suddenly there is to be this new post-mortem.'

'Ah.' He was silent until the waiter had filled their glasses and set down the bottle he'd ordered. 'It appears that the civilian doctor who treated your husband after his discharge from the British army had no experience of asthma. It is uncommon here. He has reconsidered his first opinion. Also, insufficient notice was paid to one of the findings in the somewhat superficial post-mortem report.'

'What finding was that?'

'The evidence of pulmonary œdema.' He scanned her face swiftly, nodding again at her look of incomprehension. 'It could be due to a number of causes; one of them the ingestion of an alkaloid poison. Which would suggest that someone deliberately killed him.' Again he paused.

'Go on.'

'You were present at the time of death. And you, it seems, taught junior science after a degree course which included chemistry, human biology and botany.'

CHAPTER 11

The wine she gulped—a mild Thisbe—might as well have been corrosive as she struggled to swallow. When she had stilled the trembling of her hands she dared to risk her voice. 'But that was so long ago. A lifetime away.'

Ted's life. If she hadn't been teaching at the Lady Melbray School, she would never have met him. He would have chanced on someone else and both their lives would have been different. But he would still be dead now, because she had had nothing to do with killing him.

She remembered so vividly that afternoon in the staff-room when almost everyone else had gone home; the Senior Mistress leaning against the window, staring down towards the road. 'There's a man hanging about. Don't know his face. Fairbanks, just slip down and see what he wants, will you?'

Jean, being the most junior of staff present, had gone without a word, taking her briefcase of exercise books to mark: Third Form Hygiene and Lower Fourth Biology. Old Thompson had tittered and said, 'If you think he's a child molester, Miss Barnes, hadn't one of us older fogeys better go?' But she turned a sour look on him and Jean had gone as ordered.

And the man had been Ted, perched on the top rail of the crash barrier by the gate, immaculate in a blue jeans suit and a short-back-and-sides to his wavy chestnut hair. The first impression she had of him was that he was disciplined, and the second that he had wickedly merry eyes, gold-brown.

'Are you waiting for one of the children?' she asked directly.

He didn't make any wisecrack which would have embarrassed her. At least not aloud. His eyes had said everything, and then he grinned. She had found herself laughing back because the situation was so corny and they both knew from the instant of first eye contact that each was going to be special to the other.

It had been Marcia Court he was waiting for, his sister's only child, a wild one who needed an eye kept on her, and at present in Detention. 'They thought there was a chance she'd come straight home if I arranged to meet her. I've just arrived on leave from Northern Ireland, and she'll be anxious to see what I've brought her.'

So they'd talked about the Six Counties where Jean had stayed with a schoolfriend five years back, and when Marcia came running out, pulling on her blazer, it turned out that their ways home partly coincided. Ted had taken Jean's briefcase from her hand and turned down flat Marcia's proffered satchel.

She'd left them at the top of the road to her lodgings and said goodbye. But the next day Ted was back, waylaying her out of sight of the school windows, Marcia having stayed on for tennis practice. That evening they had dinner together at a hotel in Canterbury and Ted had wanted to book a room there. She had simply said, 'I'm sorry, I misunderstood. I didn't mean to waste your time.'

Instead of being angry he had smiled at her with his eyes half shut and nodded. They had gone out several times more, and then his leave was over. 'When I've done my tour of duty in N.I.' he said, 'there'll be a stretch at Catterick. Maybe we could become engaged then. Think about it.' Which she did, constantly.

And they did more than get engaged; they were married, Jean never questioning the fifteen years' difference in their ages, taking him totally on trust as he did her. She gave up teaching after only seven terms and had never regretted it. By then, anyway, she knew she had studied the wrong subjects. With more spare time, she began to make up for lost opportunities by reading widely and taking a night school course in History of Art. Her whole life had changed. Instead of struggling to keep her head above water, she was sailing with the current, letting Ted strike out while she followed close in his wake, conscious of being loved and loving. Fulfilled, until now.

'That was all a long time ago,' she said again. She felt too tired and too miserable now to bridle at the man's outspoken attack.

'But the science you learned so well you won't have forgotten. Nor how to get hold of information you might need.'

She sighed. 'Might need, but didn't. Anyway, I certainly never studied Toxicology. I think if you're looking for a poisoner, you should pick on a sometime medical student. The only suitable person I can suggest for the role would be Colonel Moffat.' She spoke with some bitterness. 'But since he's pushing this inquiry, I'm sure he's safely above suspicion.'

'He could be bluffing. But I imagine a doctor could find a less detectable way to dispose of an enemy. Which raises the question, *was* he an enemy? And do we know where Moffat was at the time your husband died?'

'Ted was in a position to embarrass him, I think. Nothing more. But as for opportunity, Moffat could have prepared something toxic and sent it to Ted from England, without being here himself. But if it was done by swapping over the emergency inhaler for another which was doctored, then he would have needed an accomplice on the spot. Which implies me or Marjorie Rowley, I suppose.'

'Shall we consider this Marjorie Rowley? Tell me everything you know about her.'

Jean glared at him. 'Her name was on the list I made of Ted's known acquaintances. Are you sure you haven't already been to interview her?'

'Quite sure,' Clerides assured her, unperturbed. 'She is connected with the Lance Rowley you listed?'

'Wife. Lance was RAF, not army. And an officer to boot, but he and Ted weren't contemporaries, except as retired ex-Service British expatriates. Ted seemed to regard him as something of a joke. He's small and round, rather pompous and easily put out. I never knew him as a serving officer and he only made Squadron-Leader. I should say he's about sixty-five, and Marjorie a couple of years less. Ted referred to them as the Rowley-Powleys, and until just recently I always regarded them as indissolubly linked. They rattle on like a comedy double-act, but it could be that Marjorie does it with her tongue in her cheek.

'We met them at social occasions of their making, then we had to invite them back, but we didn't really have a lot in common. I think they both missed the companionship of the Officers' Mess and tried to recreate it, even including Ted who'd never taken a commission.

'It was just accidental that Marjorie happened to have called when Ted came home that day. Lance had gone to Nicosia, I remember, so no doubt she felt at a loose end. When Ted collapsed it certainly upset her, she lost her head, couldn't even cope with ringing the doctor.'

'Tell me what happened, right from when your husband came in.'

'We were in the garden room. Marjorie was enthusing over some things she'd ordered from a catalogue: canvases for working in *gros point* with coloured wools. She'd spread them over the floor and Ted wasn't in the best of tempers when he walked in on us.'

'Why that?'

'I supposed it was due to the sudden squall. He'd had to curtail whatever he'd planned to do.'

'Some water activity, you think? Sailing, skiing, fishing, skin-diving?'

'Probably spear-fishing. He used to make up parties for that.'

'He had a boat of his own, then?'

'No, he borrowed or hired one, I think. That's what I did too, whenever I wanted to sail; dinghies in my case.'

'Go on. This Marjorie had scattered the embroidery things on the floor and he walked all over them.'

'Not over them, just through them. But I never said that. How did you . . .'

'I could see him. He didn't suffer fools gladly, would you say?'

'That's true. But I'm not sure Marjorie is the fool he thought her. She does whiffle on interminably at a level that takes no mental effort, but lately—since I've been on my own—I've noticed her more. She's just saying things she supposes you expect her to say, but her mind's elsewhere. How busy, is anybody's guess.'

'Having something to conceal?' Clerides considered this.

'I wouldn't say that. More putting out her patter for the routine double-act with Lance at a bored level, and having a more worthwhile use for her mind at the same time.'

Jean paused to think over what she had said. 'I suppose what I've just noticed, without realizing its full meaning, is that they're not Siamese twins any more but coming apart.'

'Does that have any bearing on what happened on the evening we were talking about?'

'None, really. It was just a footnote to Ted's attitude towards her.'

'So when your husband arrived home, did Mrs Rowley make a move to depart?'

'No. There was a funny sort of atmosphere, as though each of them was silently needling the other. Ted clearly wanted rid of her, but for my sake wouldn't be outright rude, and she saw no reason to leave before she was ready. I suggested getting some supper for Ted, thinking she'd take the hint, but she included herself in. So we all sat down, still in the garden room, to cold chicken salad and a bottle of wine, but no one was actually hungry.'

'What did you talk about?'

Jean tried to remember. 'Trivialities. There didn't seem any common ground. I went on for a bit about the garden, and Marjorie mentioned her neighbours at Coral Bay. I don't think either of us really listened to the other. Ted certainly didn't. He seemed abstracted. Looking back, I guess he could already have been feeling unwell. He only pushed his food around the plate. If we'd been alone I might have been more aware—'

'This isn't a confessional, just a recap of the circumstances.'

'Right, then. While I was clearing the table, Ted went off down the garden. Marjorie was sitting in an easy chair with her legs crossed and swinging one shoe loose of her heel. It sounds rather elegant, but I remember thinking how absurd the pose was on a small, fat person. I must have been getting edgy.'

'And then?'

'Marjorie suddenly jumped up saying she wanted to borrow a book. She went across to the shelves and was looking through the titles. I walked out on to the terrace, and I heard Ted coughing.'

'Did he do that a lot normally?'

'No. Sometimes in the morning he needed to clear his throat several times, but this was different, as if he couldn't get enough air in. I ran down the garden and helped him back indoors. He looked grey. He sat in his usual chair, facing the open terrace. Marjorie ran to get him some water. His inhaler was in his shirt pocket and I gave it to him. He took two puffs. The wheezing had come on really badly. In all the seven years we'd been together there had never been an attack like that. He tried to get out of his chair and slid forward on to the floor.

'I shouted at Marjorie to ring the doctor. His name and number were on a list beside the kitchen phone.'

'But you say she didn't manage this?'

'She'd left her glasses among her sewing things, so she couldn't read the figures properly. She had two wrong numbers before she shouted that I'd have to come myself. Ted was breathing in a terribly laboured way by then. I chanced leaving him, but when I got back he'd collapsed.'

'How long were you away?'

'Two minutes, three. I don't know. In a crisis time goes haywire. I had to handle the whole call myself because Marjorie ran off the instant I took the receiver out of her hand. When I rushed back she was kneeling beside him holding his hand and talking to him. She didn't seem to know he wasn't breathing.'

'Did you try to resuscitate him?'

'Yes. Mouth-to-mouth, but there was no response, and all the time Marjorie was having hysterics at full volume.'

'Terrible for you. And now I'm making you go over it all again.'

'I've gone over and over it so many times. Whenever I

wake in the middle of the night I ask myself what else I could have done; whether, if I'd been on my own when Ted came back, he might still be alive today.'

'And just what do you mean by that?'

'That I'd have noticed the state he was in and headed it off somehow. Talked him into a happier frame of mind anyway. Got him to relax.'

'Blaming yourself again. Not the intrusive Marjorie?'

'She wasn't to know, poor fool.'

'But haven't you hinted that she's not the fool she appears? She was present at the meal you shared. When he became ill she ran for water. Did she force it on him? Whether on purpose or by misfortune, she delayed the call for a doctor. When you had obtained the number for her she wasn't there to take over. She went back to your husband's side, and when you were free to join them he was past saving. There you have all the elements you'd need for a good case against Mrs Rowley.'

Jean stared at him. 'You want to make a killer out of *Marjorie*? That's ludicrous!'

'Earlier you offered the choice between her and yourself.'

'That was sarcasm. She was just a statistic. I know I didn't harm him, and I've no reason to think she would; or could, either.'

'But it was she who was there when he actually breathed his last? And I'm sure you once referred to your husband dying in *your* arms. So that was more figurative than literal. I wonder who else has heard you say that?'

She put a damp hand to her head. 'Nikos, do you think we could have some coffee? This wine doesn't seem to suit me.'

'Of course.' He sanpped his fingers for the waiter and gave him the order, then turned to Jean with a crooked smile. 'It's not such a bad wine, but you have had the best part of a bottle.'

'I have? I'm sorry, I didn't notice you refilling my glass.' She gave a hopeless shrug. 'Nervy, I guess.'

'I hope it's not me that you find alarming.'

'Of course not.' She stopped and looked squarely at him. 'But you are – disquieting, I'll admit. Especially when you appear to be on the same side as me and I know that really you're just lulling me, waiting for me to let out some damning admission of guilt.' She shook her head wretchedly. 'Do you honestly believe I could have done what seems to have been done?'

He gazed gravely back, and his face was one of judgment, the face she had chiselled out of that first block of sandstone. 'Not for one moment, Jean, but I know that others might be less convinced, in view of appearances. I'm trying to assess the worst aspects for you, and to see how you'll answer if suspicion comes out into the open.'

'And as an impersonal juryman, how do you find the prisoner: guilty or not guilty?' She tried to sound jocular, but the waver of uncertainty was there.

'It's far too early to say one way or the other. We need to know much more, about your husband's activities and about the people he spent most of his time among. Not least, I think, about your friends the Rowleys and their circle.'

The coffee had arrived and Clerides took it on himself to do the pouring, raising an eyebrow as he indicated sugar and milk. In this interval Jean silently debated whether to confide one more discovery to this disturbing man. It touched on his own activities, and according to how he reacted she might be able to assess the depth of his deception, or at least whether there existed a sinister connection between him and one other on the perimeter of the mystery.

'I'll tell you one funny thing I noticed,' she offered, taking the cup and saucer he held out.

'What is that?'

'Zoë.'

His gaze remained level and inquiring. 'Who is she? Or do you mean the Greek word for "Life"?'

'She's a twenty-four-foot sailing boat I several times went out in with friends. It belongs, or so I thought, to Lance

Rowley, and normally he keeps it near his home at Coral Bay.'

'What about it?'

'I've been out in it recently, with you. Only then it was called *Zephyr II* with the original name painted over.'

She watched puzzlement, incredulity, then sudden en-lightenment pass rapidly over his face. If she had not been watching so keenly she might have missed the sequence, so brief was the flicker. Now Nikos was grinning grimly. 'The old rogue!'

'Lance Rowley?'

'No. We've never met, so far as I know. The old rogue I mean is a boatman called Baroutis. Someone at the hotel suggested his name as I wanted to hire a small yacht. At first he said everything was already booked, but when I offered good money he had second thoughts. *Zephyr II* was the result. He delivered the following morning. Not a bad little craft and well maintained, I thought. I still have her, tied up along at the Sheraton marina. So you recognized her despite the changed name? And you never breathed a word to me! What made you so positive it was the same boat?'

Jean told him about the identical white-dots-on-blue crockery with the chipped sugar basin, and the familiar cigarette burn under the plastic ice-tray in the fridge.

He smiled. 'There's no better detective than a good housewife. So you've proved some connection between your husband's friend Rowley and a boatman called Baroutis who is based on Limassol. Is there something sinister in that, apart from Baroutis hiring out a boat which was supposedly left with him for overhaul? I've heard of car repair firms doing much the same, and in this case it's easier; there's no need to turn back a mileometer.'

'There's more than coincidence to it, surely? Rowley is connected with Baroutis who is connected with you. So now Rowley is connected with you.'

'And as I said before, I have never met the man Rowley.

Cyprus is not immense, and the sailing fraternity a very small part of the community. Such tenuous connections are bound to occur. In any case, what would such a connection imply?'

Jean hesitated, sensing some undefined danger ahead, yet longing to have him dismiss her further unease. Should she mention that she had checked up on the Baroutis boatyard and found a close personal link with her dead husband? Clerides could discount that as yet another explicable coincidence. Or would he see that her suspicions regarding the diving also extended to himself, who was linked through Baroutis to Ted?

So much wine and now the coffee gave her a good excuse for withdrawal. While she splashed water over her face to freshen herself in the diminutive ladies' room, she turned the risks over in her mind and opted for caution. What Clerides didn't know that she knew couldn't harm her.

She had already given him far more information than she had intended, and learned precious little about him in return. His emphasis on her own vulnerable position had put her too much on the defensive.

When she returned to their table she gave him a warm smile. 'I have a lot to thank you for, Nikos, not least for rescuing me from my morbid imaginings. I'm sorry I've been such prickly company, and I do feel better now.'

But she declined his offer of dinner and a night of Greek dancing. There was Gregoris's little frog to finish, and if she held out on one invitation, Clerides might offer an alternative.

Almost as though he read her mind, he said, 'There's always tomorrow. Perhaps you would like to go swimming again from the incognito *Zoë*? Then you can show me how you identified her.'

'I should like that very much.'

Would she, though? It seemed likely that Ted used to go spear-fishing off that very boat. Maybe if she looked harder she could find some evidence of him there still. There was something claustrophobic about the way her horizons were constantly closing in, bringing his death into focus in whichever direction she looked.

CHAPTER 12

During the uphill drive home she had plenty to ponder. Jigsaw pieces were floating in her mind, needing only to be turned to fit into the whole. Lance's boat, renamed by Baroutis, hired by Clerides, which she would be swimming from tomorrow—diving from, probably; Ted's diving gear in the chest at the Baroutis boatyard; and a missing piece which she knew she had seen but could not for the moment put her hand on. It was there, on the edge of her memory, but still evasive. Something to do with Clerides, diving and the boat. And it could connect with Ted. What was it?

As soon as she entered the house she remembered, and went straight into the kitchen. The memento Clerides had given her after their dive together: she had rinsed it under the tap and left it to dry on the windowsill. A small knobbly pebble or bent piece of metal. She'd taken it as a whimsical joke and not really looked at it twice. But he'd meant her to, she was sure of that now. By giving it to her he had been making some significant move. And he would have expected a reaction. The very fact of her not reacting must have been some kind of answer to him. It was essential that she find the thing and take another look.

Elpida would have dried it off and put it in a place of safety, but where? She tried the knife drawer, the glass cabinet, the shelf for her indoor begonias. Not there.

She went through the house, hunting in all the obvious places and a few of the unlikely ones. After that, the frankly impossible places—the bathroom cabinet, the fridge, her handkerchief box.

Of course, if it was a stone Elpida would have put it with her sculpting things. Jean went out to look on her workbench on the side balcony, and it was nowhere there. But the beginning of the small green frog was. It rebuked her. She thought of the boy's face lighting up next time he saw her, and crestfallen when she shook her head.

She had come back to work on the frog, but concentration was impossible until she knew what Elpida had done with the Clerides pebble. She exhausted what, knowing Elpida, was the most unlikely possibility of all—that it had been thrown out with the rubbish. Carefully she sorted the refuse on sheets of newspaper on the terrace. Nothing. It only remained for her to go and ask Elpida herself.

Jean went out of the house and down the village street. Elpida's widowed sister was sitting in the last patch of sunlight by her door, working on a drawn-thread tablecloth. She beamed when Jean came hurrying along. 'You wish Elpida, missus?' she asked. 'She go car riding with my son, fine driver. Back soon. Just to cemetery to see mess they make.'

She was unconscious of having made any gaffe. Jean herself had carefully averted her eyes both times as she passed the iron gates on the stony hillside. Whatever horror had been removed from the ground was unconnected with her memory of Ted. She did not wish to see or know of it. Let the official ghouls do their job and leave her untouched. She would not even claim there was sacrilege in opening the earth and dead flesh.

'I wanted to ask her something,' she said vaguely.

'You all right?' the sister demanded, peering.

'Yes, fine. A little tired.'

'I tell Elpida and she come at once.'

'If it isn't any bother. I've lost something, you see, and it could be important.'

'I tell her. She come fine.'

Well, that was all she could do for the moment. She hoped that when Elpida did drop by she wouldn't be full of details about the state in which the diggers had left the cemetery. It would be a *miserere* plus Cassandra in full flood.

As she turned away the roar of the nephew's over-revved Panda rose from the hollow below. She waited and it came up in a cloud of dust, he beaming and red-faced, Elpida crepuscular as befitted the solemn occasion. 'Ah, Kyría,' she said descending tragically, and folded Jean damply in her arms.

'Elpida, I just came down to ask if you noticed a pebble on the kitchen windowsill last night?'

'No pebble.' Elpida came straight down to earth. 'But there was an old coin. I didn't know what it was, but I gave it a good scrub. It came nice then. Real gold, just like in the museum.'

'Oh no!' An ancient coin, which Clerides had meant her to connect with their dive from *Zephyr II*. Probably valuable. And she hadn't acknowledged its worth.

'No? I did wrong, then?'

'Not you, Elpida, no. I hadn't realized what it was. So where did you put it?'

'Just where I found it, on the same spot. It will be there now.'

'I'm afraid it isn't.'

Elpida drew herself up and wound her black shawl about head and shoulders. 'I show you. We will go in the car.'

Delighted, the nephew dusted off a seat in the rear and made room for Elpida beside him. They accelerated in low gear up the remaining eighty yards to the old schoolhouse.

Surveying the empty windowsill, Elpida was astounded and indignant. 'We never have robbers in Kalidrofi,' she protested. 'Somebody bad has come up from Limassol, or even Larnaca. It is since these Lebanese come, no one is safe.' Jean was glad that she stopped short of suggesting a Turkish raid from beyond the Green Line.

'I'm sure the village would know if any strangers had been here,' Jean soothed, sorry now that she had possibly started up a major scandal in local affairs. 'It has probably rolled off into a corner somewhere. Or a bird saw it shining and went off with it, like the Jackdaw of Rheims.'

'Jack who is this?' So Jean had to explain the story, which was all rather exhausting and time-consuming, when she could have been getting on with the frog for Gregoris.

Elpida said a respectful goodnight and went plunging off down the village street on foot, but at least Jean now knew the memento had been a coin. She needn't tell Clerides she had already lost it. A few oblique remarks should elicit what sort of coin it was, its age and provenance. But why give it to her at all? A coin—as payment? For what?—no, he wasn't that crude. It had a different significance.

Could he have picked it up off the floor of the sea bed as he'd said? Surely not. Perhaps he'd bought it off some fisherman down at the harbour. She shrugged it off for the moment.

Slipping on her overall, she switched on a spotlight over the balcony worktable. With the change of activity she achieved a shift of mind from past to future. Tomorrow had its own commonplace demands. She began to plan the basket of food she had persuaded Clerides it was her turn to provide for the outing. There would be a fresh salad, a pot of the special pâté from Yannakis, sliced cheeses, rolls and butter, wine, yoghurt and one of her own quince crumbles defrosted from the freezer. Nothing complicated: Clerides wasn't Marjorie.

While she planned, her fingers were busy chiselling, rubbing at stubborn lumps with damp wire wool. The frog was emerging, a complacent, full-throated Romeo of the swamp. Gregoris was going to love him.

Creativity brought its customary reward. By bedtime she was soothed and ready for sleep. She lay relaxed and waited. In the recesses of her mind something stirred and came awake.

One implication of her accepting Nikos's invitation had been suppressed, much like the unfinished garments which Madame Bovary had buried at the back of her cupboards, finally accepted as beyond her skills to complete. Now, while Jean's eyes adapted to the dark, her mind too had to make adjustments. She had to face what she had suppressed, and come to terms with it.

Last time, underwater, he had kissed her. Not a passionate kiss, because with their masks and his scuba gear there was inevitable clumsiness, but a kiss had been his intention and she hadn't rebuffed him. She remained as mystified by her own complex reaction then as by his motivation, but alarm had certainly been a part of it, and not only on account of the physical fear of drowning.

She felt that by that one outrageously dangerous act he had somehow identified himself with the sea and her love-fear for it, having much the same character and the same power to affect her. Why do that just then, under those risky conditions? To underline the threat that she already sensed him to be?—that he was playing some sinister game with her? And, significantly, once safely aboard again he had displayed no special tenderness towards her nor shown any need of returned affection.

Anyway, affection wasn't what she'd felt. I'm not some magazine heroine, she protested—a droopy, drippy widow with sentimental longings. The response had been pure chemistry, a reminder of what her body had been built for.

There was something about the man Clerides—reckless, ruthless, a *winner*—that echoed Ted; only, in the end Ted had lost out. Two of a kind, yet different; but the same response from me. Physical. Desire happens; there's no pretence and no guilt in it.

Maybe I should be glad that I'm coming alive again. It's a kind of proof that some day the zombie phase will end and real life reassert itself. So what do I do then?—say 'Sorry, Ted, but I'm not dead like you'? Go ahead and take what I want? But at least not until I've repaid my debt to you, love, rogue as you must have been. Somehow I'm going to find out who, if anyone, got at you.

Tomorrow, by accepting Clerides's invitation to dive, what was she committing herself to? Would he assume too much, assured by his robust male ego that what she had proposed was more than a partnership in investigating her husband's death?

She hadn't the sophisticated skills to deal with casual affairs, conditioned as she'd been to a monogamously grooved existence. She had assumed that bereaved she would remain alone, inviolate. That assumption could have been quite faulty. She had miscalculated her own weakness. She could be overwhelmed and then discounted. She could be made to suffer, because it wasn't in her to snatch the moment and lightly wave it goodbye. Tomorrow could immerse her in very deep water, except that now she was aware of herself in a new way and so forearmed.

She wished, spreading apricot jam on toast for breakfast next morning, that she could casually tell Clerides she had lost the coin, his love-token or whatever; but such airiness wasn't in her repertoire. If she admitted its loss she would sound apologetic, so instead she would stay stumm, avoid the subject, keep solidly to the investigation.

'I don't know why I'm giving myself a holiday,' she said, taking the passenger seat beside him in the Miramare car park. 'I should really be hounding the Rowleys. Didn't we agree that if I wasn't the guilty one then Marjorie must be?'

'I don't know that you accepted the notion, or that we simplified it that far. It must really depend on what they discover in London.'

She turned quickly to him. 'Where does London come in?'

'Apparently the full chemical analysis can't be done locally. The nearest forensic department of that type would be in Athens, but Cyprus still looks to Britain before Greece for anything highly technical. Take for example this crazy system of driving on the left.'

'Nikos, are you trying to tell me that they are flying Ted's body to London for the post-mortem?'

'Yes.' His profile was inscrutable as he drove, more graven and stony than ever.

'Does that mean they've found something which deserves looking into further?'

'Jean, it happened over two months ago. This is a hot climate. There wouldn't be anything as precise as stomach contents left. It's their only chance of finding anything at all.'

She had tried not to think of the body's decomposition. *Tissue slurry*. That was the term she'd once read in some textbook and even then it had sickened her. 'You said stomach. So they do suspect poison by mouth, rather than something he breathed in.'

'Yes, it's a new angle to consider. And I'd been puzzling how a lethal capsule could have been inserted in the inhaler. Pulmonary œdema, we were told the other day, so I thought of irritant gases and insecticide sprays. But an alkaloid poison taken by mouth, that's quite different.'

'It could still be insecticide,' Jean said with quiet horror. She was remembering the little pressure pump with the long curved nozzle which she used for her indoor plants. Inserted down the throat of an unconscious victim it could introduce the vapour direct into the stomach without leaving traces on tongue or mouth linings. The spray always stood, ready filled, on the shelf in the garden room, tucked behind the biggest pot of begonias. She couldn't remember what base the poison had but it might well be nicotine, the most dangerous of alkaloids. Nor could she remember when last she saw it. She only knew that there had been no white fly for many weeks, so she hadn't needed to check. If it had disappeared, that meant something sinister. And if it had not been removed it would be there for the investigating police to find; with her fingerprints all over it.

'I can't picture your husband willingly tucking into insecticide,' Clerides said drily. 'Unless, of course, you disguise it in your salad dressing. Are we to risk sharing your salad today, by any chance?' Black humour sat easily on his predatory features.

'We are indeed having salad, and he did at his final meal,' Jean said hollowly, shocked by his insensitivity. But to be fair, Clerides wasn't to guess what new horrors had just risen in her mind. 'However, on that occasion the salad was dressed in the serving bowl and well tossed. We all had some, and neither Marjorie nor I felt any ill effects.'

'Then your husband walked down the garden, out of sight, and you heard him coughing. Of course, it could be something toxic he'd come across there. You don't grow nicotianas, by any chance?'

She did, from seed, because of their wonderful scent at night. And two years back, instead of the variety *affinis* which she'd ordered, the supplier had mistakenly sent *Nicotiana tabacum*—the large-leaved plants from which tobacco was harvested. When prepared, a distillation of the juice would produce a brew so lethal that even handling the pure extract could cause almost instant death. It would require some laboratory equipment, but who would believe that she couldn't obtain and use that?

Clerides had pulled up at the marina and was studying her with a frown. 'Am I to understand from your silence that you do grow nicotianas? I meant it only as a joke.'

'In bad taste,' she told him.

He laid his hand unexpectedly over hers. 'I am truly sorry. Let's forget this disagreeable business for the moment. We could worry over a dozen different methods when only one was used. One poison and one killer. Which will come to light through scientific examination. Meanwhile we wait in patience and take reasonable precautions to see that nobody else comes to harm.'

She looked up in alarm. 'You think there's risk of a second killing?'

'How can we tell, not knowing the reason for the first? We must go carefully, and any clue we discover must be kept between the two of us. There could be danger if the guilty one thinks we're getting too close to the truth.'

'Yes, I see.' It sounded complaisant, but she was disturbed. Keeping their suspicions a secret could sound like protection of the guilty party. And you had to be very sure of the one person you confided in, to go on feeling safe yourself.

'Now let's get aboard. I've a mind to sail westward along the coast, if that appeals to you. Then we can anchor offshore somewhere near Aphrodite's Rocks and swim with snorkels. Unless you want to go deeper with air bottles?'

'I'd rather snorkel, I think. I'll go below now and put our lunch in the fridge.'

But as she stepped on board a face appeared out of the cockpit and a small, dark youngster stood up, nodding to Clerides who waved towards him. 'This is Marcos, Jean. He works for Baroutis and I've taken him on as caretaker-crew. He doesn't speak much English. Just pretend he's not here. I warned him to bring his own food.'

He didn't speak much Greek either. When she greeted him he smiled awkwardly, wiped a hand across his mouth and then down the side seam of his shorts. It seemed he wasn't a mastermind.

However, a third party present was some sort of guarantee of Clerides's proper intentions, Jean reflected. And it would excuse him from making any advances he hadn't his heart in!

He couldn't have been more proper, and as promised, no reference was made to forensic topics. His conversation was light and knowledgeable, so that in responding she had to keep her whole mind on the subject.

His familiarity with English was quite incredible and she questioned him about his years in the Home Counties as a boy. His father had worked in banking in the City, his mother had died when he was seven and an aunt kept house for them in Windsor where he had gone to school. Later he'd boarded for two years at Eton College, in New House, before the whole family had returned to Athens. Which explained a lot, she decided, including his polyglot mixture of intellectual arrogance and old-fashioned courtesy. With such a background it was remarkable that he was content to work for an insurance company in Athens.

They hugged the coastline, tacking to make the most of a fresh south-easterly breeze. He had chosen the best direction both for speed and scenic beauty, once past the headland of Akrotiri. Several times he pointed to the cliffs and demanded what some large building or ruin might be and she told him, unsure whether he was simply curious, hiding his own familiarity with the area or testing out hers. There were several shallows where she warned him of underwater hazards, but for the most part he had an instinct for interpreting surface signs and the water here had a glorious clarity so that rocks were discernible some way ahead.

At the Rocks of Aphrodite they dropped anchor and snorkelled to the sandy bottom, collecting tiny shells. Clerides left her to swim free, only giving her a hand up to climb aboard at the end.

They had their lunch in late afternoon, and when Jean expected him to turn for home Clerides said, 'I have a suggestion. We are more than half way to Paphos, and Coral Beach is not a long way after that. We could leave the boat there with the lad and return by taxi. What do you think? I have a wicked fancy to walk in on your friends the Rowleys and let them see *Zephyr II*. What do you think their reaction would be? It's a poor seafarer who doesn't know his own vessel.'

The deviousness of the man! Right from the start, Jean thought, that is what he had decided to do. Which explains why this time he's brought Baroutis's lad along. The picnic, the swimming, his autobiography and charm were all mere cover for getting me to make this introduction to the Rowleys, so that he can start taking them to pieces bit by bit, just as he does with me!

And he had the gall to ask what she thought! He deserved

her veto on it, except that she found the prospect intriguing. He was a shrewd judge of people, and it could do no harm to hear whether his opinion of Marjorie and Lance coincided with her own. She might also have her curiosity satisfied about *Zoë-Zephyr II.*

CHAPTER 13

It was clearly the wrong time to call; although, Jean saw, it might well be ideal for Clerides's purpose. They seemed to have interrupted a first-class marital row, Lance visibly puffed out with suppressed rancour. Marjorie, unduly flushed, was for the moment too busy covering up the situation to jump to any awkward conclusions about their unannounced arrival.

'Why, how lovely to see you both,' she gushed, coming forward and seizing Jean's hands as though afraid she might precipitately turn tail and leave her to a resumption of Lance's fury. 'And—er. Come in, Mr—'

She'd been drinking, Jean realized. Maybe it was becoming a habit. Certainly she had sounded pretty high one evening on the phone.

'Nikolaos Clerides.' Jean provided the introductions, mentioning Nikos as a friend from Athens, in insurance, and the Rowleys as friends in the retired Services set.

Lance eyed the newcomer with mildly suspicious petulance, feeling cheated—Jean thought—of a present discharge of spleen, but he quickly went into his host routine, rather overdoing the urging towards the drinks cabinet.

'Jean, m'dear, what'll it be? Sun's well over the yardarm. Gone down in the sea, actually. Heard it hiss m'self. Now, Martini with vodka, isn't it?'

'Martini straight would be just right, thanks.'

'Ice, twist of lemon, eh? Mr—er, Clerides. How 'bout you?'

'Brandy, thank you, with water. Just the right relaxer after a day's sailing.' He smiled wickedly at Lance's back, then accepted the glass held out to him, with a look of bland ingenuousness.

'Been at sea all day? Just what you needed, Jean. Put the roses back in your cheeks. H'm, now I come to look at you, you're positively tanned.'

'We started out early,' she told him, 'and snorkelled a bit on the way. It reminded me of those wonderful foursomes we used to have on *Zoë*. Mr Clerides has a hired boat from Limassol.'

'I hope you don't intend sailing all that way back tonight?' Lance demanded.

Clerides gave a wide, wolfish grin. 'Actually we thought of going back by taxi. I've left a crew man on board. Will there be any difficulty about the mooring, do you think?'

'Depends if you've bagged one that's normally in use. No officials just at this point, but we do respect each other's rights. You're welcome to tie up at my place, actually. *Zoë*'s away having a job done at the moment. I'll come down before you go and help you move your boat.'

'I haven't got a drink,' Marjorie said querulously. Lance darted her a venomous glance and went across to the cabinet again. They heard the bottles moved about but his hands were hidden from view. He brought back a vaguely pink mixture which Marjorie sniffed with disgust and set down at a distance from her on the side table. 'I'll just get some eats,' she offered and went out. She was gone some little time.

There was an awkward silence. Jean cast about wildly in her mind for some topic that was harmless. In the event Clerides, who seemed perfectly at ease, just beat her to it. 'You heard, of course, they'd exhumed Ted's body?'

Lance looked desperately towards Jean, in case she should make some protest, but, reassured, turned to the other man. 'I knew about the order, but not what the results are. Natural causes, I trust.'

'Oh, it's much too early to say. But they were interested in the chemical contents, sent the whole body, sealed, to London for analysis. Sounds like a thorough check for poisons, I'm glad to say.'

This has nothing to do with me, Jean swore silently, drawing back into herself. Leave them to it. I don't even know the rules of the game. I'm not sure poor Lance does either. He's gone quite pale. Nikos is a man-eater.

What exactly did he expect to do here, marching in under false colours as a friend of Ted's? His use of the christian name had made her feel instantly quite sick. If she had any courage she would stand up and walk out, put an end to the man's manipulations.

'Shall I—shall I go and help Marjorie?' she asked vaguely, but neither man seemed to hear her. Lance was on the edge of his seat, struck motionless.

'Poison? Are you sure? It was bronchial asthma Ted suffered from.'

'But it is the stomach remains that had most interest for the pathologist. Ted must have eaten something that upset him, don't you think?'

Lance put his glass down unsteadily. 'Moffat never mentioned anything about poison.'

Ah, Jean thought; Moffat, of course. Those two were the source of the original mischievous whispers.

'It seems,' Clerides went on innocently, 'that there are certain foods which produce asthmatic symptoms.'

'You mean things he was allergic to? But he was tough as old boots. He told me the only marked allergies he had were to quite obscure things he wasn't likely to come across. He was a fit man, in his prime. He wouldn't have dared to dive otherwise. I mean, the risks he'd take . . .'

'That was the sort he was,' Clerides said warmly in old pal tones. 'Anything a bit of a challenge, anything that was a little out of the ordinary, he just had to do it.'

'You men,' Marjorie said damningly, appearing from the doorway. 'The risks you take. You get away with something

a bit dodgy, and instead of sitting back and thanking your
lucky stars that you're still unscathed, you go out after more.
Not just the physical risks, like Ted, but—'

'*Marjorie!*'

'No! I won't be quiet! I've had enough of being quiet. I
told you. I told Ted; he had to let you get out before he
dragged us all into trouble. Well, he's gone, and I'm bloody
glad he is! Now you'll have to wash your hands of it.'

The silence following her outburst was not as prolonged
as Jean expected. While Lance sat petrified, Clerides leaned
slowly forward and replaced his glass on the low table. 'It's
a pity you feel like that, because I had a proposition to
make. But clearly that would be out of order.' He sighed
quietly. 'As you say, with Ted gone it's close of play. Nothing
more to be said.'

All the same, his hooded eyes opened for a moment and
made contact with the man's opposite, then he looked down
again.

Tight-lipped and rebellious, Marjorie presented a choice
of salty biscuits smeared with pâté or cream cheese. Her
usual fine hand at such things was missing, but she had
spent time covering the flush of her cheeks with paler face
powder and in so doing had smeared her lipstick. The effect
was grotesque.

'I expect your garden's looking lovely just now,' Jean
said. She had decided to introduce a topic that was impec-
cably safe.

'Hasn't Jean made a success of that place, Mr—er? I'm
sure I'd never find the time to keep it all going like she does,
though it might be fun planning it. I often think I'd like a
real garden here, but we make do with the roof and the
patio. It's not like at home where you can go to a garden
centre in any town and get just what you want—'

'Mr Clerides isn't terribly interested in growing things,'
Jean put in to stem her flow, 'except perhaps investments.'

The ends of Nikos's mouth turned up. 'I'm more of a sea
dog, actually.'

She stared at him. Descending to the Rowley-Powley level, he was even picking up Lance's clichés.

'Which reminds me.' Their host rose, smiling stiffly. 'We were going to get you tied up at my mooring, weren't we? Shall we go down and see to that, Mr Clerides, while my wife looks up the taxi number for Jean to ring?

Marjorie looked uncertain. 'How long will you be?'

'About half an hour, I should think, but don't order the taxi for as soon as that. We don't want to hasten our guests on their way.'

The funny thing was that by now he seemed to mean it. Maybe he would pour out his marital complaints to the ready-listening Clerides in the belief that he had been a confidant of Ted's. If he didn't freely volunteer information, she was sure Clerides would obtain it just the same, through the casual-sounding question and the half-truth of being already in the know. Insidious man, he had pretended it was the boat's changed name that had made him curious, but she had the feeling that really he was fishing in far deeper waters, and her own role in this was less as unwilling accomplice than as victim of a skilled con artist. She watched their backs as they left, Clerides tall and jaunty, Lance fussily concerned.

Marjorie planted herself on the satin-striped settee, clasped hands between her knees. 'Aren't men the bloody limit? Have you noticed I've started swearing? I never used to say things like "bloody", but he really makes me. Oh Jean, I thought maybe he would give up here now and we could go back to England. I do so miss it, and we're getting older all the time. I get frightened. What will happen to us when we get sick and feeble? This awful heat. I'm beginning to hate the sun, d'you know that? Long for rain, all the different sorts. Even the sooty Lancashire kind that makes everything greasy and black. Just to be able to go back and live like I used to as a girl!'

'You can't go back in time,' Jean warned her. 'Things in England have changed too, less soot in Lancashire for one thing. I suppose Lance just loves it here.'

'Well, he did. I knew he'd tire of it in time, but he thought if he stayed on a few years more he'd have made enough— saved enough, I mean—to get somewhere a bit better in England. House prices are sky-high there, you know. Isn't it disgusting that English people can't afford to live in their own country any more? After following the flag all his active life, it's so unfair! I just want to have a bit of my own life, in a village with other women who like doing the things I do, somewhere I feel I belong. But it's always been what *he* wants. It makes me want to—'

She crimped her fingers and made a diabolical face, then suddenly burst out crying. Jean went across and sat beside her, an arm across her shoulders. 'Here, have my hanky.' They sat in silence while Marjorie sniffed herself back under control.

'Will you trust me in your kitchen to make us a pot of coffee?'

'Oh, I couldn't let you do that. We'll both go.' With occupation for her hands, Marjorie was regaining confidence. She set the percolator plopping, found a pretty cloth and laid out some Worcester china on the breakfast bar. When Jean, watching her closely, decided she could face questions, she asked, 'What did you mean by saying that you thought now he would give up here. Why now especially?'

Marjorie was getting a better grip on herself. Perhaps she had cried part of the alcohol out of her mind. She thought a moment before she replied and then did so with the air of a child lying and proud of herself for doing it. 'Well, *Ted*, you see. They were so close. Lance misses him.'

Why shouldn't that be true? Jean asked herself. Ted the younger, dynamic leader; Lance, the less able, needing a push to get him going. Symbiotic, in a way. But that wasn't the whole story. It wasn't Ted himself that Lance missed. No, but Ted's death had caused something to stop, some project they had going which Marjorie had feared could bring disaster on them. And something which while continu-

ing had prevented the Rowleys returning to England as she
wished.

She must have looked on Ted as Lance's evil genius, the
man who stood between her and her heart's desire. Had she
really reproached Ted with this? Had she even, on the last
evening—while Jean was putting together the simple supper
she'd served in the garden room—made a scene which so
upset him that he had an asthma attack far more severe
than anyone thought possible in his case?

No, she was on the wrong tack there. Ted had *eaten
something* that killed him. That is what the pathologist had
suspected at the local post-mortem, and why the body
substances had been sent all the way to England for further
analysis. They must know the kind of poison; what they
needed to find out now was where it had originated. Nothing
to do with Marjorie making him angry.

The men came back from the boat, Clerides with an air
of grave satisfaction, Lance almost bouncing with breathless
importance, and Marjorie made fresh coffee for them. Preoccupied with this, she was so clearly, Jean thought, the
ideal candidate for a WI chairwoman. That was the life
she longed for, and which Ted had suborned Lance into
depriving her of.

She said as much to Nikos as they were driven back to
Limassol in a long black Mercedes saloon that looked suited
to a Mafia funeral. 'Maybe,' he said.

'You're rather short on conversation suddenly.'

He hadn't given her much idea of his tête-à-tête down at
the boat except to confirm that Lance had been disconcerted
at first sight of *Zoë-Zephyr II*, then admitted he'd let Baroutis
borrow it for hire. He hadn't yet mentioned this to Marjorie
but he was thinking of selling. Getting a bit stiff in the joints,
not so keen on sailing these days.

It seemed to Jean small reason for the expression of
complicity on the two men's faces when they came back.

'Well, what did you think of the Rowleys?' she asked.
'Rather pathetic, aren't they? I don't see myself that it's

any use following them up for clues to Ted's killer. It was
a long chance, imagining that Marjorie was involved just
because she was there. She even had a motive of sorts, but
she hasn't the necessary knowledge or the means to kill
anyone by poison.'

'Tell me what motive.'

Jean explained how Lance's involvement with Ted had
prevented Marjorie's return to England and what she
thought of as her rightful element. 'Not much of a motive,'
she allowed.

'I disagree. An intense woman pushed to the end of her
tolerance, and drinking too much, her judgement impaired.
And then, you see, you are wrong in thinking she hadn't
the knowledge or the means. The knowledge was in the
bookcase right under our noses: the definitive work on
indoor plants which would certainly have contained the
information to inspire a would-be poisoner. And the means?
—three very healthy specimens of *Dieffenbachia*, commonly
known as the.Leopard Plant. Quite a small quantity of the
leaf, when chewed, could cause swelling that blocks the
breathing passages.

'You served salad with the cold chicken that night. I
imagine it wouldn't have been difficult to cause a distraction
and add extra chopped leaf to your husband's plate, while
he was occupied with opening the wine.'

'But that would mean she had it with her, ready to use.'

'Premeditation, yes. Put yourself in the place of Mrs
Marjorie Rowley who has endured years of frustration and
resentment, brooding on the evil influence of this man who
stands between her and happiness. Why not enjoy imagining
a horrible end for him? And then go further, play at it,
finally attempt the thing itself?'

Jean shuddered and sank lower in her seat. Clerides
glanced sideways and for once his smile was gentle. 'Not
everyone is calm like you, or so forgiving.'

I am anything but calm inside, Jean thought. Aloud she
said, 'If I seem forgiving it's because there is nothing to

forgive. I don't believe anyone wanted to harm Ted. And if you're thinking of Ted's affair with Maritsa Kakouris, it doesn't really affect me. We had a good marriage and he deprived me of nothing by it. It is quite something that he delayed so long before jumping into bed with her. She's very attractive.'

'And these deceptions of your so-called friends? Marjorie Rowley's amiable front when she really resented and de-tested everything that came under your husband's influ-ence?'

'If I'm to be easily upset by deception, what should I feel about you, Nikolaos Clerides—if that really is your name?'

He made a comic, quite un-Zeuslike grimace, but he made no attempt to defend himself.

'Anyway, I never looked upon the Rowleys as my friends. Acquaintances, connections of Ted's, that's all.'

'So who are your real friends?'

She refused to admit to him that she had none, and his question forced her to look further for an answer. 'My neighbours, I suppose. Elpida, Georgios, little Gregoris and his parents, Elpida's awful nephew . . .' Already she was smiling as the list grew.

'Tell me about them. The theatrical Elpida I have met, but the others—'

And again, she realized later, he had manipulated her, eased the unease he'd already aroused, and left her secure once more. As a gesture of independence she struck back suddenly on to uncertain ground. 'That ancient coin you gave me last time we swam, where did you actually find it?'

'I told you, it was on a sandy rock at the bottom.'

'You told me, but I didn't believe you.'

He laughed aloud, showing his splendid white teeth. 'Then I must come clean. Nothing so heroic. I found it in a crack of the deckboards the first time I took out *Zephyr II*.'

'You did actually book her from Baroutis?'

'Oh yes, having no idea that she wasn't his to hire out.

It seems that he has some kind of hold over Lance Rowley
—perhaps an unpaid repair bill, or knowledge of an irregu-
larity, such as minor smuggling—enough, anyway, to put
pressure on him to lend the boat when nothing else was
available. Lance rather muffed his cover story but the facts
were evident.'

'Baroutis seems a rough character. I saw him once in a
hotel bar and a friend told me who he was.'

'He's hardly a hotel type.'

'No, but he'd wandered in rather drunk and full of bile.
It's a long story and nothing to do with Lance.' She smiled
to herself at memory of the man spitting out the words,
'Whore!—just like a whore. Anybody's!' And according to
Spiro he had been talking of his caïque, commandeered by
some high-handed tourist who had dismissed him as its
skipper.

Nikos had lapsed into silence, nodding in time with some
tune he hummed under his breath. She went back on the
attack. 'That coin on Lance's boat, how do you suppose it
got there?'

'It could have fallen from the pocket of someone stripping
to swim, or it came with a load of fish from the bottom
somewhere. Your guess is as good as mine.'

Yes, she thought, it is. And I know something you don't,
because you haven't seen inside the diving chest in the
Baroutis boat shed: wicker skips used for hauling to the
surface the big fish Ted and his men speared on their dives
from Lance's boat. But Clerides had suggested smuggling
as the hold Baroutis had over Lance. Would that be the
money-making project Ted had assembled the group for?
Watertight parcels from some illegal traffic dumped in the
sea at an agreed point by a larger passing vessel, to be
retrieved later by an innocent-seeming party of scuba divers?
Which might have been why Ted hadn't cared to have her
come along. Risky, whatever the contraband. She hoped
devoutly that drugs hadn't been involved. That was a filthy
traffic.

'I was hoping,' Nikos said absently, staring out into the darkness ahead, 'to make contact with the MO, Colonel Moffat, but Lance Rowley tells me he has "scuttled back to England". A curious way to put it, I thought.'

Moffat. In a flash Jean made the connection between him and the drugs which were fresh in her mind. Could there be a link? Had that dull, coffin-faced medical officer been running a drugs ring with Ted as his leg-man? And was his reason for facilitating Ted's discharge a way of ensuring Ted would be free to stay on here when his tour of duty was over, and continue the traffic? If that were so, wouldn't it account for Moffat's wish to know who had committed murder, since he might himself be next on the list? And having set the inquiry in motion, wouldn't he be wise to get away before he could be implicated?

'Yes, here I think.' Cutting through her speculations, Clerides leaned forward and tapped on the driver's glass partition. The Mercedes swung off the road and alongside a small taberna hung with a string of coloured lights. 'Time to eat, Jean! I'm ravenous, aren't you?'

CHAPTER 14

Nikos had insisted on their taking the inland road to drop Jean off first. Her little Morris would again be stranded at Limassol, but he would drive up to fetch her tomorrow at a convenient time. She didn't protest: it had been a long day and suddenly she found herself exhausted. As the taxi turned down the village street she saw that, unusually, the house lights were not on to receive her. Then she remembered that Elpida was away, spending a few days with her sister-in-law in Pissouri. Over-zealous on protocol, she wouldn't have allowed Georgios the house keys.

'I shall come with you and check that everything's all right,' Nikos decided, but when he had satisfied himself that no one had been in, he seemed in a hurry to be gone, promising to phone at ten the next morning.

It was when Jean returned to the kitchen for drinking-water that she noticed the thin edge of white paper under the door to the garden room. This was Georgios's domain when no one was at the house. The sliding glass doors were left open and the inner doors secured. Too well schooled by Elpida into using only the rear access, he hadn't thought to post his note through the flap on the front door.

Jean pulled at the paper but it wouldn't budge, so she undid the door, smoothed out the crumpled note and tried to decipher it. A hard-leaded pencil and several folds over Georgios's eccentric spelling made it almost illegible. Something, she thought, about two men. *Asti*-something? *Enas astifilakas?* That was a policeman. There had been two men here, one from the police. They wanted to speak with her. Georgios had—blank, blank—*tó kypo? He'd shown them the garden!* One man was very interested in the flowers. They would return tomorrow.

Oh God, what did this mean? Had they already made up their minds that she was the poisoner, having the means easily to hand? And how many plants would they have listed in her garden as being capable of killing? The hydrangeas weren't open yet, but there were larkspur, aconite, delphinium, wistaria, as well as the ubiquitous oleander. Why hadn't she stuck to wholesome apricots, grapes, carobs and figs like the rest of the village? This need for flowers could seem sinister to policemen always on the lookout for criminal intent.

While she was in the garden room she went across to the shelf of begonias. Alternating with trailing evergreens, they were large, lush double flowers of brilliant colours, all set in troughs and various glazed pots. Behind the largest should be the long-spouted pressure spray loaded with insecticide. She moved the pots aside and parted the green tracery but the spray wasn't there. Apart from a few loose grains of earth the shelf's surface had been wiped clean recently and no lighter ring showed where the base of the can would have stood. So it might have been removed by herself or Georgios some time ago. Or taken this very day for analysis of the contents.

She no longer felt like going to bed. It was pointless when she would only lie there and churn her anxieties until she was sick with fear. Just a month ago she wasn't in any way uneasy about her own part in Ted's death. True, she had left him for a few minutes to sort out the phone number because Marjorie was so incompetent, but she would have had to do that if she'd been on her own.

The trouble was that she hadn't been alone, and there lay the source of her fear. If Marjorie hadn't come, would Ted have recovered? Could that wretched woman, full of her own distress and frustration, really have taken matters into her own hands and, having failed to persuade Ted that Lance should be dropped from whatever schemes they shared, had she decided to make sure he'd have no further influence over her husband?

It was pitiful, the state that woman must secretly have been in and the misery she had given way to only today, admitting that with Ted gone Lance was still staying on at Coral Bay, when perhaps she'd risked so much in opening the way for their going back to England. Only she hadn't admitted anything of the sort: it was Nikolaos Clerides who had put the evidence together and made a murderer of her.

Just as the police could make a murderer of me, she reminded herself.

But it has to be one of us and I know I'm innocent. Sorry as I am for her, if the police come for me, I shall tell them. Nothing can bring Ted back, and in her case I don't feel any need for revenge; but if it comes to a choice of her or me, then she must face up to what she did.

Jean went slowly out into the garden. All its wonderful night scents hung heavy on the still air; the enchanting scents of her poisonous flowers. The earlier breeze, so pleasant on the shore, had dropped and deposited a surly lid of cloud pressing down the heat of the exhausted day. She felt it in her own head, pulsing with a dry insistence.

She reached for the pool lights and the blue tiles came winking up at her through the clear water. Only the little spurts from the circulating pump caused any movement at all on its surface. She dropped her clothes where she stood and slid softly into the water, not caring to disturb the stillness with a dive.

The water was as warm as the air. She had a curious sense that she could fold it about her like a downy quilt and sleep in it. For a while she lay floating, then rolled over and swam strongly for the pool's far end. She continued, varying her strokes, length after length under the timeless dark, until her body was as exhausted as her mind. Then she crawled out by the steps, picked up her discarded clothes, put out the lights and went dripping indoors. The day was over, and she had had enough.

At some time during the night she awoke whimpering. The pressure spray can had dissolved in her hands even as she tried to force it down the back of Ted's throat. He lay still beside her, not breathing, his eyes closed and pennies laid on them. But not pennies at all. They were some more ancient coin, thick and roughly shaped, dull gold. And then, as she watched, Ted's face began to change, to elongate, take on deep grooves between nostrils and mouth. 'Nikos?' she said. 'Nikos, what shall we do with the body?' But he only smiled, still watching her through the coins, and she knew they would have to weight it and sink it in the sea.

She sat up and heard thunder in the mountains. But it wouldn't rain. For hours it would rumble around and then a great wind would come howling down towards the sea, filling in the stale emptiness of the night before. Dawn wasn't far off. She dressed and went out to work on the little green frog.

When old Georgios eventually turned up, uncertain whether she could have grasped what he'd written, she offered him coffee but he wouldn't join her. She knew that

that was due to his sense of propriety, not to any fear of accepting drink from her hands, but her own cup started shaking just the same so that she had to set it down.

'Tell me about the visitors,' she invited, trying to make it sound happy and casual. 'What sort of men were they? What plants did they like most?'

But Georgios was at best inarticulate, at worst dumb. This wasn't one of his good days; the thunder had got to him too. She was sure he did his best, but when he went off to water the shrubs she still had no clear idea of the men she was due to be interviewed by.

They came early, at ten minutes past eight, parking their grey Subaru fifty yards farther down and walking back. Little Gregoris, laying the dust with a hose outside the taberna, reported to his father, and Yannakis in turn told his wife to run down for Elpida.

'She's gone to Pissouri. You know I told you yesterday. And don't suggest her sister will do, because she's worse than useless. I'll go across myself, take some fresh bread.' She tore off her apron, rolled a hot loaf in a cloth, smoothed her hair and whisked out of the door before Yannakis could protest. 'Gregoris,' he roared, needing to give instructions to someone, 'don't dawdle. You'll be late for the school bus.' He went out and glowered in the direction of the old schoolhouse but the two strangers had already gone in. He caught the whisk of his wife's skirt rounding the garden end to get in by the rear.

They were quite polite, Jean granted, but decidedly distant. She couldn't equate them with any English police of her experience, but then she had never come across anyone at home above the level of sergeant. Neither of them wore uniform but the one called Aleko struck her as having some medical knowledge. He would be the one, probably, who had shown such an interest in the flower garden.

She found her mind was working slowly and she needed to be on her guard. It was a welcome interruption when

Eleni from the taberna suddenly moved in on them with a tray of coffee. Behind the visitors' back she put a finger to her lips to restrain Jean from remarking on her unexpected arrival. The men started bobbing about, moving chairs and tables, immediately reduced to inadequate males in a females' situation.

When they were reseated and had their coffee poured, the older one, Tsangaris—whose rank Jean had failed to register—explained that the inquiry on her husband's death was due to a clerical oversight at the time of his burial; a euphemism she appreciated.

She nodded gravely, stirring her coffee and laying the spoon precisely in the saucer. The man frightened her. Dark and sleek like a seal, outstandingly handsome, yet he totally lacked charisma. If he were to reach out and touch her she would be frosted right through. She forced her mind to return to what he had said. 'So you will need to start again from the beginning and ask how it all happened?'

'Exactly.' Tsangaris gave his deadly smile. 'Anything you can tell us about your husband's activities prior to his death could be of the greatest assistance.'

'I'll do what I can, of course, but I'm afraid I don't know about most of his day. He had intended going to sea, I think, but a sudden change in the weather made him alter his plans. I wasn't expecting him home and hadn't prepared a meal, but I put together a salad with some cold chicken, and a friend of mine who was here had some with us.'

'Was your husband hungry?' This question from the one who'd been curious about the garden. A medical man?

Jean stopped to think. No one had asked her that before. Well, was he? 'I don't think he was. He left about half his meal on his plate. Perhaps when I suggested getting him some supper he thought that would be a hint for the other lady to leave. As it was, she didn't.'

'Could we have the name of this lady, Mrs Mather?'

Jean wrote it down for them and added the address at

Coral Bay. 'Her husband has a sailing boat. It may be the one my husband intended going out in that day.'

'And your husband did not wish the lady to stay on. Would you say that they were not on good terms?'

'That's exaggerating it. I think they had little in common. To be quite frank, he found her boring.' She looked up to see his eyebrows raised. 'Mrs Rowley was inclined to go on and on about cooking or embroidery.'

'Ah.' That seemed reason enough to him. 'How long elapsed after eating before your husband began to display signs of discomfort?'

Now they were reaching the nitty-gritty. On what she said in the next few sentences would rest the case against herself and/or Marjorie Rowley. She tried to answer with complete accuracy, and her recent discussion of Ted's movements with Clerides helped her to put it across in good order. The younger man made a few notes, stroked his chin and grunted. 'Did your husband not mention anything that had happened during the day?—anything that would be a clue for us to follow through? You see, we do need to know something of his activities, as this has some bearing on his state of health.'

'I'm sorry I can't be of any help there. I can only suggest you talk to Mrs Rowley. Her husband was away at the time, but she may have known if Ted was going to use the sailing boat. All I can say is that he returned a day or two before he had intended to, and that he was rather put out at the enforced change of plan. He might have been tired, but I took it at the time that he was merely tetchy.'

'Tetchy, Mrs Mather?'

'Irritable.'

'I see. Thank you. You have been very helpful. And the coffee was most welcome.'

'Is that all?'

'For the moment. It is possible that things will come to light later which you will be able to explain to us. Then we may call again.' He stood and began to move towards the door.

Jean, relieved of tension, was almost instantly flooded with suspicion. Why no questions about the garden, the potentially lethal plants? Was this anticlimax some move to trap her into indiscretion? They had been altogether too correct, too mild. Now, as they reached the outer door, one of them would look back and then would come the barbed question.

The younger one was turning with a stiff, controlled face. He was about to confront her with irrefutable proof of her guilt. Something inside her shrank away.

'Mrs Mather, is it possible for me to use the toilet?'

She was still stifling hysterical laughter when Nikos rang from his hotel. 'Is something wrong?' he asked sharply, hearing a strangeness in her voice.

'Not really. Or, more accurately, not immediately. I've just had the police here asking questions. Nothing unexpected until the end; just Ted's movements as far as I knew them on his last day.'

'And at the end?' He sounded apprehensive, much as she'd been.

'Could one of them use the loo.'

He didn't laugh, but she heard the dry humour in his voice. 'Even policemen are human. It has not shaken you, this inquisition?'

'No. I'm fine. And I don't want you to bother coming up for me. There's something I want to get on with here, then later this morning I'll get a lift down for the car.'

'Are you sure that's convenient? I must admit that makes it simpler for me. There's the boat out at Coral Bay, and a storm could be blowing up for this evening.'

'Certainly you must see to that. I'll wish you good sailing.'

There wasn't a great deal to do to finish the frog for Gregoris. She found two cue-tips from the snooker room, trimmed the edges to make them fit into the creature's eyelids, painted them a speckled orange with black centres and left them in the sunlight to dry. Then she carefully wiped the stone over with a damp cloth. It was one of the best carvings she had done.

The lorry for the *froutaría* was still being loaded with oranges. Jean called down to the driver and asked for a lift. He was delighted and went into the taberna for a duster to ensure she wouldn't mark her skirt on the passenger seat. He kept up a cheerful monologue all the way down to the city where he dropped her off by the National Bank and she walked across to the hotel car park. The little Morris was there as before except that the passenger seat was filled with flowers, a brilliant bouquet of lilies, carnations and roses in orange, yellow and white.

Very flattering of Nikos, but had he meant her to be uneasy that anyone could so easily open her locked doors? Why was it that even in paying a compliment there had to be something of menace in what he did? Or was she being unusually sensitive?

And had he deliberately made her choose between returning straight home or letting the flowers wilt without water? It was a nuisance, because she intended spending the main part of the day here; however, there was a solution.

She drove out to the small hotel where so often she and Ted used to meet up after she'd been out dinghy-sailing. Spiros wasn't to be found in the bar but his deputy knew her and provided a bucket of water for the flowers. She selected a fish *meze* from the cold buffet and had only just settled at a table when Spiros materialized with a chilled bottle of *Aphrodite* and asked to sit down with her. This was an unexpected bonus and she welcomed the chance to bring him up to date with her news. As ever, he was a good listener, and when he had anything to say it had a point. She broke off her recital of the post-mortem's suggestion of poisoning to compliment him on the food.

'It's good? But then I have a good kitchen manager, so it should be. Perhaps I will have some too.' He refilled her glass so that she wouldn't be cheerless while he was away.

Sitting sipping, she watched the big man ponder over the

selection and take the chef's advice as if he were the newest
guest to arrive. Deliberate, modest and responsible, he was
almost the opposite of Ted. Perhaps that was why the two
men had had time for each other. She found his company
reassuring because although he seemed to understand her
he didn't make her feel obvious. Between them there was a
respectful distance which she believed would always be
there however well they got to know each other.

'I have been remembering something you said to me last
time we met,' she said on his return: 'how finding the
method would lead to the person, or finding the person
would explain how it was done. Well, now I think I know
a little of both, and I'm not sure that I want to take it any
farther.'

He looked at her almost owlishly, without blinking.

'You have said it seems to be poisoning, but you gave no
idea of who might have done it.'

'And I shan't, unless there is any likelihood of me being
accused myself.'

He looked down at his plate and became preoccupied
with a loop of fried octopus.

'You disapprove, Spiros.'

She was aware of him choosing his words carefully before
he answered. 'I think perhaps there is danger for you in
that. Especially if this person knows you know. Do the police
also appear to suspect the same one?'

'From what the police say and do, it looks as if they're a
long way from forming any theory. It wasn't until this
morning that they called to check on Ted's movements for
that day. They've only just acknowledged that perhaps it
wasn't natural causes.'

'They may be slow, but they will certainly not be casual.'

She was disappointed in him, having turned to him for
comfort and having received a warning. 'What do you
suggest, then? Should I busily begin sowing suspicion elsewhere, with the risk that everyone thinks I am trying to
distract attention from my own guilt? I am the widow and

the heir. If everything comes out in the open, I am also the
deceived wife who was on the scene and best able to poison
him. I actually prepared the last food he is known to have
eaten, and my garden is full of plants that could have had
a fatal effect.'

She had given up any pretence of eating and Spiros too
laid down his fork. 'This poison, what exactly is it? Do they
know yet?'

'No. The local pathologist has had the whole body, with
what remains of the stomach's contents, sent to London for
analysis. But whatever poison it was, it caused pulmonary
œdema which wasn't due to asthma. He couldn't take air in,
collapsed, failed to respond to mouth-to-mouth resuscitation
and—simply died.

She looked up to catch a look of absolute horror on the
man's face opposite.

'Spiros, what is it? Does that mean anything to you?'

'No, nothing.' He shook his head, reached for the bottle
to pour her more wine, but his hand was shaking. His eyes
didn't meet hers and, sickly, Jean knew that Spiros had lied.

CHAPTER 15

Nothing, Jean told herself as she began to drive home, was
the same as before Ted died; least of all herself. Even Spiros
could no longer be relied on to tell the truth. She hadn't
challenged his denial that Ted's death by poisoning had
deeply disturbed him. It was bad enough that it had done.

She'd slightly changed subject by returning to the theme
of the lost insurance policy, while the hotel man sat opposite
immersed in his own thoughts. When she took her leave of
him he held on to her hand between both his own. 'Please,'
he said insistently, 'don't take any risks. Particularly,
don't . . .'

'Don't what, Spiros?'

He looked at her miserably, shook his head. 'Don't trust anyone at all. It is better that you do not make any inquiries of your own. The police will do everything that is necessary. I am worried that you may be in danger.'

Which was almost the opposite of what he'd said before. Then he had suggested she try to work out the who and the how of Ted's murder. So why change track when he heard that the means of death could have been poison? Was his concern only on her behalf, or was he afraid of suspicion widening to include someone else? But at least the advice he gave was good: she had no intention of trusting anyone, and now, to be on the safe side, that included Spiros himself. It made her feel doubly alone.

She wished she knew what Nikolaos Clerides was up to. He'd said he was bringing the sailing boat back from Coral Bay. No, correction: what he'd actually said was that the boat was *at* Coral Bay, and there would probably be a storm blowing up by the evening. Maybe he'd only intended driving over there and securing it properly so that the lad on board could go home.

Suddenly it was vital to know where he was, as if he was stalking her in the dark and she would have to dodge to avoid a blow. She swung left, taking a back street that would return her to the coast road.

Her hands on the steering wheel were slippery with sweat. The heat was increasing with the afternoon as the clouds pressed slowly lower, but it wasn't due only to that. The source of the coming storm was in herself.

If she drove now out to Coral Bay she could see whether *Zephyr II* was still tied up there. If it was, she would have to keep her eyes open for Clerides. Such a devious man; if he implied he'd gone for one purpose, it would more likely be for some other.

Vividly she recalled his coming back with Lance from checking on the boat's mooring. There had been a look of such smug complicity on the Englishman's face. And some message had previously passed between the two men while they were all four together. She had to remember what it was they had been talking about. There was a part of the conversation she must have missed because she'd been so preoccupied with Marjorie.

Of course! It was when Marjorie, furious about Ted's influence, burst out, 'Well, he's gone and I'm bloody glad he is!' And then, to Lance, '*Now you'll have to wash your hands of it!*'

To which Clerides quietly said, leaning forward and replacing the glass, 'It's a pity you feel like that, because I had a proposition to make. But clearly that would be out of order. As you say, with Ted gone, it's close of play. Nothing more to be said.'

That was when the two men had exchanged glances, and the subject had been dropped.

Nothing more? What he'd meant was 'nothing more in front of the women'. How stupid she'd been. It was anything but 'close of play'!

Jean found she was standing on the accelerator, and cut speed just before the next bend rocked her little car on its squealing tyres. Damn Clerides! He'd gone in where Ted left off. He was going to run the show in his turn. It had to be that, because no one in his right mind could imagine Lance being the one in charge of anything where Clerides was involved. So how long had Clerides had this in mind? All the while he worked on her, Jean, to get him introduced into the Rowleys' confidence? Even before he left Athens?

Well, this new development had laid to rest for ever the fiction that Clerides was anything to do with insurance. They hadn't been able to trace the second policy with an Athens company simply because there had never been one. It was all lies, his credentials had been forgeries. Worst of all, she'd been the gullible fool who helped the man to pick his safe way to the centre of the web Ted had spun. No matter what he truly was, the result must be disastrous. If a detective, then whatever underhand business the men had been running would be exposed with total publicity. And if he was some kind of crook—her first instinct about him—then the web would be extended wider yet and the wretched Rowleys would be more deeply enmeshed than before.

And her own part in this? She was surely irrelevant. Hadn't that become more apparent to Clerides the longer time he spent with her? And was that why, seeming at first to be attracted (in order to gain her confidence) he'd later established a distance between them, been less often available, dropped the earlier tenderness? It was shaming. It was one thing to be fooled on the intelligence level, but another to be conned into thinking oneself desirable!

When he had first approached her, he had been in the dark too. But yesterday he had known enough to make a deal with Lance. In the meantime, then, he had found out what the name of the game was. How? Who had helped him after he'd discovered she was completely ignorant of Ted's secret source of income?

Now the car was running parallel to the sea, and on its right side shone the ghostly plastic tunnels of the banana groves. She could smell the greenness as she passed. Just five kilometres short of Coral Bay, and still she had no idea what she would do when she reached there.

Lie low and watch, she told herself. Check on the boat first.

But *Zephyr II-Zoë* wasn't among the yachts and dinghies. The Toyota hired out to Clerides was, however, parked on a protected shoulder of the road. Which surely meant that he had come by land and gone away by sea, leaving the car to be returned to Limassol later.

But perhaps she was assuming too much in supposing that he intended taking the boat back to where it belonged. Why was it that she had this odd feeling that it had been planted here as a base camp, convenient for going farther west? Somewhere in their past conversations together there had been a mention of the north-western coastline. It was after they had dived together, and he had asked about Ted's interest in scuba.

With a sudden onset of nausea she remembered now: her own naming of coastline towns on the limit of the Green Line and beyond. She had almost boasted that Ted was diving off the shores claimed and patrolled by the Turkish invaders. And she had even quoted the depth at which he had used the underlined decompression tables for divers. One hundred and thirty feet!

Diving had to feature in what Ted had been doing clandestinely, since Clerides had been fishing for such information. And then there was the coin Clerides had given her. Gold, Elpida had declared it when she'd scrubbed it clean; and ancient, just like ones she'd seen in the museums. Clerides had been testing her out with it, to see if she had any knowledge of the operation.

When he discovered that she hadn't, he went elsewhere for what he needed. Now he and Lance were hand in glove. If she visited the Rowleys' house now, she would probably find that Lance was away from home too. The two men would be out to sea together, well on their way to the latitude of the Green Line, to an anchorage of over one hundred and thirty feet. And Lance, being in the know, would already have divulged the position of some priceless ancient wreck which Ted had come across sometime in the last two years while spear-fishing with his friends.

This all added up to Clerides being more than a con man. He was a treasure-hunter, and possibly the customer in Athens to whom Ted had been supplying the finds as he systematically raised them, working alone or with a single co-diver. Not Lance, of course. He was too old and too unpredictable for that sort of game. He would most likely be lookout man, ready to recall the divers when any official-looking patrol boat was sighted, so that they appeared merely to be sailing or fishing with innocent intent.

And what they were up to wasn't innocent. Underwater archæological excavation had to be registered with the authorities and performed under licence. She wasn't sure, but it seemed likely that the finds would be claimed by the

State of Cyprus. If not as legal owners, then as first-option buyers. And not only would the official authorities be on the lookout for buccaneers, but the Turks too, guiltily on the defensive about their new shoreline, would have regular patrols to ensure there were no encroachments. Caught in the middle, Ted—or now Clerides—could be arrested by either side, or even be responsible for provoking a new international dispute! And running that sort of danger, she recognized, would be meat and drink to either man.

But why should Lance take Clerides out now, when all coastal shipping had been warned of coming gale-force winds? Had pressure been put on him, or was his greed, frustrated so long by Ted's disappearance from the scene, forcing him past native caution? Certainly a visit to Marjorie at this moment must provide an answer.

She ran the Morris into an unmade road at an angle to the Rowleys' bungalow to come on it from the terrace end. The chairs there were empty, grouped round the matching cast-iron table, but the umbrella was still aloft, its heavy white fringe already ripped by the vicious spurts of wind which were the tease before the fury. Jean reached up and pressed the stud to lower it, then lifted off the upper half to take indoors. It was possible Marjorie's radio hadn't been tuned to the gale warnings, and she would be really upset if the sunshade was left out to be shredded. Already on the roof tendrils of creepers were whipping about and then snapping back against the trellised walls. Lance at least was enough of a sailor to recognize the early signs of a storm. He must have been mad to go out with Clerides now. Or under duress.

Jean tapped on the half open patio door and called out, 'Marjorie. Anyone at home?'

There was a soft thud from somewhere inside the house and then silence. The wrong kind of silence. Jean sidled in and laid the umbrella down. She listened again. Three distinctly different clocks were ticking away unseen, but nobody answered her second call. If Marjorie was unwell

—or hitting a solitary's bottle in Lance's absence—she might well prefer not to be disturbed. Hard luck, Marjorie, Jean decided; disturbed she would have to be.

'Marjorie, I know you're there. It's Jean. I'm coming in.'

Again there were brief, indistinct sounds almost instantly stilled. They came from the direction of the Rowleys' double bedroom. Jean went up to the door and tapped on the panels. One thing was certain: Marjorie wouldn't be holed up in there with a man. Such things were unthinkable. She pressed down the door handle and pushed. The room was locked.

Suddenly there was a rising wail of anguish. 'Oh, wait and I'll let you in. Are you alone?'

'Completely. What's wrong, Marjorie?'

There followed the click of a key turning and the door opened on to a room in disorder. The curtains were fast closed as though it was night, and the overhead light was on. Wardrobe doors and dressing-table drawers gaped. Across the bed were strewn various outer garments. On the carpet towards its foot, where its slide must have produced the first soft thud, lay a half-packed suitcase. Marjorie stood, face averted, behind the door, hands in disordered hair.

'You're packing!' Of course she was. Anyone half-sighted could have grasped that. Still Marjorie made no reply.

'But why, Marjorie?' Another idiot question. Clearly she'd had enough. Some final straw had produced the proverbial result. Marjorie's famed submission was at an end.

The moan that came from her was wordless but said all. She turned to Jean a face red and swollen with crying; and marked with a blue lumpiness across her left cheekbone.

'Marjorie, how did that happen?'

'Lance did it!' the woman shouted. 'Would you believe it? My *dear* husband, God help me!' Her shoulders shook and she sank back on to the edge of the bed. Jean followed her and sat alongside, one arm about the quivering, fleshy waist.

'Something must have upset him badly. Lance is always so—'

'De-ceitful. You can't go by appearances. I ought to know.'

'So you've decided to go away. Where?'

'Anywhere for the moment. Back to England as soon as I can get a flight.' Marjorie snuffled, blew her nose and drew herself stiffly upright. 'I can't imagine why you're interested. It was your husband first got mine into this awful mess. You could have stopped him. Ted would have done anything for you.'

'So now it's all my fault. And I don't even know what this "awful mess" is that you're talking about. Except that it must be connected with the reason for Ted's discharge from the army, but it can't have been a big scandal since the CO and Major Moffat—as he was then—knew about it and they never brought charges.'

'Oh, that! That was only the beginning. Bananas.'

Jean stared at her. Marjorie didn't usually employ slang. 'Who was bananas?'

'No, just *bananas*. Not who. They were taking loads of unripe ones out to a ship that used to lie off the west point. I don't know where they were destined for finally. Maybe Crete; they're trying to grow them there, aren't they? Anyway it was something to do with the Common Market and someone getting subsidies for them outside Cyprus.'

'You mean they were *smuggling* bananas?' It sounded ridiculous, but so much more innocent than drugs.

'It wasn't smuggling. Lance explained it to me. It was just providing intermediate transport. And the shippers paid well. They weren't contravening any regulations then. The bananas were experimental crops and no one expected much of them.'

It still sounded like smuggling to Jean. It was also quite definitely conspiracy to defraud the EEC—something sophisticated entrepreneurs might chuckle over, but being found guilty would mean a prison sentence and a criminal record for life. Would fuddy-duddy old Lance really have risked that? Ted would, like a shot, she knew.

'I see. This is news to me,' Jean said. It would take a little getting used to. How wise of Ted to have kept it to himself! But at least this project seemed less risky than the other options she'd been considering possible. 'So has Lance gone out with a load now?'

'A load?' Marjorie looked up frowning from examining herself in the wardrobe mirror. 'God, I look terrible! I can't go anywhere like this. What is this load you're talking about?'

'Bananas. You said—'

Marjorie stared at her, exasperated at her incomprehension. 'Jean, that was *two years ago*! When Ted got his discharge the CO managed to suppress the scandal, and it's all tied up now with regulations. Outside government controls, Cyprus bananas just aren't obtainable any more. Those that aren't marketed locally are officially exported. To Jugoslavia mostly, I think. Anyway, Lance said that was all small beer now.'

So it was bananas out; something else in. 'Well what are they up to now?'

Marjorie straightened, tight-lipped. 'Heaven alone knows, but nothing good, you may be certain. And that Greek you brought here is in it up to his neck, so don't play the little innocent. You just want to know what I'll give away, don't you? Well, I know how to keep my mouth shut, and that's about all I do know, because Lance doesn't discuss his business with me any more. We have absolutely nothing in common. I'm going now, leaving him for good. Or as soon as my face gets back to normal.'

'You should lie in a warm bath,' Jean suggested. 'It will help you relax. I'll make up an ice-bag for your cheek. Have you any witch hazel to dab it with?'

'Don't people in films use beefsteaks?'

'I think that was for black eyes, and it's old-fashioned anyway. Cold water and plenty of it is much better.'

Marjorie marched towards the bathroom, snatching up a kimono robe on the way. At the door she turned. 'Jean, can I come and stay with you? Just for a few days, no more. I really can't be here when Lance comes back with that man. I do think you owe it to me, after all the trouble your husband has caused.'

She didn't wait for an answer, but disappeared, bolting the door firmly after her.

CHAPTER 16

Marjorie took her time in the bathroom, finally issuing startled as the full storm struck with sudden and frightening force, making the little house shudder and sending loose objects flying about the garden to crash against its outer walls. 'Oh, my head,' she wailed. 'I didn't need this.'

Jean came back from fighting with a wooden shutter that had developed an activist life of its own. 'There's no chance of your getting away tonight,' she told the other woman. 'In fact I'd be grateful myself to stay on till the worst is over. When do you expect Lance back?'

That started Marjorie off again, so Jean sought the universal remedy and poured her a generous brandy, topping it up with dry ginger. 'You did say something about "them" coming back. Who else will be with him? We both need to know, if only to have our stories sorted out.'

'I don't know what you mean.'

'Well, there has to be a reason for me being here. And then, although you look much better now—splendid, in fact—'

'My face? It will be no surprise to Lance,' Marjorie said bitterly. 'I shouldn't have tried to cover it up. As for the Greek, I won't see him. I shall stay in my room. You're

welcome to sleep here. Have the second bedroom. It will do
the others no harm to use the floor or the settee.'

'If they do get back. Do you have any idea where they
were going or why? It looks as though they took the sailing
boat.'

'I have no idea at all,' Marjorie declared grandly. 'Oh
God, that wind!—and we're supposed to be sheltered here.
It must be hurricane force. Was that thunder?'

It wasn't possible to tell, there was so much crashing and
roaring as all about them the house's fabric withstood forces
never taken into their calculations by architects designing
lotus-eaters' havens.

Thank God, Jean thought, the old schoolhouse up at
Kalidrofi had survived worse over the decades. With any
luck the gales sweeping down from Turkey and joining
turbulence over the Tróodos mountains would rush at roof
level over the foothill villages. Most of the damage would
be wreaked on the open fields and the fruit farms. Here, on
the flat littoral, anything could happen. Out at sea— She
shuddered. 'Marjorie, at least you must know what time
they left here.'

'Of course I do. Mid-morning. The Greek had phoned
earlier and Lance went down to the moorings to meet him.
I knew they were up to some new stupidity. I warned Lance.
I told him that if he went he wouldn't find me here when
he got back. He—he was so *rude*! Jean, you couldn't
imagine . . .'

She didn't want a repeat recitation of their domestic fight.
Jean went across to the bookshelves and started searching
among the maps. Marjorie stopped in her outpourings and
looked affronted. 'What are you doing?'

'I thought I might see what charts Lance had taken.'

'Well, you won't find any there. He was a Navigating
Officer, you know. He has a cabinet full of charts and things
like that in the little room he uses for a study. Though what
he ever studies these days is a mystery. The cabinet's locked,
but the key's on a ledge at the back.'

'Thank you. Do you mind if I take a look?'

'Do what you like with the rubbish. It's always been in the way.' Marjorie was reduced to petulance. Balked in her intention of a dramatic departure, she was left without a role.

The key wasn't where Marjorie had said, but Jean had her nail file and the lock wasn't a complicated one. She opened the mahogany door and found a stack of shallow drawers, each labelled with its contents. The one in most constant use was smudged with fingermarks so that the writing was illegible. She pulled it out and examined the papers lying inside. They were all original sea charts for the coastal waters of Cyprus, and they included the northern stretches claimed as Turkish since the invasion. The ones Lance had taken on board would be photocopies of BAC 775 and 776. Depths were all given in fathoms, of course; which meant multiplying by six to get feet. They'd still used feet when she had begun with British Sub Aqua, but all modern diving manuals quoted depth in metres. The change was meant as a simplification! Small comfort to someone suddenly panicking underwater and needing to convert decompression tables.

She scanned the two charts rapidly. To the north and west of Cyprus the sea bed dropped much more slowly than to the south of the island. Above a depth of 130 feet or more in the vast bight of Morphou Bay, a small boat with lowered sails would be hard to see from land; in bad weather it would be invisible. As for distance, making full use of the boat's engine, they couldn't reach Khrysokhou Bay in under twelve hours. Say, midday to midnight. No, with the storm at sea worse than here, Clerides must have been forced to give up a couple of hours back.

She returned thoughtfully to the lounge where Marjorie had recovered enough to be nervously shaking up cushions and fidgeting chairs into different positions. 'Who left this garden umbrella in here?' she demanded.

'Sorry, that was me. It was flapping itself to bits, so I took it down. Marjorie, you must have some idea what Lance and Clerides intended doing. I mean, going off in a storm of this severity . . .'

'It hadn't started then.'

'But you knew they were going a long way. Or you guessed as much.'

'Why should I guess?'

'Because obviously it wasn't the first time Lance had gone off at short notice. Didn't he do so sometimes with Ted? As you reminded me, Lance was a navigator; he'd be absolutely essential for getting to a plotted locality. But what worries me is how they'll manage when they get there—if they do.'

Marjorie looked uncomfortable, concern warring with outrage. 'Oh, they'll be all right. The devil looks after his own.' But it didn't sound convincing.

'Look,' Jean said, 'if they've landed and are coming back, they can't possibly get here across country before early morning, even if they have a car laid on. And they'll need to rest first. We've got all the night ahead of us and quite a bit of tomorrow, I guess. So let's have a meal, play cards or something and then turn in for the night.'

'I couldn't possibly undress,' Marjorie wailed. 'Suppose the roof blows off.'

As if in corroboration, the kitchen shutter tore loose again, was whipped back and shattered glass across the floor. Reaching to catch it on the rebound, Jean put her fingers through the jagged edge of the broken pane. She gave a brief glance out at the weirdly livid sky and heaved the two parts of the fastening together. They rasped into place. The sounds of storm grew less. She stepped back on glass, and let Marjorie put adhesive bandages round the finger ends of her right hand.

It was then that the electric power failed.

'Candles,' Marjorie announced after the first gasp of horror, and went straight for them in the appropriate cupboard. Jean smiled to herself. It looked as though, under pressure, the WI spirit had come through.

They had a supper of cold lamb sandwiches and tinned soup heated on an old camping gas ring which Lance had turned out of *Zoë*'s galley. Afterwards, without radio or tape-player, and safe topics of conversation having seemingly been exhausted, the night yawned empty ahead.

As a bridge player, Marjorie scorned to play Canasta or any of the other card games Jean was familiar with. Which left the bookcase, and then Jean was immediately confronted by the thick tome on the care of house plants which Clerides had mentioned to her.

On a wrought iron and glass bench beside the curtained window she recognized the *Dieffenbachias*' spear-shaped, blotchily striped leaves and shuddered. It seemed to her impossible that for hours now she had forgotten that Marjorie was Suspect Number One in a case of murder by poisoning, but she had done, even to the extent of sitting down to a meal with her!

It was stupid to be afraid. Marjorie had enough on her mind to leave no room for homicidal intentions, at least not in Jean's direction. If anyone was in danger it would be Lance. If Marjorie had really killed Ted, it had been a crime inspired by crazed resentment, wishful dreaming put into desperate action. At present Marjorie had need of Jean so wouldn't want to be rid of her; but pushed too far over this seagoing operation—which she showed signs of being—she could be a serious threat to the men when they returned.

Jean forced herself not to eye the *Dieffenbachias* with suspicion mentally photographing their outlines, counting the number of their leaves. Deliberately she moved away and took the first book that came to hand. Marjorie had picked up a piece of crochet work in corded cotton and was stabbing away with a fine metal hook as if punishing it. Jean watched her curiously. 'What are you making?' It was surely too English-suburban for this Mediterranean bungalow.

'Set of chair backs.' Marjorie displayed it proudly. 'Made up of lots of circles, do you see? I have a nice mulberry velour suite in store at home that it'll look lovely on.'

Jean did see, quite vividly. She saw Marjorie ensconced with her women's handicrafts circle, daintily at afternoon tea, homemade scones and cakes on a lace-doilied three-tier collapsible stand. Lance wasn't a part of the scene, dismissed to smoke his pipe in the garden perhaps, or in the potting shed if it rained.

Nothing, it seemed, was going to dissuade this ordinary-seeming little woman from her determination to break with abroad. She had made up her mind some time ago, at the point when she had started on the crochet work. Jean looked assessingly at the finished pieces spread on their tissue paper wrappings. How rapid a worker was Marjorie? When had she begun? Perhaps as much as two months back?

'If you don't mind, Marjorie,' she said rising, book in hand, 'I think I'll turn in while there's a slight lull. It's bound to start racketing again, and I'd like to have dropped off by then.'

'I don't think I've any chance of sleeping. I'm too much on edge. You'd better take one of the candles, but do be careful, won't you? If a fire started it would spread everywhere in a wind like this. The countryside's tinder-dry.'

It wasn't a comforting thought to retire with, especially since without the bungalow Marjorie would be one step nearer her heart's desire. Jean said good night and left her, fervently hoping that her reawakened housewifely instincts would prevent any sudden rush of pyromania.

She awoke to hear a car door slam outside. The wind was still buffeting the house but with a more dogged persistence as though already tiring. From now on, if things kept to the usual pattern, the worst would blow itself out before dawn and not reach the same pitch until sundown tomorrow.

There were men's low voices close under her window. Lance and Clerides? No; the second voice spoke indifferent

English, so not the man from Athens. The car's engine beat altered and it drew away. The storm roared loud as an outer door was opened. Lance had come home alone.

Jean slid off the bed and felt for her shoes. In the kitchen there was a scraping of chair legs and then cursing as Lance moved in, crunching on broken glass. 'What the hell—?'

'Lance, it's Jean. Don't jump. We couldn't sweep up the glass properly because the light's gone. How did you get on?'

'We had to give up and put in before the Cape. Not soon enough for me, I can tell you. That Clerides fellow's like the mad Dutch johnny in the opera. Know the one I mean? I took a taxi straight back. Lord, but I'm bushwhacked.'

He stared round in the gloom. 'Glad things aren't too bad here. There's a lot of damage on the roads. Anyway, I think you'll find the electricity's back on. I saw the glow in other houses as we drove down the lane. Where's Marjorie?'

As he spoke he heaved on the refrigerator door and was rewarded as the little bulb came on. 'See that?' He reached in for a can of beer and tore off the lid.

'I left her in the lounge. She didn't think she would sleep if she went to bed. Have a look.'

Marjorie had slept through everything and was still out to the wide, head thrown back, mouth open, making little throaty gurgles on each drawn breath. 'Better not disturb her,' Lance whispered hopefully.

'Why don't you just creep off to bed? She'll find you there when she wakes. I'm in the guest room.'

'Yes, well, I'd better, I suppose. Dead on my feet, Jean. What a day and a half it's been!'

Jean hesitated. 'So where is Mr Clerides?'

'He went on by taxi. Had to promise a sheikh's ransom to make the man turn out, but Clerides never takes no for an answer. Did the same for a cab for me.'

Went on; not back? 'How far, then? Beyond Khrysokhou Bay?'

'Yes; as near the border as he can get. The caïque will

have tried to put in somewhere on the Greek Cypriot side. He'll hang around until he spots it. Rather he than I.'

It was exhaustion, Jean saw, that made him so easy to pump. He hadn't realized she was fencing in the dark; must suppose Clerides had confided more to her than he had done.

'Maybe I should go and help,' Jean suggested. 'In the morning.'

Lance didn't answer, just lifted a hand in salute and disappeared round the door of the main bedroom. 'In the morning,' Jean had said, but it was almost three already. Best to go now while the trail was fresh. And in the official morning Marjorie would wake to discover her husband snug in the marital bed. Far best to leave them to sort that out in private.

Out on the terrace Jean was almost swept off her feet. The cast-iron furniture had all ended piled under the far wall in a broken tangle of bougainvillaea and the remains of the television aerial. Her breath was blown back in her throat, stinging with sharp grit from the seashore as she made her way, hanging on now and again to whatever was stable.

The little Morris was still upright where she'd left it, but covered with a debris of stones and wrecked foliage. She swept the windscreen clear with her forearm and started up the engine. It fired. With half a tank of fuel, all she lacked was ballast.

Not being familiar with the westernmost point of the island, she turned back to Paphos and took the main road north. So why am I doing this? she asked herself as the car swerved with the wind broadside on and the steering-wheel pulled at her bandaged fingers. What is the point of following this dreadful man? The answer took the best part of her harebrained journey to resolve.

She had to admit finally that it was due to a slow build up of anger ever since she had realized what he actually intended: nothing more nor less than a cold-blooded take-over of Ted's operation. Somehow, in Athens, he had learned of underwater treasure discovered off Cyprus, had possibly been purchasing or handling individual artefacts singly or in small numbers as they were retrieved. (How otherwise would he have obtained the ancient coin which he gave her, expecting her to react by recognizing its provenance?)

And somehow, almost two months after the event, he had heard that the operation was adrift, and Ted no more. So he had had the effrontery to think he could come and replace him, with no more excuse than sheer greed. Ted had done it for adventure, because of the unquenchable buccaneer in him, but this man was out to make money, when he seemed already to have more of it than most. And not only had he totally disregarded whatever dispositions Ted had already arranged, but he had expected her, newly widowed, to welcome him, reveal the wreck's whereabouts and help him set up as the new boss. Such arrogance was doubly insulting.

Whatever the rights and wrongs of Ted's activities—and if the underwater site was in sea disputed between the Turkish invaders and the true Cypriots, then ownership was certainly a delicate matter neither authority would be in a hurry to claim—the planning and expenses had been Ted's and his team's. Even thieves respected each other's territories, didn't they?

She was never going to let that odious man get away with it! She had only to learn a little more of his intentions, find out the precise location of the diving, and then she would blow the whole operation to the authorities, get him caught in the act. She could surely make a deal with the Department of Antiquities: details of the operation against immunity from prosecution for the original team. Then Lance could be sent off with a golden handshake, and Marjorie return to England, to the provincial respectability she craved. The treasures would end up where they should rightfully be; and Clerides too, in jail.

But beating the man wouldn't be easy. She would need to go along with him, pretend she knew more than she actually did or else he wouldn't need her. He was confident enough of his ability to charm. She had to admit too that she hadn't been impervious to his dangerous fascination. Let him think she was still something of the hypnotized rabbit, but a rabbit with a valuable carrot to trade.

A signboard beside the road announced the approach to Kato Pyrgos and she realized that for some minutes now the sky overhead had ceased to lighten. There was a bitter stench of burning vegetation freshly doused. This was the second fire she had seen on the way and it had almost reached the outskirts of the town before they'd had it under control. Weary men were still beating at patches of smoking turf.

She pulled up at the first taberna she saw, and at once she was in luck because, exhausted from fighting against waves and wind, Clerides too had made his taxi stop as soon as Kato Pyrgos came in sight. She walked into the restaurant and he was there still, at a table, drinking coffee.

'Jean!' Clerides exclaimed, for once taken aback, and his chair tipped as he rose suddenly, extending an arm in welcome. 'What on earth are you doing here?'

Much what she had earlier asked herself, she thought ruefully; but for this man there should be a different answer. 'It's due to your magnetism, of course,' she said drolly, and saw the delight pass from his face as he accepted the level of sarcasm.

'How could I doubt it? But also?'

'Just keeping a watchful eye on proceedings. As is only natural, I retain a mild interest in my husband's investments.'

'Indeed.' He set a chair for her opposite his own. The waiter was already hovering for her order. She asked for orange juice and coffee, and was rising ready to select her breakfast from the counter when Clerides forestalled her.

'The lady has been travelling through the storm,' he told the man. 'Bring a selection across.'

Masterful as ever, Jean reflected; but at least I surprised him the once. She would have to go cannily now because the wily Greek would instantly know she was bluffing if she miscalculated at all.

'You've been injured,' he said, sounding concerned. 'Shall I get a doctor to see you?'

'It's nothing. I was clumsy with a broken window at Marjorie's.' She brushed his offer aside. 'So what damage has the storm done to the boat?'

'Very little, fortunately, but it has meant altering our plans.'

'I'm glad you said "ours". I think it's time you consulted my wishes.'

'I have been prepared to do so all along, but when I sounded you out . . .'

'With the coin?'

'—you chose not to know what it was about.'

'I needed to be a little more sure of you first. You could have been anyone.'

'And how sure are you now?'

God, the man was mocking her! 'I think I have all the information I require. So at least we can dispense with the phoney second-insurance story. You wasted a lot of my time on that, because I'll admit you took me in completely.' It sounded cool and competent, but with the right amount of rueful respect. Under the table she crossed her fingers.

'Does this mean you are now ready to take me on trust?'

'At least as far as I can watch you.' Tough stuff: did she sound convincing as a gangster's moll?

'And what do you propose?'

'She swallowed and wiped her fingers on the paper napkin. 'An equal partnership,' she said with assumed confidence, when she could no longer put off answering.

'*Equal?* Literally fifty-fifty? That would be quite out of the question. Now if you were prepared to be patient and see what transpires, I would certainly do as I had always intended and make you a most generous present . . .'

'Present be damned! You can't give me what's already mine by rights!'

'Yours? That is scarcely accurate. At present it belongs to no one but the fishes.'

Jean forced down another sickening mouthful of cheese with ham. Now he was out in the open: admitting it was all about underwater treasure, just as she had worked out for herself. 'You appear to forget,' she said icily, 'that this is my husband's operation. You are a complete outsider unless I choose to invite you in.'

Clerides made a little collection of bread crumbs and teased them about with the tips of his long fingers. He was still smiling, and taking his time over what to say next. 'Unfortunately—and I trust you will forgive me for speaking of anything so obviously painful to you—your husband is no longer with us.'

He was waiting for her to come back on this, so there was no escaping the obvious follow-up if she, was to stay in character. Jean took an audible breath. 'My husband is dead, leaving me as his sole heir.'

The Greek's timing was impeccable. The deep eyelids hooded his gaze as he seemed to consider the implications of this. Jean began to believe that they were on the point of reaching some kind of compromise. Then he raised his head and fixed her with a predator's stare.

'I was at some distance when your husband was murdered. Poison is a woman's weapon. You should be careful what moves you make at the moment. I understand that a police inspector has already visited you for your preliminary questioning.'

CHAPTER 17

'You—you *bastard*!' She was shaking, whether with anger or loathing she couldn't tell. It took all her will-power to hang on to the edge of the table and not throw her hot coffee in his face.

'You know I had nothing to do with that. I—I loved Ted!'

He lifted his shoulders and grimaced. 'What do I know? If I am questioned . . .' He threw out a hand, palm up.

The swine! He could make up any story he liked about her inviting him in on the deal and then welshing on their agreement for some personal reason. A lover's tiff, even! He could claim that she'd been ready for any advances, even that *she* had required him to make love to her. The faithless widow, the murderous wife. Who would accept her word against his? It would have been obvious to any one interested in watching that she had spent a great deal of time in the Greek's company, voluntarily, and much of it had been without a third party present.

He sat back, head tilted assessingly. 'All I wish to point out to you, my dear Jean, is that your position is a vulnerable one. You cannot afford to attract further attention. It is not safe for you to run any risks at the moment, while you are already an object of interest to the civil authority. You may leave any dubious business to me. And since I shall be the one taking all the risks—delivering the goods, so to speak —I am indisputably the one in charge of the operation. Totally. Do I make it quite clear?'

'You do not. Nor do I agree!' (Careful, Jean, you're so het up you're going to say something unforgivably hostile at any moment.)

She counted up to three in silence. Still trembly, she lifted her cup and found she needed to use both hands for affecting

to be casual. 'Equal risks: equal shares. That is my proposition: half or nothing. Any risk you take, I take too.' She
stared him out, or that was the intention.

He seemed to be smiling again behind his eyes, but his
mouth was wolfish. 'Do you really mean that, I wonder?
But why not? You are a very courageous woman or you
would not have followed me here at such a moment and
under such abominable conditions. You do really tempt me
to take you at your word.'

'Do that, Nikos.' She spread butter lavishly to hide the
tremor of her hands, and forced herself to look up at him
with a confident smile. 'We shall make quite a powerful
team, you with your derring-do and me with my knowledge.'

'Ah. Knowledge. But perhaps you bring it just a day or
two too late.'

She stared at him. He smiled again. 'The ex-Squadron-
Leader Navigating Officer—I hope I have the title correctly,
because to Mr Rowley this is certainly important—has been
most obliging, for a consideration, of course. I now have the
exact bearing for the wreck. If I am to accept you as an
equal partner in the enterprise I shall enrol you as my
companion for the preliminary dive. That will be this evening, if you accept the assignment. And provided, naturally,
that the weather permits our putting out to sea.'

But *Zoë-Zephyr II* had been run in to shore on the other
side of Cape Arnaoúti because of the storm. They could
never get her here by the evening. So there had to be a
second boat. She thought Lance had mentioned one; a
caïque, wasn't it? Why then had they needed the sailing-boat
at all? Yes, of course, to take away the spoils, so that the
caïque could continue innocently fishing.

'Did you catch up with the caïque?' she demanded. 'Was
it damaged at all in the storm?'

'She's a sturdy old tub.' He laughed deep in his throat.
'Not pretty, and certainly not comfortable, but then you say
you wish to share my hardships, so it will suit you well. The
beach she's run up on is a mile or two from here. I checked

her over before coming on to Kato Pyrgos. We can load the equipment later today, but for the present I suggest you enjoy a siesta, as I intend to do. I've taken a room here, and I'm sure when you ask with your customary charm they will find somewhere for you to put your head down. I would not wish to compromise you by making this arrangement for you.'

Again that subtle reminder of her vulnerable position, and again the mocking undertone behind the considerate words.

She stood up. 'I'll go now and see what's available. Then I must do some shopping. I haven't anything for an overnight stay.' She went back to the bar counter and the man who had brought her breakfast appeared from behind an archway. 'Lady?'

It appeared that there was no second bedroom available for guests, but there was a small store room at the rear. At present it had been partly cleared ready for repainting the walls. If the gentleman would assist him he would bring a spare bed down from upstairs. He regretted that until eleven he would be on duty alone, and a twisted back prevented him managing the removal without help. Perhaps the lady would explain the position to her friend?

Jean went back to Clerides. 'If it wouldn't compromise either of us too badly, do you think you could help bring down a bed from upstairs? The waiter has disc trouble and he's single-handed.'

Clerides had stood up politely, cigar drooping from between his fingers. He crushed it out now and half bowed. 'I should be delighted to assist. Please don't let us delay your shopping. In return you could perhaps seal our equal partnership by making a small purchase for me?' He picked up the broken cigar band from the table and held it out. 'This is not the metropolis, but there must be a tobacconist who stocks something similar.'

'Of course. I'll do what I can.'

She knew from the start that the quest was hopeless. The

little general store where she bought and equipped a new sponge bag directed her to a shop where cigars were sold, but the gilt band Clerides had handed her was unfamiliar there. She was persuaded to sniff three or four different brands and make a choice from them aided by the shop-keeper's anxious advice.

About half an hour after leaving the taberna she was back, left the cigars with the waiter to take up for Clerides, and retired to her makeshift bedroom. Its small, square window was boarded over from outside, and a greasy pull-string had no effect on the single hanging bulb, but as she opened the door light from the kitchen passage slanted in. She made out the paler shape of the bed isolated in the centre and, against the farther wall, stacks of crates and cartons shrouded with what looked like old curtains. Up-stairs no doubt Clerides fared better, but he had come first and they were equal partners. She was glad that in this he hadn't insisted on deferring to her as a member of the pampered sex.

In total darkness she felt her way to the narrow bed, its sheets holding the bitter smell of the fire that had blown towards the village. By now she was tired enough to relax the moment she stretched herself out. For only a minute or two her mind recounted brief scenes from the last twenty-four hours. She felt consciousness drop away while she murmured, 'Wind's dropping. Tonight—tonight we go to sea.' And so she slept.

She awoke suddenly to the same total darkness. It was utterly silent, and with the window boarded she had no way of knowing what time it was. Her watch, pushed under the pillow, must have fallen to the floor. She started to reach out, feeling for it across the bare boards, when she froze.

She was not alone. It was no sound that had awakened her but a touch. Someone, changing position in the bed beside her, slid a cool arm over her thigh. She lay barely breathing and the movement came again, deliberate and prolonged. She remembered the shape of the bed, its narrowness, how she had felt her way blindly to it.

No man had an arm as long as that which was trailing over her lower limbs, and now slithered off at the outer edge of her thigh.

She lay petrified, not daring to breathe, then stealthily and slowly she lifted the upper sheet. Teeth clenched, in a single frenzied movement she rolled away, fell to the floor, scrambled up and reached the door, opened it, stumbled through, slammed it and screamed and screamed, with her back against its panels.

The waiter came running and behind him customers from the bar. Clerides came leaping down from upstairs, tucking his shirt in his trousers. 'For God's sake, Jean, what is it?'

'Snake,' she managed to get out. 'There's a snake in that room. In my bed!'

'Here, take her.' Clerides pushed her into the arms of a woman who had appeared from the kitchen quarters. 'Give her brandy.' She was hustled away, still rigid with horror.

When she felt able to move, the woman took her upstairs, and she found herself sitting on Clerides's bed. His panama hat, tilted on a bedpost, confronted her with a sardonic air. All right, so I screamed, she excused herself silently; but at least it brought help. What else could I do?

As she sat there, the woman's arm about her, there was a loud crack from below and almost instantly after a ragged little cheer from the onlookers. 'There, the monster's dead,' said the woman. 'You are quite safe now. Your friend has shot it. It must have fled in here from the fire. People were in and out all the time fetching sacks and things to beat out the flames in the grass.'

They had laid the thing out along the bar counter. Greygreen, mottled and thick as a man's wrist, its flat head and gaping mouth were detached from the bloody wreck of its neck. The men had reassembled it to measure its length. When Jean went forward to look they made way and fell silent. Then one of them—a fisherman from his appearance —congratulated her.

'*Vipera Lebetina*,' Clerides announced from a far corner of the room. 'The Levant Viper. Not a pleasant experience. If you hadn't wakened in time, you could be dying by now. We should celebrate.' He banged his fist on the table. 'Drinks for everyone!'

Jean went across and accepted the chair he offered. 'I understand you shot it, and saved my life. Thank you.'

Clerides grinned. 'A cliché delivered with cool dignity. It was different in the old films I've seen. Shouldn't you swoon into my arms?'

'Not so cool when I felt the thing slither over me,' she assured him.

Clerides hummed and patted the back of her hand as it lay on the table. His touch was hard and dry. She stared at his brown flesh and for a moment saw it speckled green and smoothly scaled.

'Would you care to keep on my room now? There is still an hour and a half before we need to set out. For myself, there are things I must do.'

'I've slept enough, thank you. But it would be more quiet than down here. You seem to have started a party.'

He laughed. 'Then I'll settle my bill and get out before they take me for an Onassis.'

There was a storm-lantern now on the floor of the room she had slept in. She looked cautiously around at the shrouded shapes against the far wall as she collected her few things, holding her breath as she slid one hand under the bed to retrieve the watch.

In Clerides's room the panama hat had been removed and someone had left a tray with food and coffee. Just after four Clerides sent up a message that it was time to leave. They could use Jean's car, he told her. He had already taken the liberty of loading his own things in the rear. They seemed to consist mostly of provisions.

He had changed into clean but sun-bleached denim slacks, a white T-shirt and a peaked navy cap, making Jean conscious of the crushed cotton suit she had lived in since the start of the previous day. As soon as they were at anchor she would slip into the swimsuit she'd bought in Limassol and dive into the sea.

Dive—the word brought her to a sharp halt. If, as equal partner sharing all risks, she was to dive with Clerides—to a minimum depth of 130 feet—what would she use for equipment? There was none in the car. So did he mean her to stay on deck and monitor his dives as he went down alone? But there would be other men with them; it wasn't safe to dive singly to such a depth. With Ted she had never ventured lower than eighty feet herself.

Almost as if he read her mind, Clerides said, 'You can have the boy's wetsuit. You are both the same size, with certain necessary differences.'

The caïque was already afloat, having been run down the beach on a double track of heavy sleepers. Four men were waiting with an inflated rubber dinghy and immediately started loading the provisions from Jean's car.

'Give Andreas your keys,' Clerides ordered, nodding towards the more villainous-looking of the two remaining on shore. In Greek he instructed the man to leave the car locked and hidden behind the taberna, with the keys 'in the usual place'.

While the two men waited he checked the receipts for fuel. 'Both tanks full,' Andreas assured him. 'Seven hundred litres, fifty of them in cans.'

Clerides grunted and signed a paper, was wished '*Kaló taxídi*,' and nodded to Jean to board the dinghy while he held it steady. She crouched, reaching over the stowed goods, ready to go forward, but Clerides clicked his tongue. 'Get it started.'

She took the far side of the rear and grasped the starter cord, waiting for him to push the dinghy free of the shingle and roll over the side. Then she heaved and the outboard spluttered into life. 'So,' he said, adjusting his position to distribute the weight more evenly, 'our adventure begins. Does it excite you?'

She didn't answer because she couldn't. The wind of their bumpy passage thrust the breath back down her throat. From the shore the sea had looked choppy, but she hadn't been prepared for the way the cockleshell boat was thrown about on its fifty-yard passage out to the caïque. She clung on and watched the sky lurch down and away, the waves build over her then swing her up on their crests, toss her back into the next trough. Yes, she was excited. She was terrified and fascinated and it seemed that everything she had ever felt about the sea was intensified here a thousand-fold. This was the moment she had always known would arrive. If ever the sea claimed her it would be today.

CHAPTER 18

The young man who gave Jean a hand up the ladder was the same one who had caretakered on *Zoë-Zephyr II* at the Sheraton marina: Baroutis's lad, which surely meant that this too was a Baroutis caïque, possibly the one the old boatman had been mourning the commandeering of that night in Spiros's bar. Which seemed a lifetime ago now.

And his lad was also, it became evident, the 'boy' who shared Jean's body size, and whose wetsuit she was to borrow. Clerides sent him for it and it was laid out for their inspection. Brand new, so she wasn't surprised that Clerides complained the boy had little experience and expressed satisfaction that now he would feel safer diving in the company of someone who knew what it was all about.

All? Jean asked herself. Who ever knew all about any aspect of the sea? When she went down with Clerides later it would be in a depth she'd no knowledge of. She was familiar with her own reactions down to a level not much more than half of the one he intended, and even there she experienced a metaphysical oppression from the great mass of water above her. And in this man's company, a man who affected her as deeply and as strangely as did the sea itself —suppose she panicked. Suppose something went wrong, could she cope with it? Suppose he even meant her some harm?

He was being very methodical with the equipment laid out in the cramped little cabin, examining the face masks, pulling with his full weight on the harness, checking every link and buckle, the readings on the air cylinders, the response of each valve. 'This set is for you,' he told her, indicating a buoyancy jacket, weight belt and set of bottles. They appeared perfect, and he was satisfied that they were. The other set, which he allocated to his own use, had a more worn appearance. One of the bottles needed repainting and showed streaks of outer rust.

He waved her to a seat and, while the engines throbbed and the boat began to make shuddering headway, spread a sheet of wallpaper, face down, over the central table. He started to sketch and to explain as he went. He had already seen a plan of the wreck which Lance Rowley had received from Ted when the wreck was first located. This was its outline as it lay at present below, on the crest of an under-water ridge. On sinking, the vessel had broken its back and the forward end had tipped over into the abyss, spilling the central, hold and its contents over an area of some fifty metres square. The hull's stern could have remained almost intact below its weight of shed metal, for the ship had been carrying copper from Cyprus in 3-metre ingots shaped like the hides of a bullock. In addition there had been ingots of silver and glass, and Greek amphoras, once presumably sealed with wines, oil and other commodities, in transport to whatever port the ship was destined for.

'Where?' Jean asked him.

Clerides looked up. 'For what it's worth, my guess is that the ship intended sailing east–west, from the Phœnician coast to the Cyclades and Mycenæ via the southern Turkish coast and Rhodes. I believe the copper was Cypriot, but that will become clear when we have lifted some of the ingots for assaying. And the date?—certainly BC, perhaps one century, maybe more.'

'Two thousand years old,' Jean marvelled.

'At least. And what I am hoping is that under the metal some of the original structure of the ship will have been preserved. Wood rots in sea water over the centuries, but even an outline of the hull . . .'

His enthusiasm was infectious. Jean felt her own curiosity aroused in response. Perhaps with such an exciting end in view the dive would be less of an ordeal.

'Have you checked the depth?' she asked.

'Between 38 and 42 metres. Which brings us to the diving times and decompression requirements. I want to limit our first exploration together to a maximum of twenty minutes, surface to commencement of ascent. So, to be on the safe side, be prepared for total immersion of almost an hour.'

Jean reckoned that Ted's estimate of 130 feet was inside the limits Clerides had just quoted. She would have to keep her wits about her to memorize everything now in metres. She watched while he took a fresh sheet of paper and ruled it into columns, the first representing durations of dive at a depth of maximum 42 metres.

'By the time we've completed the project, we shall require decompression stations at 15, 10 and 5 metres. A line will be dropped from the boat with these depths marked and a permanent light attached at each point, together with spare air cylinders at the two lowest markers.'

'If we're within six miles of land,' Jean said thoughtfully, 'isn't there a chance that patrols on the coast will see our lights at night?'

'The boat carries normal lighting for the purpose of fishing, and nets will be ready to cast at a moment's notice. There will be no Divers Down flag hoisted, and all our operations will take place to the port side, away from sight of land. At the approach of any hostile vessel the underwater lights can be doused from the boat's cabin. We have two lookouts. Any more questions?'

'Decompression periods at the three stations.'

From memory he wrote them out, covering total periods of dive-to-surface of thirty, forty-five and sixty minutes. 'I'll make a waterproof copy of this for you to wear on your wrist,' Clerides promised, 'but we shall stay within sight of each other and if there is any doubt in your mind at any time, make the appropriate sign for wishing to ascend. Shall we go over the sign language together, now?'

They did so, and he caught her out on two communications. Ted had been less careful as an instructor. When she had dived off the British coast as a student things had been more happy-go-lucky still. She had no criticism to make of her new diving partner.

'Happy?' he asked. 'If so, I'll go on deck now and check our position while you change. Put on some long johns underneath. It's cold down there. I've left you a new pair in that package.' He gave her a hard stare, nodded and departed.

Fine, she tried to persuade herself. He has it all off pat. She wished she had memorized the decompression tables underlined in Ted's out-of-date manual. Only one rough figure for the 130-ft depth stayed in her mind: for a thirty-minute stay from surface to beginning of ascent, approximately the same total of minutes spread in positive geometric progression between the three stations. As the figures Clerides had quoted were nearly the same it seemed she could trust him. At least on that one score. It was not his intention to make her suffer 'the bends' from faulty decompression.

In all this plethora of technical information, one aspect the man hadn't covered was the purpose of the dive. What did he intend they should do down there, apart from observation? Would she be obliged actually to remove some of the treasures? The answer was clear when, clad in the

wetsuit, she went on deck. There was a wire cage of equipment in process of being lowered over the side.

'Camera and lights,' Clerides explained, grinning
wolfishly. 'All that's missing is music. Would you care to
take down a Walkman headset with you?'

'I fancy we'll be too busy,' she countered drily. She stared
around. There were three crew men; Baroutis's lad and the
two who had brought the provisions from the beach. While
she and Clerides were underwater, for the space of an hour,
they would put on a show of fishing and do whatever was
necessary to keep in touch with the real operation below.
She hoped they were loyal. But the Greek wasn't a fool.
They would be here with a mere sweetener in their pockets;
the rest of their cut would be promised for when the project
was completed. They stared back at her curiously, the boy
with a touch of resentment, because hadn't she deprived
him of a more active role?

He went below at a flick of Clerides's head and returned
with her set of bottles, then while the harness was fitted and
rechecked, brought the Greek's.

The boat was tossing and rolling as she lowered herself
to the water. Earlier, when she had gone snorkelling with
Clerides, it had been hot and fairly calm. This was different,
a grey lid of cloud making it premature dusk and the wind
gusting trickily again as the temperature dropped. There
were a thousand things she would rather be doing than
falling back now into the water, looking up at the sky for
the last time, losing it as the sea closed over her head and
her ears filled with the sound of her own artificial breaths.

Clerides was moving alongside. He reached out and held
her hand. They started downwards together, seeing all
warm colour drain away, into a realm increasingly grey-
blue.

A squeeze on her hand drew her attention back from the
lost circle of pale water above. The man pointed and she
made out the darker line hanging down into the depths
which they would enter. She signalled that she had under-

stood and then he loosed her hand, leaving her free to sink at will, make her own observations. His far hand was running down the line that lowered the equipment.

They passed the depth markers, each light affixed being of increasing brightness. She signalled that she had registered the position of the spare air cylinders on the 10-metre depth where Clerides pointed, and she reached out to touch their reassuring bulk.

Full fathom five. After that, denser darkness, with a descent of three times the distance they'd already come: a slow descent while their bodies, weightless as astronauts', became accustomed to the doubling, trebling, quadrupling of atmospheric pressure; longdrawn minutes of leaving security farther behind. It seemed an eternity to reach the end of the line.

Beyond the regular bubble of her own exhaust valve she could hear no sound of a second diver, but suddenly the general greyness was pierced by a light which focused on a rocky wall ahead, throwing up a silver shower of fish gusting past like blown willow leaves. In the delicate shades of life on the rock-face animal and vegetable were barely distinguishable, crustaceans mimicking the mineral with rough-textured, pinky-purple colouring.

The light panned around as Clerides turned. She saw his black shape, seal-supple but encumbered by the bulk of the twin air cylinders, bent over the crate of equipment as he unpacked it like a Christmas hamper, all in slow motion: one for you, one for me. At last a lamp to fit on her own head, and an immense reel of surveyor's tape to hold. He himself was equipped with an underwater camera.

Why go to such trouble over a simple act of pillage? Maybe he would produce a glossy illustrated catalogue for his rich, collector customers, make it look legit. Had to establish provenance, that was it. Typical of him to create a really upmarket sales promotion. Upmarket. Downwater. She suppressed an urge to laugh out loud. Have to keep her mind on practical matters.

Right, so she was there to take measurements of the wreck
—what remained of the wreck. Somebody please say where
the damn thing is.

Clerides didn't seem too sure of that himself, signalling
her to stay by the line while he finned off for a reconnaissance. The foreglow from his lamp became dimmer and
disappeared as he followed the curve of the cliff on his right.

Left alone, she began to sense a strange euphoria; with
her mouth full of rubber, she felt an urge to talk—and
nobody there to hear her. She began to lope from fin to fin,
balletically but without a floor to spring from. She let
her feet rise and turned backwards head over heels, felt
immediate vertigo. Instead of the great mass of sea pressing
down on her from above there seemed an immense void she
could fall through, upwards. She recognized something
wrong in her mind, forced herself to be reasonable, closed
her nasal passages and popped her ears. It did no good.

Clerides would be back soon. Since the storm—which
didn't happen only at the surface—sand deposits would
have shifted, might have completely covered over what Ted
had seen two months before. They might have to search
and dig, go away empty-handed. Ted's wreck would
have removed itself from the Greek's greedy reach all on its
own.

His light was suddenly glowing up ahead. He beckoned
and languidly she finned after him. Some hundred metres
on, they struck off at an angle from the cliff-face. A few
seconds more and he pointed down, his light beaming on
to the undulating sea floor.

They moved in close, lay over the bed of sand and he
began gently stroking the debris away. A solid shape began
to emerge, barnacled and rough-surfaced but distinctly
bellied.

If it had been smooth it would have been like a child-sized
pigeon. Funny to think of an amphora as a bird. Nice if it
took flight and went up to the surface on its own, saved
them a lot of trouble with air-bags. The whole floor of the

ocean here could be covered in these things. In her mind's eye she saw flocks of them like ghostly emigrating swallows rising all round on rudimentary wings.

Stupid fantasy. It must be the effect of the depths. She wasn't the right sort to come down here. Ted always said it took a certain kind of person. Ted said, said, said. Ted . . . said . . .

Clerides finned back to her, took the reel of tape and pushed the ring from the end of the tape between her fingers. He pointed to where he wanted her to take up her position. As he finned slowly away, careful not to raise more detritus, the tape ran out after him. His light became dimmer but her own was still bright. Too bright, when she felt so tired, must get her head down. Down among the dead men.

No, *mustn't*. Not here. Drown. Something wrong. Wrong gas!—Clerides.

It worried her that there was something she was expected to do. The ring on the end of the tape. Measure.

With her free hand she scrabbled about for the exposed amphora, the beginning of a handle under the rim. She just managed a half knot round it with the end of the tape and let herself float off. Sorry, couldn't wait. Her eyes must have closed because she never saw the rock until she hit it, head on. And then, blessed dark; the lamp had gone out.

Air, she thought. Have to have air. Get this thing out of my mouth. But, blundering to remove it, she lurched against the crate, remembered the line and reached over her head for it. Now, upwards. That was it. Up. Weight belt off. It fell noiselessly away as she hit the clasp, and she was rising, half sleeping, rushing through the water, almost forgetting to expel the air in her lungs but remembering vaguely there was something to wait for. Something . . .

Shoals of small, silver fish flashed past like constellations. So alive.

She felt all energy draining from her leaden limbs. Now her head was dissolving in the buzzing ache that was taking her over; it must be part of the sea's digestive process,

she supposed. She had always known in her deep
subconscious . . .

More fish flew past in a blur, and smaller forms of life
like dry sand blowing in a storm. Behind the mask she
screwed up her eyes to protect them from the scratchy
burning that was to come; confused.

It *was* sand. Now she was running uphill in sand, clawing
to find a hold and falling back as it poured away between
her fingers.

The buzzing in her head reached down inside to meet
rising nausea. Sick. She would be sick and inhale her own
vomit. She was going to die.

She had to surface. Rolling, her left leg dragging lifeless,
she heaved on the line, was encased in a globe of light which
folded round her in swathes of golden velvet, deadening the
body's distress. She didn't mind any more. She could pull
off her harness, free her mouth and roll down the soft,
enticing folds.

Hard against her mask struck the black, iron bulk of a
spare air cylinder. Uncomprehending, she stared at the
hostile frog-face of the spare mask, pushed it away and her
fingers folded round the attached black mouthpiece.

Hurry, *hurry*! Oh God, she was going to pass out. Clumsily
she made the substitution for her own mouthpiece,
swallowed salt water and began to retch. She was mewing
weakly. The sounds reached her through the bones of her
head.

And then when the nausea peaked to its climax her
stomach turned over and relaxed. She was breathing good
air, slowly coming clear of the buzzing grey mist. If she
could only rest here a while, get her mind straight, she'd be
able to take one good breath to get back to the surface, away
from that murderous man.

Clerides—not Zeus at all. The face in the stone! Elpida
had been wrong. Not Zeus, father of the gods, but Poseidon,
merciless god of the underwater.

Pancakes of air rose beside her. The other diver was

following her up fast. He wouldn't let her escape. Instead of floating unconscious on the sea bottom, she'd got out and away, reached uncontaminated air. *Almost* away. She wasn't safe yet.

She took a breath and relinquished the mouthpiece, unbuckled the harness that held her bottles and moved upwards unhampered. She remembered to expel the air slowly, still at two atmospheres of pressure, saw her own small bubbles wobbling upwards above her, watched the circle of daylight clarify and come closer. Safety.

A rush of larger bubbles flew up her body, then her ankles were seized and she was being pulled back down, forced by a greater strength, an overwhelming weight.

She tried to kick back, but the man had too strong a grasp on her. She had to let out more breath. If she did it again, at this depth, she would reach the point of needing to take more in.

He was moving up her body, hand over hand as he had come up the rope line. As his mask came almost level he reached out for her throat. She hadn't the strength to claw at his supply tube.

There is no terror like underwater panic. The water grew greyer. She sank away into blackness.

CHAPTER 19

Inspector Tsangaris lay back in his chair with half-closed eyes. Under his long, deceptively girlish lashes he observed the man before him. Spiros sat forward, elbows on knees, hands limply clasped between them, head drooping.

'I must ask you to make a written statement,' Tsangaris warned him. 'But before then, let us go over it all again. The Englishman Mather, how well did you know him?'

With savage satisfaction Clerides turned the small Morris

west and south along the coast road towards Pólis; her car, souped up by the dead husband and taken over by himself, just as the man's operation had been. He barked, midway between cough and bitter laugh. Any car handy would do when he had need of one, and by God he needed one now. There was a lot to get done, things and people to sort out before too much became public knowledge.

Andreas would have to make the final disposals back at the boat—including the fish catch. He'd smell out local suspicions, discover who would help cover things up, who would need gagging. One advantage was that everyone locally who'd known about the caïque's sortie would be aware that whatever had happened out in Morphou Bay happened in waters the Turks considered theirs. Nobody —especially officials—wanted to stir up trouble over the sovereignty of North Cyprus while high-level political solutions were on the cards; and secret hopes would be that the boat's crew had been putting one over on the occupying powers.

Grim-faced, he paid little attention to the burnt scrubland on the first part of the route back to Pólis. However disastrous to local interests, the fire had abetted him, making him the hero of the snake episode. That and the celebration rounds of drinks at the taberna had provided him with a fund of goodwill. Next time the caïque went out 'fishing' there'd be less speculation, more blind eyes.

He turned in his mind where to dump the little car. Good as it was, he was accustomed to something more powerful. If he left it with Rowley and picked up his hired Toyota it meant going out of his way, and time was of the essence. Also the fact of having Jean's car would make a nonsense of claiming she hadn't caught up with him.

He needed sleep. In Paphos he would pick up a taxi, could dump the Morris in the museum car park. No, outside Maritsa's lace and silver shop. There was a grim sort of humour in that; get Mather's onetime mistress wondering what his widow was up to in her neighbourhood.

Then he could catch up on lost sleep on the way back to Limassol. Once there he would need all his wits about him. Police anywhere required very careful handling to circumvent their instinctive Them-and-Us prejudice. His story would have to be watertight if he was to manœuvre them into doing what he wanted. But first there were two phone calls to make before he reached his hotel. Those, then a bath and a change. After that the final move, and the whole thing was in the bag. Apart from one almost disastrous slip-up, he could congratulate himself on pulling it off with style.

He instructed the cab-driver where eventually to set him down, tipped his panama hat over his eyes, lay back against the rear cushions and sank into an exhausted sleep.

Almost an hour later he made the first of his phone calls from a taberna on the outskirts of Limassol, and the answer he received was far from satisfactory. His brows met in a single black line. He clamped his jaw tight before he could trust himself to reply. 'That is directly against my instructions,' he ground out coldly.

The other man's voice came back patiently and without bluster. 'I regret it was impossible. I could not insist, you understand; only advise. And in the circumstances, the idea was not unreasonable. I arranged transport, of course.'

'So when may we expect . . ?'

'Sometime this evening, I should imagine. Between six and seven.'

'Very well. I will see to arrangements at this end. Let me have your account immediately, and it will be settled before I leave for Athens.'

'Idiot!' he muttered, dialling a Nicosia number. This time the conversation was entirely satisfactory and he did most of the talking. It consisted mainly of lists: a rough estimate of objects recoverable from the sea bed, and details of extra equipment required for the operation. Next, he told himself, back to his hotel, a bath and a change of clothes, then a visit to the police. He remembered the name of the officer who had questioned Jean about her husband's death. It was Tsangaris, Inspector Stavros Tsangaris, but before he met him it would be as well to check on the man. It was for occasions like this that he had cultivated his Acting-Sergeant acquaintance, met over drinks in the taberna opposite the Yermasoyia Section Station.

In a fresh white safari suit Clerides looked in to inquire for his new frined, and having waited for the end of a heated discussion about infringements of the pedestrian crossing for Dasoudhi beach, was told that Marcos had been called to headquarters; a matter concerning the Englishman's poisoning.

'There is some development, then?' Clerides asked with apparently mild interest.

The indiscreet constable checked himself, looked critically at the respectable turnout of the man from Athens and then decided he would already be well enough informed for it to make no difference. He shrugged. 'Someone has confessed, it seems. A hotelier from near here. We are waiting for details.'

'Ah. So I must also wait—to crack my bottle of wine with Marcos. When do you expect the good sergeant back?'

The constable shrugged his shoulders. 'It seems he knows this Spiros, calls in there sometimes for a seafood *meze* with his girlfriend. Perhaps they will need him at headquarters for a day or two while the man's being questioned.'

'I see.' He didn't entirely, but he was beginning to have a suspicion. He nodded towards the telephone. 'If Marcos calls in, tell him Nikos Clerides was asking after him. I've been away, but I'm back now, and as thirsty as ever.'

'Sure. He'll be glad to know.' Especially if the well-dressed Greek would be paying.

Time I went along and played a fly on the wall, Clerides told himself. But first he would have to spy out the lie of the land, have a plausible reason for approaching Tsangaris.

Twice there was no reply when he phoned the old school-house at Kalidrofi. He could picture the cool, spacious rooms, tiger stripes of afternoon sunlight filtering through slatted shutters, inner doors left ajar, the kitchen tidy and silent while the insistent bell rang on unheeded. With Jean gone the place would be deserted. He seemed to remember that the village woman Elpida had departed on a visit. Only the old gardener would be about, watering the plants and damping down the sand on the street outside. He might even hear the phone ringing indoors and later be able to confirm that Clerides had indeed tried to contact the lady of the house.

Whatever he had expected at Limassol Police headquarters, it was not to have the Interview Room door open and a handsome, middle-aged Apollo step out to inspect him, nod and say, 'Mr Nikolaos Clerides, from Athens? Yes? Perhaps you would wait in another room. We had been hoping you would save us the trouble of looking for you. I shall be with you shortly.'

'So why me?' Clerides asked aloud, when he had been ushered into a small side office and left alone. According to the indiscreet constable at Yermasoyia it was the hotelier Spiros who was being interrogated, however true or untrue might be the rumour of a confession. To the best of his knowledge Clerides had never set eyes on him. But it didn't mean that the man hadn't observed Clerides. So where? And doing what?

He was left for twenty minutes to mull over how he might be affected: just the right length of time to prick a man's confidence, he thought wryly. Some might panic, but he had his story ready, the part of it he was willing to release.

'Mr Clerides. Inspector Tsangaris.' The policeman came in silently behind him as he stood at the wire-meshed window. 'Please sit down.'

It was a mellow voice, handsome as the man's smooth, dark face. His hair, brushed straight back from a broad forehead was combed close like a shiny cap of black, rippled plastic. As Jean had done before him, Clerides was conscious of a chill as he met the Inspector's unfathomable eyes. 'What can I do for you?'

It was a perfectly amiable question, and it ignored his previous statement that the police themselves had been on the lookout for Clerides.

Well, let him play it that way. 'I am becoming increasingly concerned,' Clerides said sombrely in reply, 'about Mrs Jean Mather, an English lady resident at Kalidrofi. She was to have kept an appointment with me last evening at the Miramare Hotel and she failed to arrive. Since then I have rung her house several times but without a reply. Because there has been a recent tragedy in the lady's life I am naturally anxious. Not that she struck me as a hysterical type of woman when we met. In fact I was impressed by the lady's natural dignity and the way she handled her grief.'

Tsangaris was watching him impassively and made no move to interrupt his flow. Nevertheless, it would have been a mistake to go on too long. For such an initial request for help, he had surely said enough.

The Inspector gestured towards a chair at the central table and drew out one for himself opposite. 'You are concerned,' he repeated and seemed to consider this. 'What is that to do with us?'

'I hoped there might be some simple way you could check for me whether the lady has met with an accident, or whether for some reason she has been called away and was unable to get a message to me. She didn't appear the sort to be uncivil.'

Tsangaris lowered his gaze to the polished floorboards and brooded. After a few seconds he shrugged. 'Is it not possible—and I do not wish to be discourteous in putting forward this suggestion—but has it not crossed your mind that the lady, so recently widowed, might have had second thoughts about her appointment with you?'

Clerides would have liked to see his expression then. Was there some hint of mockery in the ultra-polite words? He shifted his weight on the chair. 'You are aware of Mrs Mather's circumstances, then?'

'To some extent. To some extent your own as well, but —insufficiently, shall we say?'

Clerides sighed, reached into the breast pocket of his safari tunic and slowly sorted some of the papers until he found one he handed across to the policeman. 'That will explain my interest in Mrs Mather's affairs. It concerns an insurance taken out on the life of her late husband, but until now she has been unable to lay her hand on the relevant documents.'

Inspector Tsangaris read through the paper and tapped its heading with a forefinger. 'You will have no objection if we contact this address for substantiation?'

Clerides inclined his head. 'None whatever.'

The inspector settled more comfortably into his chair. 'And why, Mr Clerides, have you brought your disquiet over Mrs Mather's whereabouts to this office, even asking for me by name? You must know that I have no personal responsibility for what happens in Kalidrofi.'

'I understood from Mrs Mather that you had visited her there and were involved in ordering the exhumation of her husband's body.'

'Ah, you were in touch with her as recently as that. Doubtless, then, she will also have confided to you that Edward Mather was most probably killed by poison?'

The heavily sardonic tone overlying the courteous phrasing was being replaced by a more direct attack. Clerides sucked in his lean cheeks, unknowingly making his appearance more wolfish, before he replied, 'Regretfully, yes. And I am also aware that Mrs Mather prepared a light supper for her husband shortly before his death.'

Tsangaris nodded blandly. 'A supper at which a third party was present—Mrs Marjorie Rowley, a friend in common to both.'

Clerides stared unblinkingly back, and neither face gave any hint of emotion. Inspector Tsangaris fingered the paper that authorized the other to represent the Athens assurance company. 'It would certainly be of interest to you whether the Englishman died by misadventure or as a result of foul play. In particular you would wish to be certain that no one could benefit financially from committing murder.'

'You understand my position perfectly, Inspector.'

'And you appreciate that I can give you no certain guidance over which lady would be the more likely to commit such a crime, if indeed a crime was committed?'

'That advice would depend, surely, on the progress of your investigation—on which of the two is eventually proved to have the better motive, the means and the greater opportunity.'

'I don't know whether you are a gambling man, Mr Clerides, but if so I think I can tell which lady you will have placed your money on. And if your suspicions are proved correct, it could be of advantage to the company you represent.'

'Neither my opinion nor the conditions for payment on the life policy can matter to your investigation, Inspector.' Clerides felt it time to shrug off too close an interest.

At last Tsangaris permitted himself a faint smile. 'And in any case we may have a wider choice of suspects. It is unlikely that you can give a positive answer to your directors in Athens for some time yet. I should perhaps warn you that we now have a witness who claims Mr Mather experienced some sickness before his arrival home on the evening of his death.'

Clerides raised his eyebrows. 'Indeed?' So that was what the hotelier had said in his statement. If he was to be believed, that would exonerate Jean Mather. 'And is there evidence of what Mather actually ate to cause the upset?'

The inspector's smile broadened to display perfect teeth. 'The witness is torn between two desires. While gallantly concerned to deflect suspicion from the widow, he remains adamant that no blame should attach to himself or his hotel. He insists that the toxic substance had been ingested before

Mather called briefly on him, and that the Englishman was violently sick before continuing his journey home. He also had some difficulty in breathing and used his asthma spray.'

Clerides nodded disbelievingly. 'How convenient for Mrs Mather. But hasn't this witness been suspiciously slow in coming forward?'

'He claims he volunteered the information only when he realized its relevance. As you know, Edward Mather was thought to have died of natural causes until the recent post-mortem suggested otherwise.'

'Suggested? Is there still no firm evidence?'

Inspector Tsangaris appeared to hesitate as if weighing the wisdom of confiding so much. But he had all the marks of an experienced interrogator: Clerides knew that the pause was intended to have him on tenterhooks. 'The—the, er, contents of the stomach and so on were sent for a second opinion to the UK, to the Metropolitan Force's Forensic Laboratories at Lambeth, London. We have just received their telexed report. The result of the analysis . . .'

The inspector's languid recitation tailed away as he searched through papers in the file he had carried in with him. 'Ah, here. Ye-es. Somewhat complex, but it would appear that there is a substance called saxotoxin sometimes present in planktons. Under certain rather rare conditions these can multiply rapidly, giving rise to "red tides". The toxin builds up in the bodies of mussels, cockles and scallops which feed by filtering plankton. The early symptoms of this type of poisoning are loss of feeling in the hands, nausea, tingling of the tongue, weakness of arms and legs, difficulty in breathing; ultimately paralysis and death.'

He smiled bleakly. 'Traces of partly digested mussels containing saxotoxin were detected in the—er, slurry of the remains. Am I explaining this to your satisfaction, Mr Clerides?'

'I think so. Shellfish poisoning, acting on Mather's asthmatic condition. So it could have been a death by misadventure after all.'

'And the meal prepared by Mrs Mather was a *chicken* salad. Mrs Rowley confirms that fish formed no part of it, and I am not at present considering collusion between the two women. So you see, it was unnecessarily noble of our witness to divert suspicion to himself. And decidedly incautious, particularly as his hotel restaurant is noted for the serving of fish *meze*.'

'But the witness denies providing the mussels or whatever which caused Mather to vomit?'

'Just so.' A slight flicker disturbed the corners of Tsangaris's mouth. 'His intention of diverting suspicion from the lady appears to have recoiled on his own professional reputation, which inclines me to believe he didn't know the poison was one found in fish. Unless, of course, it is a clever double-bluff.'

'But if Mather had helped himself from the seafood buffet, his would not have been the only case of food poisoning reported at the time.'

'Exactly.' The Inspector's voice took on a purring quality. 'No similar cases were reported. So perhaps Mr Mather's serving was specially selected for him, as it would have been if he took his meal privately in the witness's company.

'Which once more puts forward our not-so-truthful voluntary witness as our prime suspect. Unless, of course, some member of the hotel staff with opportunity also had an overriding motive. I shall keep on at the man Spiros until he admits that Mather was offered refreshments. Then we shall be close to finding out who could have known that in advance and seized the chance to tamper with the food.' Tsangaris seemed positively amused at the case's convolutions.

Clerides nodded, satisfied that the case as it stood could safely be left in the inspector's hands. Somewhere above him would be senior officers who would be pressing for a speedy solution. It looked as if the man Spiros, in trying to protect Jean Mather, had dropped himself into quite a load of sewage. Either he or someone of his staff would be finally taking the rap for Mather's death, whether officially accepted as accidental or premeditated murder.

The inspector was rising now, the file tucked under one elbow. 'I must ask for your discretion, Mr Clerides. I should regret any premature disclosures to the general public at this point.'

Clerides assured him that his information would go no farther. 'I am most grateful for your confidence, Inspector.'

'My pleasure, to be of assistance.'

Such politeness throughout, Clerides thought wryly; and such a potentially dangerous man. He had not expected to meet with sophistication of this kind among CID on the island.

CHAPTER 20

Once he had checked that the police were insufficiently interested in his affairs to put a tail on him, Clerides headed the new hire car—this time a blue Mercedes—towards Kalidrofi. Before the turn for the village he cut his speed and cruised down past the taberna, giving a lazy wave through the open window in the direction of its terrace. There was no answering wave but he knew he was observed. The small boy who lived there even came out into the road and stood looking after the car to make sure where it was going.

He pulled up opposite the second of the two sentinel palm trees. Flooded with golden sunlight, the big house looked asleep, its ground floor shutters pulled across but not latched. As far as he could tell from a first glance, it had suffered no damage from the storm although he had passed swirls of flattened grass and broken branches in several of the orchards on his way up.

He took his time getting out, stretching, jingling Jean's keys on their ring before selecting the correct one for the

main door. The little boy was still in the middle of the
road, watching every movement. Later, Clerides decided, he
would go over and give an order to be delivered, but only
after he had made a good search for the hidden safe Ted
Mather must have had built in at the time of the renovations.

An old English long-case clock in the tiled hallway had
stopped. He opened the front and reset the weights, felt
satisfaction as its deep, slow ticking resumed. The only other
sound was the humming of the refrigerator through the
archway to the kitchen. He opened a few windows then
systematically went from room to room, turning back car-
pets, shifting pictures, tapping walls.

Nothing; and already an hour and twenty minutes had
gone by since he arrived.

He took stock of the contents of the freezer, found a wicker
basket and went across to the taberna with it on his arm
and a list of provisions. There he put on a good show of
unfamiliarity with domestic requirements, and the little
boy's mother came out of a back room, wiping her hands
on a towel, to help him. When she had added up the total
and he was peeling off notes to pay her she ventured to ask,
'Mrs Mather has not come back?' Men in the rooms beyond
suddenly stopped talking.

'Later on,' he told her, smiling. 'She has been staying
with friends down at Paphos. They had their house damaged
in the storm. She's helping them to clear up.'

The woman made a clicking noise of sympathy with her
tongue and shook her head. 'Here we were more fortunate.
The worst of the winds missed us.' She would have known
from the gossipy Elpida that the Rowleys lived at Paphos.
He thought that by the time she had passed on his information the village would probably accept him in a caretak-
ing role. Elpida herself was evidently still on holiday. He
went back to the old schoolhouse and set out the makings
of a meal.

At a little after seven, when the sun was off the narrow
village street, he heard the sound of tyres and a quiet car

engine ticking over outside the front door. As he reached it, Jean was just being helped out of the rear of a dark limousine. He went forward swiftly to steady her.

'You don't have to treat me as an invalid,' she said, laughing up at him. I'm completely recovered,' but he folded her in his arms and half carried her into the house.

'It was heartless of me to leave you back at Pólis. I have worried every moment since. And when I phoned that wretched doctor, only to be told that you were determined to travel back today, I imagined every kind of accident on the way.'

'It doesn't seem to suit you, saving my life. Who would have thought that you'd take it so to heart? Will you always feel as responsible for me now?'

'There is nothing I should like to discuss with you more,' he said with mock seriousness. 'But later, after you've eaten. And then perhaps you would show yourself briefly in the village to set Kalidrofi's communal mind at rest. Meanwhile I shall be making a really splendid *omelette baveuse* if that appeals to you, accompanied by a green salad with olives and tomatoes. Sit and talk to me while I do the magic bit with the eggs.'

When they were seated opposite one another at the table on the terrace he raised his glass to her. 'You are really looking wonderful, considering what happened. To you, Jean.'

'I feel pretty good now. Thank God you swam after me and dragged me down again. I'd no idea how long we'd been underwater, and anyway, in that drugged condition, I had completely forgotten about decompression rules and "the bends", barely knew where I was at all.'

'You started to fight me like a wild cat and suddenly you'd gone limp. I realized then that you'd been breathing polluted air. They were my cylinders you were wearing and one had been doctored with me in mind. I swapped both pairs over because mine were newer and I trusted the valves completely.'

'Thank heaven you did. If it had been you collapsed I wouldn't have been able to cope with you underwater, and you'd gone much farther from the safety line. It doesn't bear thinking of. So, Nikos, to us both!'

They decided to go across to the taberna for their coffee and celebrate with some of the French cognac kept for special occasions.

'I suppose,' Jean said, as later they strolled back under the stars, 'I shouldn't feel like this, so glad to be alive. Nothing's changed. Ted's still dead, and we can't prove anything, can we?'

'That rests with Inspector Tsangaris. I dropped in for a word with him today,' Clerides confided. 'It isn't for general consumption yet, but he's looking into some fish dish your husband had on his way home. You can rest easy. He doesn't take you seriously as a suspect any more. I can't see how he could ever have done.'

'That's a relief, but who was Ted eating with, and where?'

Clerides told her and she was incredulous. 'It must have been accidental—a freak portion that Ted was unlucky enough to take. It's unthinkable that Spiros could have intended him any harm. If you'd met him you'd know . . .'

'Take it easy. I wish now I hadn't said anything. I thought you'd be glad to know you at least were in the clear.'

'Yes, but I knew I wasn't to blame. Surely the inspector can't believe Spiros capable of murder? Even if it's proved accidental, that's going to harm the hotel. I wish there was something I could do.'

'Just stay clear of the whole thing, Jean. Leave it to Tsangaris. And remember, as your husband was the only one poisoned, it does look very suspicious.'

'Maybe others ate polluted fish, were slightly upset and recovered. Ted might have got over it but for the effect it had on his asthma. It has to be accidental, Nikos, or else he ate something elsewhere.'

'If it's any comfort to you, your friend Spiros denies your

husband ate anything at his bar. It's up to the police to prove otherwise.'

They hesitated inside the hall. 'It's late,' Jean said in a small voice.

'Is that my dismissal? I'd hoped—'

'I shall be all right now. Thank you for being so considerate. I don't want you to think I'm ungrateful.'

'And I certainly don't want gratitude. Maybe someday something else. Good night, then.'

She called him back as he opened his car door. 'Nikos, what happened to my little Morris?'

'I left it at Paphos and came on by taxi. Ring the Kakouris lace shop. It's parked outside. If nobody offers to drive it back we can fetch it tomorrow.'

'Thank you again. Good night.'

When the sound of the Mercedes had died away the night seemed suddenly cooler. Or had that happened when he as good as accused Spiros of wanting to kill Ted?

Jean went through to the kitchen where Nikos had insisted on washing up their few dishes. As she was putting them away she heard the low birdcall Georgios always made to warn her he was in the garden. He rapped on the loosely closed shutters and pulled one open to put back the shed key on the inner sill. The sight of his wrinkled brown hand coming through made her suddenly aware of an overlooked possibility.

'Georgios, hullo. How are you?'

The old man's face appeared, nodding. He wasn't one for much speech, but he grinned.

'Tell me,' she encouraged him, 'did you ever see a lumpy old coin there, just behind the taps?'

'Yes.'

'Do you know what happened to it?'

'I put it with the others.' He began to turn away.

'Wait! Can you show me where they are? In the garden, is it?'

She followed him and they went to the corner where she

had arranged a vista through the evergreens, a curving path that ended at a column with her first carving on it, the crudely fashioned head of Zeus (or was it now Poseidon?)

Georgios lifted the head off and pointed down the hollow drain pipe which, coated with matt paint, stood on its end and served as its stand.

'Lift it off, can you?'

Georgios put down the carved stone and picked up the heavy cylinder in his arms. He moved back and deposited it a few feet away. Jean peered close to see what lay on the flagstone base. The small pile of coins settled more widely. She reached out and picked one up. Part of Ted's secret hoard. She remembered him, every night before undressing, emptying his pockets on to the table beside his bed. More than once in his last weeks, he had grunted, picked up a single object, tossed it in his hand and then gone, whistling softly, for a walk in the garden.

'You once saw my husband put something in here, so you looked. Is that it?'

Georgios nodded.

'So you knew to put the other one with them.' Like a child's money box, she thought.

'They are very old,' Georgios offered unprompted. 'So they belong to him.' He nodded towards the face in the stone.

'I see. You were quite right. Thank you, Georgios.'

'It is good that you are back. Sleep safe.'

'Good night.'

He had left her without replacing the column and the head. Perhaps he expected her to count the collection. She fetched a terracotta pithoi and scooped the coins in. Then she sat staring at the square flagstone base.

She remembered well how Ted had encouraged her to display the carving, how they'd chosen its site—or how he had manœuvred her into choosing the place he wanted. She had been back in England for a fortnight, and when she returned he was full of the idea, had placed flagstones in various positions to mark where the head could be placed. And this was the site she'd selected, because the others were quite wrong. Clever old Ted; had her eating out of his hand.

So what was underneath?—as if she couldn't guess!

The flagstone was heavy but not deep. Although she couldn't lift it, she found she could push it far enough to uncover the steel cover of a manhole. No need to go farther. On a slight elevation, it had no connection with a drain. This was the entrance to Ali Baba's cave, the place Ted had prepared to receive the larger treasures from the ancient wreck while in transit to his customers. It could still be empty or she could be standing over a fortune, with only Clerides as her means of unloading the treasure. Unless she confessed to the authorities and sold the whole team down the river.

She pushed the flagstone back and left the rest for Georgios to see to in the morning. Going back into the lounge she now registered what had faintly disturbed her on coming home: some of the chairs were out of place. Clerides must have moved them in her absence. Both she and Elpida always replaced the castors meticulously on to their indentations in the thick carpet.

Why should Nikos need to move the furniture at all? And one of the pictures was crooked as if hurriedly replaced. So while he waited for her he had done more than prepare a meal; he had searched the house—as Maritsa Kakouris had once searched—for a hidden safe.

It was ironic that Georgios should have led her to it that very same day, the simple old man having unwittingly discovered what couldn't be reached by the clever man from Athens.

What was to be done about Clerides? Who was this man who claimed to be in the police's confidence, posing as an insurance investigator but certainly more interested in making a fortune from raiding underwater wrecks? Never quite what he seemed and so, surely, no friend of hers. Yet he had saved her life when she'd believed he was out to kill her. Well, he needed her to help him survey the wreck. It didn't mean she was as precious to him as he sometimes liked to make out. As for her own feelings—they were irrelevant. And totally unreliable, she told herself.

Could he possibly have set Spiros up to take the blame for his own crime of murder? He could well have been on Cyprus for much longer than he implied. It was a horrific thought that she could be closely involved with her own husband's killer.

She would never sleep tonight while these questions buzzed in her mind. But she didn't need sleep anyway; she'd spent a whole day tranquillized when they'd come ashore from the dive. That was a day she had to catch up with if she was to check on Clerides.

After taking her ashore, once he'd revived her, he must have gone back to dive again, this time alone, to complete the photography and pick up any artefacts exposed to view. Then he'd come here ahead of her to find out what treasures Ted already held at the house. Nowhere in that self-seeking portrait of the man was there any saving grace to account for the terrible fascination he could exercise. It's just some morbid fancy in me, she decided. I'm a fool for a rogue, twice over. He is nothing to me; can never mean anything. Except danger.

So what was he up to now? If she'd had her car she would have driven down after him. Or, better still, she would have gone to Spiros's to find out what kind of frame-up had led the police to him.

She heard the long-case clock in the hall strike midnight. Too late to do anything. And then, through the open windows came the unmistakeable roar of a small car driven *con brio*. Elpida's nephew, ever ready for something a little special. He would be delighted to run her down to Limassol.

CHAPTER 21

At Spiros's bar she was met coldly by his daughter. While a score of tourists roistered round the floodlit pool she squared up to Jean, hands on hips and her pretty young face dark with anger. 'We want no trouble here. Go, please.'

'Believe me, I want to help. The police are quite mad if they think Spiros could—'

'My father was your husband's friend.'

'And he trusted him. As I do. We have to find out who really did that terrible thing. Did Spiros tell you anything at all before they took him away?'

'They did not take him. He went voluntarily, to save *you*, because otherwise you would have been arrested. To avoid that he told them your husband was already sick here first.'

'Was that true?'

The girl hesitated, unwilling to commit herself.

'If he was, then he could have come here like that. But where from? Did your father give you any idea—? I thought Ted intended sailing that day and the weather put him off, but his friend Mr Rowley was away in Nicosia. I don't know who else could tell me.'

The girl shook her head, less belligerent now and wishing she could give the Englishwoman some clue to ensure she went away.

'But I *do* know,' Jean suddenly burst out. 'Of course I do! The boatyard. That's where he kept his diving gear, and where he hired the caïque from. Someone there may know.'

'But it will be closed now,' Elpida's nephew objected when she went back to the car.

'Sometimes they go out fishing at night. We could try.'

'Why not?' The boy gave his wide, roguish grin. 'And if we find nobody there, we go for a long drive. I have petrol and you can pay me for it.'

'For the moment just the boatyard. I'll show you where to leave the car. Then I'll continue on foot.'

By night the harbour route seemed more circuitous, but it was partially lit by high-strung lamps which gave the black wasteland a greasy, orange patina and left pools of deep shadow between. The Baroutis sheds appeared to be in darkness, but as she approached the timber sliding doors she saw there was a narrow gap large enough to squeeze through. She stepped inside, her sandal tipping a saucer left on the floor. There was a stale odour of raw fish, and somewhere close in the darkness a cat mewed pettishly.

She stared round the interior, letting her eyes adapt to the gloom. Six square, grimed panes dimly showed paler sky, but at the far end, up a wooden stairway, light from a single naked bulb shone through the windows of a small office. To reach it she passed the chest where Ted's things were stored. She knew now that the deep wicker baskets had been meant to lift ancient treasures, not harpooned fish. The handrail shook loosely as she mounted the stairway. She halted, startled by its rattle. Somewhere ahead was the muffled sound of a radio, a subdued, monotonous droning.

Before opening the door she stood with her knuckles against the panel, ready to knock. No, she told herself; just appear.

She walked in, and the figure sprawled over the table made no effort to get up. The monotonous music she'd heard came from no radio but was the drunken misery of the man. She left the door open behind her and went round the table to him. His only acknowledgement of her was to groan as he lifted his head and his eyes slowly focused.

'Mr Baroutis,' she said quietly, 'I am Jean Mather.' She lowered herself on to the rickety chair at right angles to him.

'Major,' he said stupidly.

She was going to correct him but he went on. 'Sarj'major. No, Warrant Officer. Call him Mister.' Even in this state he had made the connection with Ted's name. 'Kill him!' he said.

The sound that came from him then sent a cramping chill through her: neither a laugh nor a sob, but choking savagery.

Jean couldn't move. From the corner of her eyes she saw the stricken face of Elpida's nephew appear low down in the doorway. She should have known he would follow her in. Well, no matter what happened now, at least there would be a witness.

'Stelios Baroutis,' she said as firmly as her voice would allow, 'my husband is dead. You killed him, didn't you? With shellfish.'

Blearily he stared at her. 'Bad fish.' He rubbed a large hand wearily over his eyes.

'The police think Spiros did it.'

But Baroutis had lost touch. She tried again. 'Why, Stelios? Why did you have to do it?'

He laid his head down on the table and spread both hands flat alongside. She didn't have to ask any more. This was grief, not anger. She remembered the other time she had seen him, in Spiros's Bar, and she heard again Spiros's voice explaining their connection. He'd gone then to Spiros because the hotel man had been at school with his dead younger brother.

'Tell me,' she coaxed, 'about Kostas.'

It took a long time. She had never seen a grown man weep before, but there were moments when she had to wait while he fought to get the words out.

Just the two of them, and so many years between. Kostas had been more like a son. All he'd had was Kostas, the caïque and this shed. He talked about their childhood; their father; a wooden camel he'd once made for the boy; his quickness at school; how women turned to look after him, he was so alive; strong, and he swam like an eel.

But nothing yet about how he came to drown.

'Poor Kostas,' she said. 'So young, and the sea took him.'

Baroutis went suddenly wild. His bunched fists swept the table and he started a hoarse bellowing in Greek. It was too fast and too colloquial for her to follow, but so loud that the boy listening on the stairs must surely catch every word, unless he'd taken fright and gone by now.

The crazed man became aware of her shrinking away and seized her arm. 'Lady,' he shouted—and she realized he was less under the influence of drink than of terrible emotion —'he kill my Kostas! Your man, so clever, diving, and the cheap old machine it poison the air. So Kostas go mad down there. They bring him up—too late! Drowned! They say trouble for me too, and Kostas dead anyway, so put weights on. Send him down again. Sail away. We all say Kostas fall overboard, hit head. Nobody find him. No—grave to bury him.'

She understood now the measure of his grief. They had to hide how Kostas had died—from carbon-monoxide poisoning when the faulty compressor had allowed its own exhaust to mix into the stored air. The diving party had no licence for underwater exploration. If a doctor had seen the body subsequent inquiries would have revealed what they were up to and their chances of sharing a fortune would have been lost. It had happened back in late winter, and months afterwards when he'd come on a 'red tide' Baroutis had seized on the chance for revenge. Perhaps he had experimented with feeding poisonous mussels to one of the stray cats of the boatyard and then he'd made up a special dish for the man he held responsible.

She shook his hand off angrily. 'And you nearly killed me, the way Kostas died. You didn't get rid of the faulty compressor. You deliberately used it to part-fill one of the air bottles, and you let me go down to my death!'

'No!' He shook his head in confusion. 'Not you. The man from Athens. *His* air. He take my boat. I spit on him! What is money?'

'He gave me the new bottles, his own. So it was me you nearly killed. I could have stayed down there at the bottom. I would be dead now!'

'Lady, truly—' He spread his big hands. 'Come. Come and I show you.' He lunged past her and made for the stairs. She tried to bar his way but he seized her and pulled her after him. There was no sign of Elpida's nephew now.

Baroutis knew his way across the building in the dark, and he still kept the grip on her arm. 'See.' He stopped abruptly and she cannoned into him. Throwing aside an old canvas cover he revealed a dark mass of metal the size of a large car engine. 'Lady, no more now!'

Tears were rolling grotesquely down his face again. He reached out sideways and came up with a curved iron bar. Jean pulled away as it whistled down at arm's length and clanged on the machinery below. The clangs rang on and on, echoing off the walls in the semi-darkness, and cringing away, hands over her ears to stop the sounds of crazed destruction, she became aware of figures moving behind her, around her, enfolding her and drawing her away.

'You're safe, thank God,' Clerides breathed fervently. 'Twice in three days, that is—too much.'

'Don't hurt him!' she called out. 'He's—' but they seemed to know. Only enough force to restrain him; and powerful as he was, he was almost at the end of his strength by now. She heard him still quietly sobbing as they led him off. 'Tell her. No harm. Too many dead—at bottom of the sea. No more now.'

Out in the air again, Elpida's nephew hopping from foot to foot, ecstatic at his own heroism, volubly anxious that everyone should know the full tale. 'Mrs Mather, good to see you. We heard it all.'

She looked around, bemused. 'Tell me then, how did you all meet up? No, Nikos, you tell me.'

'When I came down from seeing you at Kalidrofi I called in on Spiros's daughter to see if there was any help I could give. What you said made me think the police could have got the wrong man. I left her my phone number at the hotel. After you'd seen her, saying you were coming down here, she was afraid you would run into danger and she rang me. By then I'd guessed your husband would have been with the boat people that last evening before dropping in on Spiros, so I buzzed Tsangaris.'

'And *I* followed you,' the nephew interrupted, 'to see where you went. Then as I returned to the car I saw Mr Clerides. I'd seen him in our village, but I didn't know his name then. We came up here together and listened downstairs while you were talking in the office with the boatman. He's mad, isn't he? He killed your—'

'Right, young man,' Clerides checked him. 'Shouldn't you make sure that your car has all it should have before those policemen start examining it too closely? Mrs Mather will ride back with me.'

He drove with his free arm round Jean. 'It's all going to come out now,' she said fearfully: 'Ted's finding the wreck and starting to sell off the treasures; you pretending to be an insurance investigator. There'll be trouble for us all.'

'I don't see why.'

'But the diving's illegal . . .'

'Not since this afternoon, and conveniently backdated. I have a little pull with the Department of Antiquities in Nicosia, especially after the list of treasures I've promised them. Anything slightly irregular can be kept under wraps.'

'You mean you're not—'

'A crook? M'm. My colleagues might disagree over that. I once occupied the Chair of Archæology at Athens University, but now I'm freelancing. And, as you guessed, by chance I became a customer of your husband's.'

'And there is no second insurance policy?'

'That was sheer deceit. I was determined to discover the wreck, so I came to Cyprus myself. With your husband's death the only link I had with the artefacts was lost. I phoned my brother in Athens who is a director of the Life Assurance Society. He provided the temporary credentials and I invented the story to go with them. Once I'd met you, I regretted the deceit very much, but I had expected to be dealing with someone entirely different. Suddenly there was more to my quest than tracing the whereabouts of sunken treasure.'

'And you found what you were looking for.'

'What I've been seeking for a very long time, yes.' He gave a sidelong smile and tightened his arm about her. 'As for the other precious things, it was you who first said that treasure at the bottom of the sea belonged to the fishes. In a way I think I agree. Whoever brings it up again into the air has a lot to answer for. But I do try to preserve the fragile past in the best way I can.'

'I'm so sorry I mistrusted you. But I was right to! I feared the worst, but hoped . . . All along I've had such ambivalent feelings about you.'

'Shall I disappoint you now by proving respectable?' He gave his familiar wolfish grin. 'Jean, let's celebrate. We'll go along to Spiros's and set up a Welcome Back. When daylight comes there will be lengthy statements to make for the police. But when that's done we've all the time in the world.'

THE
DIAMOND JUBILEE
BOOK OF SCOUTING

1907—1967

Publication approved by
The Boy Scouts Association

PEARSON—LONDON

Published 1966

Printed for the Publishers, C. Arthur Pearson, Ltd., Tower House, Southampton Street London, W.C.2, by Blackie and Son Ltd., Bishopbriggs, Glasgow